Reason™ 5 Power!: The Comprehensive Guide

By Michael Prager

Course Technology PTR
A part of Cengage Learning

D1340975

COURSE TECHNOLOGY
CENGAGE Learning™

Australia • Brazil • Japan • Korea • Mexico • Singapore • Spain • United Kingdom • United States

COURSE TECHNOLOGY
CENGAGE Learning™

Reason™ 5 Power!: The Comprehensive Guide
Michael Prager

Publisher and General Manager, Course Technology PTR: Stacy L. Hiquet

Associate Director of Marketing: Sarah Panella

Manager of Editorial Services: Heather Talbot

Marketing Manager: Mark Hughes

Executive Editor: Mark Garvey

Project/Copy Editor: Kezia Endsley

Technical Reviewer: G. W. Childs IV

Interior Layout Tech: MPS Limited, a Macmillan Company

Cover Designer: Mike Tanamachi

Indexer: Valerie Haynes Perry

Proofreader: Kelly Talbot Editing Services

For product information and technology assistance, contact us at
Cengage Learning Customer & Sales Support, 1-800-354-9706

For permission to use material from this text or product, submit all requests online at **www.cengage.com/permissions**
Further permissions questions can be emailed to
permissionrequest@cengage.com

All images © Course Technology unless otherwise noted.

Reason is a trademark of Propellerhead Software AB.

All other trademarks are the property of their respective owners.

Library of Congress Control Number: 2010939134

ISBN-13: 978-1-4354-5861-1

ISBN-10: 1-4354-5861-3

Course Technology, a part of Cengage Learning
20 Channel Center Street
Boston, MA 02210
USA

Cengage Learning is a leading provider of customized learning solutions with office locations around the globe, including Singapore, the United Kingdom, Australia, Mexico, Brazil, and Japan. Locate your local office at: **international.cengage.com/region**

Cengage Learning products are represented in Canada by Nelson Education, Ltd.

For your lifelong learning solutions, visit **courseptr.com**

Visit our corporate website at **cengage.com**

Printed in the United States of America
1 2 3 4 5 6 7 14 13 12 11 10

This book is dedicated to my wife Jeannie and our families for their never-ending love and support throughout the years.

About the Author

Michael Prager has been involved with music technology since 1994 and has worked for Guitar Center Management, Cakewalk, Steinberg, Disney Interactive, Spectrasonics, Q Up Arts, Sony Classical, the Columbia College Hollywood, and *Keyboard Magazine*. Michael has worked on various ArtistPro instructional DVDs and is the author of several books and CD-ROMs from Course Technology, including Reason *2.5/3/4 Power!, Reason CSi Starter, Reason CSi Master, Mac Home Recording Power!*, and *Sampling and Soft Synth Power!*.

Michael resides in Redondo Beach, California, with his wife Jeannie.

Acknowledgments

It's been a real pleasure to come back to Reason after writing the first edition of this book years ago for Thomson Learning. My thanks to Mark Garvey for his continuing friendship and correspondence. Of course, this book would not read as well as it does without the superior editing work of Kezia Endsley and G.W. Childs; a happy thanks to you both. A big thanks to the gang at Guitar Center Management. To my buddies at Propellerhead and Line 6, every time I think you've created the best software and hardware out there, you go and make it even better. To my tech buddy in crime, Greg Ripes; your friendship and knowledge are worth their weight in gold.

And a hearty thanks to you, the reader. Without your enthusiasm and creativity, books like this would not be possible. I truly hope you enjoy *Reason 5 Power!* and refer to it often when writing your first or next hit song.

Contents

Chapter 6
The Reason Mixer (reMix) 147

Chapter 7
Redrum—Close Up 167

Chapter 8
Kong—Close Up   201

Chapter 9
Dr. Octo Rex—Close Up   235

Chapter 10
Subtractor—Close Up   261

Chapter 11
The Malström—Close Up   293

Chapter 12
Thor—Close Up   315

Chapter 13
NN-19—Close Up   351

Chapter 18
The MClass Mastering Suite—Close Up   489

Chapter 19
The Combinator—Close Up   501

Chapter 20
Automation   515

Chapter 21
ReWire   531

Chapter 22
Mixing and Publishing Your Reason Songs   555

Appendix A
ReCycle! 2.1   571

Appendix B
ReFills   581

Introduction

Welcome to *Reason 5 Power!* This is the third edition to a very popular series of books that explains how to use one of the hottest music programs around, Reason. Introduced in 2000, Reason includes software synthesis, loops, and beats, and a killer-sequencing engine, which has revolutionized the electronic musician and the music of today. You name the style of music and format, and you can be sure that Reason played a key role in its creation. With its easy-to-understand user interface and synthetic palette of sounds and textures, Reason is surely going to become your program of choice in the very near future.

What You'll Find in This Book

This book will provide all of the information you need in order to use Reason to its maximum creative potential. Some of the subjects that you'll find in this book include:

- An overview of the Reason interface.

- An up-close and detailed explanation of each Reason device, including synths, effects, and the sequencer.

- An explanation of how to create songs within Reason.

However, another great benefit that this book offers is additional information that will surely help you beyond the reaches of Reason including:

- Selecting computer and hardware for your Reason studio.

- Proper mixing techniques.

- Mixing down your music.

So it goes without saying that this book is not just about Reason, but all of the other "important stuff" that you'll need to know in order to get the most out of Reason.

Who This Book Is For

This book was created to suit the needs of both beginners and advanced users of Reason. Within these pages, just about every part of the program is explained in explicit detail and should get you in the know quickly and easily.

How This Book Is Organized

This book is organized in a way that is meant to take readers from the beginnings of setting up a Reason studio to the more complicated intricacies of the program itself. As mentioned before I will also share several tips and tricks along the way that will help you get the most out of Reason in a way that's easy to understand. However, there's no need to read this book from left to right, so feel free to jump around from time to time and learn about what you want to specifically know as there are several points of interest through the entire book. The chapters are arranged as follows:

- **Chapter 1:** This chapter will introduce you to Reason and different related topics such as MIDI and digital audio.

- **Chapter 2:** This chapter will help you put together your Reason studio and take you through the steps of installation.

- **Chapter 3:** This chapter is great for beginners, as it takes you through a guided tour of Reason by making use of the demo song.

- **Chapter 4:** In this book, there's no wait to create, as this chapter will help you create your first Reason song.

- **Chapter 5:** This chapter is meant to take you into the brain of Reason, better known as the sequencer.

- **Chapter 6:** Here's where you'll find it's all in the mix, as this chapter will introduce you to the mixer of Reason, called reMix.

- **Chapter 7:** You say you've got a beat fetish, but you're rhythmically challenged? That's no problem, as Redrum will give you the sounds and rhythms you need.

- **Chapter 8:** Want to take your drums to the max? The Kong Drum Designer is just what you're looking for.

- **Chapter 9:** Today's music is heavily built on rhythmic bits of audio called loops, and Dr. Octo Rex is the loop monster.

- **Chapter 10:** One of the first software synths that Reason offers you is the Subtractor. This chapter will focus in on how to use it and program different sounds.

- **Chapter 11:** Leave it to Propellerhead software to create its own form of synthesis. The Malström uses graintable synthesis to create sounds that will knock you out.

- **Chapter 12:** Thor is a soft synth that resembles something from an Emerson, Lake, and Palmer concert, but without the patch cables. This synth in a word: awesome.

- **Chapters 13/14:** Want to add some real sounds to your music such as voices and strings? The NN-19 (Chapter 13) and NN-XT (Chapter 14) are up to the challenge.

- **Chapter 15:** With all of this future music, Reason includes a separate sequencer called the Matrix, which is a retro styled control voltage sequencer.

- **Chapter 16:** No synthesizer is complete without an arpeggiator, and the RPG-8 is one of the best.

- **Chapter 17:** Need to spice up your mix with distortion, delay, and a bit of reverb? The real-time effects of Reason will provide everything you'll need.

- **Chapter 18:** The MClass Mastering Suite is a host of effects used to clean and polish your Reason songs and make them CD-ready.

- **Chapter 19:** Want all of your favorite Reason synths and patches ready to go in a one-click function? The Combinator makes this possible and then some.

- **Chapter 20:** Learn all the ins and outs of automation in this chapter.

- **Chapter 21:** This chapter will show you how to use other popular music applications such as Pro Tools, Cubase, and SONAR with Reason by using a unique feature called ReWire.

- **Chapter 22:** When it's time to mix your music, this is the chapter to turn to. Here, you'll learn how to mix down and publish your music.

- **Appendix A:** So you have loops that you'd like to use with Reason? ReCycle! is the solution and you'll read all about it here.

- **Appendix B:** Everyone needs new sounds eventually and Propellerhead already thought of that and introduced them as ReFills. In this appendix, you'll learn how they work and, more importantly, how to create your own.

1 Introduction to Reason 5.0

I t is truly an exciting time in the history of music when you can have at your fingertips a creative tool as powerful as Reason 5.0! Propellerhead has created a complete dream studio for your computer that would satisfy any hardcore synth user, and they've made it so intuitive and enjoyable to use that before you know it, you will find that it has become a direct extension of your creative self.

Since the release of the first version of Reason in 2000, the program has found its way into the hands of some of the most innovative musicians, composers, and electronic music producers in the world; it can be heard on countless dance and techno recordings as well as numerous film scores. And with every new version released, the buzz just won't die down! This is due in large part to the ingeniously conceived, easy-to-understand graphical user interface (or GUI) which, combined with the ever-expanding wealth of fantastic sounds, makes Reason an ideal music-creation tool for both amateur and professional musicians alike.

This chapter outlines the basics of the technology behind Reason 5.0 and covers the following topics:

- An overview of Reason 5.0

- MIDI and how it relates to Reason

- Digital audio basics and how they relate to Reason

What Is Reason 5.0?

Reason is music-composition software that was conceived, developed, and released by Propellerhead Software in 2000. It supplies the best of both software synthesis and sequencing for creative music production aimed at the electronic music scene. Within Reason lies the capability to produce, sequence, and professionally mix and master electronic music that consists of every element from glossy synth leads to acid-drenched bass lines to bone-crunching "four-on-the-floor" drum loops. As you can see in Figure 1.1, it's all here and available at your fingertips.

Aside from synthesis, Reason also houses a powerful arsenal of real-time effects that rival just about any hardware-based effect module found in any professional studio.

Figure 1.1 Reason 5.0—the electronic dream studio.

The list of effects ranges from reverbs to delays to chorus and other popular effects, such as vocoders and distortions. In addition, Reason 5.0 includes a complete world-class mastering suite to push your mixes to the next level. All of these tools are ready to go at the click of a mouse button and can be used in just about every creative way possible.

Here's a quick rundown of what Reason is and what it's capable of:

■ **Virtual Synthesizers**—Reason's sounds are produced by virtual synthesizers and sound modules. These synths emulate the look and feel of hardware synths and sound modules found in a music production studio. Everything from drum machines to analog synths to samplers can be found within the Reason interface.

■ **MIDI Sequencing**—Sequencing refers to the ability to record a performance using Reason synths, drum "machines," and so on. These performances are then stored on your computer and are available to edit and play back.

■ **MIDI Editing**—Once the performance has been sequenced, editing those performances within Reason is where some of the real magic of computer music takes place.

With editing, you can make both broad and intricate changes to the feel and sound of your song.

- **Routing and Mixing**—Just about any device in Reason can be virtually routed to another device by using the mouse and your creativity. Once you route the devices to other devices, Reason provides a virtual mixing board that resembles most popular hardware mixers found in studios. These virtual mixers can be used as master mixers for your entire song or as sub-mixers for other devices within Reason.

- **Real-Time Effects**—A good real-world music studio is nothing without the help of a healthy dose of hardware effects to produce cavernous reverbs and teeth-grinding distortions. All of that potential can be found within Reason by supplying real-time effects that use your computer's processor to create ambiences that you never thought were possible.

- **Synchronization**—Aside from creativity, the name of the game in computer music is expandability. Propellerhead has created its own proprietary format called ReWire to allow Reason to be used with many popular pro-audio software titles like Pro Tools or Cubase.

In case it's your first time working with a program like this, it's best to first get your hands around some of the terminology and jargon by taking a quick tour through computer music history.

MIDI and Reason

MIDI is short for Musical Instrument Digital Interface. It is a communication protocol that was developed and implemented in 1983 by most of the major synthesizer manufacturers at the time, such as Roland, Korg, and Yamaha. The simplest way to explain what MIDI does is to describe a scenario in which a simple connection is made between two keyboards.

1. Assume that you have connected two keyboards via a MIDI cable, as shown in Figure 1.2. You are all set to transmit a MIDI signal from one keyboard, called the "master," to the other keyboard, called the "slave."

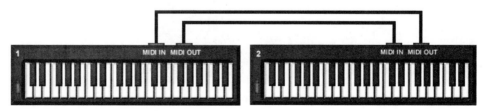

Figure 1.2 Two keyboards can be connected via MIDI.

2. Press the Middle C key on your master keyboard. This sends a MIDI signal to the slave keyboard. This MIDI signal contains a series of messages telling the slave that a note was pressed, which note it was, and how hard you pressed the note. In MIDI terms, these events are called Note On, Note Number, and Note Velocity.

3. The slave keyboard responds to this data by playing the corresponding note on its own keyboard, using the parameters specified in the MIDI message from the master keyboard.

4. After playing the note on your master, you release the key, which sends another MIDI signal to the slave. This signal also contains a series of messages, including Note Off and Note Number.

5. The slave keyboard receives this message and releases the corresponding key on its own keyboard.

If you wanted to create a full music production using MIDI in the previous 10 years or so, a boatload of hardware was required in order to compose, create, edit, and mix a piece of music. If you walked into any studio in the 90s, you would have seen racks and racks full of processors, synthesizers, and probably a few ADAT tape machines, not to mention a huge mixing console in the middle of everything. Just have a look at Figure 1.3.

Figure 1.3 Back in the "good ol' days" of recording.

Fast-forward to the present and you'll find that, for the purposes of recording audio, just about every studio has switched from tape machines to computers. It is also much more common to find studio musicians using software-based synthesizers rather than large costly hardware synths (see Figure 1.4).

Figure 1.4 Welcome to the virtual studio.

Reason is a top-rated solution for the computer musician because it offers so many possibilities for composing and playing music:

- Reason is a fantastic MIDI sequencer, with every feature you could want for creating music using MIDI.

- Reason has a large selection of virtual synthesizers, drum machines, and sound modules suitable for nearly every style of music.

- Reason supplies a fantastic virtual mixer as well as real-time effects and mastering tools that rival just about any hardware rack effects.

MIDI Is Not Digital Audio   It's important to note that MIDI is not the same as digital audio. MIDI is essentially a language that transmits performance commands from one device to another.

On the other hand, digital audio is created by capturing analog signals and converting them into digital files.

Reason does record digital audio, but not in the same way as a DAW (digital audio workstation), such as Steinberg's Cubase or Avid's Pro Tools. Reason can record samples of audio, such as a snare drum or guitar riff, and then use those samples in musical and rhythmic ways with the provided drum machines and sampler. However, Reason can't be used to record a full, linear vocal track or a guitar track. This is where you would want to use Pro Tools or Cubase. Reason is designed to integrate seamlessly with your favorite DAW software via Propellerhead's ReWire technology, discussed in detail in Chapter 21, "ReWire."

Upon its initial release, MIDI allowed keyboard players to link up and access several keyboards simultaneously. This allowed keyboardists to "layer" their sounds and create thick and heavy orchestrations in a live or studio setting. But that was just the beginning.

In the mid 80s, computer manufacturers began to develop a way of using a computer to communicate with keyboards and other peripherals via the MIDI standard. Although many computer companies integrated to MIDI by way of external hardware (remember the Commodore 64?), the now defunct Atari computer company released the 1040ST. It was one of the first computers to incorporate MIDI by including an interface on the side of the computer that sent and received MIDI signals (see Figure 1.5).

Figure 1.5 The Atari 1040ST.

Software companies were also starting to see the potential impact of developing programs to help record MIDI events and play them back as a sequence of events, hence the term *sequencing*. One of the first programs to make it out of the starting gate was called Pro 24, released by a then small German software company called Steinberg. This program could record, edit, and play back MIDI events on multiple "virtual tracks." These virtual tracks are not like audio tracks on a tape machine because they simply record and play MIDI data events, which is much different than audio events. Don't worry—digital audio will be explained later in this chapter.

What's That Name Again?   If the name Pro 24 doesn't ring a bell, it's probably because it doesn't exist anymore. Steinberg stopped development on the Pro 24 to make way for its flagship program, Cubase, a very popular program that you'll take a look at toward the end of this book.

Let's have a look at a typical MIDI sequencing setup (see Figure 1.6).

1. The first component needed in a MIDI sequencing setup is a controller keyboard that sends and receives MIDI messages.

2. This master keyboard is connected to a MIDI interface, which receives and sends MIDI messages to the computer, the master keyboard, and any other MIDI peripherals (or slave devices) in your sequencing setup.

3. The MIDI interface is connected to a computer running a MIDI sequencing program. This program can receive, record, edit, and play back MIDI messages to the master and slave devices.

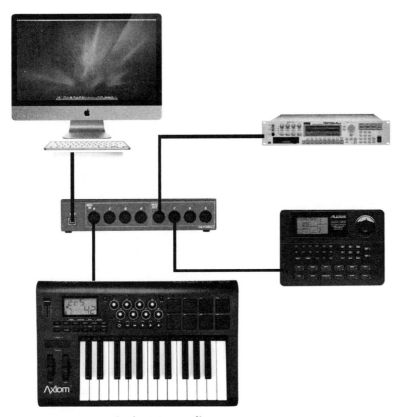

Figure 1.6 A typical MIDI studio setup.

Where Can You Learn More About MIDI?   Although Reason is a very capable MIDI sequencing program, the fact is that this book can't realistically cover every aspect of MIDI. For everything you might need to know about MIDI, check out *MIDI Power!, Second Edition* by Robert Guerin (Thomson Learning, 2005).

Digital Audio and Reason

When you get right down to it, Reason has virtually nothing to do with *recording* digital audio, as it is strictly a MIDI sequencing program. That said, Reason certainly does dip its big toe in the pool of digital audio, as all of its virtual synths and sound modules rely heavily on the existence and functionality of digital audio.

■ The Redrum drum module synth uses digital samples in order to play back acoustic, electronic, or heavily processed drum sounds (see Figure 1.7). These digital samples are stored on your computer's hard drive and then loaded into RAM when used in Reason. And now with Reason 5.0, you can actually record your own drum and percussion samples.

Figure 1.7 Redrum is the virtual drum machine that techno dreams are made of.

■ The Kong is a drum module synth that differs in many ways from Redrum (see Figure 1.8). New to Reason 5.0, the Kong is a drum designer synth that allows you both to sample your own drum sounds and/or use its synth engine to generate drum sounds. Kong also provides several powerful editing tools and effects to craft your drum sounds. And finally, it bears a striking resemblance to the classic Akai MPC hardware drum machine, which has been used on more hip-hop tracks than can be counted.

■ The NN-XT and NN-19 sound modules are Reason's sample playback modules. They both play digital samples of real instruments, such as guitars, vocals, drums, and orchestral instruments (see Figure 1.9). As with Redrum, these sound modules store the samples on your computer's hard drive and are loaded into RAM when used, or you can simply record your own samples.

Figure 1.8 The Kong Drum Designer is retro in look, yet includes a futuristic feature set.

- Dr. Octo Rex is a sound module that plays digitally sampled loops, which are stored and accessed just like the samples played by NN-XT, NN-19, and Redrum (see Figure 1.10).

- Reason's virtual synths, called the Subtractor, Malström, and Thor (see Figures 1.11, 1.12, and 1.13) are software emulations of hardware synths. Through a process called *physical modeling,* which you'll learn about later in this book, all these synths produce sound by using different forms of synthesis.

- Once you have completed creating and mixing a song in Reason, you must then export your audio mix as a digital audio file. As you can see in Figure 1.14, Reason has many exporting options.

Just the Tip of the Iceberg   This section contains just a brief overview of the sound modules in Reason. Each module has its own dedicated chapter in this book.

Much like an analog tape recorder, your computer has the capability to record sounds, such as voice, guitar, drums, keyboards, kazoos, or whatever other instrument or sound you can think of. These sounds are then translated into digital data (called

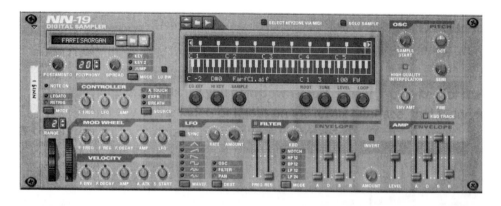

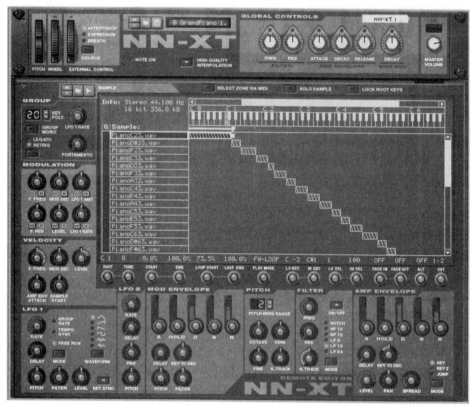

Figure 1.9 Whether you like your samplers easy or complex, the NN-19 and NN-XT will meet your needs.

samples), which are then stored on your computer's hard drive. This data can then be played back and heard through your computer's speakers.

Thanks to enhanced and intuitive graphical user interfaces (or GUIs), using a computer to record and play back audio in a virtual studio is similar to the look and feel of an analog studio, but the actual process of accomplishing this task within your computer is much different. This section outlines the basics of how to record both analog and digital sound.

Figure 1.10 Loops come alive in Dr. Octo Rex.

Figure 1.11 The Subtractor is a fantastic virtual analog synth for creating driving bass lines and dreamy pads.

Figure 1.12 The Malström Graintable Synth is in a class by itself.

Figure 1.13 Thor is a soft synth that combines different forms of synthesis along with effects and sequencers.

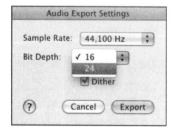

Figure 1.14 Reason offers many audio mixdown options.

Analog Sound—Frequency and Amplitude

A sound can simply be defined as a vibration that is capable of being detected by a human ear. When our eardrums vibrate, we are "hearing a sound." The rate at which our eardrums (and the sound-producing object) vibrate is called the vibration's *frequency*.

Frequency is measured in units called Hertz (or Hz), named after the German scientist Heinrich R. Hertz. A Hertz is defined as the number of vibrational cycles that a sound produces in one second. A single Hertz is equal to one cycle per second, which is far too low a frequency for the human ear to detect. The Hertz unit is usually combined with metric system prefixes to produce various subdivisions. These are commonly known as the kilohertz (kHz), the megahertz (MHz), and the gigahertz (GHz).

A finely tuned human ear is capable of detecting a broad frequency range, from about 20Hz to 20kHz (20,000Hz). The range narrows as we grow older and as our hearing is dulled due to the effects of listening to loud noises over long periods of time. It's important to treat your hearing like gold!

So how does the frequency spectrum translate into musical terms? Consider a stringed instrument, such as a cello, which has a pretty wide frequency range, as an example. When a note is bowed on the lowest string, the string vibrations are very slow, as the diameter of the string is quite thick in comparison to the highest string. This produces a very low frequency vibration, which in turn means that the sounded note is very low in pitch. On the other end of that spectrum, if the cello player were then to play a note on the highest string, the vibrations would be much more rapid, creating a tone with higher frequency and pitch.

Frequency also has a counterpart element, called *amplitude*, which is simply the volume of the sound and is measured in units called *decibels*. Every sound has a frequency and an amplitude. If you play one piano note softly, the frequency is constant and the amplitude is low. If you play the same note again, but press the key harder than before, the frequency will be the same, but the amplitude will be higher, producing a louder sound.

The graphical plotting of the frequency and amplitude of a sound is called a *waveform*. Frequency is represented on the horizontal axis, and amplitude is on the vertical. A very simple waveform with low amplitude looks something like Figure 1.15, and that same waveform with greater amplitude looks like Figure 1.16. If you were to draw a waveform with a low frequency, it would look something like Figure 1.17, whereas a higher frequency would look like Figure 1.18.

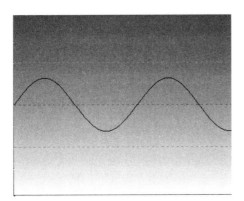

Figure 1.15 A simple waveform with low amplitude.

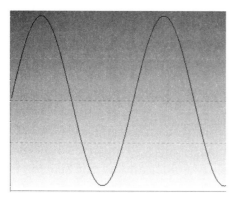

Figure 1.16 A little bit louder now.

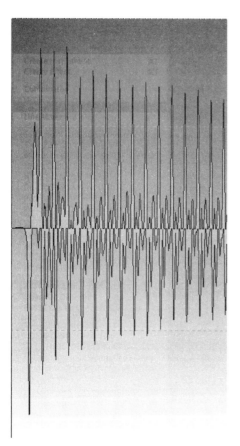

Figure 1.17 A waveform with a low frequency.

But sounds in the real world are most often not simple waveforms. They are typically much more complex, because there are numerous frequencies and amplitudes occurring simultaneously in just about any sound. With that in mind, look at Figure 1.19 to see a complex waveform. This figure is from a program called WaveLab.

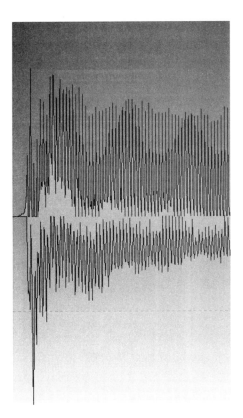

Figure 1.18 A waveform with a high frequency.

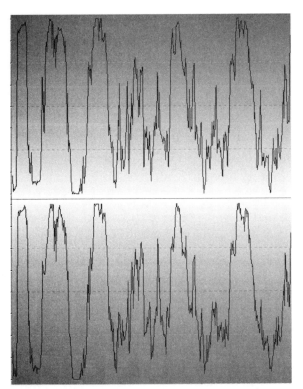

Figure 1.19 Here's a much more complex waveform with a variety of frequencies and amplitudes.

Space—The Final Dimension

In addition to frequency and amplitude, the third and final dimension that defines sound is *space*. It can be thought of as a counterpart to amplitude, as it is space that defines the amplitude of a recorded sound through time. For example, say you are recording your hand clapping in a medium sized room with the microphone placed in proximity to your hands. The recorded sound will be very loud and present, as there is very little space between your hands and the microphone. Next, try recording your hand clapping again in the same room, but standing much farther from the microphone. The recorded sound will be much different from before, not only in amplitude, but also in character.

For certain instruments, a little space is needed in order to accurately capture their entire frequency range. A good example of this is a recording of an orchestral ensemble within a large auditorium, where the microphones are typically placed a good distance from the instruments.

For other instruments, such as drums or acoustic guitars, very little or no space is ideal for accurately capturing their frequency range. However, a commonly used technique for adding ambience or character to a recording of these instruments is to place an additional microphone far away from the instrument. This "ambient mic" is then mixed in with the proximity microphones, resulting in an interesting recording.

Digital Audio and Sampling

Although both analog and digital audio generally have the same purpose and application, the technology behind how the two are recorded is very different. Frequency and amplitude are still both important in digital recording, they are just processed in another way, using a technology called *sampling*.

In 1928, an AT&T engineer named Harry Nyquist theorized that he could accurately record a waveform by sampling its frequency and amplitude electronically twice in one cycle, and then play these samples back perfectly replicated. Although this theory was to become the basis of digital audio as we know it, Nyquist unfortunately didn't have the available technology to prove his theory. Nevertheless, the Nyquist theory has been proven to some degree, and it is this theory that makes it possible to record audio digitally. Impressive show, Mr. Nyquist!

By using the Nyquist theory, you can simply describe the process of sampling.

1. Amplitude is measured as voltage values and then captured as numeric data called *bits*.

2. These bits are essentially binary data comprised of ones and zeros, each one representing "on," and each zero representing "off." Although bits can represent large numbered values, in computer terms these values translate into long strings of ones and zeros.

3. The more bits, the more possible measurements of amplitude. This essentially will mean more volume potential to musicians.

4. The rate at which these bits are captured is described as a frequency measured in kilohertz. This is called the *sampling rate*.

5. The higher the sampling rate, the better the overall clarity of the captured bits.

Earlier in the chapter, it was stated that a human ear could detect sounds ranging from 20Hz to 20kHz. Wait a tick, isn't the frequency range of a CD much higher? Yes, this is true, as a CD has a sampling rate of 44.1kHz, which is more than twice the hearing potential of a human ear.

Recall, though, that the Nyquist theory that states that a waveform must be sampled twice during each cycle in order to reproduce the waveform accurately. This means that in order to reproduce the waveform clearly, the sampling rate has to be doubled in order to accurately reproduce a waveform, which would give you a potential of around 44.1kHz. Ta da!

Bit Depth?   If you're just getting into digital audio, you should familiarize yourself with the jargon related to the field. At the top of your list should be *bit depth*.

Bit depth relates to the number of data bits that are needed in order to accurately capture analog signals at different amplitudes. As you read in the previous section, these bits are represented in the simple binary language of zeros and ones. For example, an 8-bit recording could have approximately 256 amplitude levels that would be represented as a rather long string of zeros and ones in binary (for example, 00001100, 10100010). A standard 16-bit recording would have nearly 65,535 amplitude levels that would be represented in a virtually endless string of zeros and ones.

Although a commercial audio compact disc has a standard bit depth of 16 bits, the professional recording studio typically records audio at a much higher bit depth, usually 24. This is to ensure that the recorded audio is being captured at its highest potential. The more bits available to digitally capture a sound, the more accurate that captured sound will be in terms of dynamic range.

You'll learn much more about this and other digital audio terms as you get deeper into Reason. Pretty soon, you'll be able to sling techno terms like a pro!

As you can see, Reason has a lot going on under the hood. Now that you have all of the Mr. Wizard stuff out of the way, it's time to install Reason, take a guided tour of the program, and start making some music!

2 Installing and Configuring Reason

Before diving into making music with Reason 5.0, you first need to consider installing, configuring, and optimizing the program. Although this might sound like a chore, it's really a simple task. I have installed Reason on a number of computers and operating systems, and could pretty much do it blindfolded at this point. But worry not; I'll lead you through this chapter with both eyes open, so you can breathe a sigh of relief.

This chapter covers the following topics:

- Equipping the ideal Reason studio

- Choosing a computer to use for Reason

- Installing Reason and configuring it for both PC and Mac

- Making small adjustments to let Reason rock your computer

The Ideal Reason Studio

With all that Reason is capable of, you might imagine it requires the latest in cutting-edge computing power. You will be surprised to learn that the actual requirements for a killer Reason studio are not so high. In this game, you are going to learn one important governing rule: keep it simple. Let's have a look at what goes into an ideal Reason studio (see Figure 2.1).

- A computer that meets the system requirements listed on the Reason box

- A controller keyboard that can send MIDI signals

- A sound card (internal or external)

- A microphone for sampling

- A pair of speakers (self-powered or with a separate amplifier)

- A mixing board (this isn't an essential component to get you started, but it couldn't hurt)

That wasn't such a long list, now was it? Let's examine these components.

Figure 2.1 Here's a typical Reason studio that is ready to rock and roll with the best of them.

What's Under the Hood?

Whether you are buying a computer off the shelf at your local computer store, having a computer customized and built to your specifications, or making a brave attempt at buying the parts and building your own system, there are five factors (or commandments, if you will) that will ultimately determine the performance you will get from Reason.

Here are the five commandments of computer building (you can say these out loud in your best Charlton Heston voice if you want):

- Thou shalt choose a central processing unit (or CPU) that will be fast enough to get thy music grooving now and for a long time to come.

- Thou shalt purchase an abundance of Random Access Memory, or RAM, that will permit thy music to contain a sea of funky loops, drums, and samples.

- Thou shalt purchase a large hard drive to ensure that thy music can be saved in abundance.

- Thou shalt purchase a DVD burner to back up thy precious music created within Reason.

■ Thou shalt select a proper sound card to ensure that thy music sounds freakin' awesome.

Oh yes, there is one more commandment—one that's very important but not spoken nearly enough:

■ Thou shalt have fun doing this!

CPU (Central Processing Unit)

The CPU is where all the real-time processing for your computer is handled. Installed on the computer's motherboard, the CPU handles and regulates the flow of information throughout the entire computer, and, most importantly, gives you the juice you need to make Reason rock and roll inside your computer.

The only problem with selecting the right kind of CPU for your computer is that there are so many to choose from. Consider the following list of available CPUs for both PC and Mac.

■ **Intel** has developed and released a long line of CPUs for the Windows platform. At the time of this writing, the Core i3/5/7 processor series is the most current and can range in speeds from 2.26 to a blistering 3.33GHz.

■ **AMD** is another company that has developed many CPUs for the Windows platform. AMD's current hot rod of choice is the Athlon II series, which can run at speeds comparable to the Intel "i" series, which is more than enough juice for Reason.

■ **Apple** has a well-known reputation of pushing the envelope of computer evolution and development. A few years ago, they introduced computers that utilized Intel processors, and these can be found in all of the current Apple systems, including the MacBook, MacBook Pro, Mac Mini, iMac, and Mac Pro computers.

How Much Is Enough?   How much processor power should you get? The simple answer is to purchase the fastest processor you can afford. In PC terms, the fastest i3/5/7 or Athlon II will do very nicely; with Apple computers, get the fastest Intel processor you can find and afford. Keep in mind that "bigger is always better" when it comes to buying or building a computer.

RAM (Random Access Memory)

Computers use two kinds of memory: permanent and temporary. Permanent memory can save and store data when the computer is powered down; temporary memory (called RAM, for Random Access Memory) stores data only when the computer is turned on. RAM stores and processes data while the computer is turned on, but it loses that data when the computer is turned off. When it comes to Reason, the primary function of RAM is to store the temporary data that is loaded up within a Reason song file. Simply put, if you are using any samples, loops, or drum machines within a Reason song, that information is held in temporary memory, or RAM.

The best rule of thumb here is to make sure that you have a lot of RAM installed in your computer. It will help Reason run more smoothly, and it will help prevent computer crashes that can sometimes happen due to a shortage of RAM. It's best to have at least 2GB of RAM. This will give you plenty of headroom to work with. Just keep in mind that more is always better (and RAM is quite affordable these days), so feel free to splurge.

Hard Drive

Your computer's hard drive is your medium for permanent data storage. Among other things, it holds your operating system, your applications, and, above all, your Reason song files. The hard drive is also where you will eventually store the digital audio mixes of your Reason songs.

The first key to purchasing a good hard drive is to go with a well-known brand name. Western Digital, Seagate, and Hitachi are all well-known and respected brands. Next, make sure that the drive meets the following list of requirements that will allow it to achieve good performance with Reason (and most other music-creation software):

- **Transfer rate**—How much digital data can the hard drive transfer per second? You'll want to make sure the hard drive has a transfer rate of at least 10 megabytes or higher per second.

- **Seek or access time**—How fast does the hard drive access information? The hard drive must have a seek time of 10 milliseconds (ms) or less in order to be used for digital audio.

- **Rotation speed**—How fast does the hard drive rotate? Many hard drives have a rotation speed of 5,400 rotations per minute (RPM), and will do just fine for Reason. But, if you're willing to go the extra mile, look for a hard drive that has a rotation speed of 7,200 RPM or better.

There was a time not so many years ago when a "large" hard drive of 4 gigabytes (GB), like those found in top-of-the-line Power Macs in 1998, was pretty darned impressive. Today, programs such as Reason can use up that much storage space in no time. In order to give yourself plenty of room to work with, look for a hard drive with at least 500GB of storage space. You might even consider popping in a 1TB (terabyte) drive or better because prices are so good these days.

Thinking Ahead   Let's take a moment to consider an ugly fact of computing life: hard drive crashes. Like earthquakes, hard drive crashes are nearly impossible to predict. But they happen; and in all likelihood your hard drive will crash one day, no matter how well you care for your computer. But there's a cheap, easy remedy: back your hard drive up to CD or DVD frequently. If you don't own a DVD burner, run right out and buy one as soon as possible. You'll be saving yourself from the future panic attacks and gray hairs that come with hard drive crashes.

If you're not into the idea of burning CDs or DVDs, you might also consider a thumb drive, which is essentially a stick of RAM that acts as a USB hard drive when plugged into one of your computer's USB ports. They're super cheap and easy to find at your local computer or office supply store.

One Drive, Two Drive, Red Drive, Blue Drive   Should you install two hard drives? The short answer is yes; a second hard drive is very helpful. You can perform quicker backups by copying data from one hard drive to another; and after all, as the saying goes, "two heads are better than one." But is this *necessary* for Reason? Not really, because the digital audio involved in a Reason song is stored in your computer's RAM, essentially making your second hard drive superfluous.

But if your intention is to use Reason in conjunction with another Digital Audio Workstation (or DAW) program, such as Record, Cubase, Logic, or Pro Tools, a second hard drive will certainly be needed. It doesn't even have to be installed in the computer, because there are several fantastic external hard drives that support USB, FireWire, and eSATA.

Because the prices of computer hardware are so reasonable these days, I would say if you have the cash, go for it; but remember that you can always upgrade your computer at a later date.

Sound Card—Your Digital Audio Connection

The quality of your sound card determines the fidelity of all audio recorded into your computer (the analog-to-digital conversion) and played out of your computer (the digital-to-analog conversion). Your sound card is responsible for both playing back digital audio in Reason and providing the capability to create real-time performances within Reason while the program is running. To put it simply, the sound card is just about the most important part of your studio, with the possible exception of your creativity.

Because there are so many cards available, you need to make sure yours supports one of the driver formats discussed next. The driver is software that comes with the sound card and that closely integrates the sound card with the operating system. This will ensure better accuracy and performance from Reason, because it will decrease the latency effect that can occur when using Reason as a real-time performance tool. If you are on the prowl for a new audio card, your timing couldn't be any better because there are many affordable audio cards with mind-blowing features and reasonable price tags. For example, it's now possible to purchase a 24-bit/96kHz sound card for well under $200 at your local music shop.

The Latency Effect   *Latency*, simply put, is the time lag between striking a note on your instrument and hearing that note played back through your studio speakers.

For example, on the Fourth of July, you see the fireworks explode in mid-air, but you have to wait almost a full second before you hear the explosion, depending on the distance between you and the fireworks. That is *latency*, plain and simple. But fireworks latency is a result of distance. In computer synthesis, the latency effect occurs primarily because it takes a certain amount of time for your sound card to process the audio information before your speakers can generate the sound.

ASIO Drivers. In 1996, the German company Steinberg developed and released a driver format called ASIO, or Audio Stream Input/Output. ASIO started a trend in digital audio technology by introducing an affordable way to use both the processing power of the computer's CPU and the DSP (Digital Signal Processing) of the sound card to produce a real-time audio performance in both PCs and Macs (although the current Mac operating system has eschewed ASIO in favor of Mac's own CoreAudio driver technology—more on that next). To make things even better, Steinberg made the ASIO source code available to any company who wanted to write and design ASIO drivers for their audio cards and programs. The ASIO technology took off like a rocket to Mars and is currently supported in several audio cards and numerous digital audio programs, such as Reason. If you are using a PC, you definitely want to be using ASIO drivers whenever possible for one reason above all others: ASIO offers latency times substantially lower than DirectX or MME for that matter, which is the worst of the bunch.

DirectX Drivers. If you are on the Windows platform and your sound card does not support ASIO drivers (it's pretty hard to find a card that doesn't these days), you will need to use the card's DirectX drivers instead. Developed by Microsoft using their DirectSound technology, DirectX is a common driver format. The driver is included with every consumer and professional digital sound card on the market today and is very easy to use and configure for pro audio and computer gaming.

WDM Drivers. In 2001, Microsoft released yet another driver format: WDM (Windows Driver Model). Built from the technology in the Windows XP operating system and supported in latest Windows 7, the WDM format is another in a long list of drivers supported by Reason.

CoreAudio Drivers. In 2002, Apple announced that they were releasing their own audio driver technology called CoreAudio, which essentially performs the same tasks as ASIO or WDM, except that it was designed and optimized for OSX. This driver format has quickly gained popularity in the Macintosh community due to its ease of use, and it has performance and latency characteristics comparable to those of ASIO.

Which Sound Card Should You Purchase? It's almost impossible to say because there are so many cards to choose from that support the driver formats discussed here. The answer, for you, will depend largely on your needs and your budget.

Would You Like a PC or Mac with That?

The PC/Mac debate is reminiscent of that old beer commercial where the drunks get into a shouting match of "Taste's Great! Less Filling!" I own and use both PCs and Macs on a daily basis in my studio. Each platform has its advantages and shortcomings. Here's my take on some of the differences:

- **Operating systems**—When Windows 98 was first released, it instantly hooked users with its intuitive graphical interface, and many people felt that it had the Mac's OS 8.5 beat by a mile. The introduction of Windows 7, with its very user-friendly interface and more new features than you can shake a stick at, sealed the deal even further for many Windows users, although many studios, especially those with Pro Tools systems, were sticking with the Mac OS. The landscape changed with the current version of Mac OSX. Although OSX was initially not quite ready for pro audio applications such as Reason and Cubase, it still had a slick new look to it that was addicting to use. Now with the current release of OS 10.6, "Snow Leopard," I certainly feel that the Mac OS is a worthy competitor to Windows.

- **Available software**—Let's face it, there is simply a lot more software available for the PC than for the Mac. But unless you are a computer gaming fanatic, most of these software titles are irrelevant, because they are not meant for music composition. In fact, it is worth noting that there are now two popular professional DAW software titles, MOTU's Digital Performer and Apple's Logic Studio, which only run on Mac.

- **Price**—No matter what the pros and cons of PCs and Macs may be, the choice is usually going to come down to a matter of price. Until recently, PCs were known for being much less expensive than Macs. A complete PC that will do a decent job with Reason can be purchased for as low as $600, including a monitor. This doesn't include the price of Reason or a really great sound card, but it will certainly get you started and keep you going for a long time to come. Macintosh began to meet the

PC price challenge a few years ago, with the introduction of the iMac and Mac Mini computers. These fantastic little systems start at around $699 and come with a somewhat decent sound card, and, like the budget PCs, the iMac and Mac Mini will get you up and running and keep you going for a good long while.

If you're thinking about buying a new computer and are wondering if perhaps it's time to switch platforms, I suggest that you stick with what you already know. The whole point of buying Reason, and this book, is to enjoy being creative with Reason, not to do battle with a new operating system at the same time. Reason simply works great on both platforms, and that's really all you need to know.

Running Windows on a Mac?   For several years, Mac users wanting to dabble in the land of Windows have been able to do so by using programs such as Parallels, which would essentially start Windows from within Mac OSX. While this is a neat idea, it can use up quite a bit of CPU power and RAM in order to run it. Now, Apple computers can run Windows natively using a fantastic new program called Boot Camp. Once installed, the Mac will ask which operating system to use upon starting the computer. It's a pretty new concept that is starting to gain a lot of momentum in the music community.

For more information, please visit http://www.apple.com/macosx/bootcamp/.

Choosing the Right MIDI Keyboard for Reason

For triggering all the synths and other instruments in Reason, it's important to have a MIDI keyboard of some kind. It could be a keyboard with its own built-in sounds, such as a Yamaha or Roland, or you could choose a MIDI controller keyboard, which is simply a MIDI keyboard without built-in sounds. If you have not purchased a keyboard yet but are intending to, I recommend purchasing one without built-in sounds. Why? Think of it this way; once you start using the synths in Reason, are you really going to need additional sounds from another keyboard? Probably not, because the synths in Reason will certainly give you the sounds sets that you will need to get the job done. Another disadvantage of getting a keyboard with built-in sounds is that Reason does *not* sequence external MIDI instruments and devices, making the purchase of this kind of keyboard a potential waste of money.

Controller keyboards (see Figures 2.2 and 2.3 for examples) are really the right choice for Reason, offering several key advantages:

■ They cost far less than a keyboard with built-in sounds. A standard 25-key controller can be purchased for well under $200.

■ They come in a wide variety of sizes and configurations. For example, if you are a classically trained piano student and you want to use a keyboard with weighted

Figure 2.2 The Axiom 25 by M-Audio gives you the best of both worlds by supplying knobs and pads for controlling specific Reason parameters, all in a compact keyboard. Plus, it's built like a tank, so it can take plenty of abuse.

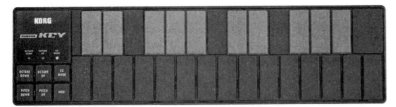

Figure 2.3 The Korg Nano KEY is a great micro solution for laptop users or musicians with space limitations. Sure, it doesn't have all of the bells and whistles of a standard keyboard controller, but at a cost of around $50, it's a steal.

keys, there are several controller keyboards of this type that are available at your local music store. A traveling musician can buy a very small keyboard to hook up to his or her laptop computer.

- Nearly all of the latest keyboard controllers support the USB (Universal Serial Bus) standard, which is great, because there is no need for any additional hardware, such as a MIDI interface.

- Many controller keyboards come with knobs and sliders that send out MIDI controller messages. These knobs and sliders can be assigned to specific editing functions within Reason (volume, cutoff, and resonance). For example, you might want to control the filters of the Subtractor or possibly the parameters of the real-time effects. Many of the major manufacturers of these controllers have already set up specific templates for use with Reason.

Read the Manual   If you are planning to purchase a USB keyboard or other USB peripheral, be sure to read the installation instructions for the keyboard prior to installing it. A good rule of thumb is to make sure that the USB keyboard is not connected to the computer unless otherwise noted in the instruction manual.

Once the drivers have been installed, you will probably need to restart your computer to complete the installation. After the computer has restarted, you can then plug in and power up the USB keyboard and it should work just fine.

Additionally, check the manufacturer's website to make sure you have the latest drivers.

Other Ways to Play Reason   Although Reason is a keyboardist's dream come true, musicians who play other instruments can get in on the action too. It might surprise you to know that I am not really much of a keyboardist. Oh sure, I play keyboards and I can plunk around on pianos, and of course I love to sound designs with synths, but my primary instrument is guitar. So, back in the "stone age" of technology, I dabbled a bit with MIDI guitars, but found little success, because they were not quite up to snuff. Fortunately, within the last few years, MIDI guitar technology has gotten much better, and I wound up using a small traveling guitar with a MIDI pickup as my "keyboard" for a couple of clinic tours. There's nothing quite like playing synth drum sounds with an acoustic traveling guitar to peak people's interest in what you're doing.

With that in mind, I offer this simple, yet effective layout to give your guitar or bass a healthy dose of MIDI without compromising playing style or feel. You'll need the following pieces:

- **A Roland GK-3 MIDI Pickup**—This is a pickup that simply attaches itself to your guitar with a basic adhesive so you don't have to drill into the guitar's body. The output of the guitar plugs into this MIDI pickup, which allows you to toggle between the MIDI pickup, the guitar pickups, or both, which can lead to fantastic and creative pads and leads. You'll be happy to know that there is a bass version of this pickup called the GK-3B.

- **A Roland GI-20 MIDI Interface**—This is the "brain" of the MIDI guitar rig. It takes the output of the GK-3 and converts it to MIDI and sends it to your Reason rig via USB. From the GI-20, you can also set your playing preferences, such as fingerpicking or strumming, and set the sensitivity.

All in all, you get a much more creative way to enter in your MIDI data into Reason. And hey drummers, check out the latest MIDI drum kits from Simmons, Roland, and Alesis. They won't set you back too much and you can enjoy laying down drum tracks with a much more live feel.

Making a Sound Decision

All of the thrills and chills that the Reason synths produce will only sound as good as the speakers you select for your rig. Speakers come in a wide variety of brands, sizes, and quality and you can bet it will take a bit of budgeting, researching, and auditioning before you're ready to make your final purchase decision.

First, you'll need to decide how much you are going to spend on a new pair of speakers. These days, you can price out a pair of speakers at anywhere between $99–$500 for a decent pair. Just keep in mind the old saying "you get what you pay for," and plan to spend more than $99 for best results. If you want a second opinion, consult the Internet for some articles and reviews on possible speaker selections.

Generally, a day's trip to your local music store will get the job done. A lot of the better-known chain stores, such as Guitar Center or Sam Ash, have their speakers set up in an isolated room so you can properly fire them up and have a listen. You can also purchase most of these speakers online with online stores.

Here are a few things to keep in mind while you are making a sound decision (pun intended):

- When you begin to audition speakers, try to find the *sweet spot* between the pair. This is the point in space at which the mix sounds properly balanced, not too heavy to either the left or the right side. See Figure 2.4 to get a better idea.

- Are you planning to buy a pair of speakers that require an amplifier, or a pair that contain their own power source? If you choose to purchase a separate amplifier, keep in mind that this will certainly affect the total price tag of your purchase.

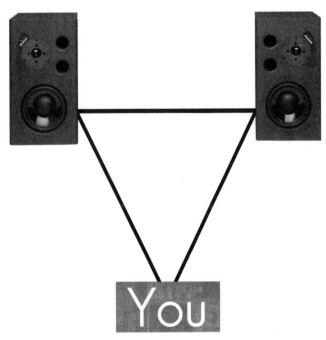

Figure 2.4 The proper speaker placement for the best possible mixing solution. Take a few extra minutes to find the sweet spot in your studio.

■ Bring along a CD of the kind of music you are planning to produce so that you can listen to that through the different pairs of speakers. Because this book is about Reason, a techno or rap/hip-hop CD would probably be the right weapon of choice for this task. Make sure that you listen to the frequency response of the low end. You don't want it to sound too overwhelming or abusive to the rest of the mix.

As previously mentioned, it might take a day or more of listening to various speakers before you reach a decision. The most important advice I can give is to let your ears be the judge. Don't be fooled by big brand names or the size of the woofers. They might be impressive to look at and tell your buddies about, but they could also end up being a bad investment.

Take Command of Your Subs   One of the hottest add-ons to any speaker setup is the subwoofer. This speaker enhances the low end of the EQ curve enough to vibrate every part of your body and enrage any neighbor or older relative within earshot. Although these are killer additions to a studio, don't rely too heavily on them for mixing. They tend to color the sound and may throw off your accuracy when mixing the bass. Not everyone has a subwoofer in his or her speaker system, so if you mix using a subwoofer, your music will sound very different when played back on a system without one. Many subwoofers can be bypassed while mixing, which is recommended. Still, because many electronic musicians may have their tracks played in clubs that use subs, they are useful tools for hearing what's lurking in the bass heavy depths of your mix.

Check Your Head(Set)   Headphones are a great solution for bedroom musicians because they allow you to work late at night without provoking police intervention or a nasty look from your significant other. All kidding aside, even though headphones are useful, you should always plan to do your final mixes using speakers rather than headphones. There are a couple of key reasons for this.

First, you need to create a natural-sounding stereo mix by adjusting the various signals and panning positions of the parts in your Reason song. This is easier to accomplish with speakers than with headphones.

Second, keep in mind that your potential audience is not likely to listen to your music on headphones. Nine times out of ten, they'll be listening to your music in their cars on the way to work or maybe at your latest rave party. When mixing a new song, it's an excellent idea to burn a test CD, run down to your car, and pop it in to listen. If it doesn't sound good there, it's back to the drawing board. So, although headphones are a good interim solution, don't forget how valuable a good set of speakers can be for your mix.

Selecting a Mixer

In your Reason studio, you might find yourself needing the ability to combine various audio sources at the same time. For example, you might have a few sound modules and drum machines that you would like to use in synchronization with Reason; or perhaps you would like to be able to plug in your guitar or mic and strum and sing along with your technophonic cacophony. Whatever the case may be, a little mixer of some kind would probably be a good investment. A couple of great budget mixers are those made by Mackie and Behringer. Both of these companies offer every kind of mixer you could want, from very simple to very complicated (see Figures 2.5 and 2.6).

Figure 2.5 The 1202 VLZ Mixer by Mackie is a good, solid unit for mixing.

Figure 2.6 The Behringer is a much more complex mixer, offering plenty of versatility.

Installing and Configuring Reason

Break out the champagne and start the party because it's time to install Reason onto your computer. The Prop heads have gone to great lengths to create a relatively painless installation procedure that anyone can tackle. Before starting, though, take a minute to make sure you have everything you need.

- The Reason jewel case should contain a single DVD.

- In your Reason box, there should be a slip of paper, which is your Reason Authorization Card. This contains your license number and your registration code, and you will need both of these to install the program and register your program with Propellerhead.

Living in the Past   Windows includes a very useful program called System Restore. This program takes a virtual "picture" of your computer setup, including your installed hardware and software, and then creates a *restore point*. This restore point can then be named and placed in a list that can be recalled later. Why is this useful? Well, let's suppose that after you install Reason, your computer starts acting a little funny—you start having unexplained crashes or lockups. It's pretty safe to assume that the installation of Reason caused some sort of conflict within the computer, resulting in the undesirable behavior. If you create a restore point before you install Reason (or any other program for that matter), you can recall that restore point at any time, restart your computer, and, upon rebooting, it will be as though you never installed Reason in the first place, thereby solving your crashing problems. At this point, you can then start to diagnose the problem by removing unnecessary hardware or additional software.

Also note that there is a program called Time Machine that performs a similar task in Mac OSX.

Crack Kills   Reason is one of the best-selling music software titles on the market today. Years of research and development went into conceiving and creating this program and others like it. Because Reason is such a hot program, you can bet that there are a lot of illegal copies, called *cracks*, floating around the Internet available for download.

Although cracked copies of software might seem tempting to download and install, it only makes things more difficult for software companies, such as Propellerhead, to stay afloat and keep producing fantastic software.

Propellerhead Software has a great reputation for addressing technical issues by updating their software titles regularly; it's important that you purchase and use an official version of Reason, because it will qualify you for technical support, product updates, and loads of free sound ReFills. Remember, software developers have to support their families too.

Installing the Program

If you've got the DVD and your license, you're ready to begin.

1. Pop the Reason program disc into your computer and wait for your PC or Mac to recognize it. On a PC, the installation program may start on its own, depending on your system settings.

2. On a Mac, simply drag the Reason folder from the disc into the Applications folder on your hard drive. On a PC, double-click the file named Install Reason and follow the instructions on the screen.

3. Launch Reason by double-clicking on the Reason icon. In Windows, you can also launch Reason from your Start menu.

4. Once the program has been launched, Reason will then prompt you to input your license number, which can be found on your authorization card (see Figure 2.7).

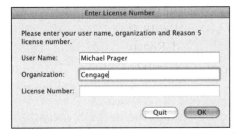

Figure 2.7 The first time you launch Reason, you will also need to enter the license number, which can be found on the little silver card in your Reason box.

5. Reason will then begin to copy the Orkester and Factory Sound banks onto your hard drive (see Figure 2.8). While this is happening, you will be entertained by several messages on your screen from Propellerhead urging you to register your software.

6. Reason should now launch and you're set to go.

Configuring Reason

After installing Reason and jumping through the authorization hoops, it's time to set your program preferences. Reason has an installation wizard that takes you through the steps of setting up your Reason studio, but you may want to alter your preferences

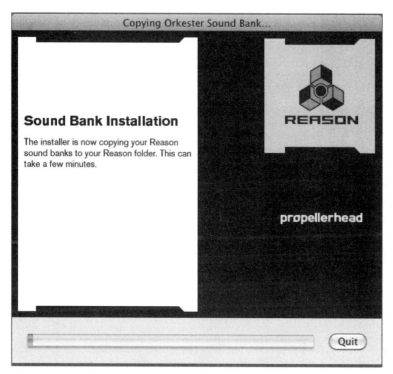

Figure 2.8 After you enter your license number, the program will copy the Orkester and Reason Factory Sound Bank ReFills to your hard drive.

further, which you do through the Preferences dialog box, which appears when you first start the program.

First, take a look at the General preferences page, in Figure 2.9.

■ The Default Song portion of the General page allows you to select the song or template song you want to see when Reason boots up. By default, Reason starts up with the built-in song selected; it's a default song template that Propellerhead has put together as a tutorial to help get you started. As you will need this in the next chapter, make sure that you have the built-in button selected.

■ On the Miscellaneous portion of the General page, you can optimize Reason to fit better with your computer (see Figure 2.10). The CPU Usage Limit assigns the desired amount of your computer's processor to Reason. Simply put, if you set your CPU to 95 percent, you are allowing Reason to use up to 95 percent of your computer's processor before you get a message stating that you have exceeded the power of your CPU. If you are planning to use Reason along with other programs in your computer at the same time, it might be a good idea to set a limit on your CPU.

■ The Use MultiCore Audio Rendering check box tells Reason to utilize your computer's multi-core capabilities (see Figure 2.11). If you own a computer with multiple CPU Cores (such as a Dual Core or Quad Core), Reason can take full advantage of this by providing more tracks and devices in your Reason song.

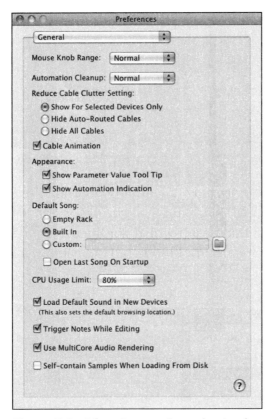

Figure 2.9 After Reason is authorized, you will need to set up the Audio, MIDI, and General preferences.

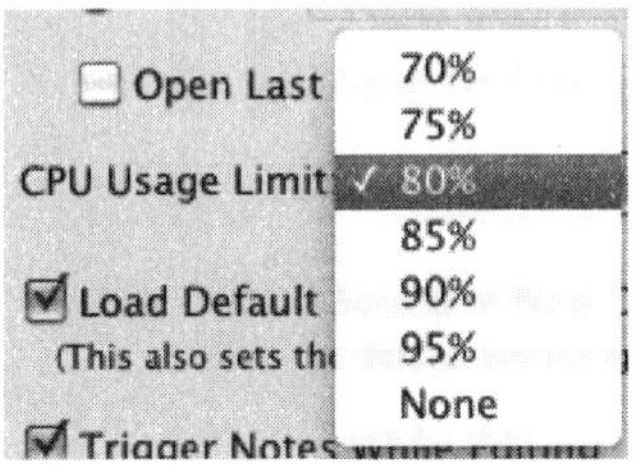

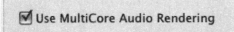

Figure 2.10 Try different CPU usage settings to optimize Reason.

☑ Use MultiCore Audio Rendering

Figure 2.11 If you have a computer with multiple CPU cores, selecting the Use MultiCore Audio Rendering check box will give you more synths and tracks in your Reason song.

Next up, take a look at the Audio preferences page, which is accessed by navigating to the Page pull-down menu and selecting Audio, as shown in Figure 2.12.

■ First, you have to select the best audio card driver for Reason. Click on the Audio Device pull-down menu, and Reason will give you a list of available audio devices that can be used with Reason.

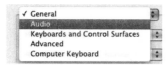

Figure 2.12 Use the pull-down menu in the Preferences window to switch between the different preference types.

- Below the Audio Device is the sample rate. Reason can work with many sampling rates, varying from 22kHz to 96kHz. If this is your first time using Reason, stick with 44.1kHz.

- Below the sampling rate lies the buffer size, which plays an active role in determining the amount of latency. As you make adjustments to the slider control, notice that the output latency decreases or increases depending on which way you go. For your first time out, it's not important to use the lowest possible setting (see the following tip), but it should be set toward the left side.

- The Play in Background option tells Reason to keep on playing, even if you are using two applications at one time. If you often use several applications at one time, this is a pretty neat feature. You can select this option if you want.

Using Multiple Sampling Rates in Your Song   One little known fact is that Reason can support multiple sampling rates within the same song. For example, if you're using Reason at 48kHz and you have some samples that were recorded at 44.1kHz, Reason will automatically convert those samples as you import them into your song.

How Low Can You Go?   The whole point of using a program like Reason is to be able to play and sequence its virtual synths and sound modules in real time. This is where making adjustments to the output latency of your audio card comes into play. An audio card's *latency* is determined by the assigned buffer size, which is found in the Audio page of the Preferences window. A *buffer* is used to hold, or collect, data temporarily in a specific location. Simply put, the larger the buffer assigned to your audio card, the more data is stored before it is sent to the audio outputs. This is what causes latency. So the name of the game here is to lower the buffer size to produce less latency.

Although it is tempting to try to use the lowest possible buffer setting in Reason, this sometimes produces bad audio results. Although you are expecting to hear audio bliss through Reason, you might end up hearing a lot of nasty pops and clicks in the playback of your Reason songs. The simplest explanation for this is that the lower the buffer setting, the higher strain it puts on your CPU. If you have a faster computer, sometimes this is not a problem. But if you are using a slower computer, it's probably a better idea to increase the buffer.

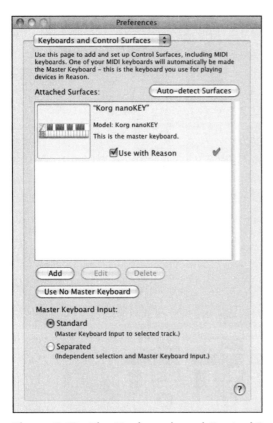

Figure 2.13 The Keyboards and Control Surfaces preferences page. Note that as I only have one keyboard in my setup, this is made the Master keyboard by default. Read on to specify how you can make any detected keyboard in your setup a Master keyboard.

The last page you'll look at in this window is the Keyboards and Control Surfaces preferences page. Select the Keyboards and Control Surfaces page from the pull-down menu (see Figure 2.13).

■ If a master keyboard has not yet been selected, highlight one from the Attached Surfaces list and click the Make Master Keyboard button.

■ If the Attached Surfaces area is empty, you may click the Auto-detect Surfaces button. If your master keyboard now appears in the Attached Surfaces list, you may select it and click the Make Master Keyboard/Use No Master Keyboard button.

■ If Auto-detect Surfaces fails, click the Add button. Choose the manufacturer of your keyboard from the Manufacturer pull-down menu, and then choose the model of your keyboard from the Model pull-down menu. Then you must select your keyboard (or the port to which it is connected) from the MIDI Input pull-down menu. If you are not sure which input to choose, you may click the Find button located to the right of the MIDI Input pull-down menu. A Find MIDI Input window will open. Now press a key on your keyboard, and the correct input should appear in the little box. Then click Choose. The window will close, and you should now see that the same selection has been made in the MIDI Input pull-down menu. Click OK.

Click on the Close Window button, which is located at the top-right side of the Preferences window on PCs or the top-left side for the Mac, and you are all set to go.

Throughout this chapter, you have looked at what goes into a typical Reason studio setup. You have also gone through the entire installation and configuration procedure. At this time, you should find yourself cocked, locked, and ready to rock into the next chapter, where you'll take a guided tour of the Reason interface and learn how versatile this crazy little program really is.

3 Getting Started with Reason 5.0

At first sight, Reason is a lot to take in—all those virtual mixers, synths, and sequencers can have you seeing double in no time. But the interface is logical, and if you've ever worked with a sequencer or recording gear of any kind, using Reason should feel familiar and intuitive almost from the start. The next couple of chapters cover the basics of navigating the Reason interface and creating music. Don't be surprised if you find yourself experimenting with Reason into the wee hours of the morning—or until your neighbors start pounding on the walls!

This chapter covers the following topics:

- Taking a first look at the devices in Reason

- Touring the Reason sequencer

- Basic routing in Reason

Reason by Default

Launch Reason, and the default song should pop up in a hot second (see Figure 3.1). As you can see, you have many virtual synths, effects, and a dandy mixer to start digging into.

First, have a listen to the groovy little tune that Propellerhead put together. You can use the spacebar on your computer keyboard to stop and start the song at any time. While the song is playing, use the navigation tools located at the right side of the program window (see Figure 3.2) to scroll up and down through the Reason Device Rack. As you scroll, take note of the basic graphic layout of Reason; it is divided into seven main sections.

- **Inputs and outputs**—These are found at the top of every song you create in Reason. As you can see, this section handles the MIDI input and the audio output.

- **The mixer**—Although you can create as many mixers as you want in Reason, there is a single master mixer in every Reason song that controls the master levels of your song.

Figure 3.1 The first time you boot up Reason, the default song loads up, which is a perfect starting point to begin honing your remixing skills.

Figure 3.2 Located at the far right side of the Device Rack, the scroll bar allows you to scroll up and down the Device Rack.

- **Effects**—Located just beneath the Reason Mixer is a real-time effect, which is routed to the auxiliary sends and returns in the Reason Mixer. There are a total of four auxiliaries available per mixer.

- **Synths**—Right below the real-time effects are the virtual synths and sound modules.

- **Reason sequencer**—At the bottom of Reason is the main sequencer. This is where your synthesizer performances are recorded, stored, edited, and then played back.

- **ReGroove Mixer**—Just below the sequencer is the ReGroove Mixer, which is used to introduce slide, shuffle, and groove to your song.

- **The Tool Window**—This handy window is used to create devices (synths, effects), edit your sequences (quantize, transposition, and so on), and select/edit the groove used with the ReGroove Mixer.

Basic Studio Signal Flow

Before you begin to tour the Reason interface, it is important to have a basic understanding of how an audio signal is routed within a studio environment. This is commonly known as the *signal flow* (see Figure 3.3).

The *signal* refers to audio coming from any piece of studio equipment (hardware or software) that is capable of generating sound. For example, audio signals can come from

- Synthesizers

- Guitars or basses

- Vocals

- Drums

In the world of Reason, the synthesizers and samplers provide the signal. The virtual outputs of these Reason synths are then routed to the mixer.

The *mixer* is used to adjust the amplitude of every signal within a studio environment. Additionally, the mixer is used to manipulate the *timbre* or character of the signal by introducing equalization and effects, such as reverb, delay, and distortion. As you read on in this chapter, you will learn about reMix, which is the virtual mixer in Reason.

Once the signals have been appropriately adjusted and manipulated, the mixed signal is then routed out of the mixer and into a pair of speakers or into a recording device of some kind. In Reason, the mixed signal is routed to the outputs of your installed audio card.

Part of the mixing process is the addition of effects to many of the individual signals. An *effect processor* is a component in your studio that accepts a signal and introduces

Instrument

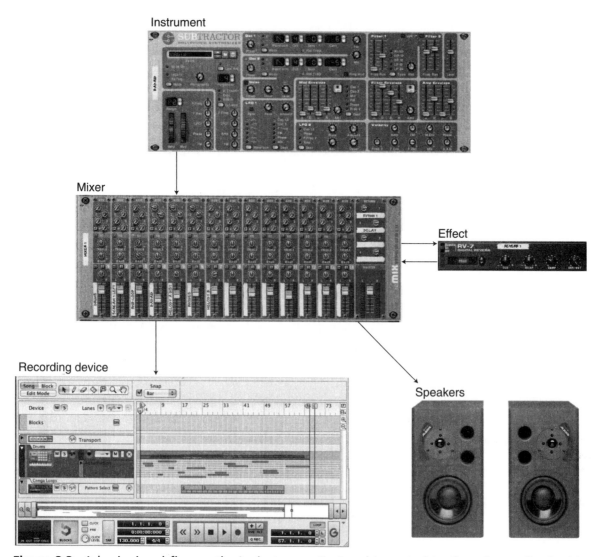

Mixer

Effect

Recording device

Speakers

Figure 3.3 A basic signal flow path. An instrument's signal is routed to the mixer, edited with effects, and then sent from the mixer to a recording device and/or speakers.

an audio effect, such as reverb, chorus, or delay. Effects are typically routed to and from the mixer through pathways known as *auxiliary sends*. Through the Aux Send, you can route a portion of any signal to any effect processor and then route the signal back to the mixer. The resultant signal is a combination of the original sound plus the added effect.

Reason's sends are located at the top of the reMix interface. The effect processors themselves are located right below reMix.

The Reason Hardware Interface

This device handles all of the routing for MIDI input devices, as well as audio inputs and outputs. The MIDI input device allows you to assign any keyboard, drum machine, or other device that sends MIDI messages to a specific device in Reason, allowing for real-time performances of the Reason synths. The Audio Out portion of this device handles all of the audio output routing capabilities of Reason. When you use Reason with a sound card that has multiple outputs or when you incorporate Propellerhead's ReWire (discussed in Chapter 21, "ReWire"), there are up to 64 audio output possibilities available. As shown in Figure 3.4, Reason automatically routes the audio outputs to the stereo left and right outputs of the active audio card.

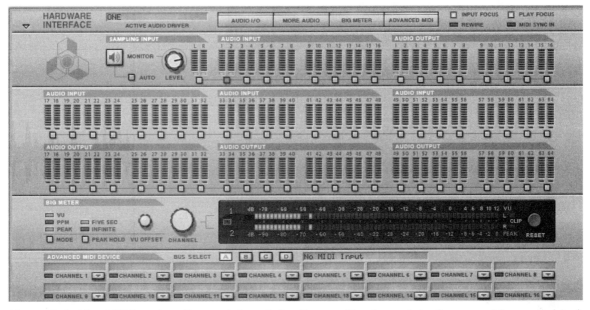

Figure 3.4 The MIDI and audio modules of the Reason Hardware Interface provide a graphical view of how MIDI and audio are routed to and from Reason.

Additionally, Reason 5 introduces the ability to sample audio for use with several of its soft synths. All of the audio input routing is handled by the Sampling Input section of the Hardware Interface.

The Reason Mixer

No matter how many nifty sound modules or incredible effects you have, you won't get far without the services of a good mixing board. Reason's mixing board, called *reMix*, is a simple yet versatile mixing console that offers many creative possibilities when mixing your synthesized masterpieces. Many of the standard mixer controls are found here, such as level, pan, mute/solo, and auxiliary sends. Reason's mixer resembles a few well-known line mixers made by the likes of Behringer, Mackie, and Alesis (see Figure 3.5). This section dives deep into the Reason mixer and shows you some cool and creative techniques that hardware mixers can't match.

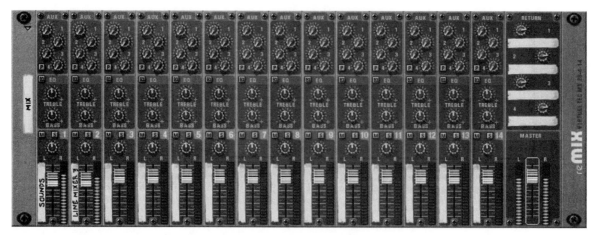

Figure 3.5 Most of the Reason modules resemble well-known hardware counterparts; reMix looks like many well-known hardware mixers.

Saving Space It's easy to be overwhelmed by the profusion of mixers, synths, and sound modules filling your screen. To conserve screen real estate, each Reason device is collapsible—simply click on the little triangle at the upper left of each device (see Figure 3.6) to toggle between the collapsed and expanded views. As you add more devices to your Reason projects, this method helps you save precious screen space.

Figure 3.6 Need to save some space in your Device Rack? Just click on the triangle in the upper-left corner of any Reason module to expand or collapse it.

Virtually Endless Possibilities Reason gives you the capability to create as many devices as you want within one song. If you want to create a Reason song using multiple instances of the Subtractor, for instance, you can do it. If you fill up all of the channels in reMix, you can create a second remix and add more devices to it. This unique virtual studio environment gives free reign to your creativity.

The only limitation that you might encounter from time to time is your computer's CPU. As you begin to add more devices to your Reason song, the CPU will need to work harder to process the data. At some point, your CPU will reach its maximum potential and your song might occasionally drop out, which sounds kind of like a CD skip.

Real-Time Effects

If the virtual synths and sound modules in Reason are the main course, the real-time effects are certainly the desserts of pure decadence. Reason's real-time effects are the virtual equivalents of studio hardware, such as a reverb, flanger, or compressor. As you can see in Figure 3.7, the Reason default song contains a real-time reverb effect. This effect can be used as an insert effect, in which the entire signal is routed to the effect and then into the Reason mixer, or it can be used as an auxiliary effect, in which only a portion of the signal is sent to the effect and then back into the mixer. If that sounds confusing, don't worry; you'll be taking an in-depth look at the routing and use of each of Reason's real-time effects. In total, Reason includes 16 types of real-time effects, ranging from reverbs, to compressors, to distortions.

Figure 3.7 The Reason effects are the icing on the cake.

What Is Real-Time? By now, you have read the phrase "real-time" at least a couple of times, and you have probably heard a lot of musicians and music magazines throw this term around. But what does *real-time* actually mean in the world of Reason? It means that you can tweak and adjust the parameters of Reason's instruments and effects and hear the results of your changes instantaneously, *while a song is playing*. To see for yourself, try the following.

Open the Reason default song, press Play, and make a few adjustments to the volume of different tracks as the song is playing. As you move the faders, you will hear the volume change. You can also change parameters of the reverb and delay, and you'll hear those changes instantly too. That's real-time.

Synths, Sounds, Beats, and Treats

Continuing down the rack with Reason's default song loaded, below the effects come the virtual synths and sound modules that make up the orchestra of Reason. You'll take a quick look at these now, but each device is discussed in a chapter of its own later in the book. You'll learn how to program those dreamy pads, stabbing leads, and pulsating bass lines.

The Kong Drum Designer

The first synth you'll see in the Device Rack of the Demo Song is the Kong Drum Designer (see Figure 3.8). This synth is a full-blown drum machine that resembles the Akai MPC, which is the cornerstone of any popular hip-hop record of the past couple of decades. Kong supplies a fantastic assortment of drums and rhythm samples, and also has the ability to sample, which gives you unlimited possibilities for easily creating your own samples.

Figure 3.8 The Kong Drum Designer is the drum machine to end all drum machines. It has a wide assortment of sounds, real-time effects, and the ability to sample.

Be sure to read all about this synth in Chapter 8.

What Are Those Green Boxes?   In the Demo Song, you'll see a neon green box drawn around the pattern box around the Pitch and Mod wheels on the Kong interface (see Figure 3.9). Whenever you see a green box around a knob, slider, or other controller, it means automation involving that controller has been recorded. If you play the song through, you'll see the wheels change value. There are several ways to program automation into your Reason songs, and you'll learn all about automation in Chapter 20.

Figure 3.9 Whenever you see a green box around a knob or slider in Reason, it means that automation has been written in.

The Dr. Octo Rex Loop Player

When you need drum, percussion, and even instrumental loops at the drop of a hat, look no further than Dr. Octo Rex (see Figure 3.10). Dr. Octo Rex is a RAM-based sample playback device based on the ReCycle technology created by Propellerhead Software. Dr. Octo Rex can import multiple specially prepared digital audio loops, called REX files, and play them back at just about any tempo.

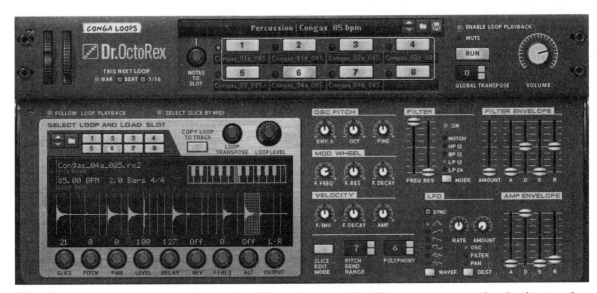

Figure 3.10 The Dr. Octo Rex Loop Player incorporates REX files to create punchy rhythm tracks.

The Reason Sequencer at First Glance

At the heart of any virtual studio lies the most important component, the sequencer. The *sequencer* is the tool used to record, edit, and play back notes and performances made with Reason's devices. In a way, it can be thought of as a virtual tape recorder, although it does not actually record audio. Rather, it records MIDI notes or impulses that are sent from a MIDI keyboard to the computer.

Sequencing has come a long way since the first encounters with MIDI, which were on the Atari 1040ST. Although I logged many hours and made a good deal of music with that computer, the MIDI sequencing programs that were available for it had very clunky interfaces and numerous crashing problems. Thank goodness for progress! Reason's sequencer (see Figure 3.11) is one of the most versatile yet easy-to-understand programs around. You'll take a quick look at the sequencer here, but for the details, check out Chapter 5, "The Reason Sequencer—Close Up."

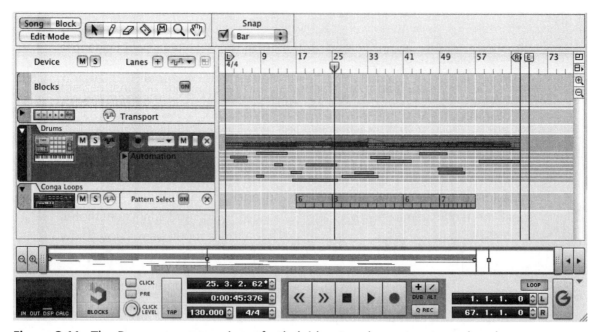

Figure 3.11 The Reason sequencer is perfectly laid out and easy to comprehend.

The Reason sequencer is divided into seven functional areas:

- The Song/Block view
- The Edit view
- The Tools (Selection, Pencil, Erase, Razor, Mute, Magnify, and Hand)
- Snap to Grid
- The Tool Window for editing your song
- The ReGroove Mixer
- The Transport panel

The Song/Block View

When a sequence has been created within the Reason sequencer, it becomes a "part." The Song view handles the "arrangement" of these parts by providing a track list, a measure ruler, and a set of "locators."

New to Reason 5 is the Block view, which builds upon the idea of creating patterns or phrases within a Reason song, saving and grouping them as blocks, and then arranging them by simply dragging and dropping them into specific parts of your Reason song.

The Track List

The *track list* is used to organize and route MIDI data to each Reason device in a song (see Figure 3.12). Each device is given its own track, which displays its sequence within your song. Looking at the default song, you can see that there are three separate tracks, each assigned to a different synth or device within the Reason Device Rack. In Chapter 5, you'll take an in-depth look at working with tracks.

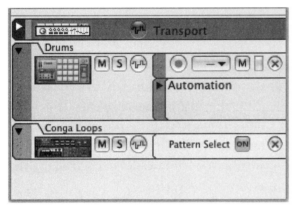

Figure 3.12 Each Reason device can have its own corresponding track in the track list.

> **Peek-a-Boo!**   You can quickly navigate to any device in your Reason rack simply by clicking on its corresponding track in the sequencer. Try it. Click on the Redrum track and the Redrum device instantly shows up in the Device Rack. This is a very helpful tool to quickly scroll through the Reason devices without having to use the scroll bar on the right side of your Device Rack.

The Measure Ruler

The *measure ruler* is used to display the linear timeline within a Reason song. As you can see in Figure 3.13, a song's parts are governed by a measure-based timeline, which is read from left to right. If you press the spacebar to start up the default song, you'll notice a vertical line moving across the measures, which is topped by a flag

Figure 3.13 The measure ruler is used to display the linear timeline within a Reason song.

Figure 3.14 If you lose your place, just locate the position indicator.

(see Figure 3.14). This is the *position indicator*; it indicates exactly where you are in the song at any given moment.

Jump to the Left; Jump to the Right   Let the default song play, and try clicking on any point in the measure ruler; the position indicator will jump to that measure and keep playing.

Reason's Locator Points

Look at the measure ruler and you'll notice two vertical markers that are positioned at the beginning and end of the default song. These markers are known as "locators." They are sort of like virtual bookmarks, indicating the beginning and end of a song or loop. Press the spacebar to start the default song and watch as the position indicator reaches the right locator. As it does, you'll see the position indicator jump back to the beginning of the song, where the left locator is sitting. You'll take a closer look at the locator points in Chapter 5, "The Reason Sequencer—Close Up."

The Edit View

The Reason sequencer has a second way of viewing the MIDI data within your song, called the Edit view. This view is used to edit the performance, timing, and synth parameters within a song. In order to see the Edit view, you must switch from Arrange mode to Edit mode by clicking on the Arrange/Edit View button in the upper-left corner of the Reason sequencer (see Figure 3.15).

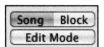

Figure 3.15 Switching to Edit mode is a click of a button.

In Edit mode, you can view and edit MIDI parameters and performance data using any of several separate data editors, called *lanes*. For example, on a track that contains a piano part, you can use the Key lane to draw, edit, or erase notes (see Figure 3.16). Or if you are using a Dr:rex Loop Player in a song, you can use the REX lane to edit its individual notes (see Figure 3.17).

To access any of these lanes, just click on their respective buttons found in the upper-right corner of the sequencer (see Figure 3.18).

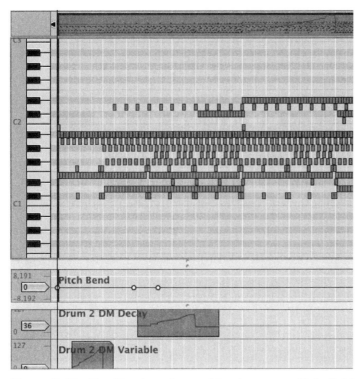

Figure 3.16 The Key lane is used to draw or edit individual notes in a synth or sampler track.

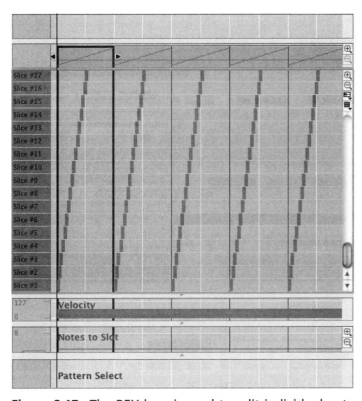

Figure 3.17 The REX lane is used to edit individual notes (slices) in a Dr:rex Loop Player track.

Figure 3.18 The Lane buttons are used to access any Lane Editor when in Edit mode.

The Editing and Quantization Tools

This next section takes a first look at the Editing tools in the Sequencer toolbar and Quantization tools found in the Tool Window (see Figure 3.19). By using these tools effectively, you can draw, erase, or edit notes, automate your mix, and correct any timing problems with ease and precision.

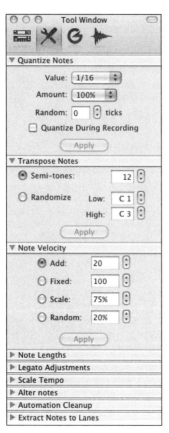

Figure 3.19 Reason's Editing tools can be found in the Sequencer toolbar, whereas the Quantization tools can be found in the Tools tab of the Tool Window.

The Editing Tools

Reason provides a set of tools that can be used in the Song or Edit modes. Many of these tools have obvious uses, such as the Pencil tool (see Figure 3.20) and the Erase tool (see Figure 3.21). A couple of the other tools have much more specialized functions, such as the Magnification tool for zoom, the Line tool for drawing straight and diagonal lines, and the Hand tool for scrolling through the arrangement in real-time.

Figure 3.20 Use the Pencil tool to draw in notes.

Figure 3.21 Use the Eraser tool to delete notes.

Quantization—Timing Is Everything

Aside from being the most important element in comedy, timing is also an absolutely indispensable element in music. Some of us are not as rhythmically inclined as we would like to be or possibly not the best synth players on the block. That's where the Quantization tools come into play. They appear on the Tools tab of the Tool Window. These tools help to correct timing problems when sequencing within Reason. For example, if you are playing a drum part and you just miss the last couple of drum hits by a beat or so, the Quantize tool can correct that mistake by shifting the misplayed notes to their correct places (see Figure 3.22). It sounds a little too good to be true, but believe me, it's a lifesaver.

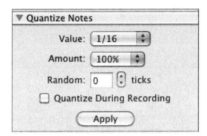

Figure 3.22 The Quantization tool is the tool of all tools for timing.

Tool Tip   Through the course of learning the ins and outs of Reason, there's a good chance that you may accidentally close a window that you need to constantly use. If this happens to you when using the Tool Window, simply select it from the Window pull-down menu of Reason. Better yet, you can show and hide the Tool Window by using the F8 key on your computer keyboard.

The Transport Panel

Below the Reason sequencer is the Transport panel. At first glance (see Figure 3.23), some of the controls look similar to those found on tape decks or CD players, but there is much more here than meets the eye. The Transport panel can be used to loop parts in songs, dictate the tempo and time signature, and help create a shuffle groove within a song, for all you hip-hop junkies.

Figure 3.23 The Reason Transport controls.

The Transport panel can also be used to control or monitor additional indicators and functions, such as:

- Display the amount of DSP (digital signal processing) used within a song.

- Indicate when an audio signal within Reason is distorting or "clipping."

- Produce an audible click or metronome track for keeping time.

- Show and hide the ReGroove Mixer.

- Activate synchronization functions.

You'll learn more about the Transport panel in Chapter 5.

Virtual Routing in Reason—Virtual Eye Candy

In addition to its power as a music composition tool, Reason offers tremendous creative possibilities with virtual routing. Just like those expensive-looking patch bays found in hardware-based studios, Reason has its own virtual patch bay that is easy to use and a heck of a lot of fun to look at. Let's get patchin'!

The visual paradigm of the Reason interface is, of course, that of a rack of equipment—just like the gear racks used in real-world studios. And, as in real-world studios, the connections between pieces of gear in the rack are handled at the back of the rack. To see the "back" of Reason's virtual gear rack, press the computer keyboard's Tab key. You'll see the backs of the devices in your rack and the cable connections between them (see Figure 3.24). This design feature, aside from being awfully cool to look at, makes routing within Reason a snap, and is unique among music software in the brilliant way it relates to real-world hardware-based studios. If you can master signal flow with one, you've mastered it with the other, and vice-versa. In this respect, Reason is terrific educational software in addition to being an enormously useful creative tool.

As you scroll up and down the default song's Device Rack, you'll notice that each of the virtual synths' audio outputs are routed to the mixer near the top of the rack.

1. Look at the back of reMix, below the Reason Hardware Interface. Figure 3.25 shows the audio outputs or reMix routed to channels 1 and 2 on the Reason Hardware Interface.

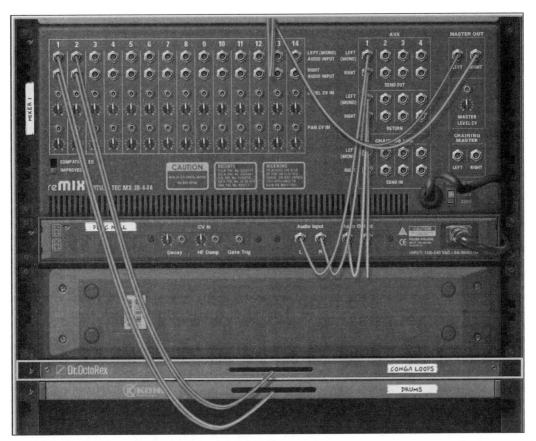

Figure 3.24   Presto! Change-o! Pressing the Tab key flips the Reason interface around.

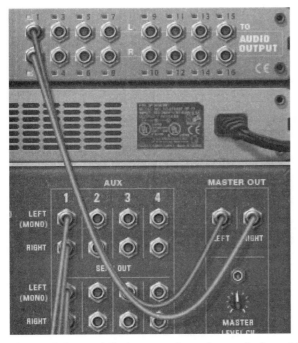

Figure 3.25   reMix is routed to channels 1 and 2 of the Reason Hardware Interface.

2. Click and hold on the left audio output of reMix, and you will see a list of options, including the Disconnect option (see Figure 3.26). Select Disconnect, and watch as the virtual cables connecting reMix to the Reason Hardware Interface disappear. reMix has been virtually disconnected from the Hardware Interface.

Figure 3.26 Click and hold any connection within the Device Rack, and you can virtually route or disconnect in a flash.

3. Now click and hold on the left Master Out of reMix and start to drag the mouse up toward the Reason Hardware Interface. A gray virtual cable appears and follows your cursor as it moves (see Figure 3.27).

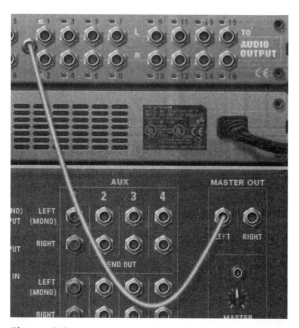

Figure 3.27 To route any device in Reason, just click and drag your virtual cable to any destination. This example is connecting reMix to channels 1 and 2 of the Hardware Interface.

4. Drag the virtual cable up to channel 1 on the Reason Hardware Interface and release the mouse. You should now see a pair of red cables connecting the mixer's Master Outputs to channels 1 and 2 of the Hardware Interface.

This example just scratches the surface of the endless routing possibilities with Reason. In later chapters, you'll learn some creative ways to use the virtual synths and other devices to create a routing frenzy within Reason.

Hide the Cables   If all these cables are confusing, you can opt not to view them by unselecting the Show Cables preference, which is located in the Option pull-down menu.

This chapter took a brief tour of the Reason interface. As you can see, there was a lot of thought put into the creation of Reason. The more you use this application, the more you'll see how much the layout of the program makes sense, and pretty soon you'll find yourself virtually routing in your sleep.

4 Creating Your First Reason Song

There are two common ways to create your first song in Reason. One way is to open the default song and erase all of the recorded tracks and use this as a starting place of sorts. Although this is a good way to begin, I believe the alternative is better. The second way is to start with a completely blank screen and create a new template and song from scratch. This method is easier than it might sound, and it's a quicker way to learn the software and free your creativity. In this chapter, you are going to create your first song in Reason by performing the following tasks:

- Creating a reMix mixer and adding some real-time effects

- Creating a couple of virtual synths and sound modules

- Creating a sequence of notes using the Reason sequencer

- Mixing your song with effects and creating a digital audio file

You are going to jump right into this, so hang on tight and you'll be just fine!

Wiping the Slate Clean

Before you can begin, you should start by getting rid of the default song and resetting the Reason preferences to create a blank song template whenever the application is launched, or whenever a new song is created while Reason is running. Follow these steps to do so:

1. Select Edit > Preferences (see Figure 4.1) for Windows or Reason > Preferences for the Mac. This will bring up the Preferences window, with the General page active (see Figure 4.2).

2. In the lower half of this dialog box is the Default Song section, where you select an empty rack, the standard default song, or a customized song. Select the Empty Rack option.

3. Close the Preferences window by clicking on the X in the upper-right corner (left corner if you are using a Mac).

4. Select File > New (press Control+N in Windows or Apple+N on the Mac). You should now see an empty song that looks like Figure 4.3.

Figure 4.1 Reason's Preferences pull-down menu.

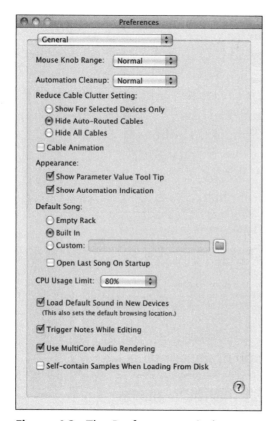

Figure 4.2 The Preferences window.

Key Commands—Your New Best Friend Key commands are keystroke combinations that allow you to perform the simplest and most complex tasks within your programs, including Reason. With the right combination of key commands, you can create new songs, save them, and cut and paste clips within Reason. They are real time savers. Most programs will also display their key commands within the pull-down menus of the program. Figure 4.4 shows Reason's File pull-down menu. To the left is the name of the function, whereas on the right side of the menu, the corresponding keyboard command is listed.

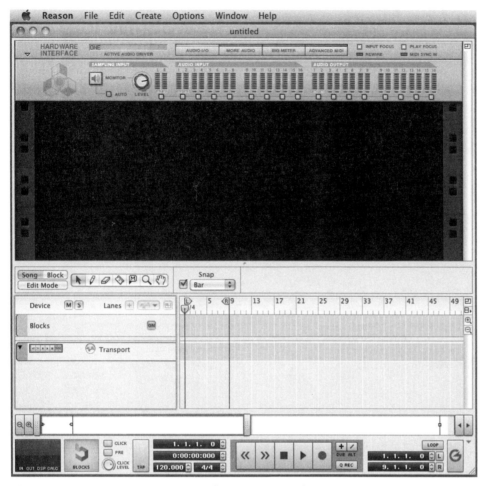

Figure 4.3   Reason now opens with an empty rack. Notice that the right locator is placed at bar 9 by default.

New	⌘N
Open...	⌘O
Close	⌘W
Save	⌘S
Save As...	⇧⌘S

Figure 4.4   Reason's key commands are listed in every pull-down menu.

Everything Is Automated   Looking back at Figure 4.3, you should note that just about every device gets its own sequencer track, including the Transport Control. This is simply because everything in Reason can be automated, which you'll take a closer look at in future chapters.

Creating a reMix Mixer

You'll set up your first Reason song by creating a reMix device and routing some real-time effects and virtual synths to it.

There are three ways to create a device in Reason. First, you can select the Create pull-down menu and choose the device you want to create (see Figure 4.5). Second, you can right-click anywhere in the black empty space in the Device Rack. This will bring up the list of devices that can be created within the program. You can do this same thing on the Mac by holding the Control key and then clicking anywhere in the empty rack space. The third way to create Reason devices is to make use of the Tool Window (see Figure 4.6). From here, you can either click and drag a device onto the Device Rack, or simply double-click on the device you want to use at which point Reason will create an instance of the device and place it onto the Device Rack.

Figure 4.5 The Create menu lets you create any type of Reason device.

Using one of these three methods, go ahead and create a reMix device by selecting the Mixer 14:2 option from the device list (see Figure 4.7).

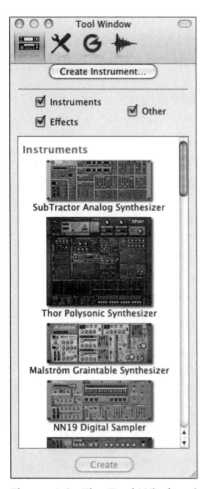

Figure 4.6   The Tool Window is another easy way to create devices in Reason.

Figure 4.7   Creating a reMix device.

Self-Routing Reason Press the Tab key to flip the Reason Device Rack around, and you'll see that Reason has already routed the main outputs of reMix into the audio outputs of your sound card (see Figure 4.8). Reason automatically routes any device you create to its appropriate inputs, taking a lot of the guesswork out of creating and routing devices. This becomes extremely handy, especially when you are new to the whole idea of routing audio.

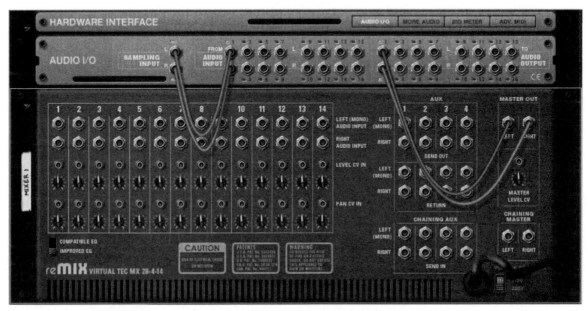

Figure 4.8 Reason can automatically route newly created devices.

Routing the Effects

After creating the reMix device, it's now time to set it up with some sweet effects.

Using the Create pull-down menu or right-clicking in the empty space of the Device Rack, bring up the list of devices. Select RV-7 Digital Reverb and that effect will appear below reMix. Add a little delay, too. Create the DDL-1 Digital Delay Line. It will appear beside the reverb (see Figure 4.9).

Additionally, I like to create sequencer tracks for my effects, as it enables me to edit the individual parameters of the effect via the sequencer. Reason doesn't create a sequencer track for effect modules automatically, but you can do this by simply right-clicking on the effect device and selecting Create Track for Reverb 1.

Look at reMix; you will see that the reverb and delay have been automatically routed to the returns, which are found in the upper-right corner of reMix. Press Tab to verify that the outputs of the reverb and delay have been routed to the effect sends and returns of reMix (see Figure 4.10).

Figure 4.9 Creating a few Reason effects is a snap.

Figure 4.10 A quick look on the flip side, and you will see that the effects are already routed to reMix.

Send/Insert Effects   There are two ways to use real-time effects in Reason—as an *Insert* or as an *Auxiliary* (or Send).

An Insert effect is used to process the entire signal of a Reason device. For example, if you were to route the outputs of the Subtractor directly to the inputs of the COMP-01 Compressor, and then connect those outputs to the inputs of a reMix channel, this would be considered an insert effect.

An Auxiliary or Send effect is used to process an assigned *portion* of a Reason device's signal. That processed signal is then routed back into reMix and mixed together with the unprocessed or "dry" signal. For example, if you have a Subtractor routed to channel 1 on reMix and a RV-7 Reverb assigned to Aux 1 in reMix, you can use the Aux 1 knob found on channel 1 to "send" a portion of your dry signal to the RV-7. Once the signal is processed by the RV-7, it is then "returned" to reMix in order to be mixed in with the dry signal on channel 1.

You'll find a lot more information on this subject in Chapter 17, "Effects—Close Up."

At this point, you can route a couple of additional effects to reMix, such as a chorus or distortion, because you have a total of four effect sends available to you. But for now, let's move on and create some synths. You can come back and add more effects later.

What's Your Name?   Renaming devices in the rack is easy, and it will help prevent confusion as you add devices to your Reason songs. To rename a device, you can double-click on the name of any track in the track list of the Arrangement window and type the name you want, as shown in Figure 4.11.

You can also double-click on the name displayed on the device itself (see Figure 4.12) and type the new name.

Figure 4.11 Double-clicking on the track and typing a new name for your instrument.

Figure 4.12 Double-clicking on the device itself allows you to change its name as well.

Is There a Dr. Octo Rex in the House?

The first virtual sound module that you are going to create is the Dr. Octo Rex Loop Player, so that you can have a steady beat to groove to. Next, you'll add a bass line along with some pads for ambience.

To create a Dr. Octo Rex device, select Create > Dr. Octo Rex Loop Player. The Dr. Octo Rex will pop up and be automatically routed to reMix (see Figure 4.13). You will see the label "Dr. Octo Rex 1" on channel 1 of the mixer, as shown in Figure 4.14.

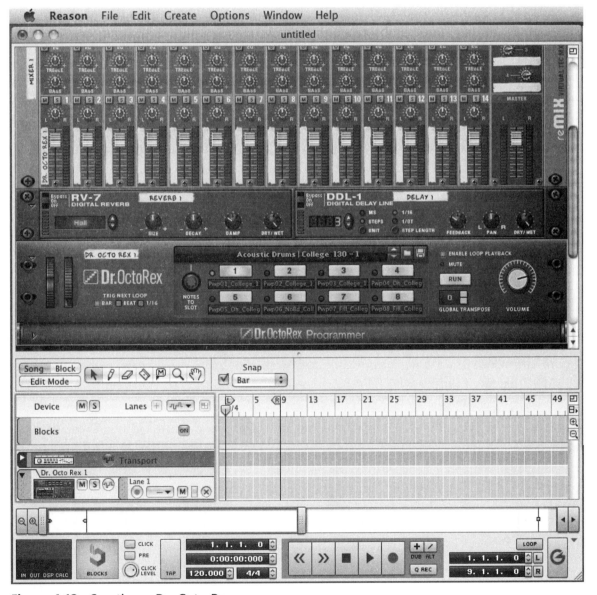

Figure 4.13 Creating a Dr. Octo Rex.

Figure 4.14   Once the Dr. Octo Rex has been created, you will see it displayed as such on channel 1 of reMix.

Each time you create a new device, Reason automatically creates a sequencer track in the track list of the sequencer interface named after the device that was created, in this case Dr. Octo Rex 1. As an additional point of interest, look below the track name. You can see an icon that looks like a keyboard, as shown in Figure 4.15. It also has at its right side what looks like a red record button, complete with a little black dot. This tells you that this track has been armed and is ready to receive and record MIDI data. Clicking on the symbol will disarm the track and you will not be able to record.

Figure 4.15   Once Dr. Octo Rex has been created, Reason automatically creates a sequencer track and sets it up for receiving MIDI data.

Looking at the Dr. Octo Rex interface, you can see that a default loop has already been loaded in. If you click on the Run button on the Dr. Octo Rex interface, it will play the loop. If this loop isn't really your style, you can easily select a new one. At the top-left center of the Dr. Octo Rex interface, there is a Patch Browser, along with a couple of scroll buttons and a folder button. From here you can preview and load REX loop files into Dr. Octo Rex.

1.   Click on the folder button to launch the browser.

2.   In the upper-left corner under Locations, you will see a file called Reason Factory Sound Bank, as shown in Figure 4.16. Click on this file to continue.

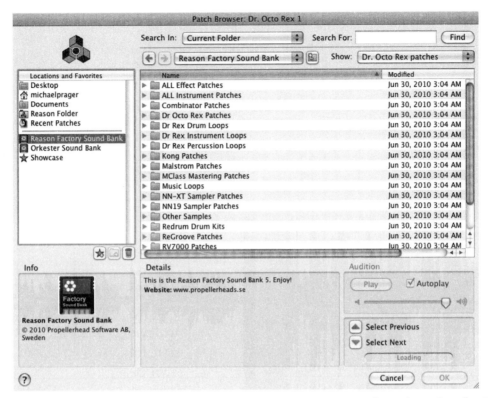

Figure 4.16 The Reason Factory Sound Bank contains sounds and patches for Reason's virtual synths.

3.   Double-click on the folder called Dr Rex Drum Loops (see Figure 4.17).

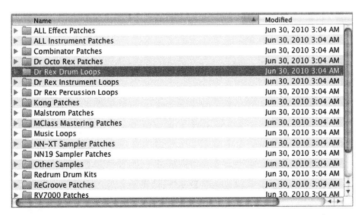

Figure 4.17 The Dr Rex Drum Loops folder contains loops and fills that are formatted as REX files.

4.   You will see a list of folders (see Figure 4.18) that contain drum loops of various styles of dance music. Depending on your mood, double-click on the folder of the style of loop you want to use.

Name		Modified
Acs01_StrghtAhead_130.rx2		Jun 30, 2010 3:04 AM
Elc29_RadioActive_120_eLAB.rx2		Jun 30, 2010 3:04 AM
Hhp65_FoSho_136_Chrnc.rx2		Jun 30, 2010 3:04 AM
Hse40_RideBeat_130_eLAB.rx2		Jun 30, 2010 3:04 AM
▶ –Beyer Lekebusch (BL)		Jun 30, 2010 3:04 AM
▶ –Bomb Squad (BSQ)		Jun 30, 2010 3:04 AM
▶ –Jason McGerr (JMS)		Jun 30, 2010 3:04 AM
▶ –Keith LeBlanc (KLB)		Jun 30, 2010 3:04 AM
▶ –Printz Board (PB)		Jun 30, 2010 3:04 AM
Abstract HipHop		Jun 30, 2010 3:04 AM
▶ Acoustic		Jun 30, 2010 3:04 AM
▶ Caribbean		Jun 30, 2010 3:04 AM
▶ Chemical Beats		Jun 30, 2010 3:04 AM
▶ Club		Jun 30, 2010 3:04 AM
▶ Down South		Jun 30, 2010 3:04 AM
▶ Drum N Bass		Jun 30, 2010 3:04 AM
▶ Dub		Jun 30, 2010 3:04 AM

Figure 4.18 Propellerhead supplies a wide selection of styles to choose from. For this example, I have selected Abstract HipHop.

5. You will see a long list of loops to select from. You can select any loop you want by clicking on it once and clicking on the Play button in the lower-right corner. If you want to listen to the loop as soon as you highlight it, click the Autoplay check box (see Figure 4.19).

Figure 4.19 By selecting Autoplay, you will save yourself a lot of time when previewing loops. You can also use the Select Previous and Select Next buttons to scroll up and down the list of loops.

6. Select the loop you want and click on the OK button at the lower-right corner of the browser window. This will load the loop into Dr. Octo Rex.

After selecting the loop that you want, Dr. Octo Rex will load it into the waveform display in the center of the Dr. Octo Rex interface, as shown in Figure 4.20. At this point, the loop has been loaded into the Dr. Octo Rex interface but not onto its sequencer track in the sequencer, so you won't hear it if you click on the Play button on the Transport. Toward the top center of the Dr. Octo Rex interface you will see a button called Preview. If you click on this button, Dr. Octo Rex will play the loop. To the right of the Preview button is another button called Copy Loop To Track. Click this button to export the loop to the Dr. Octo Rex sequencer track (see Figure 4.21).

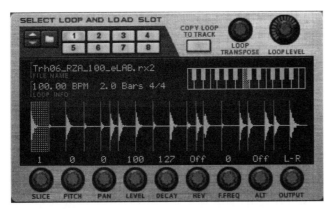

Figure 4.20 The REX file has been loaded into the Dr. Octo Rex interface.

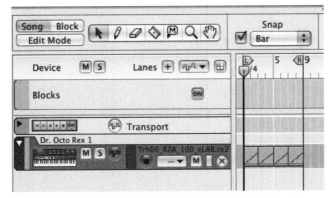

Figure 4.21 Click To Track, and the sequencer track of the REX file is loaded. Notice that the loop is copied three additional times to fill up the empty space between bars 1 and 9.

Different Loop Tempos   When you are selecting a loop for Dr. Octo Rex in the File Browser, the Autoplay function plays the loop back at its original tempo. This example uses a loop that had an original tempo of 100BPM (beats per minute). But when the loop is loaded into Dr. Octo Rex, exported to its sequencer track, and played back, it sounds much faster. The reason for this is the tempo of the song, which is found at the bottom portion of the Transport panel, is set to 120BPM. This is the master tempo for the Reason song, and the REX loop will automatically speed up or slow down to fit that tempo.

Turn on the Loop   Before proceeding, be sure to activate the loop function of the sequencer by selecting Loop On/Off, which is found on the right side of the Transport panel.

Enable Loop Playback   Once your loop has been loaded into Dr. Octo Rex, press Play on the Transport panel. Upon listening to the playback, you may hear a slight "flange," or wavy sound. This is because Dr. Octo Rex is not only playing back from the sequencer track, it's also playing the loop from the Dr. Octo Rex interface. The simple way to resolve this is to click on the Enable Loop Playback button, which is found in the upper-right corner of the Dr. Octo Rex interface. This will disable the loop playback and correct the wavy sound.

Now that you have loaded a loop and copied it to the sequencer, you can add some reverb and delay to the loop to give it some character.

1. Press Play on the Transport panel or press the spacebar on your computer keyboard.

2. Scroll up the Device Rack to reMix. You are going to work on the first track, which is called Dr. Octo Rex 1.

3. At the top of channel 1 are the auxiliary sends. As you may recall, Aux 1 is a reverb and Aux 2 is a delay.

4. Click and hold on the first Aux knob and drag your mouse upwards (see Figure 4.22). You should hear the loop playing back with a reverb effect.

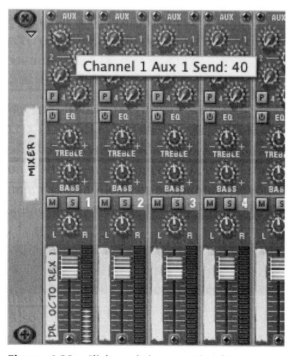

Figure 4.22 Click and drag on the first Aux knob to assign a reverb effect to it.

5. You don't want to use too much reverb on a drum loop, because it sounds a little strange, so position the Aux send 1 knob around nine o'clock. This will produce a warm and mellow reverberation effect.

6. Now add a little delay by clicking on the Aux 2 knob and setting it to nine o'clock as well.

7. You should now hear a slight reverb and delay effect on your drum loop. If you look at the reverb and delay meters below reMix, you will see they are working; the LED meters are hopping up and down.

Adding a Bass Line

The next virtual synth that you are going to create is the Subtractor. As you already got your groove thang started with Dr. Octo Rex, nothing could be better than a good ol' booty-shaking bass line.

You're going to draw in the bass line using the Pencil tool, so there will be no need for an external MIDI keyboard yet.

Click on Dr. Octo Rex to select it, and then select Create > Subtractor Analog Synthesizer. The synth is loaded below Dr. Octo Rex in the Device Rack, as shown in Figure 4.23. If you scroll back up to the mixer, you will see the name Subtractor 1 listed vertically

Figure 4.23 Loading the Subtractor.

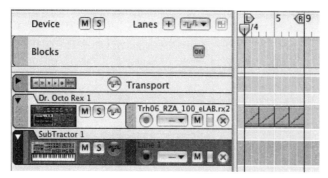

Figure 4.24 The Subtractor sequencer track has been created and is armed for MIDI input.

on channel 2. If you look at the sequencer in Figure 4.24, you'll also see a Subtractor MIDI track has been created and is armed to start recording.

Next, you will load a preset into the Subtractor by navigating to the upper-left corner of the Subtractor interface and clicking on the Browse Patch button. As in Dr. Octo Rex, the browser window opens and allows you to navigate and search for patches for the Subtractor. Click on the Reason Factory Sound Bank file (under Locations, top left) and you will now see the Subtractor Patches folder. Double-click on this folder to see several subfolders containing Subtractor patches for just about every kind of dance music (see Figure 4.25).

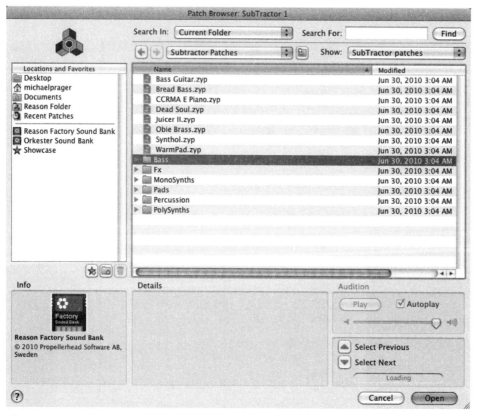

Figure 4.25 There are all sorts of patches to choose from here, but you need a bass line for this example, so select the Bass folder.

Because you are creating a bass line in this example, double-click on the Bass folder to display a long list of patches made especially for bass lines. Double-click on the bass patch called Ahab Bass. The Ahab Bass patch will appear in the upper-left window of the Subtractor interface (see Figure 4.26).

Figure 4.26   The Ahab Bass patch has now been loaded into Subtractor.

If it turns out the Ahab Bass patch is not to your liking, you can easily scroll through the list of bass patches with just the click of a button. You can re-click the Browse button and select another patch, or you can scroll through the patches in that folder by clicking the up and down arrow buttons beside the Browse Patch button. You can also click and hold on the patch name to choose another patch from the pop-up menu (see Figure 4.27). For the purposes here, try the Bass Guitar patch.

Figure 4.27   So many bass patches, so little time.

Next, you need to draw in a *clip* between the left and right locators. A clip can be thought of as a palette that allows you to draw in MIDI data. Once this has been done, you can use that clip in a few different ways, which are discussed in future chapters. For now, just select the Pencil tool, and then click and drag between bars 1–3. Release the mouse button and you've created a clip (See Figure 4.28).

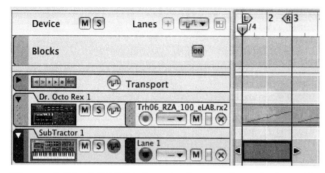

Figure 4.28 All MIDI data in Reason is stored as clips, which can then be used in several creative ways.

Click on the Selection tool, and now you're ready to sequence your first bass line. To sequence the bass line and lock in the mood and groove of your first Reason song, follow these steps:

1. First, create a two-bar loop in the sequencer in order to keep your first bass line to a manageable two bars. In the lower-right corner of the Transport panel, set the right locator to bar 3 (see Figure 4.29).

Figure 4.29 Set the right locator to bar 3.

2. Next, you need to switch views on the sequencer from Arrange to Edit view. Using the mouse, double-click on the clip you just created and Reason will automatically switch from Arrange mode to Edit mode. You should now see the Key lane and the Velocity lane (see Figure 4.30).

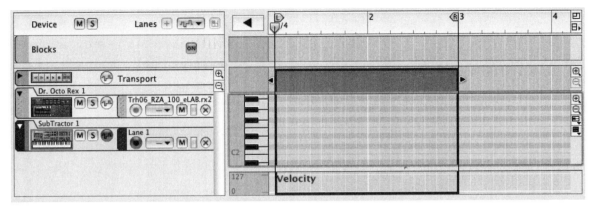

Figure 4.30 In Edit view, you can enter in notes with a mouse.

3. When sequencing MIDI events, it's helpful to see as much of the virtual keyboard as possible. Reason has a handy tool that maximizes the sequencer window; it's located in the upper-right corner of the sequencer window (see Figure 4.31). Click once on the Maximize button to enlarge the sequencer window to its fullest potential.

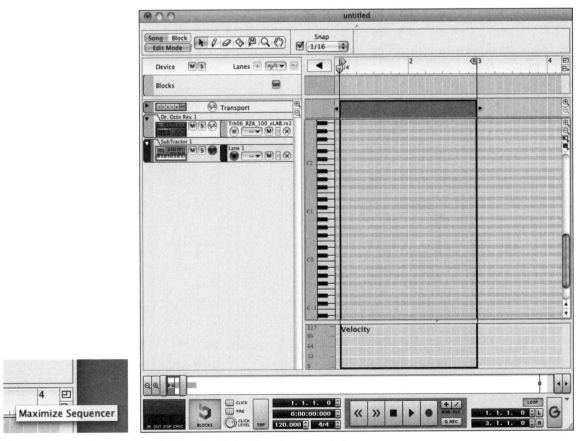

Figure 4.31 You can maximize the Edit view in one click.

4. Next, decide the note value you want to draw in (eighth notes, sixteenth notes, and so on) and select that from the Note Value menu from the sequencer toolbar (see Figure 4.32).

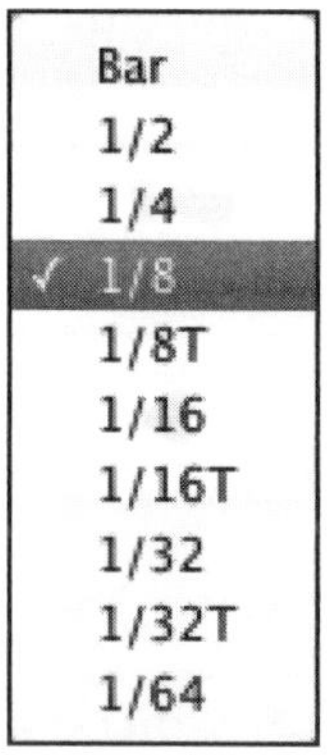

Bar
1/2
1/4
✓ 1/8
1/8T
1/16
1/16T
1/32
1/32T
1/64

Figure 4.32 Selecting the appropriate note value is a helpful time saver when manually inputting MIDI data with the Pencil tool.

5. Now you're ready to draw in a few notes. Select the Pencil tool to start drawing in your sequence in the Key lane. Because this is your first time out, keep it simple; this is a bass line, and you want it to groove, not crowd the music. When you're finished drawing notes, you should see a sequence that looks something like Figure 4.33.

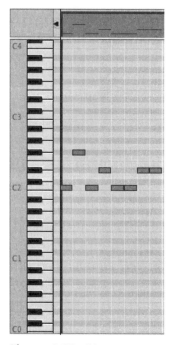

Figure 4.33 Now your two-bar bass loop is ready.

6. Click on the Maximize button to restore the sequencer window to its normal state, and click on the Switch to Arrange Mode button to see your bass line displayed in the sequencer along with the Dr. Octo Rex pattern, as in Figure 4.34.

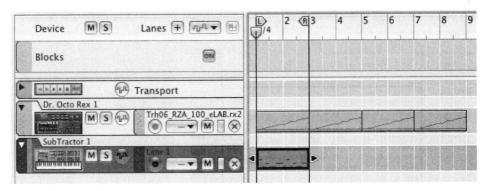

Figure 4.34 The REX loop and bass line are ready to groove together.

7. Now that a clip has been created, you'll want to make duplicates of it so that it will run the same length as the REX groove. Click on the Selection tool and click on the clip once, and then copy it (Ctrl+C in Windows; Apple+C on the Mac). Then, paste the clip (Ctrl+V in Windows; Apple+V on the Mac). This will create a duplicate clip and place it to the right of the original clip (see Figure 4.35). Paste in a couple more copies so that the bass line matches the length of the REX groove, as in Figure 4.36. Also, remember to set the right locator point back to bar 9.

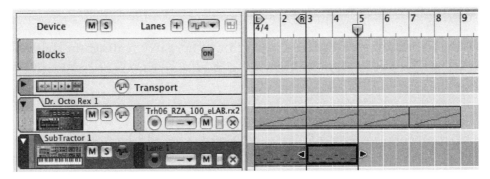

Figure 4.35 Copying and pasting clips.

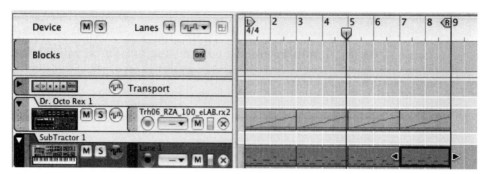

Figure 4.36   Now the clips are the same length.

8.   Press play to hear how the bass line works with your drum loop. You might want to sweeten up the mix by adding a little delay to your bass groove; scroll to reMix and turn up the Aux 2 send on channel 2 to send a little bit of the bass track to the delay device.

Now you're off and grooving!

Save Frequently   It's always a good idea to save as you work to ensure you don't lose any precious material. Use the key command or Ctrl+S on the PC or Apple+S on the Mac.

Adding a Pad

The next texture you'll add to the song is a pad line. A *pad* refers to a kind of ensemble sound that fills up the empty space, like playing chords on a guitar. The chords are held and sustained for generally long periods of time to add mysterious overtones and moods to any piece of music. A good example is a string section in an orchestra, which is used to play long sustained chords throughout film scores and symphonies.

You are going to add that texture into your groove here by creating another Subtractor synth, selecting a pad sound for it, and then drawing in some chords to give the song the mood it needs. Follow these steps:

1.   Create a new Subtractor synth. There should be a new MIDI track in the sequencer window called Subtractor 2 and it should be routed to channel 3 in reMix.

2.   To find an appropriate pad sound, again click on the Browse Patch button in the upper-left corner of the Subtractor to launch the browser window. This time, you will see all of the bass patches that you worked with in the previous tutorial.

3. In the new browser created for Reason 5.0, your sounds are never far away. Even if you are unable to see the folder you're looking for in the main browser window, you should be able to look at the top-left corner of the browser under Locations and see what you need. If this is your first time using Reason, you should see two different sound sets—the Reason Factory Sound Bank and the Orkester Sound Bank. Click on the Reason Factory Bank and then double-click on the Subtractor Patches folder in the main browser window. Finally, double-click on the Pads folder to see the available pad patches for the Subtractor.

4. Scroll down the list and select the patch called Omenous. It will load in the Subtractor window.

5. You're ready to draw in your pad clip, so draw in a Clip between bars 1–5, and then click on the Selection tool and double-click on the Clip to switch to Edit mode and use the Pencil tool to draw in a couple of chords.

Keep in mind that you want your chords to be long and sustained. Here's how to accomplish that:

1. After switching to the Edit mode, create a four-bar loop so you can draw in two sustained chords that are each two bars long. Set the right locator to 5 on the Transport panel.

2. Select the Pencil tool and locate the first note you want to draw in. Then click and hold on that note and drag your mouse to the right to bar 3. As shown in Figure 4.37, release the mouse and you will now have a sustained note. Repeat this a couple more times on different notes, so you have a nice long, sustained chord, as in Figure 4.38.

3. Repeat the previous step, and draw in another chord that starts at bar 3 and extends out to bar 5. This will give you two long sustained chords.

Now that you've created your four-bar pad track, return to Arrange mode. Now you need to duplicate this clip one time only, so use the Copy and Paste trick that you learned in the bass tutorial and repeat the pad clip once to make it equal the distance of the other two tracks.

Pads are like instant mood enhancers for music. They will set the tone and make your music sound much fuller than before. A handy tip to make the pad sound even larger than before is to add some reverb and delay to it. Scroll up to reMix, and use the Aux knobs from channel 3 to send the pad to the reverb and delay devices. You can give your pad sound a very generous helping of the two effects and turn the Aux send up to twelve o'clock or even three o'clock.

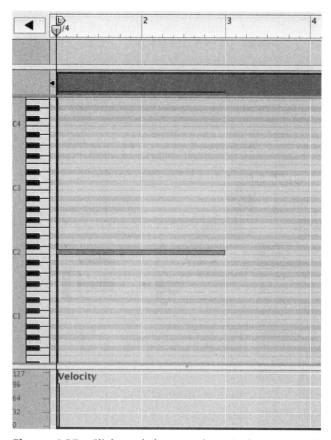

Figure 4.37 Click and drag to draw in long, sustained notes.

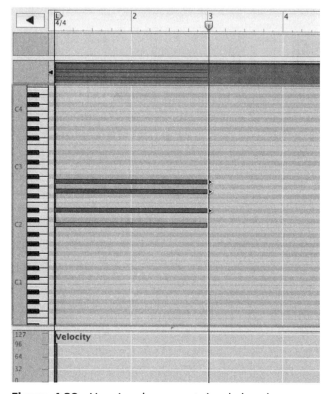

Figure 4.38 Here's a long, sustained chord.

Topping It Off with a Little Lead

You're doing great! So far you have created a grooving drum loop and sequenced in bass and pad lines. Now it's time to sprinkle a little auditory sugar on top by adding a lead line.

Throughout this tutorial, you've kept the overall tone of this song a bit on the mellow side. It's time to spice things up a bit, so you're going to use Malström and add a little acidy four-bar lead line on top of the mix.

Let's start by creating a Malström. Click on the second Subtractor, and then select Create > Malström Graintable Synthesizer. The funky green machine will appear in your Device Rack below the second Subtractor synth. It will also show up as a track in the sequencer and should appear under channel 4 in reMix (see Figure 4.39).

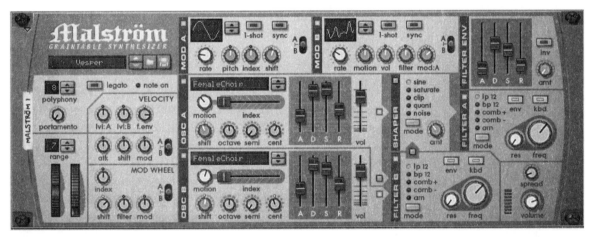

Figure 4.39 The Malström is the "new-school" virtual synth in Reason.

You need to find an appropriate lead synth patch for the Malström, so click Malström's Browse Patch button, and then click on the Reason Factory Sound Bank (found under Locations), and you should see the Malström Patches folder in the main browser window. Double-click on this folder and open the Mono Synths folder. In the long list of mono patches, find the patch called RadioHammer and double-click on it.

Just as in the previous examples, create a clip, and then switch to the Edit mode and draw in a lead line that complements the bass and pad lines. When you are finished, your sequence should look something like Figure 4.40. If it sounds a little funky at first, read on; I will give you some tips to make your lead sing.

Although the RadioHammer patch is a dreamy, acid-drenched sound that will burn its way through your mix, I thought this would be a good time to show you a couple of tricks to make this patch sound even better. Follow along as I show you how to edit your first synth in Reason.

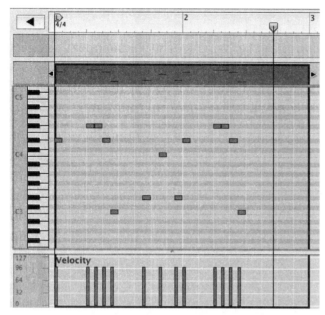

Figure 4.40 Sequencing the Malström lead line.

1. Begin by changing the Polyphony of the Malström setting to 1. *Polyphony* refers to the number of notes that can be played simultaneously by a synth or sound module. With the polyphony set to 1, only one note can be played at a time. Malström's polyphony display is in the upper-left portion of the interface. Using the arrow pointers beside the display, change it to 1 (see Figure 4.41).

Figure 4.41 Polyphony is the secret to changing any synth into a lead line.

2. Below the polyphony control is a knob called *portamento*. This controls the speed of the "sliding sound" you get between two notes. As in Figure 4.42, turn the knob until it reaches around the eleven o'clock position. This will produce a very nice note sliding effect when you play your sequence back.

Figure 4.42 The more portamento, the more slide.

3. Next, scroll up the Device Rack to reMix; you're going to make a couple of volume adjustments to the Malström. If you play the sequence as it is now, the Malström is probably a little too loud for the mix, so start by clicking and holding on the volume fader for the Malström (the fader on channel 4) and just slide it down to adjust the volume of your Malström track (see Figure 4.43).

Figure 4.43 A little level adjustment is just what the doctor ordered.

4. A neat effect you might try is to pan the synth either hard right or hard left, and then use a lot of delay and reverb to create a stereophonic effect. This is done quite easily by adjusting the pan knob to the left or right, and then using the Aux knobs to send the Malström to the reverb and delay, as shown in Figure 4.44. Voila! Instant synthesized bliss!

Figure 4.44 Pan the Malström to the left and top it off with some reverb and delay. It will give your track some needed ambience.

Putting the Pieces Together

There are two essentials for creating good dance music. First, you have to come up with some killer hooks and grooves with your synths. The second is that you must assemble them so that there is an intro, middle, and ending. At this point, you have accomplished step one with your first Reason song. As good dance music also depends on predictable beats and a generous dose of repetition, you must now assemble this tune to give it the final touch. In this section, I'm going to show you the quick-and-easy way to stretch your Reason song from 4 bars to 41. It won't be a long song, but it will be sufficient to help you understand how to arrange your pieces of music.

First, let's start with the REX loop:

1. Look at the REX track in Figure 4.45, and you will see that there are four two-bar loops lined up next to each other. First, you are going to combine all of these loops in order to create one large eight-bar loop to make it easier to copy and paste.

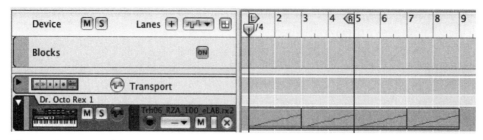

Figure 4.45 At this point, you have four separate two-bar loops.

2. Click on the Selection tool and then click and drag your mouse to the right until you reach the end of the fourth two-bar loop. Release the mouse button and all four clips have been selected, as in Figure 4.46.

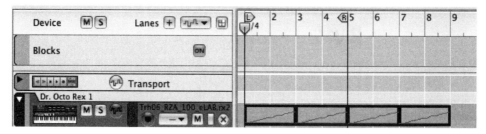

Figure 4.46 By using the Pencil tool, click and drag until all four loops are selected.

3. Next, you're going to merge the clips into one clip by selecting Join Clips from the Edit pull-down menu.

4. Copy the selection (press Ctrl+C in Windows; press Apple+C on the Mac).

5. Paste the selection (press Ctrl+V in Windows; press Apple+V on the Mac). This will place a new copy of the eight-bar loop immediately to the right of the original loop.

6. Because the copy that you made is still on your virtual Clipboard inside your computer's memory, just repeat the Paste key command three more times until the REX loop reaches bar 41 (see Figure 4.47).

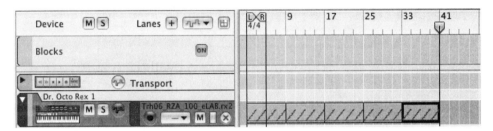

Figure 4.47 Copy and paste your REX loop until it reaches bar 41.

7. Click and drag the right locator point to the beginning of bar 41 so that you can listen to the entire track in a constant loop.

Now that the drums are laid down and arranged, you can do the same with the bass track, which is being played by the first Subtractor synth.

1. Select all of the bass clips and select Join Clips from the Edit pull-down menu, as shown in Figure 4.48.

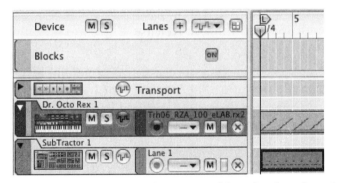

Figure 4.48 Use Join Clips to combine the four bass loops into a single eight-bar loop.

2. Using the Pointer tool, click on the bass clip and drag it to bar 5. Release the mouse button and Reason will move the four-bar clip to bar 5, as shown in Figure 4.49.

3. Using the same copy-and-paste method found in the previous example, copy and paste the bass clip until it reaches bar 37 (see Figure 4.50).

Next comes the pad that you created with the second Subtractor synth.

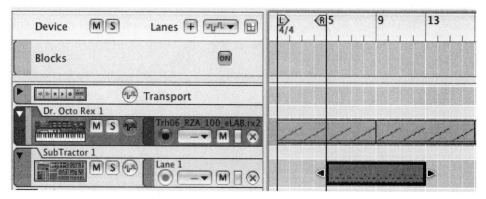

Figure 4.49 Click and drag is the name of the game when moving clips around.

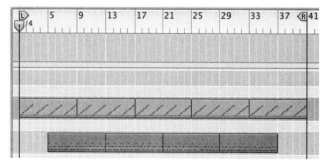

Figure 4.50 Copy and paste the bass clip.

1. Select both clips with the mouse and then select Join Clips to combine them.

2. Click and drag the pad track to bar 9.

3. Using the same copy-and-paste method that you used in the last two sections, copy and paste the pad track until it reaches bar 33, as shown in Figure 4.51.

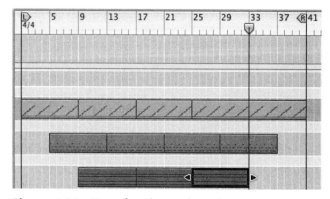

Figure 4.51 Now for the pad track.

Last on the arrangement is the lead clip that you created using the Malström synth. This is going to be a little different because you probably wouldn't want this part to play constantly through the entire song. Instead, you are just going to drop it in here and there to flavor up the mix.

1. Click and drag the lead clip to bar 13.

2. Hold down the Control key on your PC or the Option key on the Mac, and then click and hold on the lead clip. Start to drag the clip to the right, and you will see that a copy has been made and is following your pointer. Drag the new copy to bar 21 and release the mouse. This will create a new clip, as seen in Figure 4.52.

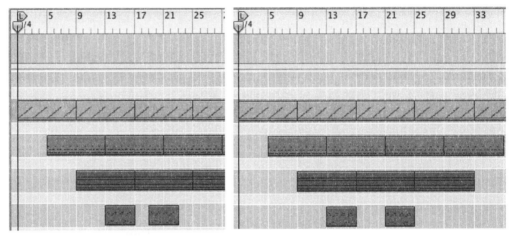

Figure 4.52 Clicking and dragging a clip while holding down the Control (Option) key will create a copy that can be placed elsewhere in your track.

3. Repeating the same step as before, create a new copy and drop it in at bar 37. After doing this, the whole song should look a lot like Figure 4.53.

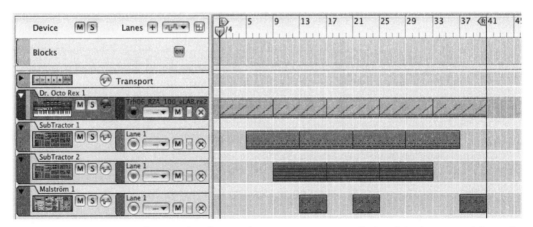

Figure 4.53 Because this is a lead, you don't want to overdo it with the repetitions, but having it play back here and there is a good use of textures and moods.

It's All in the Mix!

Last but not least are saving and mixing down your first song. Reason can create a stereo digital audio file of your song. You can then burn it onto a CD to listen to it wherever you like, or you can place it on the web so others can download it and groove along with ya. Mixdown is simple.

Mixes Galore   Aside from the standard audio file mixdown, Reason features a few other unique mixing and mastering capabilities. These other features are examined in more detail in Chapter 18, "The MClass Mastering Suite—Close Up" and in Chapter 22, "Mixing and Publishing Your Reason Songs."

When creating an audio mixdown, Reason exports the *entire* song, including all of the empty bars at the end. So, unless you like a lot of empty space at the end of your tune, you need to get rid of the empty bars by adjusting the end point position (E icon) of your song (see Figure 4.54). As in Figure 4.55, just click and drag the end point to the left until it is four bars after the right locator point. This ensures that the tail end of your real-time effects isn't unexpectedly cut off (see the note entitled "Don't Cut Off the Tail," for more details).

Figure 4.54   The end point position dictates the end of a song file.

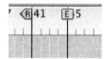

Figure 4.55   Click and drag the end point within four bars of the right locator point.

Don't Cut Off the Tail   *Tail effect* refers to the lingering sound of reverb or delay (or similar effect) after the initial sound (the hit of a snare drum, for instance) has stopped. The tail eventually dissipates to silence.

When mixing down, it's important that you extend the song beyond its ending point long enough to capture any lingering effect tails. Notice, in Figure 4.56, how abruptly the mix is cut off. Figure 4.57 shows the same mix with the tail in place; the mix was extended long enough to capture the entirety of the fading effects.

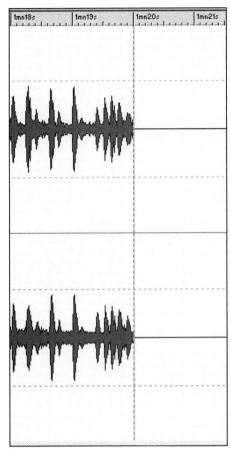

Figure 4.56 This is an example of cutting off the tail end of your mix. It doesn't look or sound good.

Now you are ready to export your song into a digital audio file. Select File > Export Song As Audio File. You will then be able to name your song, select between WAV or AIFF audio formats, and click on Save. A new window will pop up asking you to select your bit depth and sampling rate (see Figure 4.58). Reason can create a 16-bit, 44.1kHz recording, which is the standard for all commercial music CDs. Reason can also create very high-resolution digital audio files, for use in pro-audio programs or post-production. If this is your first time out, I recommend sticking with the default setting of 16-bit, 44.1kHz, and go ahead and leave Dither checked.

After you select your bit depth and sampling rate, Reason will export your song as an audio file. Depending on how fast your computer is and how many tracks you have in your song, this can take a minute or two. After it's mixed, you can quit Reason and open your digital audio file in your favorite digital audio jukebox program, such as Windows Media Player or iTunes.

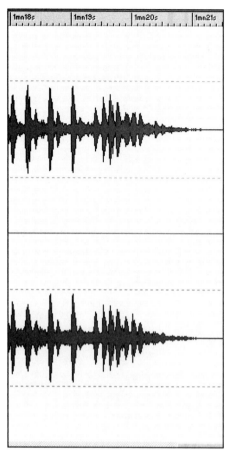

Figure 4.57 Here is the same mix without the tail cut off.

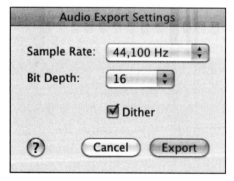

Figure 4.58 Choose your mixdown preferences and let 'er rip!

This chapter contained the step-by-step process of creating your first song in Reason. Propellerhead makes it so easy and fun to create music that it's infectious. And I'm betting you're anxious to learn more. From this point on, the chapters give you an in-depth breakdown of every synth and sound module in Reason and show you how to use these creatively in ways that will set you apart from the average "Joe Reason" user.

5 The Reason Sequencer—Close Up

The Reason sequencer (see Figure 5.1) is basically the brain of the entire program. It is the compositional tool that makes it possible to record your performances, edit them, and then play them back with accuracy and precision. This chapter examines the individual parts of the Reason sequencer and discusses how to use the sequencer to its limits.

A sequencer is responsible for performing three tasks:

■ Recording MIDI data

■ Editing MIDI data

■ Playing back MIDI data

Importing and Exporting MIDI Files The Reason sequencer can import and export MIDI files. This is a great feature for users who like to surf the web and download MIDI files of their favorite songs. Additionally, you can export your songs in Reason as MIDI files for other users to download into their favorite MIDI sequencers.

To import a MIDI file, simply choose Import MIDI File from the File pull-down menu, and then locate the MIDI with your Windows or Mac file browsers to import it. Once you import the MIDI files, just keep these rules in mind:

■ Imported sequencer tracks will not be routed to any Reason device. You will have to do this manually, and you will learn how to do so later in this chapter.

■ All of the controller data saved within a MIDI file, such as Modulation Wheel adjustments or pitch bend changes, will be imported along with the rest of the data; however, in some cases this controller data might not work as intended with Reason devices. You might have to remove the controller information, which is covered toward the end of this chapter.

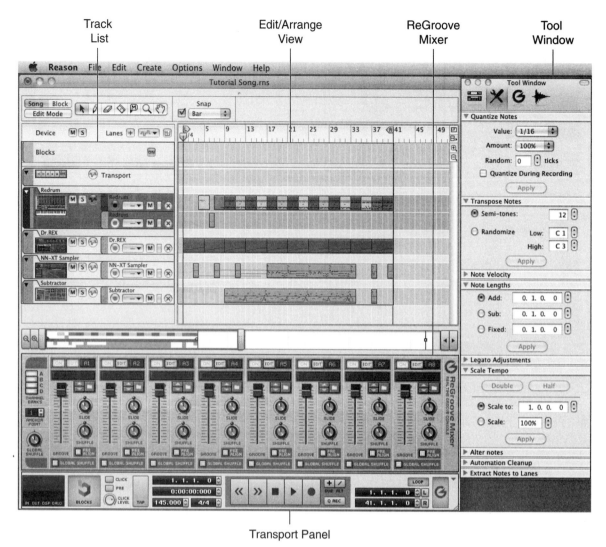

Figure 5.1 The Reason sequencer—the brain of your virtual environment. The sequencer is split into five basic sections: the Track list, the Song/Edit views, the Tool Window, the ReGroove Mixer, and the Transport panel.

To export a MIDI file, first set your end (E) marker to the end of your song. Then simply choose Export MIDI File from the File pull-down menu, and Reason will do the rest. Just remember the following:

- The tempo of the Reason song is stored in the MIDI file.

- All of the exported sequencer tracks are set to MIDI Channel 1 by default. This is because Reason is not a MIDI channel-dependent program, like Cubase and Logic are.

- All of the exported sequencer tracks will retain their given names from Reason.

The rest of this chapter explores every inch of the Reason sequencer, including the following topics:

- The basic layout

- The Track window

- The Sequencer toolbar

- The Tool Window

- The Transport panel

- Sequencing a live performance

- Sequencing written data

- The ReGroove Mixer

- Using Blocks

The Basic Layout and Tools

Before you begin your exploration of the Reason sequencer, it's important to have a general understanding of the basic layout of its common and unique views and functions.

The Song/Edit View

When you first look at the sequencer, the Song view is probably the first point of interest you will notice. This is where all of the MIDI data for your Reason song is stored, arranged, and displayed.

MIDI Data A.K.A. Clips   All of the MIDI data displayed in the Reason sequencer is also referred to as "clips." Clips are groups of MIDI data that can be easily moved around, selected, deleted, cut into smaller clips, and more.

Typically, a sequencer displays its MIDI data in a linear fashion, meaning that the information is read from left to right. With that in mind, a song begins on the far left and progresses to the right as the song plays. The timeline of the MIDI events in the sequencer is governed by the ruler, which is located at the top of the Song view and runs parallel to it. Looking at Figure 5.2, you can see that the ruler is displaying *bars*, or measure counts, for every other bar. When you read through the next part of this section and use the Zoom tools, you'll find that the ruler can display much smaller and finer increments.

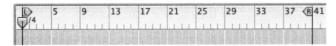

Figure 5.2 The ruler governs the timeline of your Reason song.

Several kinds of MIDI data are displayed in the Song view:

- Note information

- Controller information

- Automation information

- Pattern Change information

Life in the Fast Lanes If you're familiar with the previous versions of Reason, the sequencer in version 4 is really going to take you by surprise, because it's pretty much been overhauled and redesigned. One of the most important updates to the sequencer is the inclusion of *lanes*, which are multiple tracks of data contained within a single sequencer track. Looking at Figure 5.3, you can see a track that includes two lanes of data. The first lane is the note data, whereas the second lane is automation data for the Filter Frequency parameter of the Reason synth that this track is routed to, which is the Subtractor.

Also note that the second lane has an On/Off switch, which disables the automation data from playing back. This is also the same for pattern lanes, which you'll read about shortly.

Additionally, every lane has a Delete Lane button marked "X," which will delete just the lane and not the entire sequencer track.

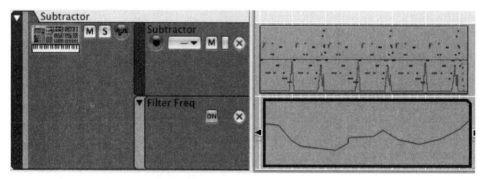

Figure 5.3 Every sequencer track can have multiple lanes dedicated to displaying and editing note, controller, automation, and pattern data.

The Song view also has an alternate viewing mode, called the Edit view. In this view, all the MIDI data in a song can be edited and new data can be created (see Figure 5.4). As you read further in this chapter, you will find that there are many creative possibilities and different faces to the Edit view.

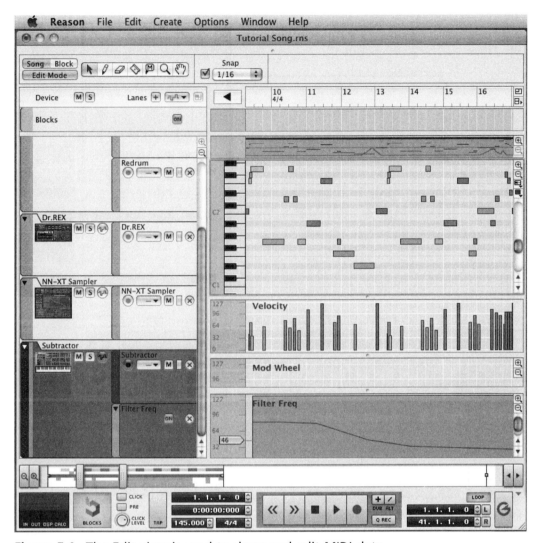

Figure 5.4   The Edit view is used to draw and edit MIDI data.

The Zoom Tools

There are four pairs of Zoom tools in the Reason sequencer. These tools help you get a close-up look at any data in the Arrange or Edit views of a particular track. They also give you a better view of an overall song.

- The first pair of Zoom tools is located in the lower-left corner of the Song/Edit view. These are used to zoom in and out horizontally on any event(s) in the Song/Edit view (see Figure 5.5).

Figure 5.5   The first pair of Zoom tools can be used to horizontally zoom in or out on any event in the Song/Edit view.

- The second pair of Zoom tools is located in the upper-right corner of the Track window. These are used to zoom in and out vertically on every sequencer track while in the Song view (see Figure 5.6).

Figure 5.6 The second pair of Zoom tools can be used while in the Song view.

- The third pair of Zoom tools is located in the upper-right corner of the Track window. These are used to zoom in and out vertically on any selected sequencer track while in the Edit view (see Figure 5.7).

Figure 5.7 The third pair of Zoom tools can be used while in the Edit view.

- The fourth pair of Zoom tools is located in the lower-right corner of the Edit view. These two are used to zoom in and out vertically on any automation data in the Edit view (see Figure 5.8).

Figure 5.8 The fourth pair of Zoom tools can be used to horizontally zoom in or out on automation data in the Edit view.

Sizing Up the Sequencer

The size of the Sequencer window can be easily adjusted in two ways:

- By clicking on the Maximize button, located just above the Zoom tool found in the upper-right corner of the Sequencer window. Note that after maximizing the Sequencer window, the Maximize button becomes a Restore button, which is used to return the window to its default position.

- By clicking and dragging on the divider between the Sequencer window and the Reason Device Rack.

Detaching the Sequencer Window   One feature in Reason worth noting is the capability to detach the Sequencer window from the Reason interface. If your computer supports dual monitors, you might find this a very useful feature. It allows you to use one monitor for the Reason devices and another for the sequencer.

To detach the sequencer, simply choose Detach Sequencer Window from the Window pull-down menu. The Sequencer window will separate itself from the Reason interface and appear in its own window. This window can then be dragged to another monitor and maximized in order to create an optimal dual monitor setup.

At any time, if you want to close the separated Sequencer window, just click on the Close Window button in the Sequencer window. The sequencer will return to its default position.

The Sequencer Toolbar

Both the Sequencer toolbar and Tool Window are used to perform numerous tasks in the sequencer. This section discusses each of these tasks (see Figure 5.9).

Let's first discuss the Sequencer toolbar by starting at the far left corner.

Figure 5.9 The Sequencer toolbar and Tool Window provide all the tools and editors to sequence like a pro.

Song/Edit View Button

These buttons are used to switch between the Song and Edit views of the sequencer (see Figure 5.10). Every time Reason is booted up and a song is loaded, the Song view is the default. Clicking on the Edit button will allow you to view any MIDI data within a sequencer track.

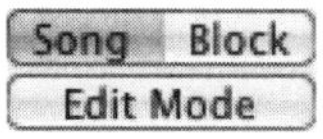

Figure 5.10 The Song/Edit View buttons are used to toggle between the two viewing modes of the Reason sequencer. The left side of this figure shows the button as it appears when the sequencer is in the Song view. The right side shows the button as it appears in the Edit view.

Block Mode   Looking back at Figure 5.10, you can also see another button called Block, which switches the Reason sequencer to the Block Edit mode. I'll cover this feature towards the end of the chapter.

Changing Edit Modes   Once you are in the Edit mode of the Reason sequencer, there are a few ways to view and edit your performances and sequences. You use the Change Note Edit Mode pop-up menu, which is located to the far upper-right of the sequencer, just above the zoom tools (see Figure 5.11). Looking at the figure, you'll notice that there are three options (Key Edit, Drum Edit, and REX Edit), and each of these editors serves a unique purpose (see Figure 5.12).

- **The Key Edit**—This editor is used to edit the MIDI data related to the Subtractor, Malström, Thor, NN-19, and NN-XT devices.

- **The Drum Edit**—This editor is used to edit the MIDI data of Redrum.

- **The REX Edit**—This editor is used to edit the MIDI data of the Dr. Octo Rex Loop Player.

Just below the Change Note Edit Mode menu is the Note Lane Performance Parameter Automation menu (see Figure 5.13). This menu is used to show and hide different controller parameters such as the Mod Wheel and Aftertouch and all of the parameters that can be automated. You'll get more in depth with this later in the chapter. For now, just be aware that these menus are available, as you'll be calling on them from time to time.

Figure 5.11 The Change Note Edit Mode menu is used to switch between the Key, Drum, and REX editors in the Reason sequencer.

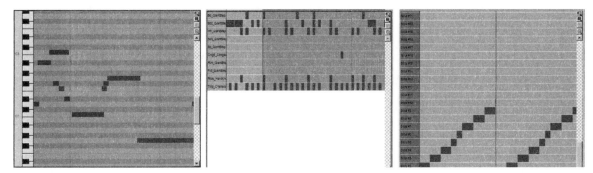

Figure 5.12 Each of these editors serves a specific purpose. The Key edit (left) is used to edit data for the Subtractor, Malström, Thor, NN-19, and NN-XT devices. The Drum edit (center) is used to edit the MIDI data of Redrum. Finally, the REX edit (right) is used to edit the MIDI data of the Dr. Octo Rex Loop Player.

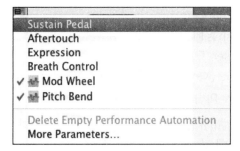

Figure 5.13 The Note Lane Performance Parameter Automation menu is used to show and hide different controller parameters such as the Mod Wheel and Aftertouch and all of the parameters that can be automated.

The Editing Tool Buttons

To the right of the Edit/Song view button are the Editing tools (see Figure 5.14). These six buttons are used to view, write, or edit data in both the Song and Edit views.

Figure 5.14 The Editing Tool buttons can be used in the Song and Edit views.

- **Selector tool**—Also known as the *pointer*, this tool is used to select an individual MIDI event or group. It can also be used to select a group of MIDI events and groups by clicking and dragging a marquee box around a group of events and groups.

- **Pencil tool**—This tool is used to draw MIDI events and groups. Additionally, it can be used to draw in controller and velocity information on an event-by-event basis. You also can hold down the Ctrl key (Option key on the Mac) and the Pencil becomes a crosshair tool that can be used to click and drag straight lines or smooth diagonal lines.

- **Eraser tool**—This tool is used to delete single MIDI events and groups. Additionally, it can also delete a group of MIDI events by clicking and dragging a marquee box around the events and groups, and then releasing the mouse.

- **Razor tool**—This tool is used to cut sequencer data by splitting clips.

- **Mute tool**—This tool is used to mute selected clips of MIDI events in a song.

- **Magnify tool**—This tool is used to get a close-up look at a group or MIDI event.

- **Hand tool**—This tool is used to scroll through a Reason song. Select it, and then click and drag to the left or right while in the Song or Edit views. The song position will shift along with you.

Keyboard Shortcuts Each of the tool buttons has a keyboard shortcut assigned to it. This makes it very easy to switch tools quickly without using the mouse. Here's a list of the buttons and their shortcut keys:

- Selector—Q
- Pencil—W
- Eraser—E
- Razor—R
- Mute—T
- Magnify—Y
- Hand—U

Snap Controls

To the right of the Editing tools are the Snap (short for "Snap to Grid") controls (see Figure 5.15), which perform two tasks:

- Assign a minimum note length value to the Pencil tool.

- Assign a minimum note length value for shifting MIDI events.

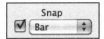

Figure 5.15 The Snap controls are used for assigning note values.

Snap supports a wide variety of note values, ranging from bar (whole notes) to 64th notes (1/64). Once a note value is selected, you can then use the Pencil, Line, or Selector tools to draw, edit, or shift clips in the Song view or MIDI events in the Edit view.

It's important to understand how the Snap works, so try a couple of exercises. Get yourself ready by starting a new Reason song, creating an instance of reMix and Subtractor, and finally creating a clip by using the Pencil tool to click and drag between the left and right locator points. When you're finished, it should look something like Figure 5.16.

Figure 5.16 The stage has been set to demonstrate Snap to Grid.

1. Double-click on the clip. This will open the Key Lane Editor for the Subtractor. The Velocity lane should also be viewable by default.

2. Select a note value of 1/8 from the Snap pull-down menu.

3. Make sure the Snap button, located to the right of the Snap Value pull-down menu, is active.

4. Select the Pencil tool and click to create a few events in the Key lane. Notice that each note is an 8th note in length (see Figure 5.17).

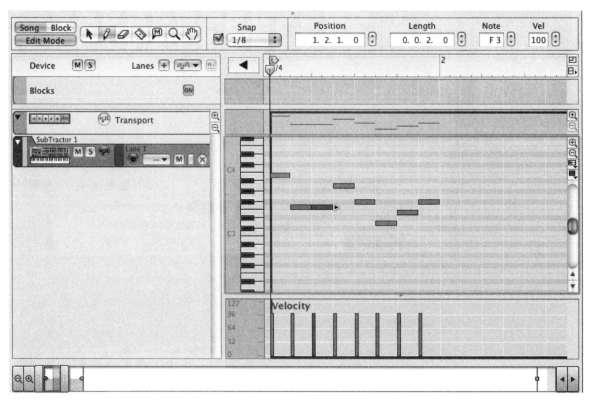

Figure 5.17 The Pencil tool can draw in 8th-note resolutions because 1/8 has been selected from the Snap pull-down menu. Note that you can click and drag to the right if you want to make the event longer than an 8th note.

5. Click on the Switch to Song Mode button.

In the next exercise, you'll use the Selector tool in the Song view. For the sake of simplicity, keep using the song you started in the previous example and make sure that the Snap to Grid button is still active before you begin this exercise.

1. Switch to the Song view and choose 1/2 from the Snap pull-down menu. This assigns a half note value.

2. Click the Selector tool. Now click and drag the Subtractor clip to the left or right, and you will notice it moving in half-note increments.

3. Choose a smaller note value from the Snap pull-down menu, such as 1/8 perhaps.

4. Try moving the clip again and you will see that it moves in much smaller increments than before.

Snap to Grid Versus Free Wheelin' Edits   Located just to the right of the Snap pull-down menu is the Snap to Grid button (keyboard shortcut S). This button turns the Snap function on and off. You have just seen how the Snap works when activated. Try turning off the Snap to Grid button and using the Selector tool to move around a few groups. You will notice that the moving groups are not governed by the Snap note value. Rather, you can move groups around freely, which is typically referred to as *free time*. This enables you to make very fine adjustments to a MIDI performance.

Additional Toolbar Features

In addition to all of the tools discussed over the last few pages, there are other tools and features that the Sequencer toolbar provides. Just to the right of the Snap tools, there may appear to be a lot of empty, unused space. I say "may" because some of these additional tools and features do not appear unless a sequencer track has been selected, at which point, some of the tools and dialog boxes will appear (see Figure 5.18).

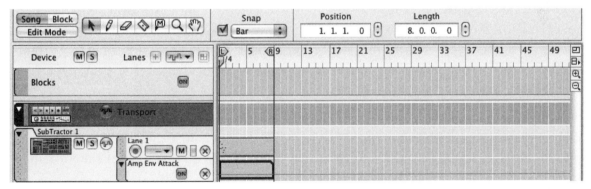

Figure 5.18 There are additional tools and dialogs in the sequencer that are only seen when a sequencer track has been selected.

The Track Parameter Automation button and pull-down menu operate in the same fashion as the Performance Parameter Automation menu that you looked at earlier in this chapter (review Figure 5.13). The purpose of this button and pull-down menu is to create an automation lane on the selected sequencer track. Looking at Figure 5.19,

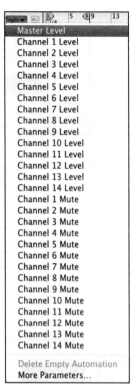

Figure 5.19 The Track Parameter Automation menu supplies a lot of the commonly used parameters for any Reason device.

you can see that most of the automated parameters are listed, such as the Master Level, and levels and mutes for all of the reMix channels. There is also an additional option called More Parameters. When it's selected, a new window will open to reveal all of the additional parameters that can be selected. Simply click to check them, close the window, and they will now appear in the Track Parameter Automation pull-down menu and an automation lane will be created for that parameter (see Figure 5.20).

Moving along to the right, the Create Pattern Lane button is used to create a lane for changing patterns with either the Matrix or Redrum, which are both pattern-based Reason devices. Note that this button is grayed out until an instance of the aforementioned Reason devices has been created.

Now, select the Pencil tool and a couple of new dialog boxes/pull-down menus appear just to the right of the Pattern Lane button.

- **Time Signature**—This dialog box is used to set a new time signature for your Reason song. To use it, simply hold down the Alt key on your keyboard (Option key on the Mac) and click on the Time Signature display in the Transport

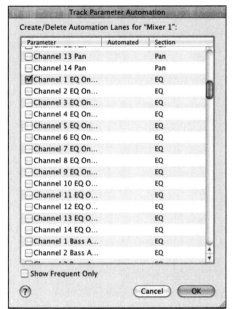

Figure 5.20 Selecting the More Parameters option will launch a new window with a list of additional automating parameters (left). Select a parameter from this list, click OK (center), and then that parameter will appear in the automation pull-down menu (right) and an automation lane will be created for that parameter.

panel. A new Time Signature lane will be created on the Transport sequencer track. At this point, select your new time signature from the pull-down menu and use the Pencil tool to draw in the new time signature along the Transport sequencer track.

- **Pattern**—This dialog box is used to select a new pattern for either the Matrix or Redrum. To use it, hold down the Alt key on your keyboard and click on the Pattern section of either the Matrix or Redrum. A Pattern Select lane will be created on the sequencer track of the aforementioned Reason devices. At this point, select your new pattern from the pull-down menu and use the Pencil tool to draw the new pattern in the lane.

- **Block**—This dialog box is used to assign any selected clip of MIDI data in a song to a Block, which is part of the Block Edit Mode. This is a brand new feature to Reason that enables you to create a dynamic arrangement of your song by assigning groups of MIDI data to Blocks that can then be rearranged quickly. This will be covered towards the end of the chapter.

Lastly, there are some additional dialog boxes that are displayed in this part of the Sequencer toolbar when you're in the Edit mode. Open any Reason song, switch to

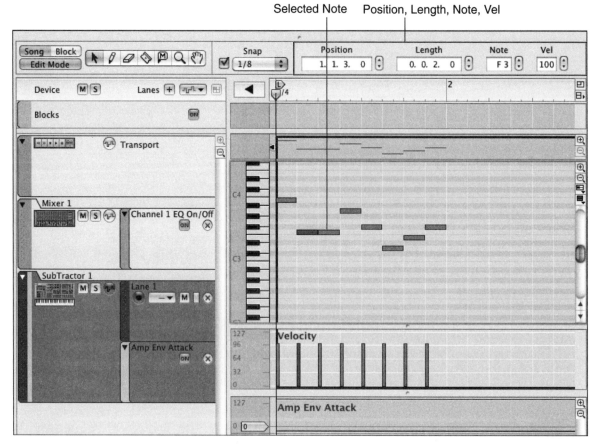

Figure 5.21 Selecting any MIDI note of any Reason device while in the Edit mode will display the Note Position, Length, Pitch, and Velocity.

the Edit mode, and select a MIDI note. At this point, you'll see the newly displayed options at the top of the screen (see Figure 5.21).

- **Position**—This displays the MIDI note's position in Bars, Beats, 16th Notes, and Ticks.

- **Length**—This displays the MIDI note's length in Bars, Beats, 16th Notes, and Ticks.

- **Note**—This displays the note's pitch in numeric form. Note that this option is not actually labeled "Pitch" or anything for that matter.

- **Vel**—This displays the note's velocity.

Note that you can also view the Position and Length options in the Song mode when a clip is selected in the sequencer.

The Tool Window

The Tool Window of Reason 5 is probably one of the best new workflow features I've ever used in a sequencing program (see Figure 5.22). It can help create new instances of any Reason device, edit your MIDI performances, or edit/alter your grooves via ReGroove, which you'll be reading about later in this chapter. In other words, it's the creative hub for your Reason destinations.

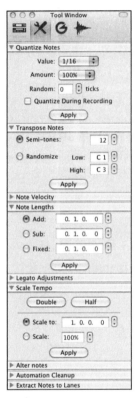

Figure 5.22 The Tool Window is used to create new Reason devices, alter your MIDI performances, or create grooves with ReGroove.

You can see that the Tool Window is divided into three tabs: Devices, Tools, and Groove. This discussion focuses only on the Tools tab for now; you'll read about the Groove tab later in this chapter.

For now, let's meet the family of the Tools tab.

Quantize

Quantization helps to correct timing problems. The easiest way to explain it is to think of quantizing as an invisible magnet that pulls and pushes MIDI events to a determined note value, which is assigned by the Quantization pull-down menu. It's an indispensable tool for rhythmically challenged (or non-robotic) people who need rhythms that are tight and punchy.

In order to use this tool, you must select a clip from any sequencer track that has MIDI note data or a group of MIDI notes in the Edit mode. Once this is done, the Apply button in the Quantize tool will become active. Assuming that you've done this, let's have a look at the individual parameters.

■ **Value**—This pull-down menu determines the note value to use for quantization. Like the Snap pull-down menu, it has a range of bar to 1/64, and all points in between. However, unlike the Snap menu, there is an additional Shuffle option, which is used in combination with the ReGroove mixer. More on this later.

■ **Amount**—This pull-down menu determines the amount of quantization to apply to a clip or to a group of selected MIDI notes. It has a range of 5% to 100%.

■ **Random**—This applies a randomized feeling to your MIDI notes in Tick increments. It has a range of 0–120 ticks. The purpose of this function is to introduce a looser feeling to your music, to avoid having it feel too tight and rigid. Think of real drummers; as much as they might try, it's difficult to hit every note right in time without some sort of variation. This introduces a randomization into their playing which is what gives the performance its charm. The Random function can help make this possible.

■ **Quantize During Recording**—When activated, this button performs real-time quantization after the MIDI event has been recorded. The amount of applied quantization is determined by the selected note value and quantization strength.

Transpose Notes

This tool is used to alter the pitch of a MIDI performance in your song. This can also be referred to as *transposition* as it can be used to introduce key changes to your song. There are two options to choose from when using this tool.

■ **Semitones**—This is used to transpose the pitch of your selected notes in semitone increments. It has a range of +/–127.

■ **Randomize**—This is used to randomize the pitches of your selected notes based within a specifically selected note range. Simply assign a From and To, and then click on the Apply button.

Note Velocity

The Note Velocity tool is used to assign varying velocities to your MIDI performances in your song. It's an important part of the creative process, because it can help introduce dynamics to your music thus making it sound much more interesting to listen to.

■ **Add**—This dialog box allows you to add a specific amount of velocity to a selected clip or group of MIDI notes. Note that this adds velocity to what has already been recorded, which simply means that if you have a MIDI note with a velocity of 80 and then use this tool to add 20, the resulting value will be 100.

- **Fixed**—This dialog box is used to apply a fixed velocity value to your selected MIDI notes.

- **Scale**—This dialog box is used to apply a scaled feeling to your selected MIDI notes. A good example of this is a drum clip that has a lot of dynamics. Using the Scale function is a great way to make those variations in velocity more pronounced.

- **Random**—This dialog box is used to introduce a randomization to the velocities of your selected MIDI notes. You want to use this sparingly, because it might create some velocities that are unpleasant to listen to.

Note Lengths

The Note Lengths tool is used to add, subtract, or fix the length of the selected clip or group of selected MIDI notes in your song. Let's say for example that you would like to take a track of sustained chords played through the NN-XT and make the notes play longer or shorter than originally recorded. Note Lengths is the right tool for the job.

- **Add**—This will add length to your selected MIDI notes by Bars, Beats, 16th notes, and Ticks.

- **Sub**—This will subtract length to your selected MIDI notes by Bars, Beats, 16th notes, and Ticks.

- **Fixed**—This will apply a fixed length to your selected MIDI notes by Bars, Beats, 16th notes, and Ticks.

Legato Adjustments

This tool is used to adjust the amount of legato between notes in your Reason song. It's a handy and quick way to make a series of notes flow evenly without gaps between the notes. It's also a tool that can be used to overlap notes, and it can be used to introduce a gap between notes.

- **Side-by-side**—This option will extend the length of a selected note to the beginning of the next selected note.

- **Overlap**—This option will overlap the lengths of a selected notes by Bars, Beats, 16th notes, and Ticks.

- **Gap by**—This option will create a gap between selected notes by Bars, Beats, 16th notes, and Ticks.

Scale Tempo

This tool is used to alter the perceived tempo of a MIDI performance. With the Scale Tempo tool, you can make a bass line or lead sound like it's playing back at half or double the tempo that it was originally recorded. Additionally, Scale Tempo will alter any automation, controller, or pattern data as well, to make sure that everything sounds correct as it plays back.

■ **Double/Half**—These buttons will double up or cut in half the original tempo of the selected MIDI notes, thus either speeding up or slowing down the tempo respectively. You can also use the Scale dialog box to create the same effect by assigning a value of 200% to double the tempo or 50% to cut it in half.

■ **Scale**—This option will allow you to alter the tempo of your selected notes by less common values than the Double and Half buttons. Simply set your desired value and click on the Apply button.

Alter Notes

This tool is a bit of an avant-garde feature, because it will alter the pitch, length, and velocity of your selected MIDI notes in a random fashion. However, this tool is not confined to a specific note or velocity range as you saw in the Note and Velocity tools. All you need to do is assign a percentage value and then click on the Apply button to see what Reason will randomly cook up for you. Just remember, there's always an opportunity to undo what you've done by selecting it from the Edit pull-down menu.

Automation Cleanup

The Automation Cleanup tool is used to optimize or clean your automation data in a Reason song. You may notice that as you begin to write in automation data and performances, it tends to get a little messy due to all of the automation points that are created along the timeline of the sequencer track. To use this tool, simply select a clip with automation written onto it, determine the Amount of cleanup needed (ranges from Minimum to Maximum), and press the Apply button. You'll take a better look at this in Chapter 20, "Automation," which discusses automation at length.

Extract Notes to Lanes

The Extract Notes to Lanes tool is used to move or duplicate a specific note or range of notes to a separate clip on a new note lane within a sequencer track. This is a useful tool to have when you are working with a device, such as a Redrum sequencer track. You can split the separate notes onto their own tracks for further editing.

The Extract tool includes the following parameters:

■ **Single Note**—This parameter enables you to select a single note to extract.

■ **Note Range**—This parameter enables you to select a range of notes to extract.

■ **Explode**—This parameter will place every note of a sequence onto its own note lane.

The Transport Panel

Although some might consider the Transport panel a separate entity from the Reason sequencer, I disagree, because the sequencer is dependent on the Transport panel in order to properly function. With that in mind, the next part of the tour is dedicated to the features and functionality of the Transport panel (see Figure 5.23).

Figure 5.23 The Reason Transport panel is vital to the functionality of the sequencer.

In the dead center of the Transport panel are the Stop and Play controls of the Reason sequencer. They look very similar to the buttons on a tape machine or VCR, and there is really no mystery as to what each button does, but there are a few variations to each of these buttons that make them more adaptable to the Reason environment.

- The Stop button stops the sequencer wherever it is playing within a sequence. Additionally, if you press the Stop button a second time, the song position returns to the Left Locater. Pressing the Stop button a third time causes the song position to return to the beginning of the sequence. This is called the *return-to-zero* function.

- The Play button makes the Reason sequencer begin playing. There are no additional features on this button.

- The Rewind button shuttles the song position backwards to any point in a Reason song. The button can be used while the song is playing or when the sequencer is stopped. When pressed once, the song position jumps back one bar, but when pressed and held, the song position scrolls back even faster.

- The Fast Forward button shuttles the song position forward to any point in a Reason song. Just as with the Rewind button, it can be used while the song is playing or when the Reason sequencer has stopped. When pressed once, the song position jumps forward one bar, but when pressed and held, the song position scrolls forward even faster.

- The Record button triggers Reason's sequencer to record MIDI data. If the Record button is pressed while the sequence is stopped, the sequencer is placed into a Record Ready mode. This means that the Play button must be pressed in order to start recording. Additionally, if the sequence is playing, you can also press the Record button to input MIDI data on the fly. This is also referred to as *punching in*.

Know Your Key Commands   The key to becoming a seasoned user of Reason is to learn the keyboard shortcuts that are linked to the graphical user interface controls in the program. Because I just went over the basic transport controls, here is a quick list of their corresponding key commands.

- The Stop button can be accessed by pressing the 0 key on your keypad.

- Pressing the Enter key on your keypad, or the spacebar, accesses the Play button. Additionally, the spacebar can be used as a way to play and stop sequences.

- The Rewind button can be accessed by pressing the 7 key on your computer keypad.

- The Fast Forward button can be accessed by pressing the 8 key on your computer keypad.

- The Record button can be accessed by pressing the * (asterisk) key on your computer keypad.

What's Your Position?   Located just to the left of the main Transport panel is the Song Position. This is a numeric readout of where you currently are in your sequence in Bars, Beats, 16th notes, and Ticks. Press Play and notice that the position indicator is constantly calling out position readings. Also note that just below this is another song position that is read in hours, minutes, seconds, and milliseconds.

If you want to jump to a specific point in your song, you can double-click in either Song Position dialog boxes, type in a value, and then press the Return button on your keyboard.

New Alt or New Dub?

Located just to the right of the main Transport panel are a couple of buttons that determine how Reason will record a new performance. These buttons are defined as follows:

- **New Dub**—Select this button and Reason will create a new Note lane in your selected sequencer track without muting the previous Note lane. This allows you to record additional notes into your sequence.

- **New Alt**—Select this button and Reason will create a new Note lane in your selected sequencer track. Additionally, it will mute the previous Note lane. This allows you to record a new take without having to listen to what was previously recorded.

Quantize During Recording

Located just to the lower right of main Transport controls is the Quantize During Recording function. When activated, this button performs real-time quantization after the MIDI event has been recorded. The amount of applied quantization is determined by the selected note value and quantization strength.

Tempo and Time

Located below the Song Position dialog box is the window in which you can make adjustments to both the song tempo and time signature.

- *Tempo* refers to the speed of the song played by the sequencer. Tempo is measured in beats per minute (or BPM) and can be adjusted anywhere from 1–999.999. This gives you many possibilities when writing and recording songs within Reason. Note: You can adjust the tempo by using the + and – keys on your keypad.

- *Time Signature* specifies the beats per bar (such as 1, 2, 3, 4, and so on), and what counts as a beat (that is, half note, quarter note, 8th note, and so on).

Tap Your Tempo   Just to the left of the tempo and time signature dialog boxes is the Tap button. This is used to set the tempo of your song by clicking on the Tap button in succession. This is a handy tool if you want to determine the tempo of a favorite track of yours and write something similar in tempo. While listening to the song, use the Tap button and click along with the beat. Reason will then set the tempo of the song.

Locators—the Key to Looping

To the right of the main Transport panel are the locator points and looping controls. If you recall from Chapter 3, "Getting Started with Reason 5.0," you learned a little bit about Reason's locator points. Although there are many ways to describe them, the easiest way to explain locators is to think of them as a pair of bookends. Just like a shelf of books, locator points act as the virtual bookends of a sequence. You have a left locator, which is used as a starting position, and a right locator, which is used as an ending position.

These locator points can be used together to create a loop for a specific number of measures.

Keeping You in the Loop   The key to any electronic or dance music is the incorporation of loops and repetition. As you will read in future chapters, there are a few virtual sound modules in Reason that will help to easily create these loops for you. For now, let's just look at the basic idea of creating a loop in the Reason sequencer.

---

1. Set your left locator to measure 1 by using the arrow keys next to the numeric values or by double-clicking on the numeric value and typing the desired value.

2. Using the same method, set your right locator to measure 9.

3. Just above the locators in the Transport panel is the Loop On/Off button. Click on it to activate the loop feature. This can also be done by pressing the / (forward slash) key on your keypad.

4. Press Play and watch as the position indicator moves to the right. As soon as it reaches the right locator point, it jumps back to the left locator point.

Once a looping point has been created, you can listen to a specific part of your song over and over in order to edit the MIDI or audio data.

Using New Alt with Looping   Be aware that if you press the New Alt button while the Loop function is turned on, Reason will still create a new Note lane on your selected sequencer track, but it will only mute the Note data between the left and right locators and not the entire Note lane.

The Click Control and Blocks

To the left of the Tempo and Time Signature portion of the Transport panel is the Click Track control. When activated, this function provides a metronome sound that is accented on the first beat of every measure. Just clicking on the Click button can turn it on, and the volume of the click can be adjusted by using the knob below. Just a word of caution: the click sound itself is quite loud, so exercise caution when adjusting the volume.

Additionally, there is now a Pre button, which gives you a measure of clicks before recording. This is more commonly known as a *pre-count*.

Just to the left of the Click Track controls is the Blocks button. This is simply used to turn the Blocks function on and off. Try clicking on it and you'll notice the following:

1. The Block button next to the Song/Edit mode buttons will be hidden.

2. The Blocks sequencer track will be hidden.

The DSP, Audio Clipping, and Automation Override LEDs

To the far left of the Transport panel are the DSP and Audio Clipping LEDs.

The DSP meter is a real-time indicator of how much of the computer's CPU is being used within a given Reason song. As you begin to accumulate more and more virtual synths, real-time effects, and equalizers within a song, this meter will tell you how much more CPU you have left until your audio "drops out."

The Audio Clipping LED is a warning light to alert you when the audio output of Reason is in danger of clipping or distorting. To demonstrate this, open the Reason Tutorial Song and turn up one of the volume faders until you see the clip LED shine a bright red. It is important to keep an eye on this, because you really don't want to clip in the digital domain. Trust me—it sounds terrible! Figure 5.24 shows a graphical example of digital clipping.

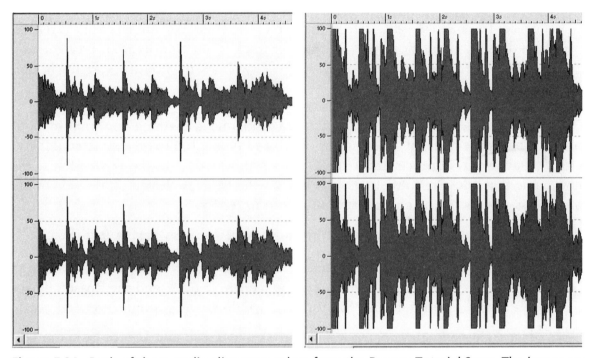

Figure 5.24 Both of these audio clips were taken from the Reason Tutorial Song. The image on the left is an example of digital audio that is not clipping. The image on the right is an example of digital audio that is clipping.

The Automation Override LED glows whenever an automated parameter within Reason is overwritten, or whenever an automated parameter is changed either during playback or while playback is stopped. In record mode, the clicking on the LED "punches out," and the previously recorded automation resumes from that point. Clicking the LED button while recording is disabled will also return any automated parameters you may have adjusted during playback or stop mode to their previously scheduled automation. You will get plenty of practice using this feature as you go through Chapter 20.

Creating and Managing Tracks

Now that you've covered the basics of the Transport panel, you're ready to move to the left side of Reason's sequencer, called the Track window. This is where all the tracks in a song are created and maintained. If you are not new to the concept of sequencing, this section should look similar to other programs you have used. If you are new to this whole game, you'll be happy to know that understanding this portion of the sequencer is a snap.

Creating and Deleting Sequencer Tracks in Reason

There are a few ways to create a sequencer track in Reason:

- A sequencer track is automatically created whenever a Reason synth device is created.

- You can right-click (Windows) or Ctrl-click (Mac) on any Reason device without a sequencer track and select Create Sequencer Track. A good example of this is reMix, which doesn't automatically get a sequencer track when an instance is created. Conversely, you can click on any Reason device with a sequencer track, right-click on it, and select Delete Track.

Once you have created a sequencer track, you can name it anything you want by double-clicking on the name of the sequencer track and typing (up to 36 characters). If you already have your sequencer track routed to a synth module in the Device Rack, the new name that you give to the sequencer track will also be reflected on the side of the module as well as on the channel it is routed to in reMix.

If you want to delete a sequencer track from Reason, you also have a few choices:

1. Highlight the sequencer track and press the Delete or Backspace key on your keyboard. Note that this will delete the sequencer track and the Reason device it's routed to. And in case you forget, a window will pop up to remind you.

2. Highlight the sequencer track and choose Cut Track and Device from the Edit pull-down menu or use the keyboard shortcut: Ctrl+X (Windows) or Apple+X (Mac). Again, this will remove both the sequencer track and the Reason device it's routed to.

3. Right-click on the Reason device and select Delete Track. This will just remove the sequencer track and not the Reason device.

The Track Parameters

After creating a sequencer track, it's time to look at its parameters (see Figure 5.25).

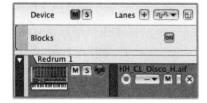

Figure 5.25 Getting acquainted with the Track parameters will make your sequencing experience a snap.

- **Track Name**—This is where the name of the sequencer track is displayed.

- **Track Icon**—This icon represents the Reason device that the sequencer track is routed to. This icon also displays incoming MIDI messages by making use of a green LED.

- **Mute/Solo**—Known simply as "M/S," the Mute/Solo buttons are used to mute or solo individual tracks from within the Track window. Also note the M/S buttons at the top of the Track window. These are the All Mute Off and All Solo Off buttons, which un-mute/solo any sequencer tracks below that are muted or soloed.

- **Record Enable Parameter Automation**—This button is used to place the sequencer track in a Record Ready mode to record automation data. Note that it is automatically activated when creating a sequencer track.

- **Record Enable**—This button is used to put the sequencer track into Record Ready mode to record your MIDI performance. Note that like the previous parameter, this is also automatically activated when creating a sequencer track.

- **Select Groove**—This pull-down menu is used to assign a sequencer track to a ReGroove channel. You'll read more about this later in the chapter.

- **Note Lane Activity**—This LED represents MIDI data as it plays back a sequence. You won't see it in action while you record, just when a sequence is playing back.

- **Delete Note Lane**—This button is used to delete a lane of data from a sequencer track. Also note that there is a New Note Lane button "X" at the top of the Track window.

Moving Tracks

Once you begin to accumulate a few tracks, you might want to organize the tracks by moving them up and down in the Track List. For example, you might prefer to have the Redrum and Dr. Octo Rex tracks at the top of the Track List, followed by the bass track, and then the chord and lead tracks. This is very easy to do; check out the following exercise, using the Tutorial Song.

1. Click in the far-left section on the sequencer track that you want to move.

2. Click and drag with your mouse until you reach the desired position.

3. Release the mouse button. The track should drop into place.

Saving Space in the Track Window Looking at the top-left corner of every sequencer track, you'll see an arrow pointing down, which means that the sequencer track is being displayed in its "expanded" mode. Click on this arrow and it will minimize or "collapse" the track. This is a great way to save space in your Track window, especially when you have 20–30 tracks of sequences playing back.

Sequencing a Live Performance

Now that you have taken your first detailed look at the sequencer interface, it's time to press forward and record your first live sequencer track. In this tutorial, you'll do the following:

- Create an instance of Redrum

- Record a drum pattern live

- Edit that pattern with quantization and dynamics

Before You Begin   Before you start this tutorial, make sure that your MIDI keyboard is turned on and connected to your computer. Additionally, make sure that the keyboard has been selected by Reason as the Master Keyboard. You can do this by selecting it from the Control Surfaces and Keyboards page of the Preferences window.

In this tutorial, you will record a drum pattern with Redrum.

1. Start a new Reason song with an empty Device Rack.

2. Create an instance of reMix by selecting Mixer 14:2 from the Create pull-down menu.

3. Create an instance of Redrum by selecting it from the Create pull-down menu. Note that a Redrum sequencer track has been created and is already armed to receive MIDI from your keyboard. Take a second to turn off the Enable Pattern Section in the Redrum interface. This will enable you to trigger and record live MIDI data from Redrum without using its pattern sequencer.

4. Because Redrum is already armed to receive MIDI data, you can press the C1 key on your keyboard. This key should trigger the kick drum sample. Also note that C#1 is typically the snare drum sample in any Redrum kit. The 10 channels on Redrum are mapped to keys C1 through A1 on your keyboard, and you might take a moment to familiarize yourself with which key triggers which sound in your Redrum kit before you start recording.

5. In the Transport panel, make sure that the Loop section is activated. Set the right locator to bar 5. This will provide you with four empty measures to record a four-bar loop. Also make sure that both the Click and Pre are turned on so that you will have a full measure count in and a metronome to play against. Also, make sure that you set the tempo to one that you're comfortable playing at. If this is your first time, I might suggest 90BPM.

6. Press the Stop button twice to send the position indicator back to measure 1. Now click on the Record button to start recording. The position indicator should begin moving to the right and will start recording MIDI data.

7. Once the sequencer starts recording data, play the kick drum sample on beats one and three until the position indicator reaches measure 5, at which time it will jump back to measure 1 and begin recording more MIDI data.

8. Once the position indicator jumps back to measure 1 and begins recording again, play the snare sample on beats two and four until it reaches measure 5, at which point it will jump back to measure 1 again.

9. Once the position indicator jumps back to measure 1 and begins recording again, play the hi-hat sample (typically found on the G#1 key) on beats one, two, three, and four until it reaches measure 5, at which point it will jump back to measure 1 again.

10. Press Stop on the Transport panel or use the spacebar on your computer keyboard to stop the recording. Notice that there is now MIDI data displayed on the Song view of the sequencer (see Figure 5.26).

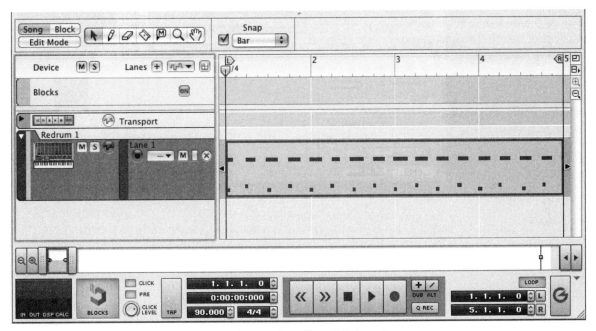

Figure 5.26 You have just sequenced your first live MIDI performance.

Editing Your Performance

At this point, you have recorded the performance. If this was your first time recording a live MIDI performance using a sequencer, the timing might not have been as tight as you wanted. In this next tutorial, you learn how to fix any timing problems and move events around by using the Editing tools.

Before you begin, make sure that you switch to Edit mode by clicking on the Song/Edit View button. Because you are working with Redrum, the Redrum Lane Editor will be displayed by default (see Figure 5.27). Use the Zoom tools to close in on the Redrum group that you are going to work on.

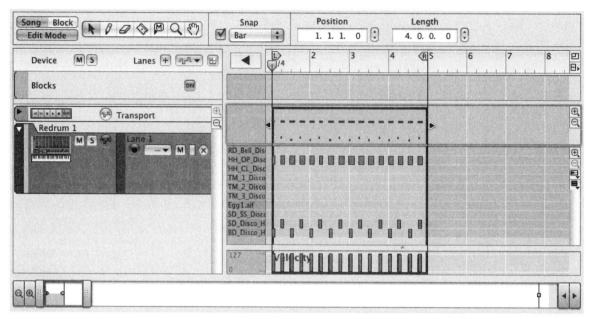

Figure 5.27   The sequencer knows which Lane Editor to display when you switch to Edit mode. In this case, the Redrum Lane Editor is displayed.

Quantize—Timing Corrections

The first thing you are going to do is correct any timing problems by using the quantization function. If you recall from Chapter 4, "Creating Your First Reason Song," you used the quantize function to help correct rhythmic mistakes made while recording a performance.

1. Looking closely at the Redrum performance, you can see many timing inconsistencies because the events don't quite match up with the vertical lines (see Figure 5.28).

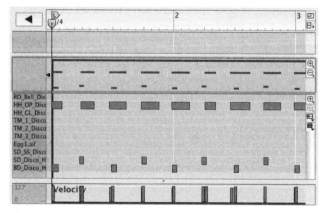

Figure 5.28   This is the drum performance before quantization.

2. Use the Pointer tool to click and drag a box around the Redrum events in order to select them all. You can also use Crtl+A (Windows) or Apple+A (Mac).

3. Next, you need to select the note value used to quantize. Start by selecting the Quantize tool in the Tool Window. Next, select a 1/4-note value. This means that Reason will nudge each note to its nearest quarter note.

4. Just below the Quantize pull-down menu is the Amount pull-down menu. This option determines the amount of quantization that will occur when the process is performed. By default, it is set to 100%, which means that the events will be moved completely to the nearest quarter note. This is fine for this demonstration, but you can try different values to achieve a different effect. This feature can help to prevent your music from feeling too robotic or unnatural.

5. Click on the Apply button to quantize your performance. You can also use the Crtl+K key command on the PC, or the Apple+K key command on the Mac.

6. Looking at the performance now, you can see the events have been nudged left and right toward their closest quarter note (see Figure 5.29). Press Play and listen to the corrected timing.

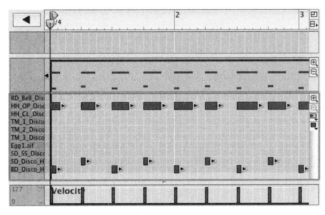

Figure 5.29 The performance has now been quantized.

Quantize While You Record   Quantizing can also be done while you are recording a performance. Just to the right of the main transport buttons is the Quantize Notes During Recording button, which, when activated, will automatically quantize your events while recording your performances.

To dig into this function a little more, try activating it and recording a new Redrum pattern like the one you created at the beginning of this tutorial.

Adding Velocity

Now that the timing has been corrected, you can add some dynamics to the performance by using the Velocity Lane Editor, which appears below the Drum Lane Editor (see Figure 5.30).

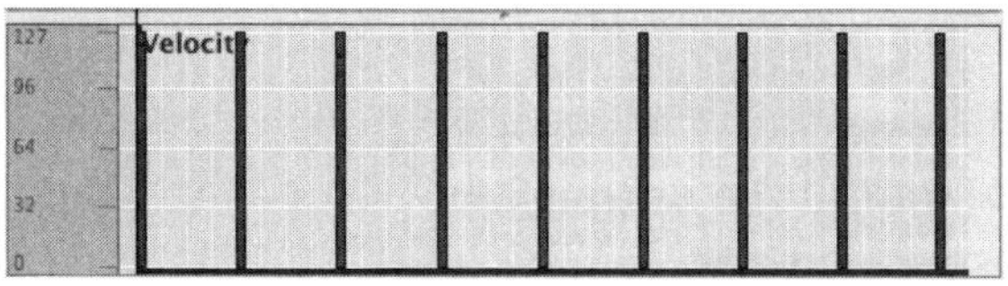

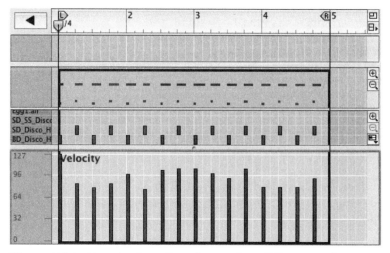

Figure 5.30 The Velocity Lane is used to add dynamics to your Reason performances.

This editor can increase or decrease the amount of velocity assigned to a recorded MIDI note. It is a great tool to use if you find that you didn't press the keys hard enough when recording your performance. In this next tutorial, you are going to edit the velocity of your Redrum pattern with the Pencil tool.

An Added Velocity Bonus In Chapter 7, "Redrum—Close Up," you'll learn about the benefits of using velocity to change the timbre and tuning of your Redrum sounds.

---

1. With the Velocity Lane Editor open, select the Pencil tool. Click and drag downwards on the velocity of the first MIDI event. Notice that as you drag down, which decreases the velocity, the color of the MIDI event changes from a dark red to a light pink (a darker color for higher velocities, a lighter color for lower velocities).

2. Use the Pencil tool on a couple of other MIDI events to alter their velocities. Try alternating between MIDI events to create a more interesting sequence (see Figure 5.31).

Figure 5.31 Use the Pencil tool to assign different velocities to the MIDI events.

Universal Edits   Edits to the velocities of a performance are *universal*. This means that a velocity edit you make to a MIDI event affects all of the other MIDI events that occur at that same time location. The significance of this is illustrated in the following example.

Looking back at Figure 5.31, you will see all of the MIDI events used to create the drum pattern. Notice how two separate MIDI events occur at the same time on each beat. For example, on the downbeat of bar one, you will see a kick drum MIDI event and a hi-hat MIDI event that are lined up vertically, which means that they trigger at the same time.

Now use the Pencil tool again to edit the velocity of the downbeat of bar one. As you make a change to the velocity, notice that both of the MIDI events change in color. This means that the velocities of the hi-hat and the kick drum are being altered simultaneously.

This can become a problem because each drum sample's velocity should be independent of the other. So how do you combat this problem? Well, there are a few things that you can do:

- You can record on separate note lanes for each drum sound. For example, you can create one note lane dedicated to the kick drum and another for the snare, and so on.

- You can use the Velocity knobs on the Redrum interface to decrease each channel's sensitivity to different velocities. More information on this can be found in Chapter 7.

- You can use the Explode option of Extract Notes to Lanes tool.

However, there is another way to accomplish this goal. Simply select the note that you want to edit with the Selector tool, switch to the Pencil tool, hold down the Shift key, and set a new velocity for the single note.

Aside from the Pencil tool, the Line tool can also be used to edit the velocities of a performance. As you may recall from earlier in this chapter, the Line tool is accessed by first selecting the Pencil, and then holding down the Ctrl key on the PC or the Option key on the Mac. Try the following example:

1. Select the Line tool and proceed to click and drag horizontally across the velocities of a few events. Release the mouse, and the velocities should change accordingly (see Figure 5.32).

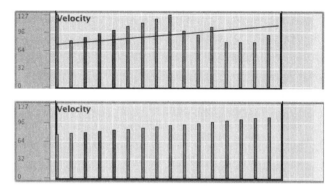

Figure 5.32 The Line tool can be used to alter the velocities of many events at one time.

2. Start at the beginning of the Redrum pattern, and then click and drag from left to right in an upward motion diagonally across the Velocity lane until you reach the end of the pattern. Release the mouse, and you have now created a fantastic crescendo (see Figure 5.33).

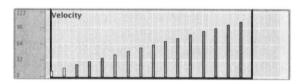

Figure 5.33 The Line tool can also be used to create crescendos, which are commonly found in dance music.

Sequencing Written Data

As you saw in Chapter 4, the sequencer can also be used to draw in events and MIDI data quite easily. This section shows you:

- How to draw and erase events with the Key and REX Lane Editors.

- How to draw in controller information.

Drawing and Erasing Events

Drawing in events with the sequencer is quite easy. Often, you might find it most efficient to write complicated performances that would otherwise be difficult to learn and execute perfectly in a live keyboard performance. It's also a handy way to write in performances when you do not have a MIDI keyboard handy, which is the case for so many traveling musicians. When inspiration hits, drawing in sequences is a real lifesaver.

Let's begin by drawing in a Subtractor sequence with the Key Lane Editor. Get yourself ready by starting a new Reason song and creating an instance of reMix and an instance of Subtractor. Also, make sure that you set your right locator to bar two.

1. Using the Pencil tool, click and drag a clip between bars one and two.

2. Double-click on the clip to switch to the Edit mode. The Key Lane Editor should open by default (see Figure 5.34).

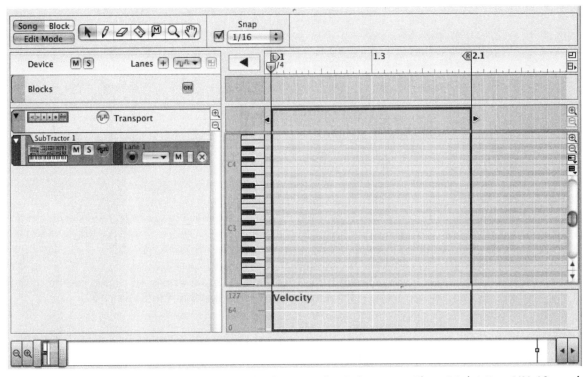

Figure 5.34 The Key lane is the assigned editor to the Subtractor, Thor, Malström, NN-19, and NN-XT Reason devices. Also notice that the Velocity lane is active.

3. Use the horizontal zoom tools (found at the lower-left corner of the sequencer) to zoom in on the individual beats of bar one.

4. You are going to write in an 8th note sequence, so select 1/8 from the Snap pull-down menu (see Figure 5.35). Also make sure that Snap to Grid is activated.

Figure 5.35 Select 1/8 from the Snap pull-down menu so you can draw 8th notes.

5. Select the Pencil tool and proceed to draw in an 8th-note sequence. For the sake of simplicity, you might want to try something as simple as a C major arpeggio (C-E-G), as shown in Figure 5.36.

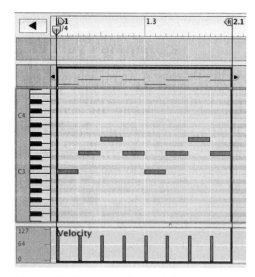

Figure 5.36 Draw in an 8th note sequence. This example draws an arpeggio line based on the C major scale. Notice that each drawn note has a default velocity of 100.

6. Press Play. You will hear the sequence play back in perfect time. At this point, you can try drawing in some different velocities for effect.

7. Click on the Switch to Song Mode button to switch modes.

Moving Events   After writing your sequence, you can easily shift the events around by using the Pointer tool. Try selecting it and then clicking and dragging on individual events to change their events and time locations. Notice when you're doing this that you can move the events left and right only by 8th-note increments. This is because the Snap to Grid is set to 1/8. If you want to make finer adjustments, try changing the Snap to Grid value to 16th notes (1/16).

Duplicating MIDI Events

After performing or drawing in MIDI events, you can very easily duplicate those MIDI events in order to create a repetition. There are a few ways to do this: use the Copy/ Paste trick that you learned in the last chapter, or use the mouse and a key command to duplicate the events and place them anywhere you want.

Let's have a look at the first method by using the current song, selecting the Subtractor track, and following along.

1.   Use the Selector tool to click and select the Subtractor clip.

2.   Choose Copy from the Edit pull-down menu (or use the Ctrl+C or Apple+C key command).

3.   Select Paste from the Edit pull-down menu (or use the Ctrl+V or Apple+V key command). This will paste the copied events right after the original selection of events (see Figure 5.37).

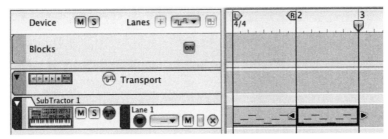

Figure 5.37   Any sequencer clip can be easily copied in the Song mode.

Now let's look at the other way of doing this.

1.   Use the Selector tool to select your clip.

2.   Hold down the Ctrl key on your PC or the Option key on your Mac, and then click and drag the events to the right.

3.   Release the mouse button. The events should now be duplicated and placed where you released the button.

For the next example, you'll use Dr. Octo Rex and the REX Lane Editor. Prepare for the example by clicking on the Subtractor in the Reason Device Rack and selecting Dr. Octo Rex Loop Player from the Create pull-down menu. This will place Dr. Octo Rex just below the Subtractor and its default patch will already be loaded.

1.   After loading your REX loop into the Dr. Octo Rex device, click on the Copy To Track button to send the loop to its sequencer track. Once you do this, disable the Loop Playback mode of Dr. Octo Rex.

2.   Double-click on the clip in the Dr. Octo Rex sequencer track to switch to the Edit mode and you will see the REX Lane Editor. Notice that the Velocity lane is also open.

3.   Select the Eraser tool and erase a few REX slices by clicking on them.

4. Time to draw in a few events. Set your Snap value to 1/16 so that you can draw 16th notes.

5. Select your Pencil tool and draw in a few REX slices in the same area that you erased earlier (see Figure 5.38).

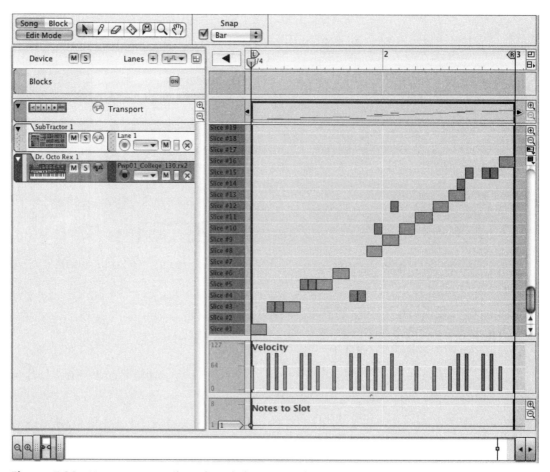

Figure 5.38 Use your Pencil tool and draw in a few REX slices. Notice that as with the previous example, a default velocity value of 100 is assigned to any drawn events.

6. Press Play. The REX loop should now sound rhythmically different.

Resizing Events

Once you begin to edit your MIDI data in either of the different lanes, you might want to resize the events that you have either drawn in or performed live. This is very easy to do. Try the following exercise:

1. Switch back to the Subtractor track.

2. Double-click on the clip to switch to the Edit mode.

3. Use the Selector tool to draw a marquee around a few of the events to select them.

4. With the Selector tool still active, navigate to the end of the selected MIDI events. Notice that the Selector tool changes to an icon with two arrows pointing in opposite directions. This is used to resize the events.

5. Click and drag to the right. You'll see the MIDI events growing in length (see Figure 5.39).

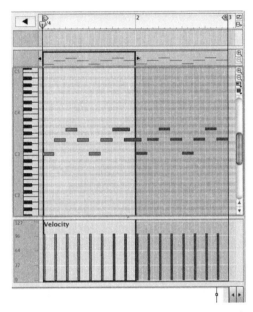

Figure 5.39 Click and drag to the right to resize the events.

6. Release the mouse. The events should now be resized (see Figure 5.40).

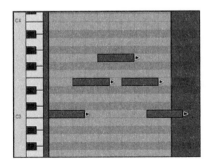

Figure 5.40 The events are now resized.

It's important to note that individual MIDI events can be resized as well as groups of events.

Drawing Controller Data

Reason's sequencer is also a great way to draw in data that controls the various parameters of each Reason device, which is done via the Note Lane Performance Parameter Editor. Although it's covered briefly in this chapter, you will find oodles of info on controller data and automation in Chapter 20.

This tutorial continues to use the setup from the last tutorial and shows you how to draw in controller data for the Modulation Wheel of Dr. Octo Rex. Before beginning the tutorial, look directly to the left of the Mod Wheel on Dr. Octo Rex, and you will see a control knob labeled F.Freq (filter frequency). Use your mouse to turn this control down to about nine o'clock. Now the Modulation Wheel will control the filter frequency in a useful way.

1. Select the Dr. Octo Rex sequencer track and double-click on its clip to switch to the Edit mode.

2. Click on the Note Lane Performance Parameter button and select Mod Wheel. This will open the editor you're going to work with (see Figure 5.41).

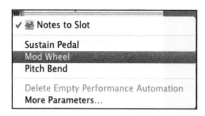

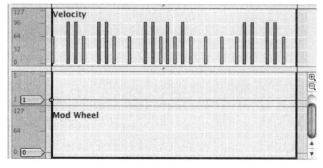

Figure 5.41 The Mod Wheel Editor is easily accessed via the Note Lane Performance Parameter button, which is located in the upper-right corner of the sequencer. Note that you can also hold the Alt/Option button and click on the Modulation Wheel in the Dr. Octo Rex interface to launch this editor.

3. At this point, you are almost ready to write in your controller data. Before you begin, select 1/64 from the Snap pull-down menu, because this will allow you to make very fine changes to the controller data.

4. Select your Pencil tool and begin to draw in some controller data for the Modulation Wheel (see Figure 5.42).

Figure 5.42 Use the Pencil tool to draw in controller data for the Modulation Wheel of Dr. Octo Rex.

The ReGroove Mixer

Even with all the sequencing tips and tricks you've learned throughout this chapter, you may end up finding that your sequences lack that feeling or vibe that you're trying for. As a result, your first few songs in Reason might end up sounding a little stale and robotic. Never fear, Propellerhead has yet again brought forth a new feature in Reason 5 that will get your songs and sequences grooving in no time. I give you the ReGroove Mixer (see Figure 5.43).

ReGroove
Channels

Figure 5.43 The ReGroove Mixer is the perfect answer for musicians who are looking to introduce a swing or shuffle feeling to their music.

The ReGroove Mixer functions in a very similar fashion to an audio mixer, except in this case the ReGroove Mixer is mixing the "feeling" or grooves between 32 accessible channels. There are several templates and tools to help you achieve the kind of feeling that you'll want for your Reason songs, so let's stop dreaming and start driving. To begin, click on the ReGroove Mixer button in the Transport panel to launch it.

Now, let's start by introducing the basic layout of the ReGroove Mixer. Looking back at Figure 5.43, you can see that the ReGroove Mixer is divided into two sections.

- **The Global Parameters**—This is the panel that is on the far-left side of the ReGroove interface.

- **The ReGroove Channels**—These are the sliders, knobs, and buttons that occupy the rest of the interface.

The Global Parameters affect the entire ReGroove interface and include the following parameters:

- **Channel Banks**—These buttons are used to access the four available banks of eight ReGroove channels each, giving you a total of 32 possible grooves within a Reason song.

- **Anchor Point**—This tool is used to set when ReGroove should begin to play back your programmed grooves. A good use for this tool is a song that has a one bar pickup and then the song begins at bar two. In this case, you would want to set the Anchor Point to 2.

- **Global Shuffle**—This knob is used to introduce a shuffle or swing feel to all of ReGroove channels. Additionally, it's used in combination with the Shuffle button found on the Matrix, RPG-8, and Redrum interfaces. Simply activate them and use the Global Shuffle knob to swing the patterns that are playing back from either of these Reason devices.

The Channel Parameters are used to affect the individual channels of the ReGroove Mixer:

- **On**—This turns the ReGroove channel on and off.

- **Edit**—This button will access the Groove tab of the Tool Window. You'll revisit this feature later.

- **Channel Number**—This displays the bank and channel number of the ReGroove channel.

- **Patch Name**—This displays the name of the patch used in a ReGroove channel.

- **Groove Patch Browser**—These buttons are used to find grooves by making use of the Patch Browser.

- **Slide**—This knob is used to slide notes back and forth in Ticks.

- **Shuffle**—This knob introduces a swing feeling, much like the Global Shuffle except this time, it applies to an individual channel.

- **Pre Align**—This button activates the Pre Align, which applies a rigid quantization to any incoming notes before they are grooved. Note that this is a non-destructive function.

- **Groove Amount**—This slider determines how strong the shuffle feeling is felt with a groove. It works in combination with the Groove tab in the Tool Window.

- **Global Shuffle**—This button links a ReGroove channel to the Global Shuffle knob.

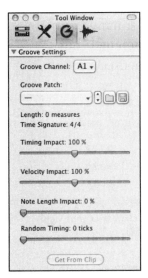

Figure 5.44   The Groove tab is used in combination with the ReGroove Mixer.

And finally, before getting into using ReGroove, let's take a hot minute to go over the parameters of the Groove tab of the Tool Window (see Figure 5.44).

■ **Groove Channel**—This is used to navigate between the different channels of the ReGroove Mixer.

■ **Groove Patch Name**—This displays the name of the selected groove. To the right are the browser and save buttons, which are used to locate and import/save grooves to use in ReGroove.

■ **Length/Time Signature**—These are used to display the length and time signature of a loaded groove.

■ **Timing Impact**—This slider determines how much the timing of a loaded groove will affect your sequences. The greater the value, the closer the sequence will reach the original timing of a loaded groove. Also note that this works in combination with the Groove Amount slider in the ReGroove Mixer, which serves as a means to scale back the Timing impact as the sequence plays back.

■ **Velocity Impact**—This slider determines how much the velocity of a loaded groove will affect your sequences.

■ **Note Length Impact**—This slider determines how much the note length of a loaded groove will affect your sequences. Note that this works only with grooves that have note lengths embedded within, which does not include drum grooves.

■ **Random Timing**—This slider randomizes the timing of your groove in tick measurements.

- **Get From Clip**—This is a neat feature that extracts the groove from a selected clip and places its parameters into the Groove tab. Let's say you come up with a killer groove on your own and you'd like to use this in another song. You can use this button to extract the groove, and then save it using the Save button.

Now that you're familiar with the parameters of ReGroove, let's dive in and see how it works.

Getting Started with ReGroove

Let's start off with something simple, like how to assign sequencer tracks to the ReGroove Mixer. To really feel the impact of ReGroove, I would suggest using a basic drum sequence. Assuming that you have this ready to go, let's begin.

You have to assign a sequencer track to a ReGroove channel. This is easily accomplished by navigating to the Note lane of a sequencer track, clicking on the Select Groove pull-down menu, and selecting a ReGroove channel to assign this track to (see Figure 5.45).

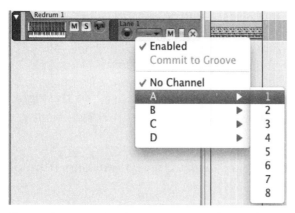

Figure 5.45 Assigning ReGroove channels is done by clicking on the Select Groove pull-down menu in the Note lane of any sequencer track.

Pretty easy huh? As you will come to find throughout the rest of this book, Propellerhead has really made a great effort to make this program easy and intuitive to use.

Commiting Yourself Looking at Figure 5.45, you'll notice the Commit to Groove option. Selecting this option applies whatever adjustments you've made with the ReGroove Mixer to your sequence. I don't suggest using this option unless you're absolutely sure that this is what you want to do with your sequence.

Now that your sequencer track has been assigned to a ReGroove channel, you're ready to explore the limitless possibilities of grooving.

Applying Groove to Your Sequence

At first listen, you won't hear any difference in your sequence, because you haven't made any adjustments to your ReGroove channel. So let's try a couple of quick parameter adjustments to demonstrate how this works. You might want to turn on the Click to really feel the impact of the adjustments.

Using the Slide knob, try adjusting this to the left or right to hear the difference in the sequence. Remember that this parameter has a range of +/–120 ticks, which is really not that much, however, the results will be heard. Have a look at Figure 5.46. On the left side is the sequence without any adjustments. The center image is the sequence with the Slide knob adjusted to –120, and the right side is the sequence with the Slide knob adjusted to +120.

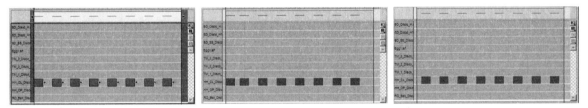

Figure 5.46 The Slide knob can make small, but mighty, adjustments to your sequences.

Now, let's have a look at the Shuffle knob. Try adjusting this to the left or right to hear the difference in the groove. This is a much more pronounced effect, so you'll certainly hear it as soon as you make some adjustments. Have a look at Figure 5.47. The left side displays the original sequence; the center displays the sequence with the Shuffle knob set to 35%, and the right side displays the sequence with the Shuffle knob at 70%. As you can see, there's quite a difference.

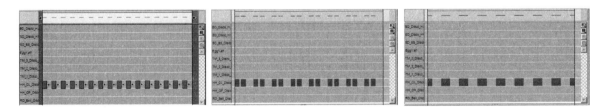

Figure 5.47 The Shuffle knob is the key to swinging your sequences to perfection.

Note that if you activate the Global Shuffle button, the LED above the Shuffle knob on the ReGroove channel will turn off, indicating that it is no longer changing the swing of the sequence. However, the Slide knob will still work even with the Global Shuffle button active.

Remember that at any time you can click the On button on any ReGroove channel to bypass the ReGroove effect to hear how your sequence sounds without it.

Working with ReGroove Patches

Okay, so after some experimenting with the parameters used in the last section, I'm willing to bet you've come up with some pretty nasty little grooves with shuffle and slide galore. Well, strap yourself in, because it's time to show you how to use the provided ReGroove patches. As with nearly all of the Reason devices, you'll find that Propellerhead has included a feast of ReGroove patches that will be sure to give your sequences something original. Before you begin, it would be a good time to set the Slide and Shuffle knobs to their default values and set the Groove Amount slider to 50%. You can also start playing your sequence back in a loop, because you're going to preview these grooves in real-time.

Navigate over to the Groove tab in the Tool Window and click on the Folder icon to launch the Patch Browser window. At this point you'll want to click on the Reason Factory Sound Bank icon in the upper-left corner and then double-click on the ReGroove Patches folder. When you're done, you should see a window that looks like Figure 5.48.

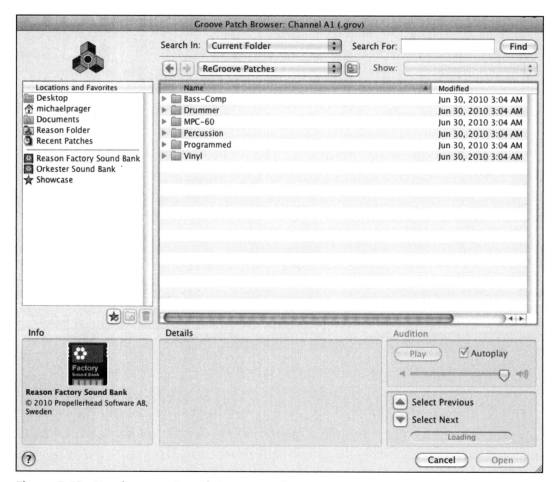

Figure 5.48 Need groove templates anyone?

As you can see, Reason supplies a healthy dose of groove patches to play with, including:

- **Bass-Comp/Drummer/Percussion**—These are grooves that were recorded live by studio musicians, analyzed, and then extracted into individual groove patches. Don't be confused though, they don't contain audio, just simply the timings and velocities of what they originally played.

- **Programmed**—These grooves were programmed by studio musicians to emulate well-known drum programming grooves for use in hip-hop or pop music.

- **MPC-60**—These are grooves that were extracted from an Akai MPC-60, which is probably the most important drum machine ever, because it had a timing and feel that has never really been duplicated.

- **Vinyl**—These are grooves that were captured from vinyl groove record samples. These samples were then analyzed, and then extracted into individual groove patches. You better believe there's some funk to be had here.

Okay, so assuming that your sequence is playing, use the Patch Browser to preview patches by simply clicking on them one time, at which point, the sequence will play with the patch applied to it. Pretty cool, huh? So once you're thoroughly versed in what the patches feel like, go ahead and click OK when you find one you like. For this demonstration, my money's on the Bobby B patch, which is located in the Vinyl folder.

Once it's been imported, you can use the Groove Amount slider to adjust the amount of groove you'd like to hear while the sequence is playing back. 50% works fine for me, but you might find that you need that extra little kick, so use whatever's comfortable.

At this point, I'm going to show you what the sliders do in the Groove tab of the Tool Window, starting with the Timing Impact slider. Looking at Figure 5.49, you can see that on the left is my sequence without any groove, the center is the sequence with the Timing Impact set to 100%, and the right is set to 200%. As I stated earlier in this section, you can use the Groove Amount slider to scale this effect back.

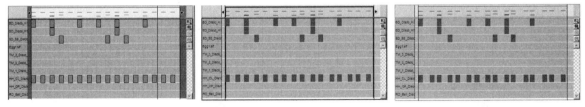

Figure 5.49 The Timing Impact slider can easily create a huge and heavy shuffle.

I'm going to leave the Timing Impact slider at 100%, so you can have a look at the Velocity Impact slider. Looking at Figure 5.50, you can see the sequence with 100% Timing Impact and 100% Velocity Impact on the left and 100% Timing Impact and 200% Velocity Impact on the right.

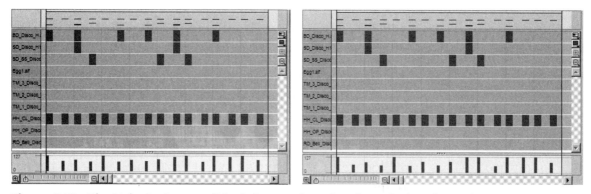

Figure 5.50   The Velocity Impact slider is imperative when introducing dynamics to your grooves.

Next up is the Note Length Impact slider, but because I'm not using a synth-based sequence, like a lead or bass line, this slider will have little or no impact on this drum sequence, so let's move down to the Random Timing slider and introduce some randomization to the timing of this groove. Looking at Figure 5.51, you can see the sequence with 100% Timing/Velocity Impact and no Randomization on the left, while on the right, you'll see the sequence with Random Timing set to 36 ticks. As this only has a range of 120 ticks, it will not create a huge difference, but you'll still see and hear the results.

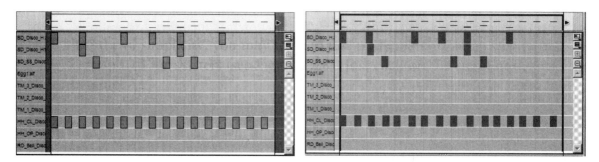

Figure 5.51   The Random Timing slider can introduce a bit more "realism" into your grooves.

Additional ReGroove Tips

Wow, there's a lot under the hood when you really start to look at the ReGroove Mixer in Reason 5. And believe it or not, there are some additional features that you should be aware of.

- **Initialize Channel**—Let's say you want to wipe the slate clean. Just right-click on any ReGroove channel and select Initialize Channel.

- **Copy/Paste**—These options are handy if you want to lock in the same groove between two instruments, like drums and bass. Simply right-click on the ReGroove channel with the groove you want and select Copy Channel. Then go to the channel you want to paste the groove to and select Paste Channel.

■ **Commit to Groove**—As mentioned earlier in this chapter, this option is a destructive edit that applies your ReGroove settings to the selected sequencer track. This option can be found in the Select Groove pull-down menu on your sequencer track. This is a neat shortcut but remember that actually alters the placement of the MIDI notes in the sequence, so be sure that you are happy with it.

Using Blocks

Brand new to Reason 5, the Block view is designed to create chunks, or blocks of song data that can be dropped in and repeated anywhere in your songs. It's a very dynamic and easy way to create variations in your songs without a lot of extra work.

In Reason terms, a *Block* is simply a group of multi-tracked information that has a typical length of 4 to 8 bars. Once created, these Blocks can be given names, such as Intro, Verse, Chorus, Refrain, and drawn in along the song timeline using the Blocks sequencer track. Doing this allows you to create a quick and easy arrangement, but it doesn't stop there.

In addition to using Blocks in your song, you can also make use of all the traditional tools and features of the Reason sequencer as you've read about throughout this chapter. This means that you can record new parts into your Reason song easily while still using Blocks. In essence, this enables you to have the best of both worlds in one environment.

Creating Blocks from Scratch

Blocks can be created in either a brand new song, or a song that's already been created with the traditional Reason sequencer. Either way you choose to create Blocks, it's really quite simple. You switch to the Block view, select your Block, and sequence in your parts. Let's look at how to create a block from scratch.

The first thing you'll want to do is start a new song, create an instance of reMix, and create some other Reason devices. Once this is done, switch to the Block view and you should see an arrangement similar to Figure 5.52.

At this point, you'll want to start creating sequences just as you've done throughout this chapter. For the sake of simplicity, I would suggest that you lay down a beat with Kong, Redrum, or Dr. Octo Rex, and then build upon that by creating a bass line and maybe a pad or two. In any case, you just want to create the parts within a Block.

Once you're done, you should have something similar to Figure 5.53.

Now that you've created your first Block, you should select a new empty Block and create a new one. Click on the Block pull-down menu, which is found on the Block track, and you'll have 1 of 32 different empty Blocks to choose from (see Figure 5.54). Select Block 2 and you'll have an empty slot to fill with new parts for your song (see Figure 5.55).

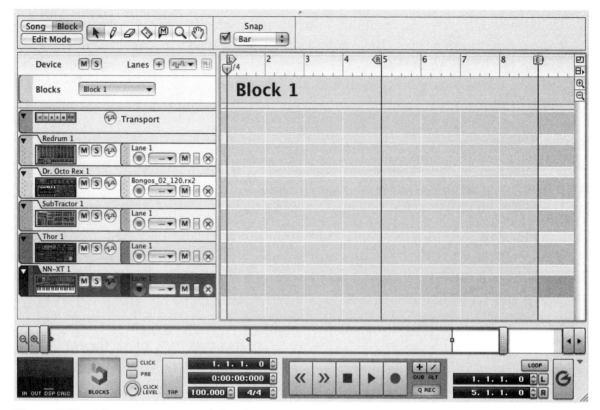

Figure 5.52 After you've created the devices you want to use for your song, switch to the Block view and you're ready to create your first Block.

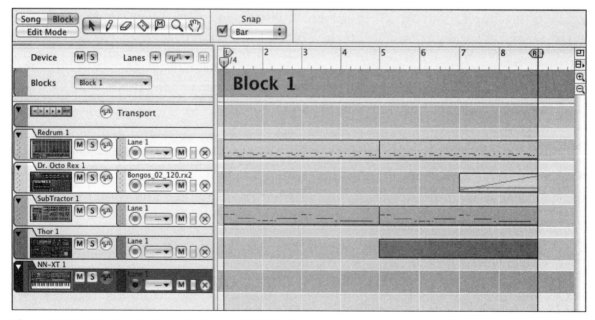

Figure 5.53 You've just created your first Block.

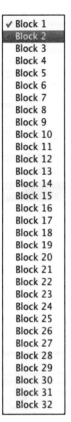

Figure 5.54 Every Reason song has 32 empty Blocks to use. Simply select the one you want and fill it up with MIDI performances from your favorite Reason devices.

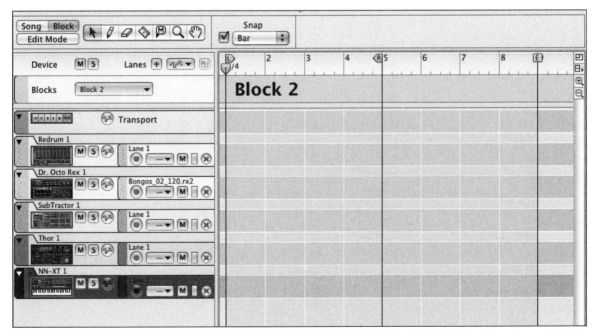

Figure 5.55 Now you have a new Block to work with.

At this point, you can fill up Block 2 with all of the MIDI performances you'd like. You can create additional Reason devices and tracks as well. Once you've finished filling up Block 2, click on the Song button of the Sequencer toolbar to switch back to the Song view.

Creating an Arrangement with Blocks

Once you collected up all of the Blocks for your song, all you need to do is create an arrangement by using the Pencil tool. Make sure the Block sequencer track is active and then try the following exercise.

1. Select the Pencil tool. Once you do, a couple of new dialog boxes/pull-down menus appear just to the right of the Pattern Lane button, including the Block pull-down menu.

2. Navigate your Pencil tool to the Block's sequencer track, and then click and drag to the right to draw in your Block (see Figure 5.56).

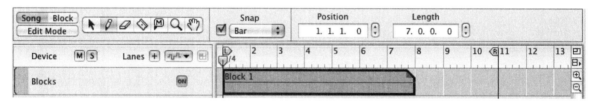

Figure 5.56 Use the Pencil Tool to draw in Block 1 along the sequencer timeline.

3. Release the mouse and you'll see that the Block has been written in along the timeline and that the parts within Block 1 are now transparently displayed in your song (see Figure 5.57).

Now that you've drawn in your first Block, select Block 2 from the Block pull-down menu, and proceed to draw in your part by clicking and dragging along the timeline. Once you've done this, release the mouse and you should see something similar to Figure 5.58.

Renaming Blocks   Let's face it, it's not that exciting to see the names "Block 1" and "Block 2" in your arrangement. I'm sure you'd rather see "Intro," "Verse," and "Chorus." This is easy to do. Just switch to the Block view, select the Block that you'd like to change, and double-click on the Block name along the Block sequencer track. Rename it, and press Enter. Once you switch back to the Song view, the new name will appear.

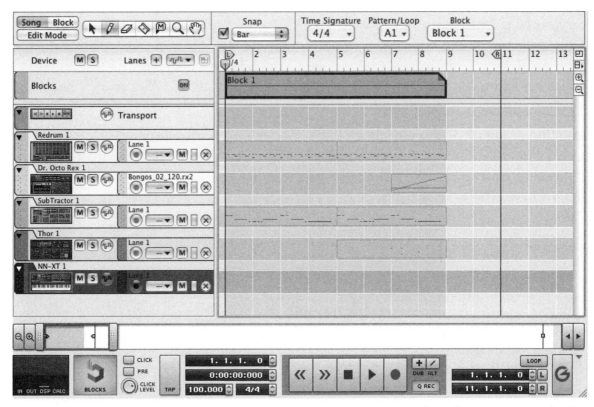

Figure 5.57 Once you release the mouse, you'll see the contents of Block 1 transparently displayed along the timeline.

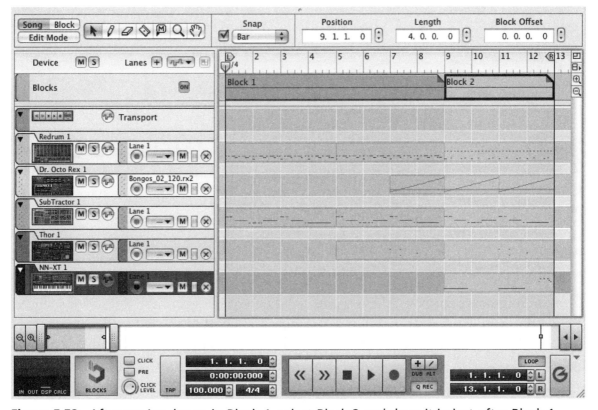

Figure 5.58 After you've drawn in Block 1, select Block 2 and draw it in just after Block 1.

Sequencing New Parts Along with Blocks

One of the best things about using Blocks is that you can still sequence additional parts with the Reason sequencer as you've done throughout this chapter. This allows you to still use Reason the way you're used to, but you also have the Blocks as a bold new creative outlet.

Looking at Figure 5.59, you can see that I've created an arrangement with the Blocks, called Intro and Chorus. I've also used the Pencil and Snap tools to create a rhythmic pattern with the Verse Block by setting it to half notes and eighth notes and simply drawn in a pattern.

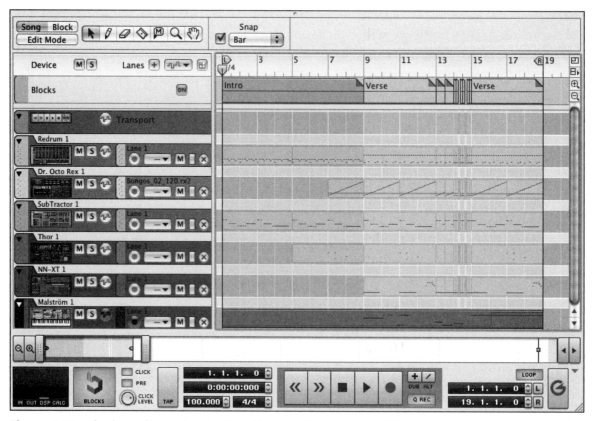

Figure 5.59 The best thing about using Blocks is that you can still use the Reason sequencer the way you normally would, but you can combine this with Blocks.

Additionally, you can see that I've created an instance of the Malström and have sequenced in a lead line in the traditional way of using the Reason sequencer.

Throughout this chapter, you have witnessed the ins and outs of the Reason sequencer. I'm betting you'll agree that there is a lot under the hood of this baby. Be sure to read through Chapter 20, which takes an in-depth look at automation and revisits the sequencer.

Now it's time to begin looking at the individual Reason devices, starting with reMix.

6 The Reason Mixer (reMix)

Reason's mixer, called reMix, is a compact yet versatile virtual mixer that allows numerous variations in signal routing. Or to put it another way, you fix it, and Reason will mix it. Because this book is for both beginner and advanced users of Reason, this chapter covers the basic concepts of mixing as well as the more advanced features and concepts of reMix. In short, there is something in this chapter for every reader. So, stick around and let's mix!

What Is a Mixer?

A mixer enables you to gather a combination of signals (or sounds) from various sources, route those signals in a variety of ways, adjust their individual amplitudes (and other sonic characteristics), and sum it all to a single monophonic or stereophonic signal called *the mix*. As you can see in the mixing example in Figure 6.1, this mix is then routed to a master recording device of some kind, such as a DAT recorder, in order to be mastered and archived. That is a very basic explanation of a mixer, but it will do nicely for now.

To get a better idea of what a hardware mixer looks like and how it works, see Figure 6.2. The Mackie 1604 VLZ3 hardware mixer is commonly found in hardware-based recording studios. The 1604 has 16 individual built-in inputs, which simply means that 16 different signals (drums, guitars, vocals, and so on) can be plugged in to it. After these signals have been plugged in, you can then make adjustments to various attributes—such as volume and equalization—on each signal. These signals are then sent, or *bussed*, to the master output section of the 1604, and from there, the mix is sent to a pair of speakers and/or a hardware recording device.

Over the years, the mixer's interface has evolved into a relatively standard layout. Here are the primary components of just about any mixer:

- **Inputs**—These are typically found at the top or rear of a mixer. This is where analog signals, such as a guitar or a microphone, are plugged in. Additionally, you will find a Trim knob that amplifies the signal by way of a device called a *preamp*.

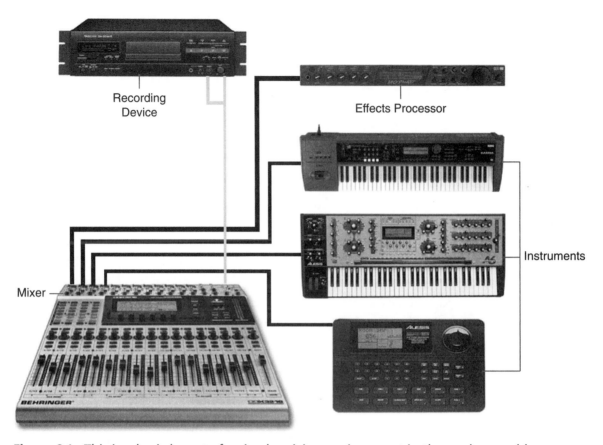

Figure 6.1   This is a basic layout of a simple mixing environment in the analog world.

Figure 6.2   The Mackie 1604 mixer is found in many project studios.

- **Auxiliary Sends**—These knobs, shown in Figure 6.3, allow you to send a percentage of your dry signal to an external effects processor, such as a reverb for your snare drum, or a chorus for a vocal track. Typically you will find between two and four auxiliaries on a hardware mixer.

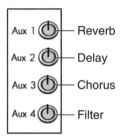

Figure 6.3 Auxiliary knobs send a portion of a channel's signal to outboard effect processors.

- **Equalization**—A mixer's EQ section is for boosting or cutting particular frequencies or ranges of frequencies within the signal flowing through a channel. As in Figure 6.4, you will likely find knobs to control the High EQ, Low EQ, and sometimes the Mid EQ as well. Some mixers offer more flexible EQing options.

Figure 6.4 With a good equalizer, you can boost or cut any frequencies. This is especially important when mixing several sounds and textures, such as guitar, drums, vocals, and synths. Each has its appropriate frequency placement, and the proper amount of equalization makes that possible.

- **Faders**—Faders dictate the volume, or amplitude, of the signal on a given channel. On a typical mixer, you'll find faders to control the volume of each individual signal as well as a master fader to control the master outputs of the signal (see Figure 6.5).

- **Master Output**—This is located at the far right side of the mixer. From here the combined signals are sent to your speakers as well as to some sort of recording device, such as a DAT machine or multi-track recording device.

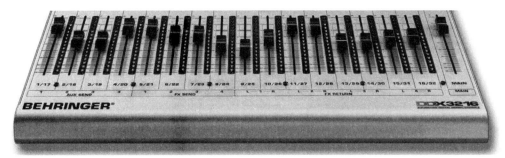

Figure 6.5 The fader section shown here can adjust the volume of the individual and master signals.

Mixing Like a Pro   There are several good books that come to mind that explain the basic and complex procedures for mixing your song. *Hal Leonard Recording Method Vol. 6 Mixing and Mastering* by Bill Gibson (Hal Leonard; ISBN#1423430537) is a good choice. Not only does Bill do a fantastic job of explaining mixing and equalization, but also there's an included DVD that will give you great audio/video examples of the topics being discussed. Trust me, it's worth the investment.

Meet the reMix Mixer

Reason's reMix mixer shares many features with the standard hardware mixer. Propellerhead went to great lengths to give Reason a look and feel that would make the transition between hardware and software seamless. The signal flow in reMix is easy to understand. Start by working your way down a single channel strip.

Figure 6.6 shows a single channel strip—reMix's channel 1. At the top of the channel are four auxiliary sends. These knobs can send a selected amount of signal to one, two, three, and four real-time effects. These effects can be heard by adjusting the Return knobs, located at the far right side of reMix (see Figure 6.7).

Below the auxiliary sends (back to Figure 6.6 again) is a two-band equalizer. This is a very basic EQ that is activated by clicking on its power button and then adjusting the Treble and Bass knobs to boost and/or cut the treble or bass.

The last section of each channel, just below the EQ, controls the level and stereo placement of any mixed signal. This section contains Mute and Solo buttons (which allow you to temporarily shut off this particular channel or leave this channel on and shut off all the others), a pan control (which places the signal from this channel wherever you like in the stereo field), and the channel's fader (which controls the volume of this channel). The next section takes a closer look at each of these components.

Figure 6.6 The reMix channel strip.

Figure 6.7 The Master section. There are four knobs for the returns and a master fader, which controls the overall signal of the mix.

Setting Levels

The first step to mixing in Reason is to set levels in your mix. To do this, start by opening the Tutorial Song, which can be found in the Reason folder. After opening it (see Figure 6.8), have a quick listen to it. I think you'll agree that the mix is a little on the flat or boring side, and this is a perfect place to start.

Look at the faders on the lower-left side of reMix. As shown in Figure 6.9, there are four separate signals, or sounds, that you can mix in this song.

Figure 6.8 Reason's Tutorial Song—a flat, dull mix.

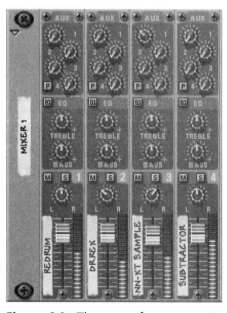

Figure 6.9 There are four separate active channels in this song: Redrum, Dr. Octo Rex, NN-XT, and the Subtractor.

Press the spacebar on your Mac or PC to play the song. Keep your eye on the Dr. Octo Rex track (which in this song is a keyboard loop rather than a drum loop) to see where the level is in the mix. If you want to know the numeric value of the Dr. Octo Rex track volume, click on the fader once, and the Parameter Value tooltip (or tooltip, for short) will open near your cursor to tell you what the value is (see Figure 6.10).

Figure 6.10 Navigate your mouse over (or click on) any parameter in reMix to cause the tooltip to display a numeric value of its level or amount.

As the song is still playing, click and drag down on the Dr. Octo Rex fader and take notice of a few modifications (see Figure 6.11.):

- The overall volume of the track has faded out of the mix.

- The track's graphic meter has dropped.

- The graphic meter of the Master Fader on the lower right of reMix has dropped.

Figure 6.11 Just like a hardware mixer, reMix can visually display level changes.

As you can guess, raising the fader will raise the volume of the Dr:rex track. Experiment with some adjustments of the individual faders.

Resetting the reMix   If you hold down your Ctrl key (Apple key for the Mac) and click on any of the faders or knobs on the reMix interface, that fader or knob will be reset to its default position (see Figure 6.12).

Figure 6.12 Ctrl-click will reset any knob in reMix to its default position. It's a real time saver!

Clipping Is Bad   While you are honing your mix-master skills with the volume faders, you might occasionally notice a bright red Clip indicator flashing in the lower-left corner of the Transport panel (see Figure 6.13). This indicates that the mixed signal in Reason has overloaded or *clipped*.

In the analog world of reel-to-reel tape machines, clipping can be a useful effect for distorting guitars and grunging up the drums. The correct term for this effect is either *overdrive* or *saturation*. Digital clipping, on the other hand, produces a very harsh and nasty distorted sound that can hurt your ears and damage your speakers.

In other words, digital clipping is bad. If you experience any clipping while mixing your signal in Reason, turn the levels down just a little bit. Your ears and speakers will thank you.

Figure 6.13 Clipping in the digital world is not a good thing, so watch your levels.

Mutes and Solos

After you experiment with the levels and achieve a mix that you are happy with, take a look at the reMix's Mute (M) and Solo (S) buttons (see Figure 6.14).

Figure 6.14 reMix's Mute (M) and Solo (S) buttons.

The Mute button is used to remove temporarily an individual signal from a mix. If you play the Tutorial Song and press the Mute button over the Redrum track, you'll notice that you can no longer hear the drums playing, but the other instruments still play. You can also tell that the Mute button has been pressed, because the M button turns bright pink.

The Solo button is used to isolate an individual signal from an entire mix. If you play the Tutorial Song and press the Solo button over the Redrum track, you'll immediately notice that the drums are the only instrument playing, and that the S button on the Redrum track is bright green. Another dead giveaway that the Solo function is in use is to look at all of the other channels on reMix, because they will be muted.

When it comes to the challenge of mixing, these two buttons are vital. The Solo button is one of your best friends, and can be used to isolate any particular instrument in your latest song. You might want to give the drum and bass tracks the most priority because they can very easily dominate the song and make everything sound muddy if they aren't properly mixed in. I can't say that this wouldn't be possible if the Solo button didn't exist, but the button sure makes this task a lot easier.

Likewise, the Mute button is also important in both the songwriting and mixing stage. A Mute button can be used creatively in many ways, such as with automation (see the tip entitled "Creativity at Work"), but it is also useful when you want to take a particular instrument out of a mix, so that you can hear the rest of the ensemble.

Creativity at Work   Although the Mute and Solo buttons might not look it, they can help to create a very interesting mix through the art of automation. Check out Chapter 20, "Automation," which covers automation in depth. Furthermore, if you want to see some cool automation at work, be sure to review the other Reason demo songs that come with Reason 5.

Panning

Panning is a mixer function that allows you to assign a channel's audio signal to a particular position in the stereo field—whether hard left, hard right, or anywhere in between. When used creatively, panning can help bring out separate voices and elements that would otherwise be buried behind the heavy thump of the drum and bass.

Notice that in the Tutorial Song, the Dr:rex channel is panned slightly to the left (see Figure 6.15). Solo the Dr:rex track so you can hear the REX file by itself. If you click and hold the Pan knob, you can drag upwards to send the Dr:rex track to the center of the mix, which is at the twelve o'clock position in reMix. Notice how the Master Level displays a balanced signal between the left and right channels.

Figure 6.15   Dr:rex is panned slightly to the left in the Tutorial Song.

Now click on the Solo button again (to release it) and try moving the Pan knob to the hard right and hard left positions. Listen to how it sounds in a full mix. Notice how heavy the REX track sounds when panned hard left or right. Propellerhead probably had it correctly panned from the start, but it never hurts to experiment or be creative with your panning.

Stereo Synths and Mono Synths in Reason   Press the Tab key on your keyboard to flip the Reason interface around and have a look at the first synth, which is Redrum. In Figure 6.16, notice that there are distinct left and right outputs for this device (hence, it is a stereo synth). If you follow the cable, you will see that the Redrum outputs have been routed to two separate inputs on channel 1 of reMix. Next, scroll down the Device Rack until you see the outputs of Subtractor (see Figure 6.17), and you will notice that there is a single audio output jack on the back of it. Follow its output cable and notice that it is routed to channel 4 of reMix.

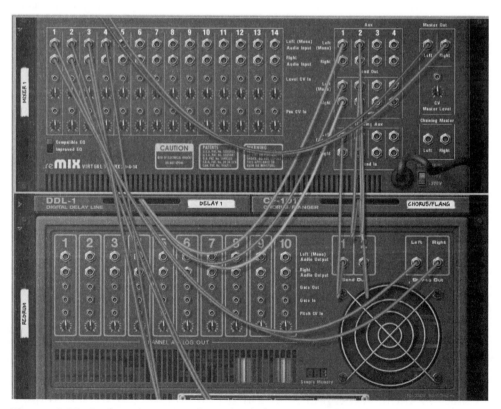

Figure 6.16   Redrum's outputs have both been routed to channel 1 in reMix.

Figure 6.17   The mono Subtractor synth is routed to the left input of channel 4.

Press the Tab key again, and notice that you have one pan control for the Redrum channel and one pan control for the Subtractor channel. This might seem a little strange to the veteran mix board jockeys out there, so let me explain.

Figure 6.18 shows how a stereo signal is routed into a hardware mixer. In a typical studio environment, a stereo signal occupies channel 1 and channel 2. Additionally, channel 1 is panned hard left while channel 2 is panned hard right.

Why is reMix different? To save space in the interface, Propellerhead has combined the left and right channels into one channel in reMix. Also, stereo signals are automatically panned hard left and right upon being routed into reMix. So, if you were to pan Redrum left, it would look something like Figure 6.19 in the analog-mixing world.

Let's now look at the typical routing of a mono synth with a hardware mixer. As seen in Figure 6.20, the pan control must stay at the twelve o'clock position in order for the signal to be heard equally in the left and right channels. The same goes for reMix in this case. Interestingly enough, the top or left input of every channel in reMix is labeled as the Mono input, so the synth will automatically be panned in the dead center when routed to reMix.

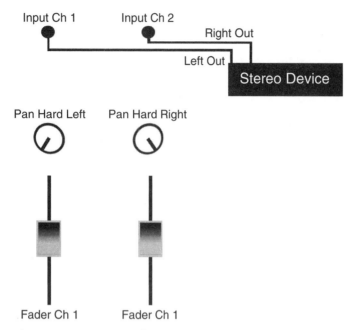

Figure 6.18 Here is how a stereo signal looks when routed on a hardware mixer.

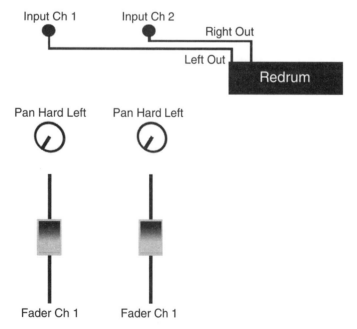

Figure 6.19 Playing with the stereo field of a synth in Reason looks a lot different from a hardware mixer.

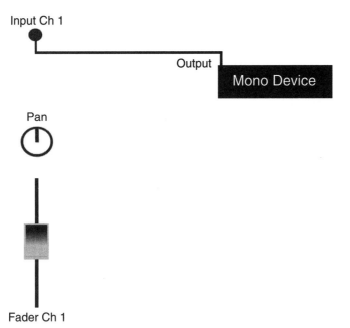

Figure 6.20 But the mono synths look and act the same in the software and hardware realms.

Itty Bitty Knob Adjustments   If you find that the knobs and slider movements in Reason are not as precise as you would like, you can adjust this in the Preferences window (see Figure 6.21) located in the Mouse Knob Range pull-down menu. Here you can specify the desired accuracy by selecting Normal, Precise, or Very Precise.

Figure 6.21 How precise do you want to be?

Equalization

Equalization (or EQ) is the process of adjusting (cutting or boosting) specific portions of the audio frequency spectrum within an audio signal. Equalization can help liven up a mix by adding punch to your bass tracks and by giving your leads and arpeggios an added crispness. Equalization can also be used to effectively remove unwanted frequencies to balance out a mix. To sum up, a good dose of EQ might be just what the doctor ordered when mixing a new track.

Although reMix's EQ section is fairly basic, it will be helpful to take a quick look at the various types of equalization that exist:

- **Shelving EQ** is the most common of all EQs. It's found on radios, entry-level audio mixers, and, more importantly, in reMix. This type of EQ is comprised of two shelving filters, called the *Low Pass filter* and the *High Pass filter*. As you might guess, the Low Pass filter is responsible for either boosting or cutting the low end of the frequency spectrum, whereas the High Pass filter handles the high end of the spectrum, as shown in Figure 6.22. On certain hardware mixers that use Shelving EQs, you might find a Mid Pass filter, which is responsible for cutting/boosting midrange frequencies and makes for a somewhat more accurate EQ section than the typical high-pass/low-pass setup.

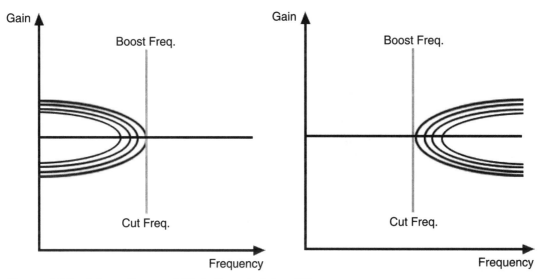

Figure 6.22   A Low Pass and High Pass shelving EQ.

- **Graphic EQs** are found in mid-level hardware mixers and in many pro-audio software plug-ins. Graphic equalization incorporates a number of separate filters, each of which controls a specific slice of bandwidth within the frequency spectrum. These filters have controls (knobs or sliders) that can either boost or cut their assigned slice of bandwidth. Although they are a bit more complicated than Shelving EQs (see Figure 6.23), the Graphic EQ is a step in the right direction toward accurately shaping your sound.

- **Parametric EQs** are the big daddy of equalizers because they are the most accurate equalizers available. As opposed to Shelving and Graphic EQs, Parametric EQs allow you the flexibility of setting the center frequency, range, and the amplitude of each band. Parametric EQs are found within the virtual mixing consoles of most pro-audio software, such as Cubase or SONAR (see Figure 6.24), and although they take a little more practice to understand, you can be sure to achieve much better results with them.

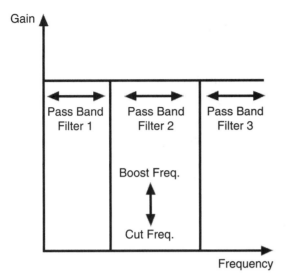

Figure 6.23   A graphic equalizer is a lot more complicated, but can achieve great results.

Figure 6.24   The parametric EQ, shown here in Cubase SX 3, is an eye-catching marvel that really works well.

Parametric EQ?—It's in There!   Reason has not one but two parametric EQs built in. First, there is the two-band Parametric EQ called the PEQ2 that can be used as a send or insert effect. You can learn all about it in Chapter 17, "Effects—Close Up." Second, there are two bands of parametric EQ built into the MClass Equalizer, which you can read about in Chapter 18, "The MClass Mastering Suite—Close Up."

The Shelving EQ in reMix is simple and easy to use. Just follow these steps while playing the Tutorial Song:

1. Select any channel with a signal and activate the EQ section of the reMix channel strip by clicking on the EQ button, found just above the Bass and Treble knobs (see Figure 6.25).

Figure 6.25 Activate the EQ section of reMix.

2. As the song is playing, make adjustments to either the Bass or Treble knobs to adjust either the low or high frequencies, respectively (see Figure 6.26).

Figure 6.26 Have some fun and make EQ adjustments to any of the active channels in the Tutorial Song.

3. If at any time you want to bypass the equalizer, just click on the EQ button again to turn it off.

Less EQ, Less CPU Reason's EQs and effects do require a certain amount of CPU resources in order to be used effectively. Located in the lower-left corner of the Transport panel is the Reason DSP meter, which indicates how much of your computer's processor or CPU is being used in your song, much like the temperature gauge on your car. If you happen to notice that your CPU meter is starting to run a little on the high side, temporarily turning off an EQ or two might save some precious CPU speed.

Auxiliary Sends and Returns

As you will see in coming chapters, Reason has a full supply of real-time effects to cater to any electronic musician's needs. In order to use the real-time effects in Reason, you must first understand the mixing basics of *sends* and *returns*, also called *auxiliaries*.

The sends are the four knobs found on the reMix console just above the Equalizers on every channel, as shown in Figure 6.27. They are responsible for sending a specific amount of dry signal from the channel to a real-time effect, such as a delay or reverb.

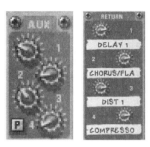

Figure 6.27 reMix has four auxiliary sends and returns.

If you have the Tutorial Song still open, look directly below reMix, and you will see a delay and a chorus/flanger loaded (see Figure 6.28). If you press the Tab key on your computer keyboard, the Reason interface will swing around, and you will see that the auxiliary sends are routed to the inputs on both of the effect units. You will also notice that the virtual outputs of the effect units are routed back to reMix. These are called the *returns*.

Figure 6.28 Follow the cables in the back of the Device Rack to see how the send effects are routed in reMix.

The returns are located in the upper-right corner of reMix. They are responsible for returning a specific amount of the processed signal back into the channel strip. See Figure 6.29 to get a better idea of how this process works.

You can use up to four auxiliary effects per instance of reMix. If that isn't enough for you, you can create another reMix and route additional effects to that device, and connect the two mixers together, in a process called *chaining*.

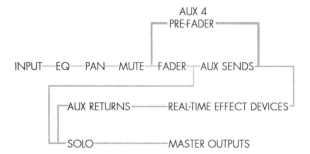

Figure 6.29 How a send and return work within a mixer.

Pre-Fader, Post-Fader   The button labeled P in the Aux Send section of reMix is the pre-fader button for auxiliary send 4. When it's pressed, any signal currently routed through Aux Send 4 will be sent to the effect before it goes to the channel fader.

By using an effect in pre-fader mode, you are essentially using it as an insert effect without any additional routing. There are a couple of real-time effect devices in the Reason arsenal that can be used as pre-fader or post-fader effects, such as the Comp-01 Compressor, or possibly the PEQ2 parametric EQ.

To see how it works, create a Comp-01 compressor on auxiliary 4, activating the pre-fader button on its channel. Next, assign an amount of signal to the real-time effect. You can now turn down the fader of that channel and you will hear just the effect. Then you can turn up the fader to hear the mix of both the dry signal and the affected signal.

---

microMIX—reMix's Little Brother

With the release of Reason 3.0, Propellerhead included a smaller, simpler virtual mixer to be used in combination with reMix called *microMIX* (see Figure 6.30). This device is more commonly thought of in the analog world as a *line mixer*, because it's used to create a simple, yet balanced mix of several signals into a stereo pair of outputs, which are then sent to a stereo input of a more complicated and advanced mixer, such as reMix. This accomplishes the simple task of saving space in the analog studio, and the same can be said for the virtual mixing world of Reason. To better understand this concept, I'll give you a possible use for microMIX.

Figure 6.30 microMIX is an important addition to the Reason family, because it provides several additional mixer inputs for creative routing possibilities. It can be used effectively with the Combinator or with just individual Reason devices.

Let's say that you're using an instance of Redrum and you would like to have a single channel for six of Redrum's ten outputs. This would enable you to properly adjust the volume and panning of several drum and percussion sounds you have loaded into your Redrum kit. You could easily do this in reMix, but you would quickly run out of open channels for other Reason devices, such as NN-XT or Subtractor. microMIX can accomplish this task with ease, because it includes the following parameters:

- Six stereo or mono line inputs

- Pan knobs

- Mute and Solo buttons

- An Aux Send for a single effect, which can be used in either Pre- or Post-Fader mode (see Figure 6.31)

Figure 6.31 microMIX provides an additional Aux Send and Return, which can be used in either Pre- or Post-Fader mode.

Another great way to use microMIX is with the Combinator; you'll explore some of the possible uses for it in Chapter 19, "The Combinator—Close Up."

As you can see, reMix is a compact and versatile mixer that offers many creative possibilities. Both reMix and microMIX have a few more tricks up their sleeves, which you will discover in future chapters.

7 Redrum—Close Up

Redrum is Reason's drum machine, with features and capabilities that go far beyond most software drum machines (see Figure 7.1). Propellerhead designed Redrum to perform both as an independent, pattern-based drum machine and as a sequencer-driven powerhouse. And with version 5, Propellerhead has given Redrum the ability to sample audio, making it even more versatile.

A Guided Tour of the Redrum Interface

At first sight, the Redrum interface might look a little confusing if you're new to computer music, but as you start to look at the interface from left to right, you are going to find that it's quite easy to understand and use. With its extensive feature set and originality in design, it'll get your creative juices flowing.

In order to become acquainted with Redrum, you'll work through some tutorials in this chapter. To follow along, set up your Reason song using these steps:

1. Load an empty Reason song.

2. Create a reMix module.

3. Create a few real-time effects, such as a reverb and delay.

4. Create an instance of Redrum. Notice that Redrum is already routed to channel 1 of reMix and a sequencer track has been created and armed for MIDI input (see Figure 7.2).

Now you are ready to begin your lesson on this rhythmic marvel!

Browsing and Loading Patches

When you first load a Redrum module a default drum kit is loaded. Of course, you'll probably want to try different drum kits, so navigate to the lower-left corner of the interface, where you can browse the drum patches (see Figure 7.3).

Click on the browser window or on the folder button located directly below it to open the Patch Browser window (see Figure 7.4).

Figure 7.1 Redrum is the groove machine that could.

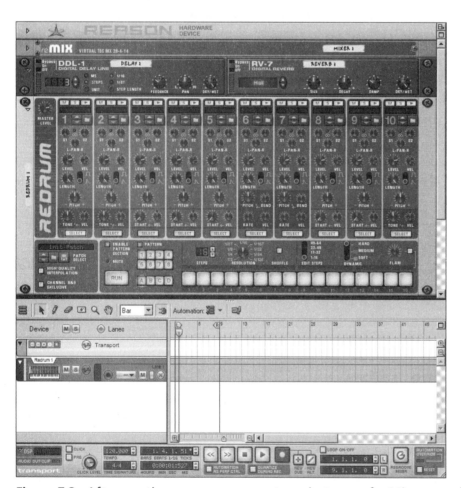

Figure 7.2 After creating a new song, create an instance of reMix, a couple of effects, Redrum, and you're all set to go.

Figure 7.3 Redrum's Patch Select area is where you access the drum patches.

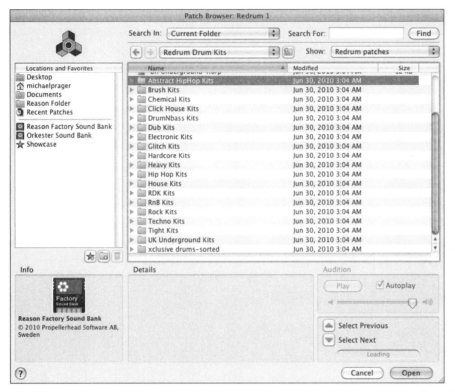

Figure 7.4 The Patch Browser window is where you locate and load Redrum kits.

At this point, you should see the Reason Factory Sound Bank ReFill under Locations on the upper-left side of the Patch Browser. Click on the Reason Factory Sound Bank ReFill, and you will then find a series of folders dedicated to each Reason module. The folder that you are interested in is the Redrum Drum Kits folder; double-click on it to display the contents.

You should now see several alphabetized folders with different styled drum kits within each one. Double-click on the Rock Kits folder to display five rock-style drum kits. Load the first kit, called Groovemasters Rock Kit 1.drp. Because each loaded Redrum kit contains 10 individual samples, loading can take five to 10 seconds, depending on how fast your computer is and how much installed RAM you have.

More Is Better   As stated in Chapter 2, "Installing and Configuring Reason," Redrum is one of several RAM-dependent synths found in Reason (like the NN-XT and NN-19). The samples and drum kits that you load into these modules will perform only as well as your computer allows.

It is wise to consider upgrading your computer with another stick of RAM. You wouldn't believe the performance boost that can be achieved with another 512MB or 1GB of RAM—and RAM is relatively affordable these days.

Time Saver   Here's a quick tip that will not only save you time, but will make you appear a little more masterful in the studio. Once a patch is loaded into the Redrum interface, you can quickly change to the next drum kit of that same style by clicking once in the Patch Name window. A pull-down menu will appear (see Figure 7.5) listing all of the other available kits within the same genre. In this case, because you already loaded a Groovemasters drum kit, once you click on the Patch Name window, you can choose from the five included kits of this style. Additionally, you can use the up and down arrow buttons located below the Patch Name window.

Figure 7.5   By clicking on the Patch Name window, you can quickly select another kit.

Just below the patch selection window are the two global setting options for Redrum (see Figure 7.6). They both are important to the overall sound quality and playability of Redrum.

Figure 7.6   Redrum's global settings.

High Quality Interpolation can greatly improve the sound quality of the sample playback in Redrum. When activated, this function employs a very advanced interpolation algorithm, which results in better audio playback, especially with samples that contain a lot of high frequencies, such as hi-hat sounds or Latin percussion.

Algorithms? Interpolation?   An *algorithm* describes the step-by-step mathematical process of problem solving. *Every* functioning part within your computer is algorithmically related, right down to the language code that was used to conceive and create the Reason program.

In digital-sampling terms, algorithms are used to capture, store, and play back audio. Because audio is not a constant, there are many variables (such as frequency and amplitude) needed to accurately capture an analog signal, and then convert it to digital bits. Using interpolation algorithmically solves these variables.

Interpolation is a key building block for algorithms in the sense that it is a calculation that estimates numerical values of a function (or action) between two or more known values. When the High Quality Interpolation function is selected in Redrum, new sets of calculations are used to determine a more precise algorithm.

The Channel 8&9 Exclusive button produces a virtual link between the eighth and ninth sound channels of the Redrum interface (see Figure 7.7). When activated, sound channel 8 works as a cutoff for channel 9 and vice versa. For example, an open hi-hat sample is loaded on channel 9 and a closed hi-hat sample is loaded on channel 8. If channel 9 is playing its sample, it will immediately be silenced when channel 8 is triggered, much as a hi-hat would behave in an acoustic drum kit.

Figure 7.7 Use the Channel 8&9 Exclusive button to make your hi-hat parts sound realistic.

The Drum Sound Channels

Next, take a look at the drum sound channels. As you proceed, note that there are a lot of creative editing features that can add interest to your rhythms.

Let's begin with drum sound channel 1, which is typically where the kick drum sample is loaded. (See Figure 7.8.)

Figure 7.8 Drum sound channel 1 is typically where the kick drum sample is loaded.

Across the top of channel 1 are the Mute, Solo, and Trigger buttons, defined as follows:

■ The Mute (or M) button works similarly to the mute buttons on the reMix mixer; it silences the particular channel on which it is active. For example, if you have a full pattern playing that includes a kick, snare, and a hi-hat, pressing the kick channel's Mute button will allow you to hear just the snare and hi-hat without the kick.

■ The Solo (or S) button works in the opposite way because it will isolate just the drum sample that you want to hear on its own. If you have a full Redrum kit playing and you just want to hear the kick drum, select the kick channel's Solo button. All of the other drum sounds will be muted.

■ The Trigger button (shaped like a right-pointing arrow) works as a sample preview button; when it is pressed, the corresponding channel will play the drum sample that is loaded within. If you press channel 1's Trigger button, you will hear the kick drum sample.

Two Ways to Trigger Samples   There is a second way to trigger samples from Redrum without having to press each of the triggers on the interface. You can set up your MIDI controller keyboard to trigger each sound. Assuming that your MIDI controller is properly set up, press the C1 note on your MIDI keyboard, you should now hear the kick drum play.

At this point, you can trigger all of the different drum samples loaded in your Redrum kit, because they are mapped out between notes C1–A1 on your controller keyboard.

Mapped Samples Explained   From time to time, you will hear the term *mapped out* used to describe how samples are assigned to specific keys on your master keyboard. In the case of Redrum, this is a very easy concept to understand because there are only 10 possible keys that your drum samples can be assigned to.

First, you need to understand that there are 10 available octaves in a MIDI sequencer, just as there are 10 octaves on an 88-key piano. Each octave uses the C key as its starting point. Additionally, every note on your MIDI keyboard has a corresponding numeric value. With this in mind, the octaves on a MIDI keyboard are identified as follows:

■   C–2 to B–2 (MIDI notes 0–11)—The lowest octave on a keyboard

■   C–1 to B–1 (MIDI notes 12–23)

- C0 to B–0 (MIDI notes 24–35)

- C1 to B1 (MIDI notes 36–47)

- C2 to B2 (MIDI notes 48–59)

- C3 to B3 (MIDI notes 60–71)—This is the center note of a keyboard, also called Middle C

- C4 to B4 (MIDI notes 72–83)

- C5 to B5 (MIDI notes 84–95)

- C6 to B6 (MIDI notes 96–107)

- C7 to B7 (MIDI notes 108–119)

- C8–G8 (MIDI notes 120–127)—The highest octave on a keyboard

Drum machine samples are typically mapped out in the C1 octave of a MIDI keyboard. Figure 7.9 shows how the individual drum samples of Redrum are mapped out within this octave.

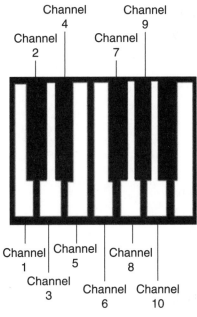

Figure 7.9 Here is how the samples of Redrum are mapped out in the C1 octave of a MIDI keyboard.

Selecting Your Drum Sounds

A major limitation of hardware drum machines is that most of them can't change their sounds. Once you buy the drum machine, you are stuck with the sounds, which, over time, will become less and less interesting.

Thankfully, this is not the case with Redrum because each channel's sample can be changed, customized, and sampled. It is all done in the sample browser portion of the Redrum channel strip, located just below the Mute, Solo, and Trigger buttons. In the display window of this section is the filename of the currently loaded sample. If there is no sample loaded, this window remains blank. Because you have already loaded a Redrum kit, the kick drum file is listed here as BD1 1 OHSH.aif.

Located just below the display window are the scroll, browser, and sampling buttons. These are the tools you use to change the kick drum sample loaded on drum sound channel 1. You can even sample a completely new sound!

The scroll buttons allow you to manually navigate through your available samples one by one. Try clicking on the Scroll Down button once and notice that a new kick drum sample loads almost instantly. Also try clicking on the Scroll Up button to return to the original kick drum sample.

Check Your List   Redrum offers a quicker method of locating samples. Just click once on the display window, and a very long list of available samples should pop up (see Figure 7.10). As you can see, there are many kick drum samples to choose from.

Additionally, you will find that a lot of these listed samples can be musically categorized by their filenames. For example, the kick drum sample named

Figure 7.10 Redrum is chock full of samples to fill every channel.

Bd2_Abused.wav would suggest that this kick drum is suitable for industrial-style music, whereas Bd2_Chemical.wav would be used in big beat Fatboy Slim type music.

The Sample Browser button located to the right of the scroll buttons opens a browsing window. From that window, you can search your computer for an entirely new sample to import to any of Redrum's 10 channels. For example, if you don't want a kick drum on channel 1, click on the Sample Browser button to find and import a new sample (see Figure 7.11).

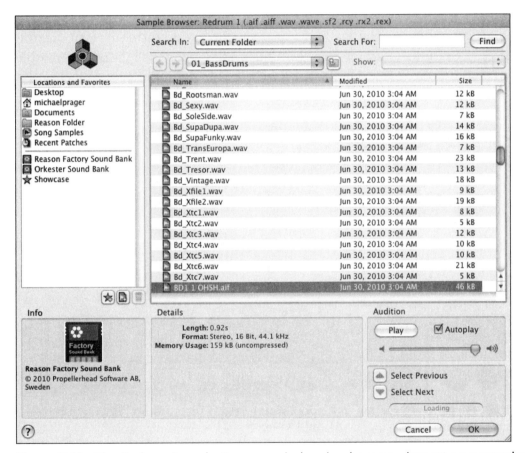

Figure 7.11   The Redrum Sample Browser window is where you import new samples.

File Formats   Redrum supports a great many file formats that can be imported into its individual channels. This leaves the playing field wide open for users who own a lot of sample CDs, because they can be used at will in Reason.

Redrum supports these audio file formats:

■   .aif—A commonly used format for the Macintosh platform.

■   .wav—The standard file format for the Windows platform.

- SoundFonts or .sf2—A file format developed and implemented by EMU and Creative Labs.

- REX file slices—A format developed by Propellerhead and implemented in a program called ReCycle!. Read more about it in Appendix A, "ReCycle! 2.1."

Additionally, Redrum supports multiple bit depths and sampling rates, and works with both mono and stereo files, so you can import your pristine quality drum samples in a flash. Just keep in mind that these samples are stored and used internally in 16-bit format.

Finally, the Start Sampling button enables you to record and edit your own custom sound for use in Redrum. Click on this button, and Reason will begin to sample your specified audio source (see Figure 7.12). Once you're done, you can click on the Edit button to launch the sample editor, or you can rerecord the entire sample.

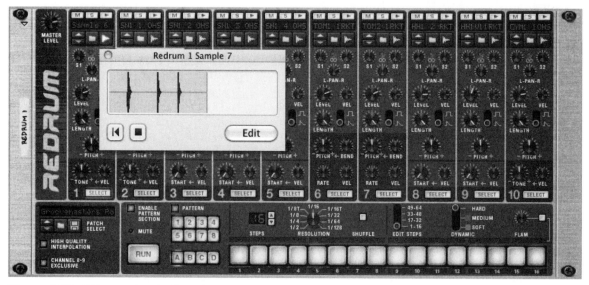

Figure 7.12   The new sampling feature in Reason allows you to record brand new samples into instruments, such as Redrum, NN-19, NN-XT, and Kong.

Sampling Tutorial   If you want to really jump into the depths of sampling audio now, just skip ahead to Chapter 13 and read the section entitled "Sampling Audio with the NN-19".

Sends and Pans

Located just below the Sample Browser controls are the Sends and Panning knobs for each Redrum channel. These knobs perform a function similar to that of the Sends and Panning knobs on reMix—they control both the amount of signal that is sent off to a real-time effect and where the signal is placed within the stereo field.

As you read further in this book, you'll find that every module has a couple of neat but subtle tricks up its sleeve, and Redrum is certainly no exception to the rule.

The Sends knobs, or S1 and S2 as they are labeled, are directly linked to the same effect sends as reMix. If you recall from Chapter 4, "Creating Your First Reason Song," reMix has four auxiliary knobs, or "sends" that send the desired amount of dry signal to one of the loaded real-time effects that are virtually routed to it. In this example, you should have a reverb and a delay effect routed to reMix that can be accessed by using auxiliary sends 1 and 2. This is the same setup for Redrum, because the S1 and S2 knobs have access to these effects as well. In Redrum terms, this means you can assign individual drum samples to their own real-time effects, which in turn can create a much more dynamic and creative mix. (See Figure 7.13.)

Figure 7.13   Both reMix and Redrum have access to auxiliary effects one and two.

The Pan knob controls where each drum sample is placed within the stereo field of a mix. Creatively using all 10 of these knobs can produce a very realistic drum mix that mirrors an acoustic drum kit. For example, give this drum mix idea a spin:

- Pan the kick dead center at the 12:00 position.

- Pan the snare slightly off to the left or right at either the 10:00 or 2:00 position.

- Pan the hi-hat (closed and open) to the left or right at either the 9:00 or 3:00 position.

- Pan the high tom to the 11:00 or 1:00 position.

- Pan the low tom to the 10:00 or 2:00 position.

Try varying the panning to come up with your own interesting combination. It's important to experiment with every aspect of mixing if you want to produce a song that is truly original and attention-grabbing. Stereo was invented for a reason, so use it!

One additional point of interest to note here is the LED located just above the knob that indicates whether the loaded sample is a mono or stereo sample. The LED lights up when the sample is stereo and stays dark when the sample is mono.

Advanced Redrum Routing with Remix
You will probably find it easier to get the sound and feel you want from Redrum if you route it as though you were mixing a live drum kit, making reMix faders available to each sound Redrum can produce. That way, you can have total volume and panning control at your disposal and many additional virtual routing possibilities—for example, using a compressor as an insert effect on the kick sound channel.

This can be very easily accomplished using Reason's virtual routing. You're going to create a submixer for Redrum, which will give you close control over each Redrum channel and leave plenty of room for other virtual synths.

1. Click once on the Delay unit (see Figure 7.14) to select it. Next, choose Mixer 14:2 from the Create pull-down menu. This will create another reMix device between the real-time effects and Redrum. Also notice that Redrum is still routed to channel 1 on the primary reMixer.

Figure 7.14 Select the Delay real-time effect and create a reMix device.

2. Rename the second reMix Redrum Submix by clicking on the virtual tape at the left of reMix (see Figure 7.15).

Figure 7.15 Rename the second reMix Redrum Submix. Note that the name has been abbreviated here.

3. Press Tab. You will see that the Redrum submix has automatically been routed to the primary reMix by way of the Chaining Master inputs (see Figure 7.16).

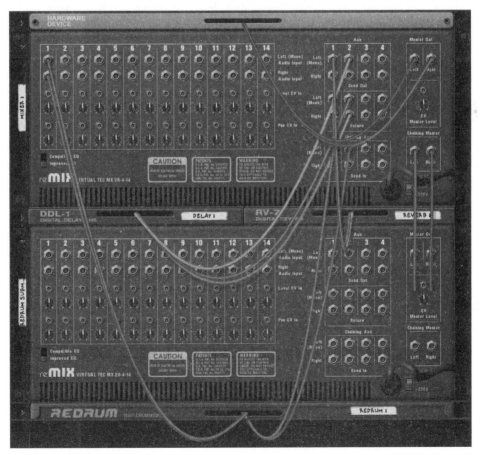

Figure 7.16 Reason has already routed the Redrum Submix to the primary reMix by using the Chaining Master inputs.

4. Scroll down the Device Rack and find Redrum, which should be the bottom device. Click and hold on the outputs to bring up the routing pull-down menu. Now select Disconnect to virtually disconnect Redrum from the primary reMix.

5. Using your mouse, click and drag each individual Redrum output to an input on the Redrum Submix, as shown in Figure 7.17.

Figure 7.17 Route each Redrum sample to its own reMix channel.

6. After completing this, press the Tab key again. You should now see each Redrum sample routed to its own fader on the Redrum Submix (see Figure 7.18).

If you now trigger any sample in Redrum, you will have total control over its volume and placement in the stereo field with the help of your handy submixer.

Redrum Levels and Dynamics

Continuing down Redrum's channel 1 strip, below the Panning knob you will see Level and Velocity knobs. These help to introduce a dynamic element to your Redrum kits. These also help keep your drum patterns from sounding as though they were played by Robby the Robot.

■   The Level knob controls the volume of each channel in the Redrum interface.

Figure 7.18   Now Redrum has its own mixer.

■   The Velocity, or VEL knob, affects the impact of the Level knob by introducing a dynamic element to the mix.

VEL Means Dynamics   The VEL knobs in Redrum can be used to effectively produce a realistic and dynamic drum performance, which sets Redrum apart from many other drums machines, whether they are software- or hardware-based.

As previously stated, the Level knob affects the volume of any Redrum channel. The Dynamic switch of the Pattern Programmer (you'll look at it later in this chapter) introduces different velocities (or dynamics) to the Redrum channels, which can then alter these volumes.

The VEL knob determines how much the volume is affected by different velocities. For example, if the VEL knob has a positive value, the volume of a Redrum channel will become louder with increasing dynamics. If the VEL has a negative value, the volume will decrease as the dynamic increases, which is called *inverting*.

Later in this chapter, when you begin to write your own patterns, be sure to add different velocities to each note. Try experimenting with the VEL knob to create a realistic drum groove.

Dynamics Means Creative Mixes   Along with melody, harmony, and rhythm, *dynamics* is an important element needed to give any form of music its edge or character. Such character makes the song more interesting. It is a governing element that cannot be ignored, but only better understood by listening to numerous styles of music as examples.

For example, because this chapter discusses drums and drum machines, consider jazz music as a blueprint to define a good use of dynamics. Check out some of jazz's greatest artists, such as Miles Davis, Buddy Rich, or Dave Brubeck. Notice how the drummer plays with the mix by introducing both loud and soft dynamics simultaneously. This alone helps make the drums and percussion pop out of the mix.

If you need something that rocks out a little more, listen to something with more of an edge, such as hard rock or alternative. You can hear that even steady rock, such as music by Rush or System of a Down, needs good dynamics to make the song memorable.

Believe it or not, even good old "four-on-the-floor" techno music has dynamics. Check out CDs by Moby or Orbital and listen for the variations in dynamics.

Think of your audio mix like a good painting—it can't be just one color, so mix it up!

Length, Decay, and Gate

Up to this point, you've looked at controls that affect the mix of the Redrum channels. As you continue down channel 1, the following sections discuss controls that will alter the actual sound of the sample.

The Length knob sets the playback length of the drum sample. In the case of channel 1, this knob controls the playback length of the kick drum. If you click and drag on the knob to decrease the length, you will hear the sample get shorter.

The Decay/Gate switch (see Figure 7.19) sets the playback mode of the drum sample. When the switch is in the down position, it's set to Decay mode, which allows the sample to play with a decay (or sustain). Additionally, when using Redrum in Decay mode with the main Reason sequencer, the sample will play the same length of time, no matter how long or short the MIDI note is held.

Figure 7.19   The Length knob and Decay/Gate switch set the playback mode of the loaded drum sample.

When this switch is set to Gate mode the sample will play for a determined amount of length, and then cut off without a sustain. When using Redrum in Gate mode with the main Reason sequencer, the sample will abruptly cut off as soon as it reaches its determined length or its MIDI note is released (whichever comes first).

Try an example of this with sound channel 1 to see its effectiveness. Make sure the Decay/Gate switch is set to Decay mode before you begin.

1. Turn the Length knob down to about its middle position, until the tooltip reads 56.

2. Play the sample using either the Trigger button or your MIDI keyboard. You will hear the slight decay effect.

3. Switch to Gate mode.

4. Play the sample again with either the Trigger button or your MIDI keyboard. It should now sound much more beefy, because it contains no sustain or decay at the end. It is simply playing the sample until it reaches its determined length.

Pitch

The Pitch knob alters the playback pitch of any Redrum sample. The range of the available Pitch is +/– one full octave and all points in between. Notice the LED above the Pitch knob lights up whenever a value greater or less than zero is selected.

Return to Zero   Remember, holding down the Ctrl key (or Apple Key on the Mac) on your computer keyboard and clicking on a knob such as Pitch will reset its value to zero.

Tone

The Tone knob controls the "brightness" of the sample assigned to the Redrum channel. Lowering the Tone value will "darken" and muddy up the sample as it plays back, whereas increasing its value will make your samples quite bright and brittle sounding.

To the right of the Tone knob is its corresponding Velocity knob, which applies the effect of the Tone knob based on the velocity values of the sample playback.

Selecting Your Channels

Beneath the Tone and Velocity knobs on every channel is the Select button. When pressed, this button selects the channel for use with the Redrum Pattern sequencer.

Not All Channels Work Alike

As you look over the other channels of Redrum, you will notice that there are channels whose parameters are similar to those of channel 1 and others whose parameters are altogether different (see Figure 7.20). Take a look at these other parameters and see what they do.

Figure 7.20 Redrum is certainly not a one-trick pony by a long shot.

Let's Get this Sample Started. Available on Redrum channels 3, 4, 5, 8, and 9, the Start knob sets the point at which the loaded sample will begin to play back. In other words, when the Start knob is adjusted, Redrum will play that sample back not at the beginning, but rather in accordance to the position of the Start knob. See Figure 7.21 for a graphical example of this function.

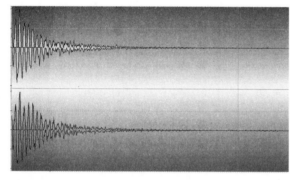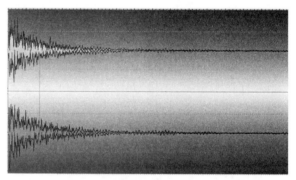

Figure 7.21 These waveforms were captured in WaveLab and graphically show at which point Redrum began to play the sample. Using a snare drum sample as an example, in the left figure the sample is played from start to finish, because the Start knob is set to zero. In the right figure, the sample is played well after its original starting point as the Start knob has been set to 9:00.

To the right of the Start knob is its corresponding Velocity control. This knob determines where the starting point of a sample will be in relation to its played velocity. Notice the LED above this knob that will light up whenever a value of greater or less than zero is selected.

When used together, the dynamic possibilities are virtually endless. I will show you some examples later in this chapter when you use the Pattern sequencer.

Bend That Pitch. Moving along to channels 6 and 7, you will find what I kindly refer to as the *disco effect*. You'll understand why in a minute. Seriously though, these parameters are used to create a pitch bend effect (see Figure 7.22).

On channels 6 and 7, you will see the Pitch knob that works as it does on the other Redrum channels. The difference on these channels is the additional Bend knob.

Figure 7.22 Channels 6 and 7 produce a disco-like pitch bend to your toms. Sorry, but the disco ball is not included.

Creating a Pitch Bend   You can use either channel 6 or 7 for this example. Without altering the position of the Pitch knob, turn the Bend knob by clicking and dragging upwards.

Now use your MIDI keyboard or the Trigger button to hear the results. Notice how the pitch starts at the top and slides down.

Now adjust the Pitch knob to either a positive or negative value and listen to the sample again.

Like I said…Disco! Disco! Disco!

Below the Pitch and Bend controls are the Rate and Velocity knobs for further editing of the pitch bend effect.

The Rate knob controls the bend time of the pitch bend effect. Setting this knob to a negative value decreases the bend time and speeds it up, whereas setting it to a positive value increases the bend time, which slows the effect down.

Its Velocity knob controls the amount of the pitch bend effect according to the velocity at which the sample is played. Try increasing the value and notice how much wider a range the pitch bend effect has when triggered.

The Redrum Pattern Programmer

Aside from great sounds, Redrum includes a fantastic pattern-based programmer (see Figure 7.23). Although this composition tool is much different from the main Reason sequencer, they can be used together at the same time, which creates a virtual drummer's paradise.

Figure 7.23 The Redrum pattern programmer is Redrum's composition tool.

Before you begin to explore the interface in depth, you need to understand what a pattern-based programmer is.

What Is a Pattern-Based Programmer?

A pattern-based programmer is comprised of a series of step-programmed drum patterns that are compiled and stored within a saved song. Redrum offers four pattern banks, each of which can store eight separate patterns (see Figure 7.24). This adds up to 32 individual drum patterns that can be created, saved, and used within one song. *Mama mia*, that's a lot of patterns!

Figure 7.24 With 32 individual possible patterns to choose from, your song won't run out of creative rhythms by a long shot.

All of these patterns are *step-programmed*, which means that each drum sound in the Redrum module must be manually programmed with your mouse one step (or beat) at a time. This might sound a little tedious to the beginning Redrum programmer, but the immediate benefit of using a pattern programmer like this is that you have meticulous control over every dynamic of each of the 10 samples in Redrum. Better yet, there are even a few add-ons of a sort that will make your drums sound even more expressive.

Run Those Patterns

There is hardly a better place to begin this tour than with the Run button, located to the far-left side of the pattern section (see Figure 7.25).

Figure 7.25 Redrum's step pattern controls are used to change patterns and stop/start patterns.

The Run button starts and stops the pattern section. Press it once, and then look to the step section and notice the "running lights" as the pattern plays through. Press it again, and the sequencer will stop. The pattern programmer can also be started and stopped from the Transport panel of the Reason sequencer. Press your computer's spacebar and notice how the Redrum sequencer starts right up.

Located just above the Run button is the Enable Pattern Section button. This links the Redrum pattern section to the main Reason sequencer. Click on it once to turn it off and then start up the main Reason sequencer again. Notice that the Redrum pattern section does not start up. Additionally, as the Reason sequencer is playing, try clicking on the Run button again. You will see that the Redrum pattern section will not start up unless the Enable Pattern Section button is active.

To the right of the Run and Enable buttons is the Pattern section. As mentioned, there are four banks: A, B, C, and D, with eight patterns assigned to each bank. This gives you 32 available patterns to program. In order to change patterns manually, just click on either a numeric pattern or one of the four banks followed by a pattern number. This will bring up the pattern stored in that location. Of course, you will not see any available patterns because you have not written any yet. Clicking on the Pattern button located just above the numeric pattern buttons will deactivate the pattern section entirely. Even with the Run button active, the patterns will not play again until you reactivate the Pattern button. This can be useful when you are using the Reason sequencer to program Redrum rather than using patterns.

Climbing the Steps of Pattern Programming Success

To the right of the Pattern section is the Redrum Step-Programming Interface (see Figure 7.26). This is where your step patterns will be written and edited. You won't believe how easy and creative it really is!

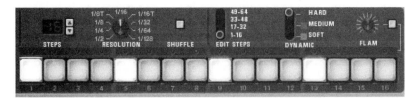

Figure 7.26 The Redrum pattern programmer interface is where you write and edit your step patterns.

Before you learn about the specific parameters that can be edited, you'll program your first pattern to get your feet wet.

1. Select the channel 1 kick drum by clicking on its Select button (see Figure 7.27).

2. Look at the 16-step pattern in front of you and decide which steps you will place your Redrum sample on. By default, each step is a single 16th note, so for

Figure 7.27 Select the Redrum channel that you want to program. For this tutorial, I have selected a kick drum sample on channel 1.

the sake of simplicity, you may want to just place the sample on step buttons 1, 5, 9, and 13 for starters (see Figure 7.28). Just click on the step buttons to light them up.

Figure 7.28 Select the steps that you want to use to write in your pattern. Because a kick drum is selected, this example uses steps 1, 5, 9, and 13.

3. Now select another Redrum channel and write in a pattern for that sample as well. Try a snare drum on steps 5 and 13 or a hi-hat on steps 1, 3, 5, 7, 9, 11, 13, and 15.

4. Now press the spacebar on your computer keyboard, or click on the Run button in the Redrum pattern section. You should hear the sample you programmed played in time with the tempo of your Reason song.

Click and Drag If you want to write in a drum roll or a 16th note pattern in Redrum, you have two choices. One choice is to click on the individual notes, which is kind of a drag when you are writing in a long string of 16th notes in a row.

> The other choice is to select the sound that you want and simply click and drag along the steps. This will allow you to write in a 16-step hi-hat pattern in no time.

Now take a look at the specific parameters that can be used in the Redrum pattern programmer.

How Many Steps Do You Need?

Although working with 16 steps is a lot of fun, as time goes on you might come to find that your patterns and song require more than 16 steps. With this idea in mind, allow me to present the Steps Spin control (see Figure 7.29).

Figure 7.29 The Steps Spin can assign up to 64 steps to your Redrum patterns.

The Steps Spin control assigns a specific number of steps to your patterns. Any value between 1 and 64 steps can be assigned using this control. Assigning specific step values to your Redrum programmer makes it possible to sequence different time signatures. For example, if you want to create a "waltz" feeling in 3/4 time, just set the number of steps to 12. Just keep in mind that the Reason sequencer must also be set to 3/4 time as well (look back at Chapter 5, "The Reason Sequencer—Close Up," to review). The number of steps can be increased and decreased by either clicking on the scroll buttons to the right of its display, or by clicking and dragging up or down in the display.

To the right of the Steps Spin control is the Resolution knob (see Figure 7.30). This knob assigns note values to your steps in the Redrum programmer. By default, the Resolution knob is set to 1/16 or 16th notes, which simply means that each step is a 16th note. Aside from 16th notes, there are many other available resolutions, such as the 16th note "triplet" setting, which produces a triplet feeling against a 4/4 time signature. There are also extremely high resolutions, such as the 1/64 or 64th note resolution, and lower values such as the 1/4 or quarter note resolution. The Resolution knob is there for your experimenting and creativity; just remember that the resolution is linked to the tempo of the Reason sequencer, so higher resolutions can sound strange at fast tempos.

Figure 7.30 The Resolution knob assigns different note values to each step.

As the saying goes, "It don't mean a thing if it ain't got that swing," and Redrum has the perfect tool for giving it to you. Located to the right of the Resolution knob, the Shuffle button applies a swing or shuffle feel to your drum patterns. Once activated, using the ReGroove Mixer's Global Shuffle knob can intensify the shuffling effect.

Give the Shuffle a test drive by following these steps:

1. Wipe the slate clean by selecting Edit > Clear Pattern.

2. Select the Redrum channel that has a closed hi-hat sound. Now write in a 16th note pattern by clicking and dragging across the steps. Make sure that the Resolution knob is set to 16th notes or 1/16.

3. Activate the Shuffle button and set the Pattern Shuffle knob to the 10:00 position.

4. Press the Run button in Redrum, or start the Reason sequencer and listen to the shuffling effect. Be sure to make changes with the ReGroove Mixer's Global Shuffle knob to hear the different shuffling feels you get with this function. Also try adding in kick and snare patterns against it.

If you increase the number of steps in your patterns, you will certainly need a way to view and edit the additional steps. The Edit Steps switch is located to the right of the Shuffle button (see Figure 7.31) and addresses this very need. Click and drag the switch up and down to view and edit all of the 64 available steps.

Figure 7.31 View and edit all of the steps in your Redrum pattern by using the Edit Steps switch.

Dynamics and Flam

As stated earlier, dynamics are the key to creating a great sounding track, no matter what instrument is used. Redrum has several features to help make control of dynamics easy.

The color-coded Dynamic switch is used to assign different velocities to each step in a pattern (see Figure 7.32). Have a look at how you can use this to create some interesting effects with just a hi-hat sound.

Figure 7.32 The Dynamic switch creates a much-needed element for any pattern programmed in Redrum.

1. Just as before, delete the current pattern by choosing Clear Pattern from the Edit pull-down menu, or by using the Ctrl+X (Windows) or Apple+X (Mac) keyboard command.

2. Select the closed hi-hat channel in Redrum and set the Dynamic switch to Soft.

3. Using your mouse, create a hi-hat pattern by clicking on steps 1, 2, 5, 6, 9, 10, 13, and 14. Notice that these selected steps are light green.

4. Now switch the Dynamic switch to Medium by clicking and dragging upwards.

5. Click on steps 1, 5, 9, and 13. Notice how the colors of these steps change to a shade of orange.

6. Press the Run button on Redrum and listen to how the dynamics change with the hi-hat. You can also click on the Shuffle button to hear the dynamics along with a shuffling feel.

7. Click and drag upwards on the Dynamic switch to change the value from Medium to Hard.

8. Click on steps 1, 5, 9, and 13 while the sequencer is still running so you can hear the effect in real-time. Notice that the color of these steps has changed to a shade of bright red.

To the right of the Dynamic switch are the Flam controls. In drumming terms, Flam describes what it also known as a *double strike* on a percussion instrument. This double strike creates a very slight drum roll sound and the Flam controls are used to recreate that effect (see Figure 7.33).

Figure 7.33 Use the Flam controls to create a realistic double strike sound on any channel.

A flam can be applied to any step or sound in a Redrum pattern by activating the Flam button and clicking on any step. After you select a step to affect, you can control the speed of the flam by adjusting its knob. Let's look at an example.

1. Cut the current pattern.

2. Press the Run button, select your kick drum channel, and set your dynamics to medium. Write a kick pattern on steps 1 and 9.

3. Select your closed hi-hat channel, set the dynamics to soft, and write a simple 8th note pattern on steps 1, 3, 5, 7, 9, 11, 13, and 15.

4. Select your snare drum channel, set the dynamics to medium, and write a syncopated rhythm on steps 5, 8, 1, and 14.

5. Activate the Flam button by clicking on it. Click on step 14 of the snare drum pattern. Listen to the immediate effect and notice the red LED above step 14 stays lit.

6. Use the Flam knob to control the speed of the effect. I suggest setting it at the 3:00 position to make the snare pattern sound realistic.

Please note that Dynamics and Flam must be applied while programming a pattern (before clicking on a step) and cannot be applied while simply playing back a pattern that has already been created (at least not without clicking on steps in the pattern).

Building the Redrum Groove with the Pattern Programmer

By now, you should have a pretty firm grasp on the Redrum interface and how to navigate through the step sequencer. Now is as good a time as any to start using Redrum as a power user should!

Because you have been probably using the same Redrum kit throughout this tutorial, it's high time that you find another Redrum kit to have some fun with. Click on the Patch Browser folder to bring up the browser window.

Ideally, you need a drum kit that can be used at fast and slow tempos effectively, so I suggest double-clicking on the Heavy Kits folder. You'll see seven Dublab Redrum kits at your disposal. Select the first kit and let's get cracking!

Listen to each Redrum channel by clicking on the Trigger buttons or by using your MIDI keyboard. There are good solid drum sounds that you can use effectively with the Redrum pattern programmer in order to create some interesting patterns. Let's start by writing out a simple pattern with the programmer using just a kick, snare, and hi-hat. Make sure that you have Bank A, Pattern One selected for this tutorial, and set the song tempo to 90BPM.

1. Select the kick drum Redrum channel, set its dynamic to Medium, and write in a simple kick drum pattern on steps 1, 4, 8, and 12. Press the Run button to start the pattern so you can hear the changes as you are making them.

2. Select one of the snare drum Redrum channels, set its dynamics to Medium as well, and write in a quick pattern line on steps 5, 10, and 13. Notice that the pattern sounds rather empty. This is where you fill in the blank space with the hi-hat.

3. Select the closed hi-hat Redrum channel, set its dynamics to Soft, and write in a quarter note pattern on steps 1, 5, 9, 13, and 16 for some variation. Notice that the groove is starting to take shape nicely as all of the blank space is filled.

Honing Your Drumming Skills   If drums are not your primary instrument, you might soon find yourself running out of rhythmic ideas for Redrum. Not to worry, because you can take a quick trip to your local sheet music store and pick up a book of drum patterns for $10–20. These books are full of pattern ideas that are sure to provide an ample source of material for months and years to come.

If you are short on funds, you might also search the Internet for drumming web pages that offer free drum patterns.

This is a good starting point because a basic groove has been set up. Now is the perfect time to add some real-time effects using the S1 and S2 knobs on each Redrum channel.

Start by giving the snare drum some reverb, which is accessible by using the S1 knob. Because the reverb is most likely set to its default of Hall, it's a good idea to not overdo it with the effect on the snare drum, because it will sound too saturated. Try assigning a send value of 40 to the snare channel. You should now hear a nice, smooth echoing reverb underneath the snare sample. Also notice that the signal meter for the reverb effect should be lit up.

You should have the delay effect loaded and ready to be used with the S2 knob. It's time to add some delay to the hi-hat track in order to create an interesting 16th note feeling. Select the closed hi-hat Redrum channel and set the S2 knob to a value of 80. At this point, you should hear a very smooth, syncopated pattern with the hi-hat. You might consider panning the hi-hat a little off to the left or right to create a stereo effect that sounds good in a drum mix.

Altering and Randomizing Your Redrum Patterns

You should now have a drum pattern that can be used as a good, solid rhythm. But this shouldn't be the only drum loop you will use in your entire song, so now you are going to create a few new patterns by using some of Reason's handy pattern edits.

1. Start by selecting Copy Pattern from the Edit pull-down menu. You can also use the Ctrl+C (on a PC) or Apple+C (on the Mac) key command. This will copy all of the written steps from Pattern 1, and allow you to move them to Pattern 2 to begin editing.

2. Select Pattern 2 by clicking on it and choosing Paste Pattern from the Edit pull-down menu. You can also use Ctrl+V on a PC or Apple+V on a Mac. This will paste the copied pattern into Pattern 2.

3. At this point, click on the Edit pull-down menu and notice how many pattern edits you have available. For starters, try something simple, like the Randomize Pattern. This can be done by choosing it from the Edit pull-down menu, or

using the key command of Ctrl+R for the PC or Apple+R for the Mac. Reason will now randomize your original pattern and also add new Redrum channels. Notice that the dynamics will also randomize, giving you a very different pattern that can be used as a fill.

4. You can repeat the randomization as many times as you like in order to find the pattern that you like best.

Upon closer inspection of the Edit pull-down menu, you will see many other pattern alterations you can perform on your patterns, so let's take a moment to discuss their functions.

- **Shift Pattern Left**—Shifts all of the active Redrum channels one step to the left.

- **Shift Pattern Right**—Shifts the pattern one step to the right.

- **Shift Drum Left**—Shifts an individual Redrum channel's sequence one step to the left.

- **Shift Drum Right**—Shifts one channel's sequence one step to the right.

- **Randomize Pattern**—As you read in the previous section, this randomly generates an entirely new pattern by adding new sounds and dynamics.

- **Randomize Drum**—Randomizes an individual Redrum channel while still adding new dynamics.

- **Alter Pattern**—Alternates the active pattern entirely without adding any new sounds or dynamics. If the Randomize Pattern effect is a little too much for your song, this is a good alternative.

- **Alter Drum**—Performs the same task as Alter Pattern, but alters a single Redrum channel.

Using Dynamics to Alter Velocities

After creating a few patterns, you can now begin to alter the actual sound and timbre of the Redrum channels themselves by working with the dynamics and individual velocities.

For this example, let's start with the kick drum and create a dynamic pattern that will modify the tone of the kick drum as the pattern plays. Make sure that you have selected Pattern 3 so you have a clean slate to start with.

1. Select Redrum channel 1, which is the kick drum. Set your Dynamic to Soft and write an 8th note pattern on steps 1, 3, 5, 7, 9, 11, 13, and 15. Press the Run button to hear the pattern.

2. Switch the Dynamic to Medium and click on steps 3, 7, 11, and 15 to alter their dynamics.

3. Switch the Dynamic to Hard and click on steps 5 and 13 to alter their dynamics. You should now have a kick pattern that has a very distinctive loud and soft characteristic to it.

4. Locate the Level and Velocity knobs on channel 1 strip. Leave the Level knob alone, but try different values for the Velocity to hear the enhancements that it produces.

5. Now locate the Tone and Velocity knobs on channel 1. Set the Tone knob to −42, which will make the kick drum sound very "lo-fi" and muddy. Now set the Velocity to a positive value, such as 45. You will hear the immediate change in the tone of the kick drum. Listen to how the tone of the kick alters with the change in dynamics.

In the next example, you'll have a go with the Start and Velocity knobs on channel 3.

1. Select channel 3, which is a snare drum sample. Set your Dynamic to Soft and write a 16th note pattern on steps 3, 4, 5, 7, 8, 9, 11, 12, 13, 15, and 16. Press the Run button to listen to the pattern.

2. Switch the Dynamic to Medium and click on steps 4, 8, 12, and 15 to alter their velocities.

3. Switch the Dynamics to Hard and click on steps 5, 9, and 13 to alter their velocities. You should now hear a very driving snare drum pattern.

4. Locate the Start and Velocity knobs at the bottom of channel 3. Adjust the Start knob to a value of 38. To really hear this effect, select the Solo button at the top of channel 3. Listen to the effect and notice how soft it sounds, because the starting point of the sample has been altered.

5. Now, adjust the Velocity knob to a value of −20. The snare drum line now sounds much more realistic; the snare sample is reacting in much the same way as a real snare drum would.

6. Click on the Solo button again, so you can hear both the snare and kick playing together. For added effect, you might also activate the Shuffle to swing it a little bit.

In this last example, you'll use the low tom channel and create a pitch bend effect by using a combination of dynamics and velocities.

1. Select channel 7, which is the low tom sample. Set your Dynamic to Soft and write a quick 16th note pattern on steps 3, 4, 11, 12, and 16. Press the Run button to listen to it.

2. Switch the Dynamic to Medium and click on step 16 to alter its dynamic.

3. Switch the Dynamic to Hard and click on steps 4 and 12 to alter their dynamics.

4. Locate the Pitch knob for channel 7 and set it to a negative value of 24. Set the Bend knob to a maximum positive value of 55. Listen to the sequence and notice how there is now a slight pitch bend effect on the tom as it plays.

5. Locate the Rate knob and set it to a positive value of 88. Set the Velocity to a positive value of 28.

6. Now listen to the tom sample and notice how it changes pitch according to the dynamics and velocity.

You've come a long way in this section—from a simple four-beat pattern to an all out cacophony of drumming thunder.

Using Redrum with the Reason Sequencer

After you have completed your rhythmic bits and pieces in Redrum, you need to use the Reason sequencer to string your patterns together in order to create a full composition. There are a couple of ways to do this:

■ You can program an automation to switch between patterns in a song.

■ You can copy the patterns into the Reason sequencer for further editing.

Let's take a closer look at each of these.

Shifting Between Patterns with Automation

Automating the patterns of the Redrum sequencer is probably the quickest way to compose your overall song structure, and it is surprisingly quick and easy to do.

In this next tutorial, you need to have at least two or three patterns already programmed into the Redrum programmer because you will be shifting between them during your automation recording.

1. Make sure the Redrum track in the Reason sequencer is armed to receive MIDI data. Also make sure that the Enable Pattern Section option of the Redrum programmer is activated and ready to go, and that Pattern 1 is selected in the Redrum sequencer.

2. Press Record in the Reason sequencer. Both the Reason and Redrum sequencers should start playing. Because you previously selected Pattern 1 in the Redrum programmer, this is what you should be hearing.

3. Let Pattern 1 play for a measure or two, and then get ready to shift patterns by just clicking on Pattern 2. As soon as the next measure starts to record in the Reason sequencer, you should hear Pattern 2 playing. Be sure to notice the automation that has been recorded on the Redrum track in the Reason sequencer (see Figure 7.34).

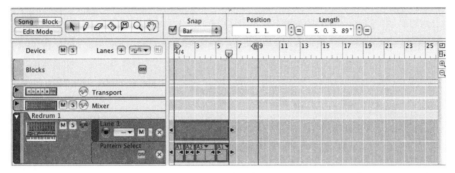

Figure 7.34 The Reason sequencer displays automation data as it is being recorded.

4. Now switch to Pattern 3. It should start playing as the new measure starts in the Reason sequencer.

5. Press Stop. Notice that there is now a neon green box around the Pattern section of the Redrum programmer (see Figure 7.35). This means that automation has now been written within this section.

Figure 7.35 When you are finished recording your automation, a neon green box will appear around the parameter that has been automated.

6. Press Stop again to return to the first measure of the Reason sequencer. Press Play to listen to the Redrum pattern play back. Notice that the patterns are changing on their own because they have been automated.

Clearing Your Automation   After listening to your recording, you might find that you don't like the way the patterns came together, so you will probably want to redo your recording. Chapter 20, "Automation," covers automation extensively, but for now here is a quick tip on resetting the automation.

Find any parameters that have an automation written in by looking for the neon green box around it. Right-click on the parameter (or Control-click on the Mac). At this point, a menu will appear and you should see an option to Clear Automation. Choose this option, and the automation will be erased from that parameter.

Copying Patterns to the Reason Sequencer

After programming your patterns into Redrum, you might decide that you want to rework them with a bit more precision than a step-programmed sequencer allows. This is where the Reason sequencer comes in handy.

1. Select the Redrum pattern that you want to copy to the Reason sequencer.

2. Set the left and right locators in the sequencer to where you want the pattern to start and stop. For example, set the left locator to measure one and the right locator to measure two, and the Redrum patterns will be copied in between.

3. Click once on the Redrum interface to select it.

4. Choose Edit > Copy Pattern to Track.

5. You should see the MIDI events for the Redrum pattern you selected in the sequencer.

6. On Redrum, deselect Enable Pattern Section.

7. Press Play. You should now hear the pattern play back from the Reason sequencer.

8. If you want to copy more patterns to the Reason sequencer, you must reset the left and right locators to the starting and end points that you want.

Turn It Off   After you have copied your patterns to the Reason sequencer, make sure you deactivate the Enable Pattern Section button in the Redrum programmer. If you forget to do this and press Play, both sequencers will begin to play again, but this time, Redrum will be playing the notes in its own sequencer as well as what it is receiving from the Reason sequencer. This will produce a very strange *flange* effect that doesn't sound very good and will most certainly cause the Audio Out Clipping LED in the Reason Transport panel to glow a bright red, which is not a good thing.

After you have copied your tracks to the Reason sequencer, you should press the Arrange/Edit View button in the Reason sequencer to see how Redrum information is displayed.

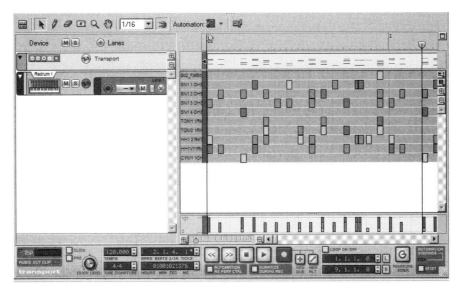

Figure 7.36 Redrum MIDI events as displayed in the Reason sequencer.

As shown in Figure 7.36, the MIDI events for Redrum look a little different from the standard Edit mode that you might remember from Chapter 5. Each drum sound has its own lane that can be edited in various ways. For example, you can now draw and erase notes, or you can re-quantize the whole sequence to create an entirely new groove.

You can now have access to different controllers and edit automated parameters with more accuracy and precision. The possibilities are virtually endless.

8 Kong—Close Up

As you have seen from Chapter 7, "Redrum—Close Up," Reason already includes a very powerful, yet versatile drum machine within Redrum. Because Propellerheads have not been known to rest on their laurels, they decided to push the creative envelope and introduce Kong (see Figure 8.1). New to Reason 5, *Kong* is an electronic musician's dream machine, as it includes a desirable feature set of sampling, physical modeling, and effect, all wrapped up in a great looking interface that looks and feels very similar to the popular Akai MPC series of drum machines.

A Guided Tour of Kong

When you first create an instance of Kong, the first parts of the interface you'll see are the Pad section and the dedicated drum control (see Figure 8.2). Additionally, you'll also see the Patch Browser buttons, the Pitch and Modulation Wheels, and the Master Level. As you will see later in this chapter, this is just the first half of the interface, but for now let's just concentrate on the basics and work our way out from there.

Browsing and Loading Patches

When you first create an instance of Kong, a default drum kit is loaded. After a while, you'll certainly want to try different drum kits, so navigate to the upper-left corner of the interface, where you can browse the drum patches (see Figure 8.3).

Click on the browser window or on the folder button located directly below it to open the Patch Browser window (see Figure 8.4).

Once the Patch Browser is open, you can locate and load any of the available Kong patches by opening the Kong Patches folder, located in the Reason Factory Sound Bank. Once you do this, you can select between standard Kong Kits, and the same Kong Kits mapped out specifically for keyboards.

Let's try a simple kit in order to familiarize yourself with the Kong interface. Open the Club Kits folder and select the Downtempo Kit. Click on the OK button in the Patch Browser and the kit will load itself into the Kong interface.

Figure 8.1 Kong is a powerful drum machine and sound-designing powerhouse with a hip and retro graphic interface.

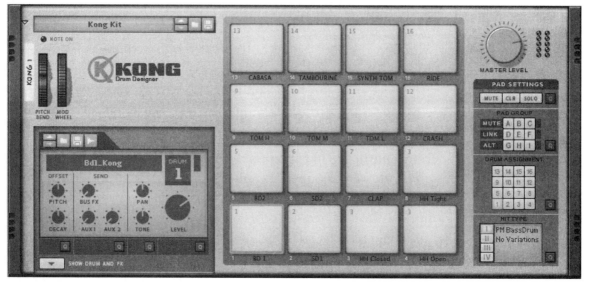

Figure 8.2 The main interface of Kong includes the Pad section on the right, the drum controls on the left, and the Patch Brower buttons at the top.

Figure 8.3 Use the Patch Browser controls to load one of several Kong patches.

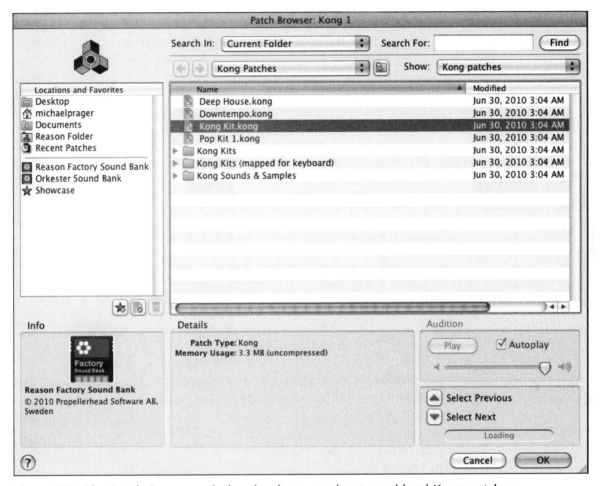

Figure 8.4 The Patch Browser window is where you locate and load Kong patches.

The Pad Section

The Pad section of the Kong interface is where you graphically trigger the individual sounds in a loaded Kong kit. Looking back at Figure 8.2, you can see that there are 16 individual pads arranged in groups of four. You can trigger these sounds by using any of the following methods:

- Clicking on them with your mouse

- Using a controller keyboard

- Using the On Screen Piano Keys (press F4 on your computer keyboard)

Mapping the Pads on Your Keyboard   The individual Kong pads are mapped in a very similar fashion to Redrum, which starts at C1 and ends at D#2 on your keyboard.

All of Kong's pads are all *velocity sensitive,* which means that they will respond and sound differently depending on how hard or soft you trigger them from your keyboard. Additionally, you can use your mouse to achieve the same effect by clicking from the bottom (softest) to the top (hardest) on each pad.

To the right of the Pad Section are the Pad Settings, which house various parameters that allow you to assign the pads, edit them, and remap them (see Figure 8.5).

Figure 8.5 The Pad Settings enable you to edit the mapping and mixing of any selected pad.

Let's have a look at each of these sections, starting with the Mute, Clear, and Solo buttons.

- The Mute button will mute any selected Kong pad. Once you press the Mute button, it and the selected Kong pad will turn bright red.

- The Clear button will deactivate all assigned solos and mutes to the pad section. For example, if you had both of the kick drum pads muted, you could press the Clear button to un-mute both with one click.

- The Solo (or S) button works in the opposite way to the Mute button, as it will isolate just the drum sample that you want to hear on its own. Select a pad, click the Solo button, and all of the other pads will turn bright red, while the selected pad will show as a bright green hue.

Just to the right of the Mute, Clear, and Solo buttons, is the Quick Edit mode button. Press this button and the Pad section will launch into a Quick Edit Mode, which enables you to perform several edits quickly throughout the entire pad section (see Figure 8.6).

Next down from the Mute, Clear, and Solo buttons are the Pad Groups (see Figure 8.7). These are used to assign different play parameters to your selected Kong pads. Using these effectively can give you a much more realistic effect to your drum samples, and they also introduce the ability to be a lot more creative with your sequencing.

Mute Groups are used to have one pad mute the sound of another pad that is assigned to the same group. For example, let's say you have an open hi-hat sample on pad seven and a closed hi-hat sample on pad eight.

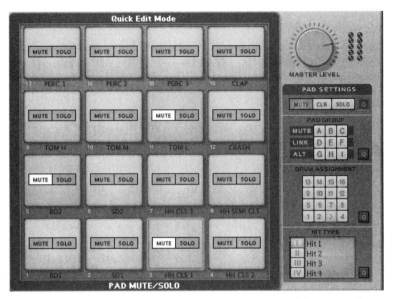

Figure 8.6 The Quick Edit Mode makes it possible to perform quick edits to several Kong pads efficiently.

Figure 8.7 Pad Groups make it possible to have your Kong performances sound realistic by incorporating Mute, Link, and Alt groups.

You can assign both of these to a Mute Group so that when you play the open hi-hat sample, you can use the closed hi-hat sample to mute it, which is exactly how it would sound on an acoustic drum kit.

Try the following exercise. Make sure you're still using the Downtempo Kong Kit before you begin.

1. Select pad twelve, which is a crash cymbal.

2. Click on the "A" Mute Group to assign pad twelve to it.

3. Select pad four, which is a closed hi-hat.

4. Click on the "A" Mute Group to assign pad four to it.

5. Play pad twelve and then pad four. You should hear the crash cymbal abruptly end.

Link Groups are used to combine, or link several pads together, so that they will be triggered simultaneously. To get a better idea of how this works, try the following exercise:

1. Select pad thirteen, which is a shaker type sound.

2. Click on the "D" Link Group to assign pad thirteen to it.

3. Select pad six, which is a snare drum.

4. Click on the "D" Link Group to assign pad six to it.

5. Play either pad thirteen or six and you'll now hear both of them played back at once.

The Alt Groups is used to create a randomization effect between grouped pads. This is certainly one of the more creative themed groups that Kong offers up.

Try the following exercise:

1. Select pad one, which is a kick drum and assign it to Alt "G."

2. Select pad five, which is another kick drum and assign it to Alt "G."

3. Select pad nine, which is a high tom and assign it to Alt "G."

4. Select pad thirteen, which is a shaker sound and assign it to Alt "G."

5. Play any of the four assigned pads and Kong will randomly play any of the four sounds.

The Drum Assignments buttons are used to assign the drum sounds of Kong to any of the 16 individual pads (see Figure 8.8). I'll get into this later in the chapter when I show you how to build your own drum kit with Kong.

Figure 8.8 The Drum Assignment pads are used to assign selected drum sound to any of Kong's 16 pads.

The Hit Type dialog box is a function that makes it possible to assign one of four hits to a single Kong pad (see Figure 8.9). This is another feature that probably won't make a whole lot of sense this early in the chapter, but it will in a very short while.

Figure 8.9 The Hit Type is used to assign one of four different drum hit types when selected.

The Drum Controls

The Drum controls of Kong are used to assign specific sounds to each selected Kong pad, as well as mix the loaded sound with send effects, panning, tone, and volume (see Figure 8.10). Additionally, you can also sample your own sounds into Kong from these controls, making for a very powerful drum-sampling machine.

Figure 8.10   The Drum controls are used to browse and load sounds for the Kong pads, as well as mix them.

Sampling Tutorial   If you want to really jump into the depths of sampling audio now, just skip ahead to Chapter 13 and read the section entitled "Sampling Audio with the NN-19."

Within this section, you can select new sounds for any selected pad, edit it, and save it using the available Browse and Save buttons. While each Kong pad has its own series of controls, they cannot be viewed until you select one of the pads by clicking on it with your mouse. Click on the BD1 pad and let's have a look at the available parameters.

- **Sample Scroll**—These buttons are used to select new samples one by one from within a selected directory. For example, as you have selected the kick drum Kong pad, the scroll controls will allow you to select a new kick drum sample. Also note that you can click on the naming dialog box within the Drum controls and select a new drum sample from a pop-up list.

- **Sample Browser**—This button is used to launch the Sample Browser, which makes it possible to search for, preview, and import new samples into your Kong kit.

- **Save**—This is used to save your sample.

- **Sample**—This button will launch the sampling function so you can record your own sounds into a Kong kit.

- **Pitch**—This knob is used to change the pitch of the selected Kong pad.

- **Decay**—This knob is used to change the decay of a selected Kong pad. This is especially useful if you have a cymbal sound with a very long decay or sustain.

- **Bus FX**—This knob is used to send signal from a selected Kong pad to one of several provided Bus effects. I will discuss this further later in the chapter.

- **Aux1/Aux2**—These knobs are used to send signal from a selected Kong pad to one of several Aux effects.

- **Pan**—This is used to set the placement of the selected Kong pad in the stereo field.

- **Tone**—This knob is used to alter the tone, or equalization of the selected Kong pad.

- **Level**—This knob sets the level of the selected Kong pad.

Just below each of these controls is a series of Quick Edit buttons that perform different types of edits on selected Kong pads along an X-Y axis (see Figure 8.11). Let's start from the far left and move to the right.

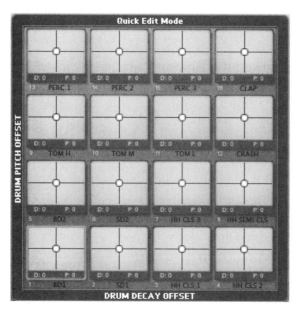

Figure 8.11 The Quick Edit buttons at the bottom of the Drum Controls allow you to edit two separate parameters across an X-Y axis.

- **Quick Edit One**—This Quick Edit button makes changes to pitch and decay.

- **Quick Edit Two**—This Quick Edit button makes changes to the bus and aux knobs. However, unlike Quick Edit One, this Quick Edit makes its changes with individual adjustments for each knob.

- **Quick Edit Three**—This Quick Edit button makes changes to the pan and level.

- **Quick Edit Four**—This Quick Edit button makes changes to the tone and level.

The Drum Module and FX

There's a whole other layer to the complexity of Kong, which is the included Drum Module and FX section (see Figure 8.12). This section is where you will select the type of synthesis that will generate your drum sounds and the real-time effects to enhance them further.

Figure 8.12   The Drum Module and FX section of Kong is where you select the type of synthesis to produce your drum sounds and assign real-time effects to them.

Click on the Show Drum and FX button to display this section and let's start exploring.

The Drum Module

At the far left is the Drum Module, where the sound of Kong is generated. Kong provides three types of synthesis to produce sounds (see Figure 8.13).

Figure 8.13   The Drum Module generates your drum sounds by using three types of synthesis. The module shown here is the NN-Nano.

- **Samples**—Kong supports several digital audio formats, including WAV, AIFF, SoundFonts, and REX files.

- **Physical Modeling**—This type of synthesis is used to generate sounds by mathematically simulating or emulating an acoustic kick drum, snare drum, and toms.

- **Analog Modeling**—This type of synthesis is used to generate sounds by mathematically simulating or emulating classic analog kicks, snares, and toms.

Let's have a look at these and discuss each Drum Module in depth, starting with the NN-Nano.

The NN-Nano Drum Module

The NN-Nano is a drum sampler that's based off the NN-XT sampler, which is discussed in Chapter 14, "NN-XT—Close Up" (see Figure 8.14). This module is used to import or record samples and to provide several creative editing options that can make your drums sound as realistic or synthetic as you would like. Note that when using the Downtempo kit, every pad uses the NN-Nano.

Figure 8.14   The NN-Nano is used to record and import samples into a selected Kong pad. It's the little brother to the NN-XT sampler.

Let's explore the various parameters of the NN-Nano, starting with the Sample Map Display.

The Sample Map. The Sample Map is used to select/edit samples and map their Hit Type to a selected Kong pad (see Figure 8.15). The NN-Nano supports multi hit samples, which enables you to create either realistic or synthetic samples for your Kong kit, as each sample is assigned to one of four different Hit Types, discussed earlier in this chapter. All of the nuances and sonic characteristics of the sampled instrument can be accurately mapped within the NN-Nano.

Figure 8.15 The Sample Map is used to import or record samples, and then map them according to their assigned hits.

Let's discuss the individual parameters.

- **Sample Scroll Controls**—These buttons are used to select new samples one by one from within a selected directory.

- **Browser**—This button is used to launch the Sample Browser, which makes it possible to search for, preview, and import new samples.

- **Sample**—This button will launch the sampling function so you can record your own sounds.

- **Add Layer**—This button is used to add a layer to a selected sample hit. For example, you could have a kick drum on Hit 1, and then use the Add Layer button to add a layer with a cowbell sample onto it.

- **Remove Layer**—This button will remove any selected layer.

- **Edit Sample**—This is used to launch the Sample Editor for any selected sample.

- **Hit**—Use this to select one of four available hit types.

- **Sample**—This displays the name of the loaded sample. You can select a new sample by double-clicking here and you can also preview the loaded sample by holding down the Alt key on your computer keyboard and clicking on the sample.

- **Velocity (Graphical)**—This is used to display and edit the mapped velocity of a loaded sample in a graphical way. Simply click and drag from either the left or right corners of a selected sample to assign its low and high velocity values.

- **Level**—This dialog box displays the amplitude of a selected sample.

- **Velocity (Numeric)**—This dialog box is used to display and edit the mapped velocity of a loaded sample in a numeric way. Simply click and drag up or down to assign its low and high velocity values.

- **Alt**—This is used to alternate between different layers within the same hit. For example, if you have three snare samples loaded onto one hit, you can assign them to the Alt function to create the alternate effect. It helps to introduce some randomization to your loaded sample.

- **Pitch**—This is used to assign a pitch to a selected sample.

- **Hit Name**—This is used to assign a new name to a selected hit.

The Global Parameters. The NN-Nano also includes a wide assortment of synth parameters that can be assigned to your selected sample. These parameters are global, which simply means that they will affect all of the hits within a selected Kong pad equally.

The Polyphony controls determine how many voices can be heard simultaneously from a selected hit. NN-Nano offers three choices (see Figure 8.16).

- **Full**—This is the full polyphony setting, which means that all hits can be heard with full polyphony.

- **Exclusive Hits**—When selected, any played hit will abruptly cut off any other audible hits.

- **Monophonic**—When selected, only one hit will be heard at a time.

Figure 8.16 The Global Parameters are provided to universally edit all of the hits within a selected Kong pad.

The Mod Wheel parameters are used to assign both pitch and decay to Kong's Modulation Wheel. This can offer some creative textures, as the Mod Wheel is a very lively sounding effect best served in a live environment.

The Velocity parameters are used to edit the following parameters to your hits based on the amount of velocity used.

- **Pitch**—The velocity modifies the pitch for a sample hit.

- **Decay**—The velocity modifies the decay time for a sample hit.

- **Level**—The velocity modifies the level for a sample hit.

- **Bend**—The velocity modifies the pitch bend effect. This is very similar to the bend parameter covered in Chapter 7.

- **Sample Start**—The velocity modifies the starting time for the sample hit.

The Pitch parameters are used to set the global pitch and create a pitch bend effect for your hits. For example, you could load a crash cymbal, and have its pitch bend up or down over a specific amount of time. The included parameters are as follows:

- **Pitch**—This knob sets the global pitch for your hits.

- **Amount**—This knob sets the amount of pitch bend. A positive value will cause the pitch to bend down, whereas a negative value will have the opposite effect.

- **Time**—This knob determines the amount of time given to the pitch bend effect.

The Oscillator (OSC) parameters are used to determine the Sample Start time. Additionally, the NN-Nano can reverse the playback of your samples by pressing the Reverse button. This creates a fantastic backward sound to your loaded samples.

The Amp Envelope (AMP ENV) parameters assign global envelope parameters to the amplitude of your hits. The included parameters are as follows:

- **Attack**—This sets the attack to your hits.

- **Level**—This knob sets the amplitude of your hits.

- **Decay**—This knob is used to determine the decay of your hits once they've been triggered. The Decay parameter includes two additional parameters called Gate and Trig modes. When Gate is selected, the Decay knob will assign the minimum decay to your hit, which will sound very abrupt only when the Kong pad is released. When Trig is selected, the hit Decay will be abrupt no matter if you hold the Kong pad down or not.

Nurse Rex

Now that you're done touring NN-Nano, let's change the drum module by selecting pad one, clicking on the down facing arrow located at the upper-left corner. A pop-up menu will allow you to select from a list of nine drum modules (see Figure 8.17). Select the Nurse Rex module and you're ready to begin.

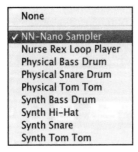

Figure 8.17 Kong includes nine types of drum modules.

Nurse Rex (see Figure 8.18) is a light version of the Dr. Octo Rex loop player device, which is covered in Chapter 9, "Dr. Octo Rex–Close Up." This drum module loads REX files and enables you to assign the slices to any Kong pad.

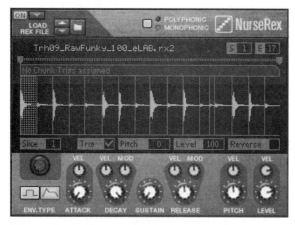

Figure 8.18 Nurse Rex is the cure for your drum sounds. Any REX file can be loaded into the interface, at which point individual slices can be assigned to any Kong pad.

Loading REX files. After creating an instance of Nurse Rex, the first thing you'll want to do is load a REX file, which you do by clicking on the Browse Loop button, which is found in the upper-left corner of the module. This will launch the Loop Browser, where you can navigate, browse, and select your REX file. The best way to do this is as follows:

1. Click on the Reason Factory Sound Bank icon.

2. Double-click on the Dr Rex Drum Loops folder to display its contents.

3. You can browse through this entire folder, which contains subfolders with loops of various styles. For the sake of simplicity and time, select the file called "Acs01_StrghtAhead_130.rx2," which is found in the root Dr. Rex Drum Loops folder.

4. Click OK and the loop will now be loaded into Nurse Rex.

Now that you have loaded a REX file, play the associated Kong pad to hear the loop play back. By default the REX file will play back in its entirety without stopping until it reaches the end of the file. This is known as the Loop Trig mode, which is one of the four available Hit Types for Nurse Rex (see Figure 8.19).

Figure 8.19 Nurse Rex includes four Hit Types, which can be selected from the Kong interface. Included are Loop Trig, Chunk Trig, Slice Trig, and Stop.

Loop Trig Mode is governed by a pair of Start and End points in the Waveform display. The range of these points can be altered by either clicking or dragging up or down on the dialog box, or simply clicking and dragging the Start and End points on the ruler along the Waveform display to the left or right. For example, you could set the Start point to 3 and the End point to 3, which will cause Nurse Rex to simply play the third slice of the REX file when triggered.

The *Chunk Trig Mode* is a Hit Type that makes it possible to assign individual slices of a loaded REX file to multiple Kong pads. This is a really great feature, as you can use a single drum module to feed several Kong pads at one time, which saves CPU and memory resources.

Here's how to do it:

1. Select Chunk Trig as the Hit Type on pad one.

2. Select the Quick Edit Mode for the Drum Assignments.

3. Set the second Kong pad to the first Kong pad by clicking on the "1" value, and set its Hit Type to Chunk Trig.

4. Set the third Kong pad to the first Kong pad by clicking on the "1" value, and set its Hit Type to Chunk Trig.

5. Set the fourth Kong pad to the first Kong pad by clicking on the "1" value, and set its Hit Type to Chunk Trig.

Once you've made your edits, your Kong set up with Nurse Rex should look like Figure 8.20. Play the pads now and each pad will play a specific chunk of the REX file. At this point you can set the size of the chunks by clicking and dragging between them to the left or right and come up with some wild combinations.

Figure 8.20 Pads 1–4 have been assigned to Pad one and set to Chunk Trig, which will allow each pad to trigger a specific part of the loaded REX file.

Slice Trig Mode is made to assign a single slice or multiple slices of a REX file to a single Kong pad. Select pad one, select Slice Trig Hit Type, and then play the pad. You should now only hear a single slice play back, which is the first slice by default. If you want to select a different slice, you must deselect the first slice by clicking on the Trig parameter to deactivate it (see Figure 8.21).

Figure 8.21   When using the Slice Trig Mode, you can set any slice of a REX file to be triggered by the Kong pad. However, you must deselect the first slice by clicking on the Trig parameter.

At this point, you can select another slice by clicking on it with your mouse, and then selecting the Trig parameter to set it as the slice that the Kong pad will trigger (see Figure 8.22).

Figure 8.22   Select any other slice of the REX file and then select the Trig parameter to set it as the slice for your Kong pad.

In addition to triggering a single slice, you can also choose multiple slices, select the Trig parameter, and the Kong pad will alternate between each of the slices (see Figure 8.23). Here's how to do it using pad one.

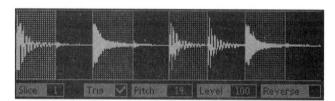

Figure 8.23   You can also choose multiple slices and have Nurse Rex play each one back in an alternating fashion.

1. Hold down the Apple key (Ctrl key for Windows) and select multiple slices with your mouse.

2. Select the Trig parameter.

3. Play the Kong pad and Nurse Rex will alternate between the various slices.

The Stop Mode is used to abruptly stop a REX file while playing back in either the Loop Trig or Chunk Trig Modes. If you want to do this, just assign one of the other available Kong pads to the first Kong pad by using the Quick Edit Mode and set its Hit Type to Stop. Now play the REX file with the first Kong pad and use the other assigned Pad to stop it.

The Waveform Display Parameters. Nurse Rex Waveform Display offers a variety of parameters that can be assigned to each slice of a loaded REX file (see Figure 8.24).

Figure 8.24 The Waveform Display parameters make it possible to reverse slices as well as alter the pitch and/or level of each slice within a REX file.

- **Slice**—This knob is used to select any slice of a REX file by clicking and dragging up or down.

- **Trig**—This parameter is used to assign a slice to be triggered when the Slice Trig Hit Type is selected.

- **Pitch**—This will alter the pitch of a single REX slice.

- **Level**—This will alter the amplitude of a single REX slice.

- **Reverse**—This will assign a reverse playback effect to a single REX slice.

The Panel Parameters. Nurse Rex offers a wide assortment of real-time parameters to twist up and turn your REX file around, which can produce some very eclectic and creative results (see Figure 8.25). Note that these parameters are global, meaning they affect the entire REX file.

Figure 8.25 The Panel Parameters are used to globally affect the loaded REX file.

- **Envelope Type**—This toggles between a Gate mode, which is set by the Decay parameters, or the ADSR (Attack/Decay/Sustain/Release) mode.

- **Attack**—This is used to set the Attack when the ADSR mode is selected. The Attack sensitivity can be modulated by using the included Velocity parameter.

- **Decay**—This is used to set the Decay when the ADSR mode is selected. The Attack sensitivity can be modulated by using the included Velocity parameter or the Mod parameter, which is linked to the Modulation Wheel.

- **Sustain**—This is used to set the Sustain when the ADSR mode is selected.

- **Release**—This is used to set the Attack when the ADSR mode is selected. The Attack sensitivity can be modulated by using the included Velocity parameter or the Mod parameter, which is linked to the Modulation Wheel.

- **Pitch**—This is used to alter the pitch of the REX file and can be modulated by using the included Velocity parameter.

■ **Level**—This is used to alter the level of the REX file and can be modulated by using the included Velocity parameter.

Multiple Hit Types   Each Kong pad can be assigned to a different Hit Type when using Nurse Rex. For example, pad one can be set to a Loop Trig Hit Type, while pads two and three can be set to Slice Trig, and finally pad four can be set as a Stop. Don't be afraid to jump in and try different combinations of Hit Types with Nurse Rex. It may be just what your music needs to give it that creative edge you've been looking for.

Physical Bass, Snare, and Tom Tom Modules

The Physical Bass, Snare, and Tom Tom modules are drum sounds that are based on the principles of physical modeling, which is a form of programming that uses sets of equations to emulate the inner workings of an instrument. In the case of these drum modules, physical modeling is used to emulate the characteristics of the acoustic kick, snare, and tom tom drums (see Figure 8.26). Before you begin this section, select pad one, and then change the drum module to the bass, snare, or tom modules.

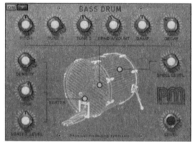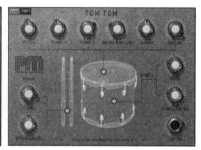

Figure 8.26 The Physical Bass, Snare, and Tom Tom modules use physical modeling to emulate the sound and feel of acoustic kick, snare, and tom tom drums.

There are several shared parameters between these modules, which I'll explore throughout the next couple of sections. For example, there is a Level parameter on each of the drum modules, and it performs the same task, which is to adjust the amplitude of the module and send it to the FX section, which you'll read about later in the chapter.

The Drum Head and Shell Parameters. Each of the drum modules shares similar parameters, such as the drum head and shell parameters, which affect the overall tone characteristics of the drums.

■ **Pitch**—This knob sets the pitch for all of the drum modules.

■ **Tune 1 and Tune 2**—Available on the Bass and Tom Tom modules, these knobs alter the harmonics of the drum, which is similar to adjusting the screws on the sides of an acoustic drum.

- **Tune**—Available on the Snare module, this knob adjusts the tension of the snare head.

- **Bend**—Available on the Bass and Tom modules, this knob creates the natural pitch bend of an acoustic drum when struck hard.

- **Damp**—This knob sets the damping for all the drum modules.

- **Decay**—This knob sets the decay for all the drum modules.

- **Shell Level**—Available on the Bass and Tom Tom modules, this knob is used to introduce the sound of the shell into the mix.

- **Shell Size**—Available on the Tom Tom module, this adjusts the length of the shell. Think of it like those drum kits you've seen with the very long and deep toms.

- **Edge Tune**—Available on the Snare module, this parameter sets the tuning of the head. Note that this only works when Hit Type 4 is selected.

- **Snare Tension**—Available on the Snare module, this parameter adjusts the tension of the snare, which is located on the bottom of an actual snare drum.

- **Bottom Pitch**—Available on the Snare module, this parameter adjusts the bottom head of the snare drum.

- **Bottom Mix**—Available on the Snare module, this parameter adjusts the amount of the bottom head you'll hear in the mix.

The Beater and Stick Parameters. The Beater and Stick Parameters are used to emulate the beater sound of the kick drum and the stick sound of the snare and toms. These parameters have a very pronounced effect and there are several variations.

- **Density**—Available on the Bass drum, this adjusts the "make" of the beater. For example, a rubber beater produces a much different sound than a traditional fabric style beater.

- **Tone**—Available on the Bass and Tom Tom modules, this knob adjusts the tone.

- **Beater Level**—Available on the Bass module, this knob adjusts the level of the beater hit in the mix.

- **Stick Level**—Available on the Snare and Tom Tom modules, this knob adjusts the level of the stick hit in the mix.

The Synth Bass, Snare, Tom Tom, and Hi-Hat

The Synth Bass, Snare, and Tom Tom modules are the complete opposite of their physical counterparts (see Figure 8.27). These particular modules are used to emulate the electronic characteristics of the analog drum machines of the 80s, such as the TR808 and TR909.

Figure 8.27 The Synth Bass, Snare, and Tom Tom modules make your drum patterns sound their most analog.

Drum Parameters. As with the physical modules, the synth drum modules share many common parameters, such as the Level parameter. Let's explore these further.

- **Pitch**—This parameter adjusts the pitch of the drum.

- **Tone**—Available on the Bass Drum, this parameter adjusts the tone of the drum.

- **Attack**—Available on the Bass Drum, this parameter adjusts the attack of the kick sound.

- **Decay**—This parameter adjusts the decay time of all the drum modules. In addition, the parameter also adjusts the Noise Decay on the Bass, Snare, and Toms, as well as the Harmonic Decay on the Snare.

- **Harmonic Balance**—Available on the Snare, this parameter adjusts the mix between the bass tone and the harmonic tone.

- **Harmonic Frequency**—Available on the Snare, this adjusts the harmonic frequency.

- **Harmonic Decay**—Available on the Snare, this parameter adjusts the decay of the harmonic tone.

- **Click Frequency**—Available on the Bass, this adjusts the click frequency.

- **Click Resonance**—Available on the Bass, this adjusts the resonance of the click sound.

- **Click Level**—Available on the Bass, this adjusts the click volume.

- **Bend Amount**—Available on the Bass and Tom Tom, this parameter sets the amount of pitch bend by assigning an upper pitch.

- **Bend Time**—Available on the Bass and Tom Tom, this parameter adjusts the time it takes from the pitch set by the Bend Amount to reach the original pitch.

- **Noise Tone**—Available on the Snare and Tom Tom, this parameter sets the tone of the noise element in the sound.

- **Noise Decay**—Available on the Snare and Tom Tom, this parameter sets the decay of the noise element in the sound.

- **Noise Mix**—Available on the Snare and Tom Tom, this parameter sets the level of the noise element in the sound.

The Synth Hi-Hat. The final drum module discussed here is the Synth Hi-Hat module (see Figure 8.28). The Synth Hi-hat module emulates the classic sounds and textures of the 808 and 909 hi-hats.

Figure 8.28 Like the Bass, Snare, and Tom Toms, the Synth Hi-hat sounds and feels like the retro hi-hat sounds found on classic drum machines.

- **Pitch**—This knob sets the pitch of the hat sound.

- **Decay**—This knob sets the decay of the hat.

- **Level**—This knob adjusts the level of the hat.

- **Click**—This knob adjusts the level of the click in the hat sound.

- **Tone**—This knob adjusts the overall tone of the hat.

- **Ring**—This knob is used to introduce a resonance into the hat sound, in order to create a metallic ring tone.

Kong Routing and FX

In addition to all of the groovy sounds and editing parameters, Kong also sports a complex, yet versatile array of routing parameters to help make your drums sound their best. From here, you can specify how to route your drum module through the Insert FX, Bus FX, and Master FX.

Looking at Figure 8.29, you can see that by default the drum modules of Kong are routed to two separate Insert FX. Just as a reminder, insert effect process the entire dry signal that's fed to it. That processed signal is fed to the Master FX/Output. Additionally, the Kong supports a single Bus FX that is fed dry signal by using the Bus FX knob on the Drum Control panel. This will give you a very solid mix of drums and effects.

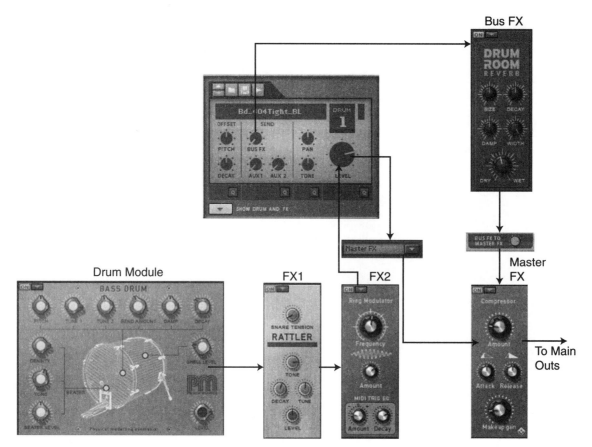

Figure 8.29 The routing of Kong offers a lot of potentially creative and interesting textures to add into your Reason songs.

Figure 8.30 The Drum Output menu enables you to route your drum sounds to the Master FX, Bus FX, or to any of Kong's 16 outputs.

Kong also offers bonus routing possibilities by making use of the Drum Output pop-up menu at the bottom of the FX1/2 Slots (see Figure 8.30).

Last point of interest here is that you can specify how much processed signal is sent from the Bus FX slot to the Master FX slot by using the "Bus FX To Master FX" knob at the bottom right of the Kong interface.

Kong Effects

Now that you have a better understanding of the routing potential of Kong, let's have a look at the real-time effects that come with Kong. As stated earlier in this section, there are two insert slots and bus slot. Additionally, there's also a master effect slot, which is used as an insert to process the entire signal when routed to the master outputs.

The first type of effects to discuss is the generator effects. These are used to enhance the Kong pads by introducing additional tones and textures to the samples and synth percussion sounds generated by Kong. They can be used as insert effects on both insert slots.

Noise Generator. The noise generator is used to introduce a digital noise tone into your Kong pads (see Figure 8.31). This is a fantastic effect for adding more crispness to your hi-hat or snare sounds.

Figure 8.31 The Noise Generator is a fantastic real-time effect that can be used to add some digital sizzle to your drum sounds.

The Noise Generator has the following parameters:

- **Hit Type**—The Noise Generator can be assigned to any or all Hit Types on a Kong pad. For example, if you were to load up a Physical Model Snare module, you could use this parameter to assign a noise to any of the four Hit Types associated with that module.

- **Pitch**—This parameter sets the pitch of the noise.

- **Attack**—This parameter alters the attack time of the noise.

- **Decay**—This parameter alters the decay of the noise.

- **Reso**—This parameter assigns the resonance to the noise.

- **Sweep**—This parameter assigns the start pitch of the noise sweep.

- **Click**—This parameter sets the noise's click level.

- **Level**—This parameters sets the level of the generator.

Tone Generator. The Tone Generator is an effects module that generates a synth tone via an oscillator, which is then mixed with the sound generated by a Kong pad (see Figure 8.32).

Figure 8.32   The Tone Generator introduces a tone to your Kong sounds, which can help create some really cool synthesis effects on top of samples or loops.

The Tone Generator has the following parameters:

- **Hit Type**—The Tone Generator can be assigned to any or all Hit Types on a Kong pad.

- **Pitch**—This parameter sets the pitch of the tone.

- **Attack**—This parameter alters the attack of the tone.

- **Decay**—This parameter alters the decay of the tone.

- **Bend Decay**—This parameter alters the decay of the pitch bend effect.

- **Bend**—This parameter assigns the pitch of the generated tone.

- **Shape**—This parameter alters the shape or tone of the generator.

- **Level**—This parameter sets the level of the generator.

The next effects covered are the FX modules, which are similar to the standard real-time themed effects you'll find all over the Reason interface.

Drum Room Reverb. The Drum Room Reverb is an effect that creates a reverberation, or echo to any audio that's fed through it (see Figure 8.33). Think of it as the ambience effect that works great with just about any drum sound, especially snares and tom toms.

The Drum Room Reverb includes the following parameters:

- **Size**—This parameter adjusts the size of the room.

- **Decay**—This parameter adjusts the decay of the reverb effect, which is also known as the *tail*.

Figure 8.33 The Drum Room Reverb effect creates a reverberation effect that's perfect for adding ambience to your drums and loops.

- **Damp**—This parameter adjusts the dampening of the high frequencies within the reverb.

- **Width**—This parameters adjusts the width of the reverb's stereo field.

- **Dry/Wet**—This adjusts the ratio between the dry unprocessed sound and the wet processed sound.

Transient Shaper. The Transient Shaper bears a lot of similarities to a compressor effect (see Figure 8.34). However, unlike a traditional compressor, this effect just alters the attack of the audio that it's processing, which is called the *transient*.

Figure 8.34 The Transient Shaper effect is used to alter the attack of your Kong pads, which are known as the transients.

The Transient Shaper includes the following parameters:

- **Attack**—This parameter alters the amplitude of the attack on the transient.

- **Decay**—This parameter alters the decay time of the effect.

- **Amount**—This parameter determines the level of the effect.

Compressor. The Compressor is an effect that is typically used to level out audio signals that are too loud in the mix and are in danger of digital clipping (see Figure 8.35). This can also be used to make your drum sounds stand out in the mix by increasing the perceived loudness without actually increasing the amplitude of the sound.

Figure 8.35 Have a drum sound with a volume issue? The Compressor can help level it out and give it a smooth sound.

The Compressor has the following parameters:

■ **Amount**—This parameter sets the sensitivity of the compressor.

■ **Attack**—This parameter is used to alter the attack of the compression effect.

■ **Release**—This parameter sets the release of the compression effect.

■ **Make Up Gain**—This parameter compensates for any volume lost by the compression effect.

Filter. The Filter is used to create a tonal sweeping effect on your Kong pads (see Figure 8.36). It's a very commonly heard, yet effective sound necessary with electronic music.

Figure 8.36 The Filter creates a sweeping effect to your drum sounds. Try putting it through a drum loop to really hear the effect.

The Filter has the following parameters:

- **Frequency**—This parameter assigns the cutoff frequency.

- **Resonance**—This parameter assigns the volume applied to the frequencies around the cutoff.

- **Filter Type**—This changes the filter type. You can choose between Low Pass (low frequencies pass through the filter), Band Pass (mid frequencies pass through), or High Pass (high frequencies).

- **MIDI Trig Amount**—This parameter determines the amount that a MIDI note will trigger the filter effect.

- **MIDI Trig Decay**—This parameter sets the decay time of the MIDI controlled envelope.

Parametric EQ. The Parametric EQ is an effect that is used to alter the equalization, or tonal qualities of the signal fed through it (see Figure 8.37). It's very similar to the EQs found on reMix.

Figure 8.37 The Parametric EQ functions just like the Tone knobs on your home stereo. It's used to enhance the bass, treble, and every frequency in between.

The Parametric EQ has the following parameters:

- **Frequency**—This parameter assigns the center frequency that will be altered.

- **Gain**—This parameter determines the gain of the center frequency.

- **Q**—This parameter sets the bandwidth around the frequency. From here, you can create a nice, round EQ curve, or a very narrow and nasal sounding curve.

Ring Modulator. The Ring Modulator is one of the more unique type effects, as it creates a very pronounced and distinctive sound that makes the hairs on the back of your neck stand up (see Figure 8.38). Basically, a ring modulator takes the input of your audio and multiplies it with another signal called a sine wave. This produces a very metallic tone that's perfect for special percussion effects.

Figure 8.38 The Ring Modulator is going to be your go-to effect for creating a unique, ringing, metallic effect. Try it on a snare or hi-hat.

The Ring Modulator has the following parameters:

- **Frequency**—This parameter assigns the frequency of the sine wave.

- **Amount**—This parameter assigns the amount of sine wave applied to the original signal.

- **MIDI Trig Amount**—This parameter determines the amount that a MIDI note will trigger the ring mod effect.

- **MIDI Trig Decay**—This parameter sets the decay time of the MIDI controlled envelope.

Rattler. The Rattler (see Figure 8.39) is another unique effect, in that it emulates the character of the snare and applies it to other drum sounds. Imagine having a snare on your tom toms or kick drum. The Rattler will get the job done.

Figure 8.39 The Rattler is used to place a snare onto your Kong sounds that don't have a snare on them, such as a tom tom or cymbal.

The Rattler includes the following parameters:

- **Snare Tension**—This parameter assigns the tension of the snare.

- **Tone**—This parameter alters the tone of the snare effect.

- **Decay**—This parameter is used to assign the decay to the ring of the snare.

- **Tune**—This parameter tunes the snare.

- **Level**—This parameter assigns the volume of the overall effect.

Tape Echo. The Tape Echo emulates the characteristics of a classic type of delay that was generated via infinite loops of tape (see Figure 8.40). This created a very distinct sound, and that sound is now a part of Kong.

Figure 8.40 The Tape Echo is quite unlike a digital delay, in that it emulates the feel and sound of the classic delay machines that were tape driven.

The Tape Echo includes the following parameters:

- **Time**—This knob sets the amount of time between echoes.

- **Feedback**—This knob assigns a number of echoes.

- **Wobble**—This knob emulates the wobbling of the tape speed. This means that the frequency of each echo will be tonally unique.

- **Frequency/Resonance**—These knobs set the cutoff frequency and resonance of the tape echoes. Think of these knobs as a filter for the delay.

- **Dry/Wet**—This adjusts the ratio between the dry unprocessed sound and the wet processed sound.

Overdrive/Resonator. The Overdrive/Resonator is a dual effect of sorts (see Figure 8.41), as it includes an overdrive/digital distortion effect and a resonator. Put these both together and you've got a mean growling snare or kick.

The Overdrive/Resonator includes the following parameters:

- **Drive**—This parameter assigns the amount of distortion.

- **Resonance**—This parameter assigns the amount of resonance.

Figure 8.41 The Overdrive/Resonator is the right effect to give your Kong sounds a gritty, snarling edge by combining digital distortion and resonance.

- **Size**—This parameter determines the size of the resonance chamber.

- **Model**—This button toggles between the different resonance bodies.

For More Info on Effects If you want to know more about the effects of Reason, be sure to jump to Chapter 17, "Effects—Close Up," where you'll get a close up look at every real-time effect device.

Kong Connections

Press the Tab key to swing the Device Rack around and you'll now see all of the Kong CV and audio connections available (see Figure 8.42).

Audio Outputs

Kong includes three different kinds of audio outputs: Main, Aux, and External.

- **Main Outputs**—Located to the far right of the interface are the Main Outputs. Kong supplied a pair of master outputs, as well as an individual output for every Kong pad. That means that you have a virtually endless supply of routing possibilities.

- **Aux Outputs**—These outputs are routed by default to the Chaining inputs of reMix and are used to integrate the aux effects of Reason with your Kong kit. For example, let's say you're using an instance of the RV7000 in your Reason song and you'd like to send the snare of your Kong kit to it. This is done by selecting the snare Kong pad and assigning a value to either the Aux 1 or Aux 2 knobs in the Drum Control panel. Note though that you need to have the RV7000 routed to Aux 1 or 2 on reMix.

- **External Outputs**—This pair of outputs is used to send audio that's routed into Kong to an external Reason device.

Figure 8.42   The back of the Kong interface offers a wide selection of CV and audio outs. There's even a couple of pairs of audio inputs to utilize Kong as an effect for other Reason devices.

Audio Inputs

In addition to the variety of audio outputs, Kong also supplies a couple of pairs of audio inputs. Both pairs are located at the bottom left and center on the rear panel of the Kong interface.

- **Audio Inputs**—These are the standard audio inputs for Kong. From here, you can route the outputs of other Reason devices and send them through the Bus FX and Master FX.

- **External Inputs**—These inputs are used in combination with the External Outputs.

Here's a quick example of how the inputs and outputs of Kong can be used. Looking at Figure 8.43, you can see that there is an instance of Kong, Dr. Octo Rex, and the Malström. You can also see the following connections:

1. The left output of Dr. Octo Rex is connected to the left audio input of Kong, which routes to Kong's Bus FX and Master FX.

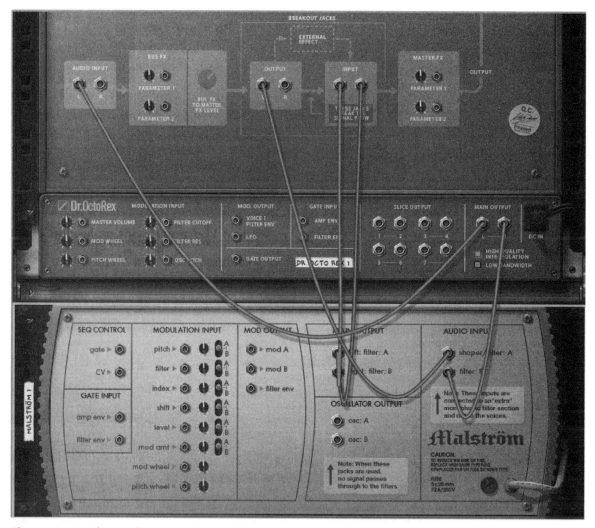

Figure 8.43 The audio inputs and outputs of Kong can be used in creative ways such as this setup, which has Dr. Octo Rex routed to both Kong and Malström.

2. The left external output of Kong is routed to the Shaper/Filter A input of the Malström. Activate these sections on the Malström interface and you can achieve some sonically wild results.

3. The right output of Dr. Octo Rex is routed to the Filter B input of Malström.

4. The Main outputs of Malström are routed to the External Inputs on Kong, which routes to Kong's Master FX.

CV Inputs/Outputs

Kong sports a wide variety of CV inputs and outputs, which are used to route Control Voltage information to and from Kong to any other Reason device. Let's begin with the Gate Inputs/Outputs.

Gate Inputs/Outputs. The Gate Inputs and Outputs are found on every Kong Pad and are used to trigger other Reason devices with the outputs and/or have other Reason devices trigger the individual pads. Try this quick exercise:

1. Create an instance of Redrum.

2. Write in a quick bass drum sequence.

3. Press the Tab key to view the back of the Reason Device Rack.

4. Connect the Gate Out of Redrum's Channel One and route it to the Gate In on any Kong pad.

5. Play the Redrum sequencer and you should now hear Redrum and Kong play the same sequence.

Modulation Inputs. Kong includes a number of CV inputs that are used to modulate its various parameters by routing the modulation output of any Reason device to it. For example, you could use the Modulator outputs of Malström and route it to Kong's Volume Modulation input.

Here are the available Kong Modulation Inputs:

■ **Volume**—Routing a CV connection to this input will modulate Kong's Volume.

■ **Pitch**—Routing a CV connection to this input will modulate Kong's Pitch Wheel.

■ **Mod Wheel**—Routing a CV connection to this input will modulate the Modulation Wheel.

■ **Bus Effects**—These CV inputs are used to modulate two specific parameters of loaded effects in the Bus EX slot of Kong, which are simply called Parameter 1 and Parameter 2. For example, if you have a Compressor effect loaded into the Bus FX slot, the Parameter 1 input is used to control the Attack parameter of the compressor and Parameter 2 input is used to control the Release.

■ **Master Effects**—These operate just like the Bus Effects, except they are routed to the Master FX slot on the Kong interface.

Sequencer Control. The final set of CV inputs is the Sequencer Control inputs. These inputs are used to route sequencer information from another Reason device with a sequencer, such as the Matrix or Thor, to the Kong. That way, you can run both devices together with the same rhythm. Just remember that the CV input of the sequencer control is used to trigger the pitch of Kong, whereas the Gate input of the sequencer control is used to trigger the note on/off and velocity of Kong.

As you have seen throughout this chapter, Kong is an amazing drum machine, capable of so much sonic goodness, yet has an incredibly easy-to-understand interface. Be sure to really dig into this Reason device and create your own Kong kits.

9 Dr. Octo Rex—Close Up

One of the more unique devices in the Reason Device Rack is the Dr. Octo Rex Loop Player (see Figure 9.1). Dr. Octo Rex is a RAM-based sample playback device based on the ReCycle! technology created by Propellerhead Software. Dr. Octo Rex can import specially prepared digital audio loops, called REX files, and play them back at just about any tempo.

Dr. Octo Rex can import the following file formats:

- **.rex**—A mono file format supported by the Mac platform.

- **.rcy**—A mono file format supported by the PC platform.

- **.rx2**—A stereo file format supported by both Mac and PC platforms.

- **.drex**—A patch format that stores several rx2 files within a single file.

There's a New Doctor in the House   For those of you long time users of Reason, you might have noticed that Dr:rex is no longer listed at one of the Reason devices. That's because Dr. Octo Rex has replaced Dr:rex. Thankfully, you'll find throughout this chapter that all of the Dr:rex features are found within Dr. Octo Rex. I'm sure that Dr:rex had a nice retirement party, though.

A New Reason to ReCycle!

Propellerhead Software began to make its mark in the audio industry in 1996 by releasing a sample-editing software product called ReCycle!. This program gave musicians the ability to import digital audio loops into their computers, slice them up, and then send these individual slices back to the sampler (see Figure 9.2). This gave musicians the ability to use an audio loop within varying tempos while not affecting the pitch. It was a real breakthrough because musicians could now use the same loops in different songs and styles and keep it all in the original pitch and tempo.

And just when musicians were starting to comprehend the concepts and possibilities that ReCycle! had to offer, Propellerhead again broke new ground in 1997 by introducing their own digital audio format, called REX. A REX file is a single audio file that

Figure 9.1 The Dr. Octo Rex Loop Player is based on Propellerhead's REX technology.

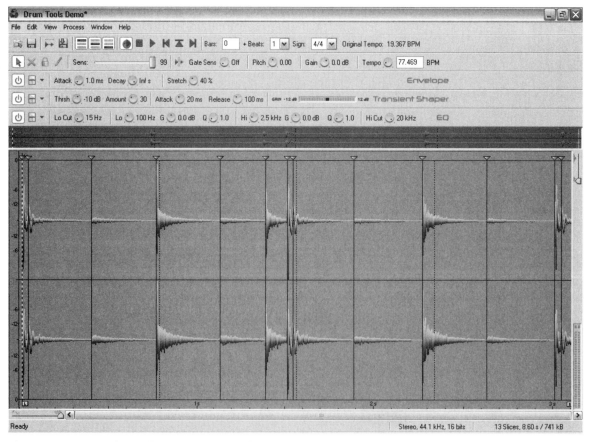

Figure 9.2 ReCycle! will breathe new life into your audio loops.

contains a number of smaller separate audio files, or *slices*. The REX file could then be imported into a digital audio/MIDI sequencing program, and the audio loop would instantly work at any tempo. Not only this, but if you were to change the tempo of your song, the REX files would instantly speed up or slow down to match that new tempo. It was just like the original concept of ReCycle!, but without the need for an external sampler.

REX files could be created within ReCycle! and became an adopted format for many digital audio programs, such as Cubase VST and Logic Audio. Since the introduction of the REX format, many companies have begun releasing new REX format titles and re-issuing older audio loop titles as well. At the time of this writing, there are literally thousands of audio loops available in the REX format.

Roll Yer Own   In Appendix A, "ReCycle! 2.1," you can learn how to create your own REX files from an audio loop.

In 2000, when Reason 1.0 was announced, it seemed only right that Propellerhead would incorporate its REX technology into this program because it's all about remixing and loops. With that, I give you the subject of this chapter, Dr. Octo Rex!

A Guided Tour of Dr. Octo Rex

Now that you have a basic idea of what Dr. Octo Rex is and the technology behind it, you can begin your tour of the Dr. Octo Rex interface. Create an instance of it, and then expand the Programmer so you can view the entire interface.

Getting Sound into Dr. Octo Rex

By default, Dr. Octo Rex loads eight loops automatically into its interface across eight different triggers or "slots," which are incredibly useful when you are trying to get to know this fantastic loop machine. If you'd like to hear the preloaded loop, press the Run button and Dr. Octo Rex will play and repeat the loop until you either press the Run button again, or just press the Stop button in the Transport panel. Additionally, you can preview any of the loaded loops by clicking on their corresponding slot numbers (1 through 8). However, you'll soon want to start trying new sounds and textures, so let's discuss how to load sounds into Dr. Octo Rex by loading a drex file.

In the middle of the Dr. Octo Rex interface is its file browser (see Figure 9.3). Start by clicking on the folder icon. This will bring up the Patch Browser so you can begin to audition and load sounds (see Figure 9.4).

Figure 9.3 Dr. Octo Rex's file browser is used to load REX loops into Dr. Octo Rex.

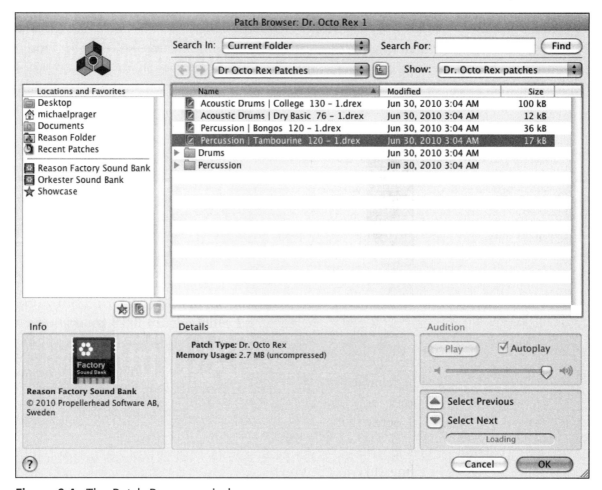

Figure 9.4 The Patch Browser window.

When the browser opens, you might not see any sound files to audition. If this is the case, click on the Reason Factory Sound Bank (on the left under Locations). Now you'll see four different folders:

- Dr. Octo Rex Patches

- Dr Rex Drum Loops

- Dr Rex Instrument Loops

- Dr Rex Percussion Loops

For this example, double-click on the Dr. Octo Rex Patches folder. From any of these folders, you can select a drex patch to import into your Dr. Octo Rex device. For example, you could open Drums > Pop > Acoustic Drums and then select the drex patch you want to import into Dr. Octo Rex style drum loop.

The Audition Tempo   The auditioning feature plays loops at the tempo your Reason song is set to.

Once you have selected your patch, click the Patch Browser's OK button or just double-click the patch file to load it into Dr. Octo Rex (see Figure 9.5). Notice also that the name of the REX file within the patch is now displayed in the Dr. Octo Rex Waveform display.

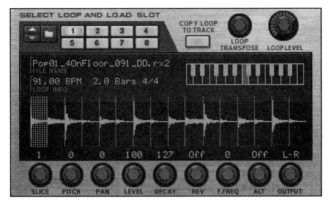

Figure 9.5 The REX file has now been loaded into Dr. Octo Rex.

Once a patch file is imported into Dr. Octo Rex, the slices that make up the REX loaded into file are mapped out over the C1 octave of your keyboard. This enables you to preview each slice of a loaded REX file by arming the sequencer track and playing any keys within the C1 octave of your keyboard (C1, C#1, D1, D#1, E, and so on).

You can also preview the slices of any of the other REX files within the drex file by first clicking on its corresponding slot number, and then clicking on the Notes to Slot button, which is the red LED located just to the left of each slot in the Dr. Octo Rex interface.

If you'd rather listen to the entire REX file play back, just click on the Run button, located at the top-right corner of the Dr. Octo Rex interface. This will play the selected REX file back indefinitely until you either press the Run button again, or you press Stop on the Reason sequencer.

While the REX file is playing back, you can switch between different slots in real-time. If you want to specify how quick Dr. Octo Rex changes between different selected slots, you can select one of three options on the far left side of the interface.

■ **Bar**—The REX file will change slots at the end of the nearest completed bar.

■ **Beat**—The REX file will change slots at the end of the nearest completed beat.

■ **1/16**—The REX file will change slots at the end of the nearest completed 16th note.

Selecting Different REX Files Within a Patch

As you'll come to find throughout this book, there's very little that Reason can't do when it comes to creative thinking and sound design. For example, let's say you load a drex patch and you like the REX files loaded onto all of the slots except for slot 8. It's very easy to select another REX file by simply clicking on the name of the REX file in slot 8 and selecting Open Browser from the pop-up menu (see Figure 9.6).

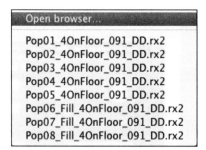

Figure 9.6 Selecting new REX files for your patches is as easy as clicking on the name of the loaded REX file and opening the Patch Browser to find another REX file.

At this point, the Patch Browser will open, and you can use this to locate, preview, and import a new REX file into slot 8.

Polyphony

Towards the bottom of the Dr. Octo Rex programmer is the Polyphony parameter (see Figure 9.7), which determines the number of REX slices your MIDI keyboard can play simultaneously. Dr. Octo Rex contains a large polyphony potential that ranges from 1 to 99. You can change the polyphony by clicking on the increase/decrease controls to the right of the display or by clicking and dragging within the display itself.

Figure 9.7 The Polyphony control assigns the number of voices that can be played simultaneously.

Adjusting the polyphony allows for some very interesting loop-editing possibilities. Because each slice in a REX file is assigned to a key on your MIDI keyboard, you can re-sequence loops using the REX Lane Editor in the Reason sequencer. This will give you a chance to reinterpret the loop by introducing a new groove and feel that includes playing different voices simultaneously. You'll learn more about this later.

The Synth Parameters

In the middle of the Dr. Octo Rex interface is the main display, where REX loops can be edited with ease. Here you can accomplish everything from transposition to pitching and panning each slice within a loaded REX file.

Just to review, a REX file contains a number of different slices of audio, which are compiled and seen as one file. The sliced nature of the REX files makes them ideal for easy editing.

The Waveform Display

In the Dr. Octo Rex Waveform display (see Figure 9.8), you can see the REX file split in a slice-by-slice view along with the original tempo of the loop. Above the waveform and to the right, Dr. Octo Rex displays the default pitch of the REX file. The default pitch for any REX file loaded into Dr. Octo Rex is C. Every aspect of the REX file can be edited, with the help of the parameter knobs above and below the Waveform display. Let's take a look at them.

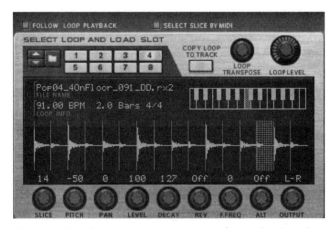

Figure 9.8   The Dr. Octo Rex Waveform display shows a graphical representation of the loaded REX file.

Located just above the Waveform display are a few of Dr. Octo Rex's Play parameters (see Figure 9.9).

Figure 9.9   These play parameters are used to preview your REX file and alter its pitch.

- **Select Slice by MIDI**—This button allows you to select each REX slice with a MIDI controller, such as a keyboard or drum machine. If you activate this button and press Play, you'll see the slice selector move across the loop from left to right in accordance with the MIDI note that is being played. Above this is the Note On indicator light, which will let you know when Dr. Octo Rex receives any kind of MIDI signal, whether from a controller or a keyboard.

- **Follow Loop Playback**—When selected, Dr. Octo Rex will display the currently triggered REX file in the Waveform display. This will change as a new REX file from a different slot is selected.

- **Copy Loop To Track**—This button sends the MIDI notes that are assigned to each slice of a selected REX file to the Dr. Octo Rex's sequencer track. If you select the Dr. Octo Rex sequencer track and click on the Switch to Edit Mode button, you will see each of these MIDI notes displayed in the REX Lane Editor.

- **Loop Transpose**—This knob will alter the pitch of the entire REX file. The range of this parameter is +/− 12 semitones.

> **Turn It Off**   After you have used the Copy Loop to Track button to send the REX slices to the Reason sequencer, you might hear a strange flange or phaser sound as you play your song back. This is because while the Reason sequencer is playing your REX file back from the sequencer track, it is also playing the REX file back from the Dr. Octo Rex interface. This is because the "Enable Loop Playback" parameter is activated. This parameter is located just above the Run button. Stop the sequencer, deactivate this parameter, and press Play again, and your REX file should now sound just fine.

Below the Waveform display, you'll find the following parameters to edit the REX file (see Figure 9.10).

Figure 9.10 Below the Waveform display are the available parameters to alter the entire REX file and individual slices of the REX file.

- **Slice**—This knob allows you to select each slice in the Waveform view by clicking and dragging the mouse up or down.

- **Pitch**—The Pitch knob transposes each slice within a REX file. Each slice can be adjusted up or down, giving you a possible pitch range of eight octaves. This is great for creating some interesting rhythmic ideas or mapping the pitches in a chromatic effect.

- **Pan**—The Pan knob adjusts the stereo position for any slice within the REX file. For example, you can set slice number 1 to −64, or hard left, while setting slice number 3 to 63, or hard right. This can create a very cool stereophonic effect, especially when you combine it with the pitch knob.

- **Level**—This knob changes the volume of an individual slice in a REX file. By default, each slice is set to 100, which is moderately loud. This allows for some very interesting dynamic changes that can affect the overall feel of the REX file when used creatively.

- **Decay**—The Decay knob adjusts the length of each slice in a REX file. By default, each slice is set to 127, which is the maximum length. When adjusted, each slice can be shortened to create a "gate" effect of sorts.

- **Reverse**—Using this knob will create a reverse effect on an individual slice within a REX file. This is really cool for drum samples in particular.

- **Filter Frequency**—This knob assigns a specific amount of the cutoff frequency of the Filter Section to a selected slice within a REX file. The Filter Section is covered later in this chapter.

- **Alt**—This knob is used to create a natural feel to the slices of your loaded REX files. This is accomplished by assigning individual slices of a REX file to one of four groups. These groups then randomize once the REX file has been copied to the Dr. Octo Rex sequencer track. For example, let's say you have a REX file with four different snare slices within it. You can use this knob to assign all of the snare slices to Alt Group 1. When the REX file is then copied to the Dr. Octo Rex sequencer track, the snare slices will randomize.

- **Output**—This knob allows you to assign the individual slices of a REX file to one of five pairs of outputs on the back of the Dr. Octo Rex interface.

Slice Edit Mode   One of my personal favorite new features of Reason 5 is the Slice Edit Mode, which is in the lower middle row of buttons in the Dr. Octo Rex programmer (see Figure 9.11). When selected, you can edit the slices of a loaded REX file by making use of a Pencil tool. Select any of the slice editing parameters by clicking on its name in the Waveform display and you can edit the individual slices. This is a powerful feature, because it makes it possible to simply draw in your edits, rather than use the knobs of the individual slice parameters, which can be a little cumbersome at times.

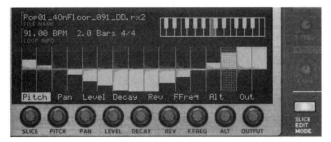

Figure 9.11 The Slice Edit Mode makes editing the slices of a REX file so simple by allowing you to use a pencil tool to edit the slices instead of the knobs.

The Oscillator Pitch Section

The Oscillator Pitch section can adjust the overall pitch of the REX as well as assign a selected amount to the Dr. Octo Rex Filter Envelope (see Figure 9.12).

Figure 9.12 The Oscillator Pitch Section can create some wild filter effects to your loaded REX files, as well as affect the overall pitch.

- **ENV. A**— The Env Amount knob is used to assign a determined amount of the Dr. Octo Rex oscillator over to the Filter Envelope. This will produce a pitch-shifting effect based on the amount of filter applied to the oscillator.

- **OCT**—The OCT knob will transpose the entire REX file up or down an octave at a time and has an eight-octave range.

- **FINE**—The Fine knob will adjust the overall pitch of the REX file in *cents*, which are hundredths of a semitone. With a range of +/– 50 cents, this is for making extremely minor adjustments to the overall pitch.

Global Transpose At the lower far right section of the main panel of the Dr. Octo Rex interface is the Global Transpose parameter. This will affect the overall pitch of all the REX files loaded within an instance of Dr. Octo Rex. It has a range of +/− one full octave.

The Filter Section

To the right of the Waveform display lies Dr. Octo Rex's Filter section (see Figure 9.13). By shaping the overall tone of the REX file, you can generate incredible filter sweeps that hurt the ears and shatter speakers. The filter can then be modified with an envelope and finally be assigned to the Modulation Wheel for dynamic control. Now let's have a look at the filter.

Figure 9.13 The Dr. Octo Rex Filter section is used to shape the character of the REX file.

Whenever a Dr. Octo Rex is loaded into the Reason Device Rack, the filter is already activated. It can be turned off and on by simply clicking on the Filter power button located at the top of the Filter section.

Once the filter is activated, you can select one of five filter modes by clicking on the individual names or simply by clicking on the Mode button:

- **Notch**—This filter can be thought of as the opposite of a Band Pass filter. It will reject the mid-frequencies while allowing the high frequencies and low frequencies to pass through. Although not the most dramatic filter effect, it still has a place in the mix for making minor changes to a sample.

- **HP 12**—This will filter out the low frequencies while letting the high frequencies pass through. It has a roll-off curve of 12 decibels per octave.

- **BP 12**—This filters out both the high and low frequencies, leaving the mid-frequencies alone to be toyed with. With a roll-off curve of 12 decibels per octave, the BP 12 can be used effectively on instrument loops, such as a guitar loop or possibly hi-hat heavy percussion loops.

- **LP 12**—This filter allows low frequencies to pass through, whereas high frequencies are filtered out. It is similar to the 24dB low pass (introduced next), but the roll-off curve is not as strong because it has a range of only 12 decibels per octave. This makes the LP 12 a perfect solution for creating a filter sweep that is low but not low enough to blow up your speakers.

- **LP 24**—Like the LP 12, this filter allows low frequencies to pass through, while filtering out high frequencies. To top it off, this low pass filter has an intense roll-off curve (approximately 24 decibels per octave), which produces a greater emphasis on the low frequencies.

A filter typically has two controls: *cutoff frequency* and *resonance*. The cutoff frequency (or *filter frequency* or *cutoff filter*, as it is also called) specifies where the filter will function within the frequency spectrum. It is a popular parameter used to create the "sweeping" effect that we hear so often in electronic music. When the frequency is used to alter a filter, it opens and closes the filter within a specific frequency range. For example, if the cutoff frequency is set to the highest position possible and is in LP 12 mode, the entire frequency spectrum will pass through. Likewise, if the cutoff is set to a lower position and the cutoff frequency is set in the LP 12 mode, say between the middle and bottom, the resulting sound will contain a majority of low-end signal because only the lower end of the frequency spectrum can pass through.

Resonance on the other hand is a parameter that modifies the filter's sound. It is used to emphasize different frequencies around the cutoff slider. When used within different positions, the resonance slider can filter out different frequencies or create fantastic "bell tones." For example, if the cutoff slider is set to the maximum potential and the resonance is set to the minimum potential, the resulting sound will be extremely treble heavy with minimal bass. However, if the resonance slider is in the middle position, the bass will be filtered out even more. If the resonance is set to its highest potential while the cutoff is set to its lowest potential and the filter is in LP 12 mode, the resulting signal will be extremely bass heavy. As the cutoff filter moves up, the bass frequencies will be dynamically enhanced by the resonance, and the resulting sound will have the neighbors pounding at your door immediately afterwards.

Watch Your Levels   As previously stated, make sure to keep an eye on the Audio Out Clip indicator, which is at the bottom left of the Transport panel, especially when you start fiddling with the filters found on just about every synth and sound module in Reason. Not only can you distort your signal, but you also run the risk of damaging your speakers and, more importantly, your ears.

To the right of the Filter modes is the Filter Envelope (see Figure 9.14). An envelope is used to modify specific synth parameters, including pitch, volume, and filter frequencies. By using an envelope creatively, you can control how these parameters are modified over a specific amount of time. But before you get ahead of yourself, take a look at the essential controls of the Filter Envelope.

Figure 9.14 The Dr. Octo Rex Filter Envelope affects the overall impact of the filter.

- **Amount**—This slider assigns a specific amount of the filter section to the envelope. By default, the Amount slider is set to 0 and will not produce any noticeable changes as it is moved up and down. This will change drastically if adjustments are first made to the Filter section itself.

- **Attack**—When a sound's envelope is triggered, the Attack parameter determines the length of time before the envelope reaches its maximum value.

- **Decay**—Once the maximum value is reached, the Decay parameter determines the length of time until the value begins to drop.

- **Sustain**—After the value begins to drop, the Sustain determines the level at which the falling value rests.

■ **Release**—Once the value has been set at its rested value, the Release parameter determines how long it will take for the value to fade to 0 after the key has been released, or in this case, after audio has passed through the filter.

A Filter Exercise   The following is a filter exercise that should help you start a few ideas brewing. Before you begin, start a new Reason song and create an instance of reMix and Dr. Octo Rex.

1. Load a REX loop with a lot of kick drum in it. For example, choose something from the House folder. After loading the REX loop into Dr. Octo Rex, press the Run button so you can listen and edit at the same time.

2. Select the LP 12 Filter mode and adjust the Frequency Filter slider to a numeric value of 25 and the Resonance to about 75. This should produce a very low-end, bass-heavy sound.

3. Raise the Filter Envelope's Amount slider to about 50. This should start to change the timbre of the sound immediately.

4. Now try working with a different combination of Filter Envelope parameters. For example, to create a percussive loop, have the Attack, Decay, and Release set to 0. Then move the Sustain slider up and down until you reach a desired effect. Click on the Run button to stop playing the loop.

5. To make this loop appear in the Reason sequencer, click on the Copy Loop To Track button. The corresponding MIDI notes should appear in the Dr. Octo Rex track. Press Play in the Reason sequencer to hear your loop.

The LFO (Low Frequency Oscillator)

Directly beneath Dr. Octo Rex's filter you will find the LFO, or Low Frequency Oscillator (see Figure 9.15).

Figure 9.15   The Dr. Octo Rex Low Frequency Oscillator can be used to alter different Dr. Octo Rex parameters.

- An LFO is capable of generating waveforms with a low frequency, hence the name LFO.

- An LFO's purpose is to modulate a parameter, such as a filter or another oscillator. This means that the LFO itself is never actually heard, just its effect on other synth parameters.

In order to hear the effect of the LFO, you must first adjust the Amount knob, located to the right of the Rate knob. Once this parameter is turned up, you can start to explore the other functions of the LFO.

Keeping It in Sync. No "boy band" jokes, please. The LFO has the capability to modify the main oscillator in either free time or synchronized time that is determined by the master tempo of the Transport panel. To activate the synchronization, click on the Sync button, located directly above the Waveform selector (see Figure 9.16). This will sync the Dr. Octo Rex LFO with the Reason master tempo. At this point, you can follow it up by assigning both a waveform shape and a destination to the LFO.

Figure 9.16 Activating the Sync option will synchronize the LFO with the tempo of your Reason song. As shown here, when the Sync button is activated, the Rate knob adjusts the rate of the LFO in note length values.

Waveforms—Take Your Pick. There are six types of waveforms that can be applied to your LFO. They can be selected by clicking on them with the mouse or by using the WAVEF. button at the bottom of the waveform list.

Let's discuss the differences between these individual waveforms:

- **Triangle**—Creates a smooth up and down vibrato.

- **Inverted Sawtooth**—Creates a cycled ramp up effect.

- **Sawtooth**—Creates a cycled ramp down effect.

- **Square**—Makes abrupt changes between two values.

- **Random**—Creates a random stepped modulation. Also known as sample and hold.

- **Soft Random**—Exactly as the previous waveform, but with a smoother modulation curve.

Destination: Anywhere. Once an LFO waveform and rate/amount has been selected, it is time to choose which parameter will be modulated by the LFO. LFO modulation can be applied to three destinations. Again, you can click directly on each one or cycle through them by clicking the DEST button.

■ **Osc**—Sends the LFO modulation effect to the overall pitch of the REX loop. Depending on which waveform is selected and how much LFO is assigned to the oscillator, it can produce a very neat "up and down" effect.

■ **Filter**—Sends the LFO modulation to the filter section of Dr. Octo Rex. This can produce a tempo-based filter sweep effect if the Sync button is activated.

■ **Pan**—Sends the LFO modulation to the pan controls of Dr. Octo Rex. When synced, this will create a tempo-based stereophonic effect.

The Amp Envelope

It takes two basic actions to create an audible sound—the generation of the sound and its amplification. This chapter has spent a great deal of time focusing on the generation of sound in Dr. Octo Rex. The amplification aspect is covered by Dr. Octo Rex's Amp Envelope feature (see Figure 9.17).

Figure 9.17 The Dr. Octo Rex Amp Envelope is used to affect the overall amplitude of Dr. Octo Rex.

■ **Level**—This slider controls the volume of Dr. Octo Rex.

■ **Attack**—When a sound's envelope is triggered, the Attack parameter determines the length of time before the envelope reaches its maximum value.

■ **Decay**—Once the maximum value is reached, the Decay parameter determines the length of time that passes until the value begins to drop.

■ **Sustain**—After the value begins to drop, the Sustain determines the level the falling value rests at.

■ **Release**—Once the value has been set at its rested value, the Release parameter determines how long it will take the value to fade out after releasing the key.

The Velocity Section

The Velocity section (see Figure 9.18) allows you to assign certain filter and amplification parameters to be modified according to the velocity at which each note (or slice)

Figure 9.18 Different Dr. Octo Rex parameters can be modified by velocity.

is played. Remember, the term *velocity* refers to how hard the note is played on your keyboard. Whether you play it hard or soft, these assignable parameters will respond according to their settings.

If you are not using a controller keyboard, you can draw the velocity data in via the Reason sequencer.

- **F.Env**—When set to a positive value, different velocities control the Amount knob of the Filter Envelope. A negative value has the opposite effect.

- **F.Decay**—When set to a positive value, different velocities control the Decay parameter of the Filter Envelope. A negative value has the opposite effect.

- **Amp**—When set to a positive value, the velocity controls the amount of volume. A negative value has the opposite effect.

Pitch Bend and Modulation

The Pitch Bend and Modulation controls are located below and above the Velocity section (see Figure 9.19).

Figure 9.19 Pitch Bending and Modulation controls are just what any good synth needs.

Get It in Pitch. The Dr. Octo Rex Pitch Bend Range is similar to Pitch controls on hardware synths—it bends the pitch of the whole loop up or down. You can click on the up and down buttons, or just click and drag in the dialog box itself, to change the range. For kicks, try selecting 24, which is the equivalent of 24 semitones, or two octaves. Now press the Preview button. While the file is playing, use a keyboard controller with a pitch shifting wheel or just click and drag up or down on the Bend wheel to hear the pitch shifting at work.

Modulation. Modulation is the "secret sauce" or essential ingredient in any form of artistic electronic music. It can be used to effectively change the timbre of a signal. The common Modulation Wheel found on most typical synthesizers can be assigned to a number of different synth parameters. When assigned, the Modulation Wheel then makes modifications in real-time to the played note according to the selected parameter and its assigned value.

The Modulation Wheel has three parameters that can be assigned to it (see Figure 9.20).

Figure 9.20 Assign different parameters to your Modulation Wheel.

- **F.FREQ**—Assigned to the cutoff filter of the Dr. Octo Rex filter section. When a value is assigned to this knob, the cutoff filter's value decreases or increases as the Modulation Wheel is used.

- **F.RES**—Assigned to the resonance control of the filter section. Depending on where it is set, the resonance control increases or decreases while the Modulation Wheel is in use.

- **F.DECAY**—Assigned to the Decay slider of the Filter Envelope. Depending on where it is set, the envelope decay increases or decreases.

The whole point of electronic music is to experiment and deviate from the norm. The Modulation Wheel is a useful tool for accomplishing that goal.

Make It Punchy!   Here's a quick DIY tutorial on using the Modulation Wheel with the three parameters. Before beginning this exercise, start a new Reason song and create instances of reMix and Dr. Octo Rex.

1. In the Filter section by default, the filter mode should be set to LP 12 mode, which is fine for this exercise. Now set the Filter Frequency slider to about 25, and set the Resonance slider to 75.

2. Press the Run button to hear your REX file in action with the active filter.

3. In the Filter Envelope, set the Amount slider to 100%. Then set the Attack, Decay, Sustain, and Release to 0.

4. In the Modulation Wheel section, set the F.FREQ knob to 32, the F.RES knob to –32, and the F.DECAY to –64.

5. Now use the Modulation Wheel with your mouse or MIDI keyboard and notice how the filter opens up as it is activated. Also notice how the Decay amount increases.

Dr. Octo Rex Connections

Press the Tab key to swing the Device Rack around and you'll now see all of the Dr. Octo Rex CV and audio connections available (see Figure 9.21).

Figure 9.21 The back of the Dr. Octo Rex offers a wide selection of CV and audio outs, as well as audio quality parameters.

Audio Quality in Dr. Octo Rex

In the lower-right corner of the back panel are two parameters that affect the quality of your loops (see Figure 9.22).

Figure 9.22 These controls affect the audio quality of Dr. Octo Rex.

- **High-Quality Interpolation**—When activated, Dr. Octo Rex plays the REX file back with a more advanced interpolation algorithm, resulting in a higher-quality audio signal. The difference is most noticeable in loops containing a lot of high-frequency data, such as a hi-hat track. This enhanced audio quality does come at the price of a bit of extra work for your processor to do.

- **Low BW**—This stands for low bandwidth, and it removes some of the high end from the playback of a REX file in order to relieve the burden on your CPU. The difference is especially evident in loops with a lot of hi-hat or Latin percussion. If, on the other hand, your loops are mostly low-frequency data, or if they've been put through a Low Pass filter, you'll be less likely to hear the difference.

Audio Outputs

The rear panel of Dr. Octo Rex offers two types of audio outputs.

- **Main Outputs**—These are used as the main outputs of Dr. Octo Rex. All of the loaded REX files will be automatically routed to these outputs.

- **Slice Outputs**—These outputs are available for routing individual slices of loaded REX files within an instance of Dr. Octo Rex. This is done by making use of the Output parameter on the Waveform display editor on the front panel of the interface. Simply select the slice you want and assign it to one of four stereo outputs.

CV Outputs

There are three CV outputs available to you to use on the rear panel of the Dr. Octo Rex interface.

- **Filter Envelope**—This is a Modulation Output that sends modulation information from the first slice of a REX file played through the Filter Envelope to any modulation input on another Reason device. For example you could route this output to the Gate CV input of the ECF-42 filter. Every time the REX file plays back, the first slice will trigger the Gate parameter of the ECF-42.

- **LFO**—This is another Modulation Output that sends modulation information from the LFO of Dr. Octo Rex to the CV inputs of any other Reason device.

- **Gate Output**—This is an output that sends out a gate signal for every slice of a REX file.

Gate Inputs

There are two CV inputs that receive gate information from another Reason Device and can be used to trigger two different envelopes, the Filter Envelope and the Gate Envelope. In this case, you could have the Gate Output of a Redrum channel trigger the Filter Envelope or Gate Envelope as a sequence plays back. Or in another example, you could use the Curve CV output of an instance of the matrix to trigger either of these two envelopes.

Modulation Inputs

To the far left in the rear panel are all of the Modulation Inputs of Dr. Octo Rex. In this case however, you'll see that there are not only inputs, but there are also input knobs to the left that specify how intense or subtle the modulation effect will be.

- **Master Volume**—Routing a CV connection to this input will modulate the Master Volume of Dr. Octo Rex.

- **Mod Wheel**—Routing a CV connection to this input will modulate the Modulation Wheel. This can be edited even further by assigning any or all three of the modulation destinations on the front panel.

- **Pitch Wheel**—Routing a CV connection to this input will modulate the Pitch Wheel.

- **Filter Cutoff**—Routing a CV connection to this input will modulate the Cutoff Frequency parameter of the filter section.

- **Filter Resonance**—Routing a CV connection to this input will modulate the Resonance parameter of the filter section.

- **OSC Pitch**—Routing a CV connection to this input will modulate the pitch of the loaded REX file.

Creative Uses for Dr. Octo Rex with the Reason Sequencer

The key to enjoying a long, creative, and fruitful future with Dr. Octo Rex and Reason is to try different combinations and ideas. Remember, anything can be routed into anything within Reason. This section goes through a few tips and tricks to fire up the synapses and get the creative juices flowing.

Before you begin these exercises, make sure that you start a new Reason song and create instances of reMix and Dr. Octo Rex. Finish preparing yourself by locating a new REX file or a drex patch from the Reason Factory Sound Bank and loading it into Dr. Octo Rex.

Cut It Out!

Although many folks like a good predictable four-on-the-floor beat in dance music, it is a good idea to introduce some variations from time to time. One of those variations includes the deletion of different slices from a REX file in order to give it an entirely different feel.

Recall that a REX file contains two file formats in order to do its magic. The first format is a digital audio format, which you see in the Waveform view of Dr. Octo Rex as a series of slices. The other format is the corresponding MIDI notes that accompany each digital audio slice. When you press the Copy Loop To Track button on the Dr. Octo Rex interface, it copies the MIDI notes to its track on the sequencer. Once the MIDI tracks have been recorded, you can simply open the appropriate editor in the sequencer and remove a few of the MIDI notes so that the corresponding audio slices will not play back.

Start by clicking on the Switch to Edit Mode button on the Reason sequencer. Because this is a Dr. Octo Rex track, the sequencer will automatically know which editor to open, in this case the REX Lane Editor. At this point, you should see all of the MIDI notes lined up in zipper fashion (see Figure 9.23) as they move upwards diagonally from left to right. To the far left of the notes is a list of numeric names for each slice. Depending on the length of the loop, there can be up to 92 slices displayed here. Navigate your mouse to Slice 1 of the Slice list and notice that the Selector tool has now become a Speaker tool, which enables you to preview a slice by clicking on the slice name. You can also click and hold on the name of any slice in the list, and drag your mouse up and down to preview the slices one by one.

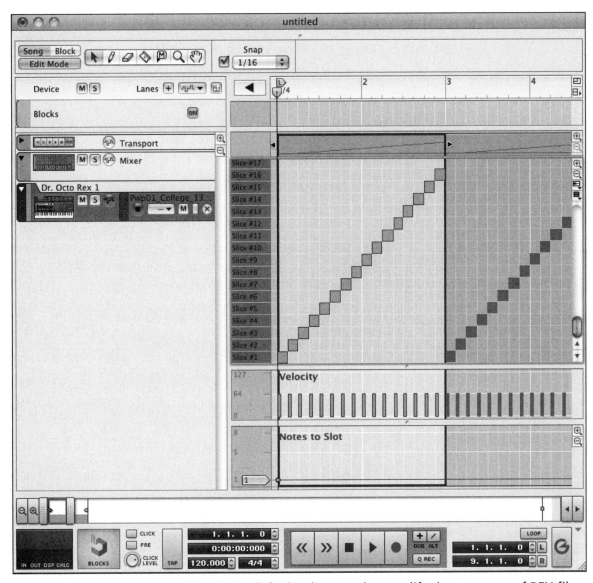

Figure 9.23 The REX Lane Editor is the default editor used to modify the sequence of REX files.

At this point, listen to each slice and decide which sound you want to remove from your loop. For example, you will probably want to keep the kick drum in order to keep a steady beat, but you can remove the snare or hi-hat sounds. Locate each of the sounds that you want to remove and then highlight them. Click Delete to get rid of them or use the Eraser tool. You can also highlight each note and use the Cut key command.

When you're finished, play the loop and see how you like the results. Getting a sound you like might take a lot of experimenting. Remember, you can always go back to the original loop by using the To Track button in Dr. Octo Rex or by using the unlimited levels of Undo.

Write Your Own Grooves

Aside from erasing MIDI notes, you can also rewrite your REX file groove in a couple of ways.

- Draw in a new sequence using the slices.

- Use a MIDI controller to record a new sequence.

By using the Pencil tool, you can redraw the MIDI notes that are connected to the different slices in your Dr. Octo Rex module. It's easier than it sounds, but it will take a little practice.

Before you begin this exercise, start a new Reason song and load instances of reMix and Dr. Octo Rex. Load a new REX file into Dr. Octo Rex, and click on the Copy Loop To Track button to send the MIDI notes of the REX file to the Reason sequencer. Then click on the Switch to Edit Mode button. You should now see the REX Lane Editor.

Select the Pencil tool from the toolbar and find the sounds that you want to draw notes for. Choose Edit > Select All to highlight each MIDI note in the editor. Now press the Delete key to erase all of the notes. As you can see in Figure 9.24, you have a clean palette to work with.

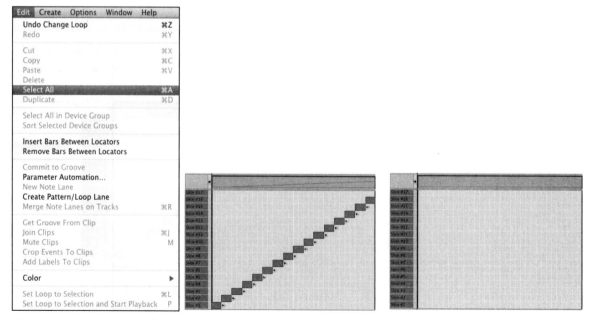

Figure 9.24 Erase all of your notes and start with a clean slate.

Next, create a two-bar loop so that you can work quickly. In the Transport panel, set your left locator to bar 1 and the right locator to bar 3. Make sure that the loop function is on by clicking on the Loop On/Off button in the Transport panel. Press the Stop button twice in the Transport panel to send the position indicator back to the beginning of the sequence. Press Play. You should now have a two-bar template to work with.

Next, choose the note value that you want to draw in. Because this is probably your first time doing this, I suggest using something simple like an 8th note. To do this, just select it from the Snap pull-down menu of the Sequencer toolbar (see Figure 9.25). Select the Pencil tool, and you can begin to draw in your MIDI notes.

| ▲ |
| 1/2 |
| 1/4 |
| 1/8 |
| 1/8T |
| ✓ 1/16 |
| 1/16T |
| 1/32 |
| 1/32T |
| 1/64 |

Figure 9.25 Select your note value using the Snap pull-down menu.

Start with Slice 1 and draw in an 8th note on each downbeat of bar 1 (1, 2, 3, and 4). (See Figure 9.26.) Press Play. You should now hear the first slice play four times. Now choose a few more slices and draw them in. As you can see in Figure 9.27, you can make a very simple yet effective rhythm with just four slices. Try it on your own with different note values and you'll be on your way to a groove.

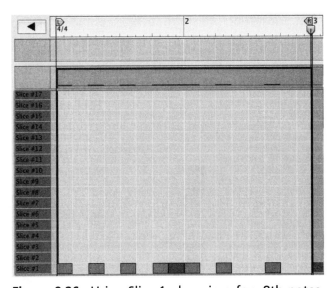

Figure 9.26 Using Slice 1, draw in a few 8th notes.

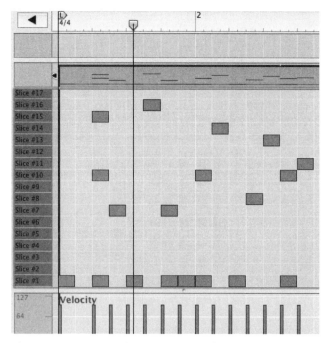

Figure 9.27 Draw in more note slices to create your new REX groove.

Old School Style   If you've sequenced in other programs, you might be accustomed to seeing a Key Edit window that looks more like Figure 9.28. As you learned in Chapter 5, "The Reason Sequencer—Close Up," Reason also has a Key Edit window, called the *Key lane*. You can draw in your new REX grooves using either the REX Lane Editor or the Key Lane Editor by selecting them in the upper-right corner of the sequencer (see Figure 9.29).

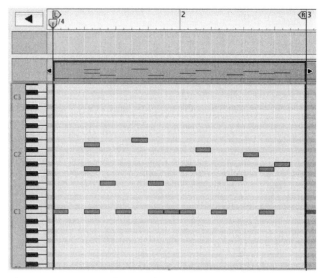

Figure 9.28 Any kind of recorded event can be viewed in any of Reason's editors. In this case, the REX slices are viewed in the Key Lane Editor.

Figure 9.29 Select the editor you want to work in. The left button is the Key Lane Editor, and the button on the right is the REX Lane Editor.

You can also input data into the Reason sequencer live (covered in Chapter 5). Just make sure that your Dr. Octo Rex track is activated and ready to accept live MIDI data. You do so by clicking on the MIDI In section of the track (see Figure 9.30). Using your MIDI keyboard, you can now play your Dr. Octo Rex in much the same way that you would play a drum machine with a MIDI keyboard. Any REX file loaded into Dr. Octo Rex is mapped across a MIDI keyboard starting with C1 on your keyboard because this is Slice 1 in Dr. Octo Rex.

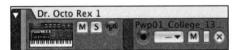

Figure 9.30 Arm your Dr. Octo Rex sequencer track so you can input MIDI data.

Just press Record. You can record a new performance of the REX file.

As you have seen in this chapter, the Dr. Octo Rex is a Reason device that takes looping to a whole new level. Next, you are going to delve into the first of Reason's three virtual synths—the Subtractor!

10 Subtractor—Close Up

The Subtractor Analog Synthesizer is Reason's workhorse synth (see Figure 10.1). Its usefulness is virtually boundless because it can be used for many textures and elements in electronic music, including leads, pads, FX, and percussion. It is also a great synth to help you create your own great-sounding patches.

This chapter explores and explains the inner workings of this wunderkind, covering such topics as:

- The basics of subtractive synthesis

- The Subtractor interface

- Programming your own patches

- Advanced programming with the Matrix Pattern sequencer

Subtractive Synthesis Explained

Subtractive synthesis is a form of analog synthesis, in that it relies on non-digital means to generate sound. Subtractive synthesis requires three active elements in order to generate sounds:

- **Oscillator**—The module that generates a continuous sound, determined by a waveform (more on this later).

- **Filter**—A device that alters the timbre of the oscillator's waveform by filtering out, or *subtracting*, various frequencies from the waveform (or combination of waveforms).

- **Amplifier**—The module that receives the altered signal from the filter and amplifies it.

Of course, this is a simplified explanation of a complex synthesis process. Understanding and using subtractive synthesis with hardware synthesizers was a constant challenge for those who desired the ambience and textures that were possible. In the old

Figure 10.1 The Subtractor Analog Synthesizer is a software emulation of a classic hardware analog synth.

days of synthesizers, a musician would have all of the required synth parts (oscillator, filter, and amplifier) in separate hardware devices encased in a modular apparatus, and the signal had to be physically "patched," or routed, from one hardware device to another. Following is an example:

1. You began with the oscillator by selecting a waveform.

2. That signal would then be routed to a filter to manipulate the frequencies of the oscillator.

3. That output of the manipulated signal could then be patched to an envelope that could adjust the Attack, Decay, Sustain, and Release of the filter.

4. The output of the envelope would then be routed to an amplifier with an envelope that would adjust the Attack, Decay, Sustain, and Release of the amplitude.

5. That signal would then be routed to a hardware mixer.

There are many other factors and modifications that can be introduced along the signal flow, all of which make analog synthesis a lot more fun to program than it sounds on paper. Additionally, you will find that Subtractor does a good job of taking away the mystery of patch programming.

Phys Ed 101   Those new to the world of virtual synths may be (quite understandably) a bit confused by the use of the term *analog synthesis* within the confines of the digital realm. Think about it. How can anything "analog," which is comprised of physical parts and patches, such as a Moog or Oberheim synthesizer, exist in the digital world, which relies on just 0s and 1s? The answer is physical modeling.

Physical modeling is a form of programming that uses sets of equations to emulate the inner workings of an instrument. In the case of subtractive synthesis, physical modeling is used to emulate the oscillators, filters, and amplifiers. The benefit of physical modeling is that the performance characteristics of the modeled instrument can be accurately reproduced. A good example of this is a guitar string that's picked too hard, causing the produced tone to play sharp. Physical modeling is a simple enough concept to understand, but a lot of thought must go into formulating and creating the equations, and then they must be programmed.

If you want to learn more about the inner workings of physical modeling, you can read all about it at this website:

http://en.wikipedia.org/wiki/Physical_modeling

A Guided Tour of Subtractor

It's time to take a look under the hood of this powerful synth. After the tour has finished, be sure to read on and learn how to create your own customized Subtractor patches and learn how to use the Subtractor with the Matrix Pattern sequencer.

The Oscillator Section

The Subtractor is one of the only virtual synths inside of Reason that actually generates sound by pure oscillation (see Figure 10.2). As you read further in this book, you will find that the term "oscillator" is associated with just about every one of the other virtual synths, but this is not precisely accurate. For example, the NN-19 and NN-XT generate sounds by using digital audio samples stored in RAM. Yet they both have an "oscillator" section in their interface. The same is true for the Malström, which is a virtual synth that generates sound by a completely unique form of synthesis called *graintable*, which you'll take a closer look at in the next chapter.

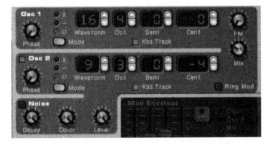

Figure 10.2 The Subtractor has two oscillators, which have 32 individual waveforms each.

An oscillator generates sounds by producing a combination of two characteristics:

- A selected waveform.

- An assigned pitch. This is done by pressing a key on your MIDI keyboard.

Oscillator 1

Oscillator 1 is the Subtractor's primary source of generating sound. You'll soon see that Osc 1 has plenty of choices to offer when it comes to variable waveforms. First, take a look at the main parameters of Osc 1.

- **Waveform Selector**—There are 32 waveforms available in each oscillator. A waveform is a "sound shape" that is generated by the oscillator, which determines the character of the sound.

- **Octave Selector**—This shifts the frequency of the waveform up and down in pitch by octaves. When an instance of a Subtractor is created, the octave is set to 4, but the actual range of this parameter is 0–9, providing a 10-octave range in total.

- **Semitone Selector**—This parameter shifts the frequency of the waveform up and down in 12 semitone steps, equaling one octave.

- **Cent Selector**—This parameter is also commonly known as *fine-tuning*. It is used to make very small tuning adjustments and has a range of one semitone.

- **Keyboard Tracking**—This button is used to change the pitch of the oscillator as it receives different MIDI notes. If this button is not activated, the pitch of the oscillator will remain constant, no matter what incoming note messages it receives. This is ideal for programming sounds that are not pitch specific, such as percussion sounds.

As mentioned, each oscillator has 32 individual waveforms, listed as follows. The first four are typically found on any hardware analog synth. The remaining 28 are unique and exclusive to the Subtractor.

- **Sawtooth**—The most complete of all waveforms because it contains all harmonics. The resulting sound is full and very bright in character.

- **Square**—This waveform contains odd numbered harmonics and has a very present hollow timbre to it.

- **Triangle**—This waveform contains a few harmonics and has a slight hollow sound to it.

- **Sine**—This is the simplest of all waveforms because it contains no harmonics (overtones). It is a very smooth and soft tone.

- **Waveform 5**—This waveform features the high harmonics. Not quite as bright as a Sawtooth wave.

- **Waveform 6**—This waveform contains several harmonics and can be used to emulate an acoustic piano.

- **Waveform 7**—This waveform is very smooth and sounds similar to an electric piano.

- **Waveform 8**—This waveform has a very sharp sound and can be used to emulate percussive keyboards like a clavinet.

- **Waveform 9**—This waveform can be used for bass sounds.

- **Waveform 10**—This waveform sounds very similar to a Sine wave and can be used for sub-bass sounds (a la Drum 'n' Bass).

- **Waveform 11**—This waveform is formant heavy and perfect to use for voice patches.

- **Waveform 12**—This waveform has a metallic ring to it, making it perfect for xylophone type sounds.

- **Waveform 13**—This waveform is very full sounding and sounds similar to a pipe organ.

- **Waveform 14**—This waveform is also very organ like but is not as bright as waveform 13.

- **Waveform 15**—This waveform can be used to emulate bowed string instruments.

- **Waveform 16**—This waveform is similar to 15, but contains a higher set of overtones.

- **Waveform 17**—This waveform is also similar in texture to 15, but contains a lower set of overtones.

- **Waveform 18**—This waveform can be used for steel string guitar sounds.

- **Waveform 19**—This waveform has harmonic qualities similar to bass instruments.

- **Waveform 20**—This waveform can be used to emulate muted brass instruments, like trumpet or trombone.

- **Waveform 21**—This waveform can be used to emulate saxophone sounds.

- **Waveform 22**—This waveform is yet another that can be used to emulate brass instruments, but with a little more character.

- **Waveform 23**—This waveform is great for creating mallet percussion instruments.

- **Waveform 24**—This waveform is similar to 23, but contains a higher set of overtones.

- **Waveform 25**—This waveform has a plectrum attack and can be used to program guitar patches.

- **Waveform 26**—This waveform is similar to 25, but contains a higher set of overtones.

- **Waveform 27**—This waveform is similar in tone to 23 and 24, but has a bell-like tone.

- **Waveform 28**—This waveform is similar to 27, but contains fewer overtones.

- **Waveform 29**—This waveform has a complex harmonic structure and can be used to program organ and metallic pad patches.

- **Waveform 30**—This waveform can be used with frequency modulation and Osc 2 to create noise patches.

- **Waveform 31**—This waveform is similar to 30, but contains fewer overtones.

- **Waveform 32**—This waveform is similar to 30, but contains more overtones.

Initialize the Subtractor   Before you begin programming the Subtractor, be sure to initialize (or reset) it by right-clicking on the interface and selecting Initialize Patch. That will reset the Subtractor to its default values.

Oscillator 2

Oscillator 2 functions in the same way as Osc 1, but has a few surprises up its sleeve. Adding a second source of oscillation to the mix can lead to an endless amount of modulation possibilities without a lot of extra programming.

To the right of Osc 2 is the Oscillator Mix knob. This knob is used to mix the amplitude of the two oscillators. Turning it clockwise will increase the volume of Osc 2 and decrease the volume of Osc 1. Turning the knob counter-clockwise will do the opposite.

Try the following example:

1. Set the waveform of Osc 1 to the Square wave and the waveform of Osc 2 to the Triangle wave.

2. Set the octave of Osc 1 and 2 to 2 for a very bass-heavy sound.

3. Turn the Mix knob clockwise until it reads 100.

4. Adjust the fine-tuning of Osc 1 to 20 Cent.

5. Arm the Subtractor sequencer track to receive MIDI from your keyboard and play a low note to hear the very solid bass sound and the wavering out-of-tune mix between Osc 1 and 2, which sounds pretty cool too.

Phase Offset Modulation

Along with generating a single waveform, the Subtractor oscillators can also generate a second identical waveform within the same oscillator. That second waveform's phase is then offset and modulated. Very complex new waveforms can be created with this process, which is called *phase offset modulation*.

To begin offsetting the phase of an oscillator, you must first select one of three modes to activate this function.

- **X:** Waveform multiplication

- **–:** Waveform subtraction

- **O:** No phase offset modulation

To better see how these waveforms look once phased, see Figure 10.3. In the image on the left, you will see a single Sawtooth waveform that contains no phase modulation at all. In the middle image, you will see that same Sawtooth waveform, but this time it has been multiplied and a new waveform has been created. In the right image, you will see that same waveform again, but this time it has been subtracted and another new waveform has been created.

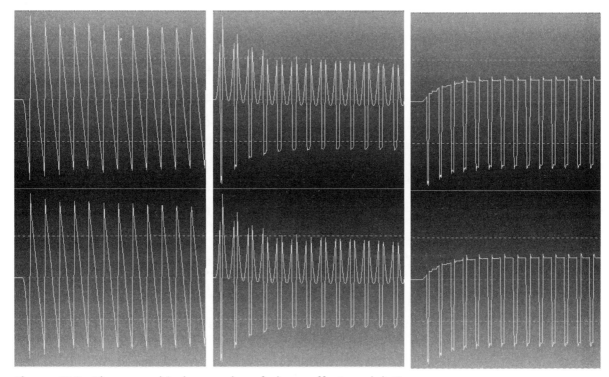

Figure 10.3 Three graphical examples of phase offset modulation.

To the left of the phase mode sectors is the Phase knob, which controls the amount of offset between the two waveforms within a single oscillator.

Learn by Example Phase offset modulation can be a difficult concept to grasp. Therefore, I suggest that using a Subtractor patch, which features this function, is the best way to learn and better understand how it works. Browse through the various patches in the PolySynth folder, and you will find several examples. Synced Up is a good patch to demonstrate phase offset.

Noise Generator

The Noise Generator can be thought of as another oscillator. But this oscillator does not generate a pitched waveform. Rather, it generates noise that can be used for several sound design and instrumental possibilities, such as "wind noises" and percussion sounds.

To activate the Noise Generator, click the power button located in the upper-left corner of its interface. Take a look at the main parameters of the Noise Generator:

■ **Noise Decay**—This parameter determines the length of time the noise will last when a note is played. Unlike Osc 1 and 2, the Amp Envelope does not govern the Noise Generator's parameters, so you can create a short burst of noise at the beginning of a sound using just this parameter.

■ **Noise Color**—This parameter controls the character of the noise. The easiest way to think of it is like a single band of EQ. If you turn the knob to the right, the noise becomes brighter. If you turn the knob to the left, the noise becomes muddier sounding and bass heavy.

■ **Level**—This parameter controls the volume of the Noise Generator.

Now try an example of the Noise Generator.

1. Choose Initialize Patch from the Edit pull-down menu to reset the Subtractor. Note that Osc 2 should be turned off.

2. Activate the Noise Generator by clicking on its power button.

3. Play a note on your MIDI keyboard to hear the mix between Osc 1 and the Noise Generator. Turn the Oscillator Mix knob all the way to the right (clockwise) to hear just the Noise Generator.

4. Experiment with the three main parameters of the Noise Generator. Once you find a setting you like, turn the Oscillator Mix knob counter-clockwise to hear Osc 1 mix back in.

The Noise Generator Outputs   The outputs of the Noise Generator are internally routed through Osc 2. Even if Osc 2 is not active, as was the case with the previous exercise, the Noise Generator can still be heard.

If you turn on Osc 2, you will hear the output of Osc 2 mixed in with the Noise Generator.

Frequency Modulation

Frequency modulation (FM) is a form of synthesis that requires two separate signals in order to generate a new sound:

- **The Carrier**—Produced by Osc 1, the carrier is used as a basic sound that will be modulated.

- **The Modulator**—Produced by Osc 2, the modulator is used to modulate, or modify, the output of the carrier. How much it is modulated is determined by the amount of FM assigned.

This is a fantastic effect that can be best explained by example:

1. Initialize the Subtractor patch by selecting Initialize Patch from the Edit pull-down menu, or by right-clicking (Control-clicking on the Mac) on the Subtractor and selecting Initialize Patch from the pop-up menu. Select the Sine wave for Osc 1.

2. Activate Osc 2 and select the Triangle wave for Osc 2.

3. Turn the FM knob to 50, and start playing some notes on your keyboard to hear the FM effect.

4. Turn the Osc Mix all the way to the left so you can just hear Osc 1.

5. Change the semitone settings on Osc 2 and notice that you can still hear the FM effect, even though you are listening to just Osc 1. As Osc 2 is a modulator when using FM, its modulation effect is still heard, even though the actual output of the oscillator is inaudible.

Because the Noise Generator is routed through the output of Osc 2, it can also be used to modulate Osc 1 through FM.

Try the following example. Make sure that you are playing a sequence of some kind to hear the effect:

1. Turn off Osc 2 and turn on the Noise Generator.

2. Turn the Osc Mix completely to the right so you will just hear the Noise Generator.

3. Play a sequence, or play your MIDI keyboard.

4. Set the Level knob of the Noise Generator to 64.

5. Set the FM knob to 24.

6. Turn the Osc Mix to the left to mix the two signals. The resulting generated sound should sound tight and nasal.

Frequency modulation is just one of those effects that has its own unique niche in electronic music. I suggest trying it on a sequenced arpeggio; it produces a killer staccato sound.

Ring Modulation

A ring modulator is used to multiply two audio signals, thus creating a new signal that contains additional frequencies. It is a unique sound that can be used to generate frequencies that are smooth and bell-like or jarring frequencies dripping with dissonance.

As you can see in Figure 10.4, the ring modulator is quite simple to show in diagram form. However, the sounds that you can create with it can be surprisingly complex in tone and texture.

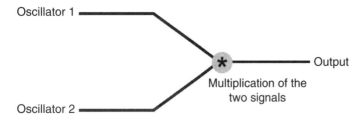

Figure 10.4 Osc 1 is multiplied by Osc 2 to create a completely original sound, which is the magic of ring modulation.

Try this exercise to see how ring modulation works:

1. Initialize the Subtractor patch before you begin.

2. Activate the ring modulator. Note that you won't hear any difference yet because Osc 2 is still not active.

3. Activate Osc 2. You will hear a slight variation in the tone.

4. Turn the Osc Mix knob clockwise to hear just the ring modulator.

5. Play some notes on your MIDI keyboard, or play a sequence of notes in the Reason sequencer.

6. Make a few adjustments to the semitone controls of either Osc 1 or 2 to start hearing the quite noticeable dissonant effect created by the ring modulator.

7. At this point, you can turn the Osc Mix knob to the left in order to bring Osc 1 back into the mix if you want.

8. Set both semitone controls back to zero and experiment with the Cent controls. This produces a very fat chorus-like effect.

The Filter Section

As you read earlier in this chapter, a filter is one of the three elements needed to shape your sounds. The Subtractor is certainly up to the challenge because there are two filters included that can run independently of each other or be linked (see Figure 10.5).

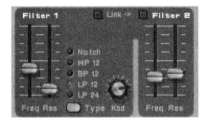

Figure 10.5 Subtractor has two filters that can either be used individually or linked.

Filter 1

Filter 1 is the Subtractor's primary filter. It has many available filter types and a Keyboard Tracking parameter, which is discussed later in this section. For now, take a look at the different kinds of filters.

- **Notch**—This filter can be thought of as the opposite of a Band Pass filter. It will reject the mid-frequencies while allowing the high and low frequencies to pass through. Although not the most dramatic filter effect, it has a place in the mix for making minor changes to a sample.

- **High Pass**—HP 12 is the opposite of the Low Pass filters in that it will filter out the low frequencies while letting the high frequencies pass through. It has a roll-off curve of 12 decibels per octave.

- **Band Pass**—Labeled as BP 12, this filters out both the high and low frequencies, leaving the mid frequencies alone. With a roll-off curve of 12 decibels per octave, the BP 12 can be used effectively on instrument loops such as a guitar loop or possibly hi-hat heavy percussion loops.

- **12dB Low Pass**—Also called LP 12, this filter is similar to the 24dB low pass, but the roll-off curve is not as steep, because it has a range of 12 decibels per octave. This makes the LP 12 a perfect solution for creating a filter sweep that is low, but not low enough to blow up your speakers.

■ **24dB Low Pass**—Also called LP 24, this filter allows low frequencies to pass through, while high frequencies are filtered out. To top it off, this low pass filter has a very intense roll-off curve (approximately 24 decibels per octave), which produces a greater emphasis on the low frequencies.

The Filter Frequency, or *cutoff filter*, as it is also called, is used to specify where the filter will function within the frequency spectrum. It is a very popular parameter used to create the "sweeping" effect that often occurs in electronic music. When the frequency is used to alter a filter, it opens and closes the filter within a specific frequency range. In order to better understand what the Filter Frequency does, try the following exercise.

1.   Load a PolySynth patch from the Reason Factory Sound Bank. Try the Analog Brass patch, which is located in the PolySynth folder.

2.   The filter is already activated. Set the filter mode to the LP 24 setting and make sure the Resonance slider is set to 0. Also make sure the Filter Frequency slider is set to its maximum setting of 127.

3.   Arm the Subtractor sequencer track to receive MIDI and play a sustained chord with your left hand. With your right hand, click on the Filter Frequency and drag the control down so you can hear the filter close as it decreases in value. Once the Filter Frequency is set to 0, all of the high frequencies have been filtered out. Try this same exercise with other filter modes, such as the Notch or Band Pass, to hear the effect.

The Resonance slider is used in combination with the Filter Frequency. It emphasizes the frequencies set by the Filter slider, which thins the sound out but also increases the sweep effect mentioned earlier. In order to better understand how the Resonance slider works with the Filter Frequency, try the following exercise.

At the far right of Filter 1 is the Keyboard Tracking knob. It can be used to bring the higher notes to the forefront in a mix by gradually increasing the filter frequency the higher up on the keyboard you go.

Filter 2

Filter 2 brings an *additional* 12dB Low Pass filter to the table. Although it might not have all of the bells and whistles that Filter 1 has, it can produce many interesting timbres that are not possible with most hardware-based synths.

To activate Filter 2, just click on its power button. Once this is done, the outputs of Filter 1 are virtually routed through Filter 2.

Filter 2 can be used in two ways:

■ The Frequency slider of Filter 2 can be used independently of Filter 1, meaning that any changes you make to this parameter will only affect Filter 2.

■ The Frequency slider of Filter 2 is linked to the Frequency slider of Filter 1, meaning that any changes you make to this parameter will affect both Filter 1 and Filter 2.

Take a look at an example of frequency independence:

1. Load the Singing Synth patch from the Monosynth folder in the Reason Factory Sound Bank.

2. Once it is loaded, notice that Filter 1 is set to BP 12. Arm the Subtractor sequencer track, and play a couple of MIDI notes. Notice the vowel-like texture of the patch.

3. Notice that Filter 2 is activated but it is not linked, so its Frequency slider is running independently.

4. Try turning off Filter 2 to hear the difference between using one and two filters. When Filter 2 is deactivated, the patch really loses its originality and sounds like a standard run of the mill synth patch.

Let's look at an example of linking up the Frequency sliders of both filters:

1. Load the Fozzy Fonk patch from the PolySynth folder in the Reason Factory Sound Bank.

2. Notice that Filter 1 is set to Notch mode. Arm the Subtractor sequencer track and play a couple of MIDI notes. Listen to the sound that is being generated from the Subtractor. There is no way a Notch filter could sound that way on its own because it has a very nasal timbre to it and has far too many mid-frequencies in the mix.

3. Notice that the Filter 2 Link button is now activated. This means that the Frequency slider of Filter 1 will affect the Frequency slider of Filter 2 as well. Note also that as there is an offset between the two frequencies; that offset will remain as the Frequency slider changes on Filter 1.

4. To demonstrate the Filter 2 Link, try making some adjustments to the Frequency slider of Filter 1. Also try deactivating Filter 2 and making those same adjustments to the Frequency slider of Filter 1 to hear the difference.

The Envelope Section

The Subtractor has three envelopes, and although they share some common parameters, you'll find that the purpose and functionality of the envelopes are quite different (see Figure 10.6).

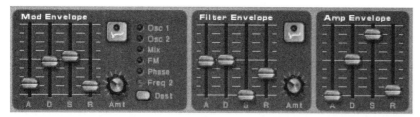

Figure 10.6 The Subtractor has three envelopes: Modulation, Filter, and Amplitude.

There are four basic parameters that all the Subtractor envelopes share:

- **Attack**—When an envelope is triggered, the Attack parameter determines the length of time before the envelope reaches its maximum value.

- **Decay**—Once the maximum value is reached, the Decay parameter determines the length of time before the value begins to drop.

- **Sustain**—After the value begins to drop, Sustain determines the level at which the falling value should rest.

- **Release**—Once the value has been set at its rested value, the Release parameter determines how long it will take the sound to drop to silence after you release the key. When Release is set at its maximum level (assuming there is a sufficient level of Decay), you will get an infinite "hold" result, where any note you strike will ring out forever, even after you release the key.

The following sections take a look at each of the available envelopes.

Filter and Amplitude Envelopes

The Filter Envelope is used to modify the Frequency parameter of Filter 1. When using it in combination with the Filter Frequency and Resonance sliders, the Filter Envelope can be used to create long, sustained filter sweeps and percussive filter-powered stab sounds.

To the right of the Filter Envelope are two additional parameters that can be used in combination with it.

- The Invert button is used to invert the functions of the individual envelope parameters at once. For example, say you are using the Attack parameter of the Filter Envelope and have assigned a positive value of 80, which produces a very slow attack. Activate the Invert button and the Attack parameter is inverted, which means the attack will be much faster now.

- The Amount knob determines how much the filter will be affected by the envelope. Increasing the value of this parameter directly affects the set value of the Filter Frequency, which in turn will affect the Filter Envelope, resulting in some very intense filter combinations.

To demonstrate the capabilities of the Filter Envelope, try the following exercise. Make sure that your Subtractor sequencer track is armed to receive MIDI signals.

1. Load the Desiree patch in the PolySynth folder of the Reason Factory Sound Bank. Notice the filter settings of this patch.

2. Use your mouse to increase the value of the Attack parameter to 55. Play a chord on your keyboard and notice the sweeping effect it produces. Because the Filter mode is set to LP 24, using the envelope with a slow attack causes the filter to first play the lower frequencies, followed by the higher frequencies. Additionally, if you increase the Amount knob, this sweeping effect will dramatically intensify.

3. Now decrease the value of the Decay parameter to 24. Play a chord and notice how the filter abruptly closes as soon as the Attack reaches its maximum value. Also notice how there is still a long sustain after the filter closes.

4. Now increase the value of the Sustain parameter to 101 and listen to how fast the filter opens and decays, but the Filter Frequency still remains open for a long while.

5. With the Decay set to such low values, the Release parameter will have virtually no effect on this patch. To hear the effect of the Release parameter, turn the Attack all the way down, increase the Decay parameter to 66, and turn Release all the way up. Now when you strike a chord and let go, the notes will continue to ring out until the cows come home.

The Amplitude Envelope is used to shape the volume characteristics of the Subtractor patch. This is useful for creating very long sustained patches (such as pads), or medium to short sustained patches (such as bass synths or percussion). The same types of parameters are available here (Attack, Decay, Sustain, and Release). The included Level slider located just above the Amplitude Envelope is used as a Master Level for the Subtractor.

To experiment with the Amplitude Envelope, try using the previous exercise as a road map to guide you through the different envelope parameters.

Modulation Envelope

The Modulation Envelope works in the same way as the Filter Envelope, but it has a different use. The Modulation envelope sends the standard set of envelope parameters to one of six destinations, including:

- **Osc 1**—This destination alters the pitch of Oscillator 1.

- **Osc 2**—This destination alters the pitch of Oscillator 2.

- **Osc Mix**—This destination controls the Oscillator Mix knob.

- **Frequency Modulation**—This destination controls the amount of FM.

- **Phase**—This destination controls the amount of phase offset between Osc 1 and 2.

- **Filter Frequency 2**—This destination controls the amount of Filter Frequency for Filter 2.

The Amount and Invert knobs work in the same way as they did with the Filter Envelope, so there is no need to waste time on that. Instead, try the following exercise to better understand the functionality of this envelope. Make sure that your Subtractor sequencer track is armed and ready to receive MIDI.

1. Load the GlassOrgan patch from the PolySynths folder in the Reason Factory Sound Bank. Notice that the Modulation Envelope is not being used at all; its Amount parameter is set to 0.

2. Set the Amount knob to 127 so that the envelope will be triggered with its maximum potential.

3. Set the Attack to 85 for a very slow attack.

4. Play a note or chord on your keyboard and listen to the pitch of Osc 1 slowly rise and quickly decay. For a faster sci-fi laser-type sound, set the Attack back down to zero.

The LFO Section

The Subtractor sports two independent Low Frequency Oscillators, or LFOs (see Figure 10.7). In some ways, an LFO can be thought of as a standard oscillator, because it is capable of generating a waveform and frequency. However, the purpose of an LFO differs greatly from that of a standard oscillator in two ways:

- The LFO can only generate waveforms with low frequencies.

- The LFO's purpose is to modulate a specific parameter of a patch, such as a filter or another oscillator. That means that the LFO itself is never actually heard, only its effect on other synth parameters.

Figure 10.7 Subtractor has two LFOs.

LFO 1

LFO 1 has many waveform choices and destinations. It is also capable of synchronizing the LFO effect to the tempo of your Reason song. First take a look at the different available waveforms:

1. **Triangle**—Creates a smooth up and down vibrato.

2. **Inverted Sawtooth**—Creates a cycled ramp up effect.

3. **Sawtooth**—Creates a cycled ramp down effect.

4. **Square**—Makes abrupt changes between two values.

5. **Random**—Creates a random stepped modulation (also known as sample and hold).

6. **Soft Random**—Exactly as the previous waveform but has a smoother modulation curve.

The Amount knob assigns the amount of LFO effect to your patch. It's fairly easy to get carried away with this parameter, so easy does it.

The Rate knob increases and decreases the rate of the LFO effect.

The Sync button synchronizes the LFO effect to the tempo indicated on the Transport bar. Also note that once Sync is active, the Rate knob displays its amount by note values rather than numerically.

Once you have selected your rate, amount, and waveform, you must next decide where to send the LFO signal. There are six possible destinations from which to choose:

- **Osc 1&2**—This destination alters the pitch of Oscillators 1 and 2.

- **Osc 2**—This destination alters the pitch of just Osc 2.

- **Filter Frequency**—This destination controls the Filter Frequency Filter 1 (and Filter 2 if they are linked).

- **Frequency Modulation**—This destination controls the amount of FM.

- **Phase**—This destination controls the amount of phase offset for Osc 1 and 2.

- **Oscillator Mix**—This destination controls the Oscillator Mix knob.

LFO 2

Although the LFO 2 might not be as complex and versatile as its bigger brother, it is welcome addition to the Subtractor interface. LFO 2 does not sync to tempo. Instead, it is *key triggered,* which means that the LFO will trigger every time a note is played on your keyboard.

The Rate and Amount knobs perform exactly the same task as they do with LFO 1, minus the Sync feature, of course.

The Delay knob is used to create an offset between playing a note and then hearing the LFO modulation. It can be used to mimic the vibrato effect of a wind or stringed instrument, which calls for long sustained notes followed by a vibrato.

The Keyboard Tracking knob can be used to increase the frequency of the LFO the farther up on the keyboard that you play.

Once you have set the individual parameters of LFO 2, you can send the effect to one of four destinations.

- **Osc 1&2**—This destination controls the pitch of Oscillators 1 and 2.

- **Phase**—This destination controls the amount of phase offset for Osc 1 and 2.

- **Filter Frequency 2**—This destination controls the Filter Frequency Filter 2.

- **Amplitude**—This destination controls the overall volume of the Subtractor.

The Play Parameters

Once you have familiarized yourself with the ins and outs of programming the Subtractor, it's time to take a look at the parameters that involve the performance side of this virtual synth (see Figure 10.8). You'll find there are a lot of interesting and creative choices that you will enjoy playing with.

Figure 10.8 Subtractor's Play parameters are used to add expression to your performance.

Velocity Control

The Subtractor is a *velocity-sensitive* virtual synth. Although this might not be as impressive to those of you who have oodles of digital synths lying around your studio, this is a significant feature to vintage synth connoisseurs; velocity-sensitive keyboards were not available in the early days of subtractive synthesis. If you played a note on, say a vintage Moog or ARP synth, that note would be generated at its maximum velocity, regardless of hard or soft the note was played.

Located in the lower-right corner of the Subtractor is the Velocity Control section, where different parameters can be made velocity-sensitive and will react according to how hard or soft a note it played (see Figure 10.9). The velocity data can be received from a live performance with a MIDI keyboard or played from the Reason sequencer or the Matrix sequencer. After you read through this section, be sure to read the programming tutorial later in this chapter. There, you'll use a few of these parameters.

Figure 10.9 The Velocity Control section is a big part of the Subtractor's Play parameters.

The different parameters that can be modified by velocity are as follows:

■ **Amplitude**—This parameter controls the overall volume of the Subtractor. When set to a positive value, a harder velocity increases the volume. When set to a negative value, a harder velocity decreases the volume.

■ **Frequency Modulation**—When set to a positive value, a harder velocity increases the Frequency Modulation parameter. A negative value has the opposite effect.

■ **Modulation Envelope**—When set to a positive value, a harder velocity increases the Modulation Envelope's Amount parameter. A negative value has the opposite effect.

■ **Phase Offset**—This parameter controls the phase offset of oscillators 1 and 2. When set to a positive value and when the phase offset is activated, a harder velocity increases the amount of phase offset. A negative value has the opposite effect.

■ **Filter Frequency 2**—This controls the Frequency slider of Filter 2. When set to a positive value, a harder velocity increases the amount of filter frequency. A negative value has the opposite effect.

■ **Filter Envelope**—When set to a positive value, a harder velocity increases the Filter Envelope's Amount parameter. A negative value has the opposite effect.

- **Filter Decay**—This controls the Decay parameter of the Filter Envelope. When set to a positive value, a harder velocity increases the Filter Decay parameter. A negative value has the opposite effect.

- **Oscillator Mix**—This knob controls the Oscillator Mix knob. When set to a positive value, a harder velocity increases the amount of Osc 2 in the mix. A negative value has the opposite effect (Osc 1 is more present).

- **Amp Attack**—This controls the Attack parameter of the Amplifier Envelope. When set to a positive value, a harder velocity increases the Amp Envelope Attack parameter. A negative value has the opposite effect.

Pitch Bend and Modulation

The Pitch Bend Wheel is an emulation of a standard pitch wheel found on most MIDI keyboards. Simply put, it is used to bend the pitch of the played notes up and down. The Range parameter, located just above the Pitch Bend Wheel, controls the range of pitch by up to +/– two octaves.

The Modulation Wheel is used to control a number of different available parameters:

- **Filter Frequency**—When set to a positive value, the Modulation Wheel increases the Filter Frequency parameter. A negative value has the opposite effect.

- **Resonance**—When set to a positive value, the Modulation Wheel increases the Resonance. A negative value has the opposite effect.

- **LFO 1**—When set to a positive value, the Modulation Wheel increases the Amount knob of LFO 1. A negative value has the opposite effect.

- **Phase**—This knob controls the Phase Offset parameter of the Oscillators 1 and 2. When set to a positive value, the Modulation Wheel increases the amount of phase offset. A negative value has the opposite effect.

- **Frequency Modulation**—When set to a positive value, the Modulation Wheel increases the Frequency Modulation parameter. A negative value has the opposite effect.

Legato/Retrig

Retrig is thought of as the "normal" setting for the Subtractor because it is the commonly used parameter for playing polyphonic patches. When Retrig is selected, the Subtractor envelopes are triggered when you press and hold down a note, and then retriggered when another note is played.

Retrig can be used with monophonic patches as well. Load a patch from the Mono-Synths folder in the Subtractor Patches folder of the Reason Factory Sound Bank. Try pressing a note and holding it while pressing a new key. Release the new key and the first note will retrigger.

Legato is a commonly used parameter for playing monophonic patches, such as leads or bass lines. With the polyphony set to 1, press and hold down a note, and then press and hold another note. Notice that the new note has no attack, as the Subtractor's envelopes have not been retriggered, as would be the case when Retrig is selected. If you add some portamento to this patch, you will get a retro vintage mono synth glide sound.

It is also possible to use Legato with a polyphonic patch. Set the Polyphony of a patch to a low number of voices, such as 3. Hold down a three-note chord and then play another note. Notice that the new note will be played with a legato effect (no attack), but it will cease to play the highest note of the chord you are playing because it is "stealing" that note in order to play the new note.

Portamento

Portamento is used to create a sliding effect between played notes. The knob determines the amount of time it will take to slide from one note to another. It can be used with either monophonic or polyphonic patches, and it is a great tool for creating some interesting effects. Try loading a polyphonic patch, such as the Glass Organ patch found in the Poly Synths folder. Set the Portamento to a value of 45, and play some chords. You will hear a slight sliding effect that makes the patch sound a little funny, but try adding some real-time effects.

Polyphony

Polyphony assigns the number of voices that can simultaneously play at one time. The Subtractor has a wide range of polyphony, from 1 to 99 voices, offering a wide range of creative possibilities. For example, when set at 1, the Subtractor becomes a monophonic instrument, which is perfect for creating scorching lead lines.

External Modulation

The Subtractor is capable of receiving common MIDI controller messages and then routing that data to a number of available parameters. When used effectively, this can create performances with a great deal of additional expression.

The three MIDI messages that can be received are as follows:

- **Aftertouch**—Also known as *channel pressure*. This is when a note is held down on a keyboard. Additional pressure can be applied to this note, which sends additional MIDI data. Many keyboards support this feature, so check your manual.

- **Expression Pedal**—Looks a lot like a sustain pedal. If your keyboard has an input for it, you can buy an expression pedal at your local music instrument shop.

- **Breath Control**—This external source is found mostly on older Yamaha keyboards, but it enables you to mimic the attack of wind instruments.

Once you have selected the external source, you can then route the MIDI data to any or all of these parameters.

- **Filter Frequency**—When set to a positive value, an External Control message increases the Filter Frequency parameter. A negative value has the opposite effect.

- **LFO 1**—When set to a positive value, an External Control message increases the LFO Amount knob. A negative value has the opposite effect.

- **Amplitude**—When set to a positive value, an External Control message increases the amplitude of the Subtractor. A negative value has the opposite effect.

- **Frequency Modulation**— When set to a positive value, an External Control message increases the Frequency Modulation parameter. A negative value has the opposite effect.

Creating Your First Subtractor Patch

Now that you have a pretty firm idea of what makes the Subtractor tick, it's time to dig in and create your first customized Subtractor patch. This tutorial takes you through a step-by-step process of programming a pad patch that will be perfect for any ambient occasion.

Setting Up a Start Point

Before you begin to program your first Subtractor patch, it's important to find a good starting point from which to begin your synthetic experimentations. If your species has only two hands and one brain, you may find it cumbersome to play keyboard while making adjustments to the Subtractor, so I suggest using the Reason sequencer to get around it. By writing in a sequence that is related to the kind of patch you are going to create, you can make the programming process much quicker and more efficient.

For this programming tutorial, you are going to create a pad patch, which is typically used for long, sustained chords. This is a perfect place to set up the Reason sequencer with a few sustained chords so that you can loop the sequence and make changes to the Subtractor in real-time.

1. Create a part and switch to Edit mode to display the Key Lane Editor.

2. Set the Snap value to 1 bar. This will allow you to draw in measure-long notes.

3. Using your Pencil tool, draw in an E major chord at measure one using the notes E1, B1, E2, G#2, B2, and E3.

4. Using your Pencil tool, draw in an A major chord at measure two using the notes A1, E2, A2, C#3, and E3.

5. Activate the loop mode on the Transport panel. Set the left locator to measure 1 and the right locator to measure 3. This will give you a two-bar loop (see Figure 10.10).

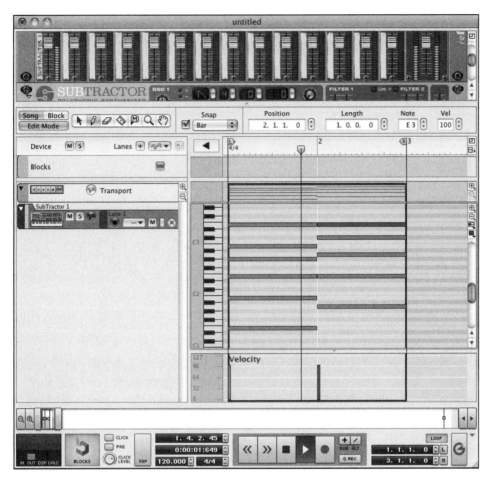

Figure 10.10 A two-bar loop has been created.

Programming Your Subtractor Patch

In this tutorial, you are going to build a pad patch by working with each section of the Subtractor interface. This will serve as a good review of everything you have learned about the functionality of the Subtractor throughout this chapter. If you have not already done so, make sure to select Initialize Patch on the Subtractor.

Programming the Oscillators

Let's start things off simply by working with Oscillator 1, and then adding in Oscillator 2. To hear the changes in real time, press Play on the Transport bar. The two-bar loop should start playing continuously.

1. Set the waveform of Osc 1 to a Sine wave. Notice the organ-like bell tone that is produced.

2. Set the Octave box of Osc 1 to 3. Notice how the tone still retains its bell tone quality, but sounds very dark and muddy.

3. Next, set the phase offset to Waveform Multiplication or X, and set the Phase knob to 44.

At this point, the patch sounds very dull, so let's add another timbre to the mix by using Osc 2. Before activating Osc 2, make sure that you turn the Mix knob counter-clockwise until it reaches a value of 44. This will allow Osc 1 to be the dominant voice in the patch.

And now, on to Osc 2.

1. Activate Osc 2 and set its waveform to a Square wave.

2. Next, set the Cent control to a positive amount of 20. This will fine-tune Osc 2 a little higher than Osc 1, which will sound much cooler later on in this tutorial.

3. Set the phase offset to the Waveform Subtraction or –, and set its Amount knob to a value of 123. If you want to experiment with this setting a little bit, try making adjustments between the values of 0 and 127 to hear how Osc 2 will fade out from the mix when set to a low value.

4. Activate the ring modulator. Notice all of the new frequencies and timbres that are introduced to the patch.

Bring in the Noise   When creating a pad, it's nice to add a little noise to the mix to give the patch a little grit on top of the synthetic smoothness of Oscillator 2. If you want to add this element to your patch, try these settings:

- Activate the Noise Generator.

- Set the Decay knob to its maximum value.

- Set the Color knob to a low value; this will dull the tone of the digital noise.

- Set the Level knob to a mid value. I suggest starting with a value of 30 and working from there.

Throughout the rest of this tutorial, you can choose to turn the noise off or leave it on. It's not an essential texture to this patch that you are creating, but it never hurts to add a little gravy now and then.

Programming the Filters and Envelopes

You now have a much more interesting sound to work with. It's time to manipulate it further by using both of the filters.

1. Change the mode of Filter 1 to LP 24.

2. Set the value of the Filter Frequency to a low amount—around 30 or so. The patch should now have a very abrupt Attack and Decay, but you should also be able to hear a very low sustained timbre underneath it.

3. Activate Filter 2 and set the Resonance slider to a high value of 90.

4. Activate the Link button. This will connect the Frequency Filter slider of Filter 1 with the Frequency slider of Filter 2.

Upon listening to the patch at this point, it might sound a little strange because it is not quite a pad sound. That's all about to change as you introduce the Filter Envelope to the patch.

Before you begin this part of the tutorial, set the Amount knob of the Filter Envelope to a value of 67. Now set the Attack, Decay, Sustain, and Release to the following values:

- **Attack**—Set to 80 to create a slow rising attack.

- **Decay**—Set to 80 as well, so the envelope will remain at its peak value.

- **Sustain**—Set to 37. This will create a fast drop off from the peak value.

- **Release**—Set to 37 as well. This will introduce a slight sustain to the envelope, but not too much.

> **Watch Those Levels** Because you are using an LP 24 filter on this patch, you will surely notice how much fuller and louder the patch is getting. That said, you might want to turn down the Level slider of the Subtractor to avoid any potential digital clipping.

Now the patch should sound much more like a pad than before. Notice how the filters fill out the sound nicely by using a slow attack on the envelope. Another texture to note is the "wavering sound" between the two oscillators, courtesy of the fine-tuning Cent value of 20. Try changing the Cent value to 0, and notice the difference.

Now you will continue working with the envelopes by using the Amplitude Envelope. Set this envelope to the following values:

- **Attack**—Set to 60 for a slow attack.

- **Decay**—Set to a high value of 100 for a prolonged peak level.

- **Sustain**—Set to 60 for a slower drop off from the decay.

- **Release**—Set to a low value of 0.

> **Save Your Work** Don't forget to occasionally save your patch by clicking on the Save button at the top-left corner of the Subtractor interface.

The last envelope to program is the Modulation Envelope, which is going to modulate the FM knob of the Subtractor. Set the Amount knob to 30, set the Envelope Destination mode to FM, and adjust the parameters of this envelope to the following values:

- **Attack**—Set to 0 for a fast attack.

- **Decay**—Set to 70 for a long sustained peak level.

- **Sustain**—Set to 10 for a fast drop off from the decay.

- **Release**—Set to 0 for a fast release.

Programming the LFOs

Adding the LFOs to this patch is what will help give it originality and character. As you know there are two LFOs in the Subtractor. In this tutorial, you will start by creating a tempo-synced LFO for the Filter Frequency; and you will then use the second LFO to modulate the phase of the two oscillators.

Begin with LFO 1.

1. Activate the Sync button to synchronize LFO 1 to the tempo of your Reason song.

2. Set the Rate knob to a value of 1/8. This will cause the Filter Frequency to modulate on every 8th note.

3. Set the Amount knob to a low value of 12. You will still hear the effect of the LFO, but it will not become too dominant in the patch.

4. Set the Destination mode to F.FREQ or Filter Frequency. Note that as you are using both filters, the LFO will modulate both Frequency Filter sliders.

5. Select the Square waveform from the waveform mode. This will produce an abrupt modulation between the maximum and minimal potential of the square waveform that will sound great when synced to tempo.

Next, take a look at LFO 2 and have it modulate the phase of Oscillators 1 and 2.

1. Set the Destination mode of LFO 2 to Phase.

2. Set the Rate knob to a value of 30.

3. Set the Amount knob to a high amount of 90.

4. Set the Keyboard Tracking to 100.

Add a Dash of Velocity In this tutorial, you're not making much use of the Velocity section, so I want to point out a parameter or two in this section that you can use if you want.

- **Filter Envelope**—Using this knob will increase or decrease the amount of the Filter Envelope according to the velocity at which your notes are played. Try adding a positive amount, such as 25, and notice how much more present the filter effect becomes.

- **Filter Frequency 2**—Using this knob will increase or decrease the amount of Filter Frequency from the second filter. Try using a negative amount such as –34, and notice how the Filter Frequency changes with velocity. Now imagine that with some delay on it.

Programming the Play Parameters

You're in the home stretch; you can finish this patch by making a few adjustments to the Play parameters of the Subtractor.

- **Polyphony**—By default, the Subtractor has polyphony of 8, and this won't do for those really large, sustained ambient chords. Begin by assigning a higher polyphony count of 16.

- **Modulation Wheel**—Assign a negative value to the Filter Frequency so it will decrease in value as the Modulation Wheel is used. Assign a positive amount to the LFO 1. This will increase the amount of LFO as the Modulation Wheel is used.

- **Portamento**—Assign a positive amount to this parameter. This will create a sliding effect that sounds great with pads and bass synths.

Another parameter you might want to adjust is the range of the Pitch Bend Wheel. For example, try assigning a value of 24 to the Pitch Bend Wheel to create some really wild pitch bent notes and chords.

Sci-Fi Sine Wave LFO Invasion

The Subtractor provides a wonderful opportunity to explore the mellow beauty of the Sine wave. In fact, the Subtractor produces a particularly warm and beautiful Sine wave. But you needn't worry that the following tutorial will lull you to sleep, because just as you begin to fall into a sine-trance, LFO 1 will instigate such insanity that your neighbors will think the Martians have finally invaded!

For this exercise, start with an empty rack, create an instance of reMix, followed by an RV7000 advanced Reverb, and finally the beloved Subtractor. Initialize the Subtractor to wipe the slate clean. No need to set up a sequence on this one unless you really want to—this can be a fun hands-on-the-keyboard experiment. (Don't worry if you're not a keyboard player—just one finger and a thumb will be fine!)

1. This exercise will sound great with some reverb, so turn Aux Send 1 up to a value of 85 or so on reMix channel 1. The RV7000's default settings are fine as they are.

2. On the Subtractor, turn the Portamento up to about 74, and turn the Polyphony down to 1. You're going old-school monophonic for this one.

3. Select sine waves on both oscillators and activate Osc 2.

4. Set the Amp Envelope Attack to 20 (for a quick but soft attack) and set the Amp Envelope Decay to 127.

5. In the Velocity section, reduce the F.ENV to 0.

Try playing some notes that are at least a couple of octaves apart on your MIDI keyboard and enjoy the retro portamento. In the upper register, it's pretty sci-fi. In the lower register, you can definitely get the glasses rattling in the cupboard with some serious sub-bass!

Now you're ready to start playing with LFO 1. If your MIDI keyboard has a Modulation Wheel on it, you might want to use it to control the amount of LFO 1 by turning up LFO Mod Wheel Amount to 63.

1. Set LFO 1 Rate to 74. Then try using your mod wheel or the LFO 1 Amount control to bring in just a bit of Theremin-like vibrato at the end of some of your notes (using the Triangle waveform). The LFO 1 Dest control should still be at its default setting, controlling Osc 1 and 2. If you find this to be enjoyable, please take your time before moving on to step 2.

2. Crank up the LFO 1 Amount control to 127 and use the Waveform button to listen to the different LFO 1 waveforms. It is quite fun to turn the LFO 1 Rate control up and down while playing with each waveform. Enjoy the freaky "sci-fi computers running amok" effect of the bottom two Random and Soft Random waveforms.

3. Before the men in black beat down your door, try turning the LFO 1 Amount back down for a moment and work the Osc 1 FM Amount knob as you play.

In the middle register of the MIDI keyboard, you may find some very vocal Theremin-like sounds as you experiment with Osc 1 FM Amount. Down low, you might just find some pure evil lurking or at least a good "spaceship door opening on Dr. Who" sound. Before moving on to the next bit, turn the Osc 1 FM Amount back down to 0.

1. Turn on the LFO Sync Enable button. The LFO 1 Rate control now shows note values. Set it for a value of 1/8.

2. Turn LFO 1 Amount all the way up.

3. Set LFO 1 Waveform to the Random waveform (second from the bottom).

4. Turn on the Click (perhaps turning down the Click Level a bit), and press Play in the Transport panel. If you are feeling more ambitious, you could set up a Redrum or Dr. Octo Rex beat instead.

5. Try playing 1/8 note rhythms simply by pressing any key on your MIDI keyboard right on the beat, holding it, and then letting go right on the beat, holding the notes (and leaving spaces) in whatever fashion feels good to you.

Too weird for pop music? In large doses, sci-fi freak-outs may well get your music labeled "experimental" (also known to some commerce-minded folks as "kiss of death"), but in tasteful doses it can be quite refreshing to the ears and contribute to a memorable production. Of course, in general the sine wave is quite musical and pleasing to the ear, fitting in naturally with all sorts of electronic music, hip-hop, pop, or even country. (Okay, maybe not country.)

Using the Subtractor with the Matrix

This section gives you a little taste of the kind of fantastic sounds you can get from the Subtractor, when using it along with the Matrix Pattern sequencer. Although you dig into the Matrix later in this book, I thought it might be fun to show you how to make the Subtractor sound like Robby the Robot.

What Is the Matrix?

The Matrix is a software emulation of what is called a *control voltage sequencer* (see Figure 10.11). This was a hardware device that was used to sequence synthesizers back in the days of "Switched on Bach" and Emerson, Lake, and Palmer. Essentially, a control voltage (or CV) sequencer sends out controlled amounts of voltage that are read by the synthesizer and interpreted as pitch and length of notes.

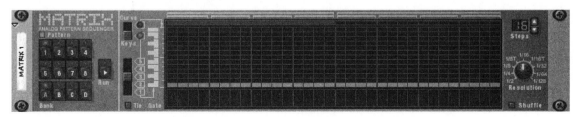

Figure 10.11 The Matrix Pattern sequencer is used to write synth patterns for the Subtractor.

The Matrix does this as well, but takes it a step further by sending pattern data, note data, gate data, and parameter control data. The Matrix is capable of storing up to 32 individual patterns that can each be up to 32 steps long, and it supports many note values, including the ability to shuffle.

For much, much more on the Matrix, be sure to turn to Chapter 15, "The Matrix—Close Up."

Connecting the Matrix

The first thing you need to do here is create a Matrix sequencer and route it to the Subtractor, and this can be done in just a couple of steps.

Make sure that you have initialized your Subtractor patch, so you can begin with a clean slate.

1. Click on anywhere on the Subtractor to highlight the interface. Doing this before creating a Matrix will create a Matrix directly below the Subtractor and automatically route it to the Subtractor inputs.

2. Select the Matrix Pattern sequencer from the Create pull-down menu. An instance of the Matrix will appear below the Subtractor. Click on the Tab key and the Device Rack will swing around. You will see that the Matrix has indeed been automatically routed to the sequencer controls of the Subtractor (see Figure 10.12).

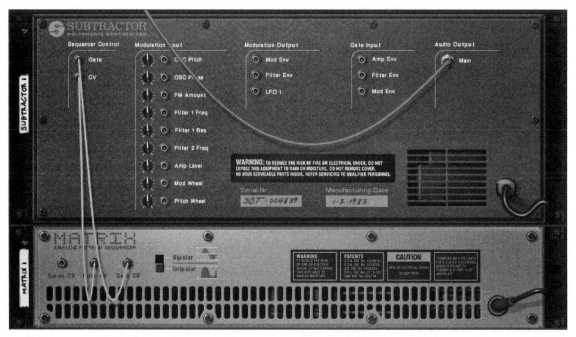

Figure 10.12 The Matrix has been automatically routed to the sequencer controls of the Subtractor.

Creating a Curve Pattern with the Matrix

Now that the Matrix has been routed to the Subtractor, you can use the Matrix to draw in a curve pattern, which will affect the pitch of Oscillator 1.

1. Route the Curve CV output of the Matrix to the Osc Pitch Modulation Input of the Subtractor (see Figure 10.13). This will allow the Matrix to control the pitch of Oscillator 1.

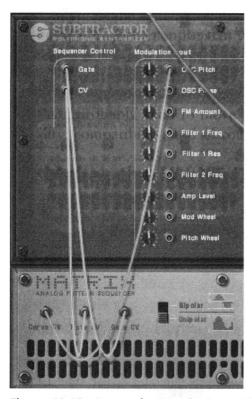

Figure 10.13 Route the Matrix Curve CV to the Osc Pitch Input of the Subtractor.

2. Press the Tab key to flip the Device Rack around again.

3. Switch from Keys to Curve mode in the Matrix by clicking on the switch located in the upper-left corner of the interface.

4. Press Play in the Transport panel of Reason. The Matrix sequencer should begin to run as well, allowing you to hear the Subtractor under Matrix control.

5. Draw in a Curve pattern for the Matrix by simply clicking in the grid section. As the pattern recycles, you should be able to hear random notes play from the Subtractor. Giving each grid a different value, as shown in Figure 10.14, can change these notes.

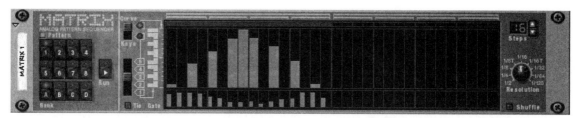

Figure 10.14 Drawing in a curved pattern with the Matrix is easy and sounds great when you need some interesting elements for your electronic masterpiece.

By now you can see that the Subtractor is a synth of many creative possibilities. It has certainly earned a welcome place in our virtual studios due to its very useful sounds and endless routing potential.

11 The Malström—Close Up

When Reason 2.0 hit the market in 2002, Propellerhead introduced a new virtual synth, based on an original form of synthesis, called the Malström (see Figure 11.1). With its handsome graphical interface and unbelievable synthesis prowess, it is likely to quickly become a permanent fixture in your Reason songs.

Graintable Synthesis

Malström's uniqueness stems from the method by which it generates sound, called *graintable synthesis*, which is essentially a combination of granular and wavetable synthesis. To better understand how this works, you need to understand these two forms of synthesis.

In *granular synthesis*, sound is generated by a specific number of short, adjacent audio segments, called grains. Grains can be generated either by using a mathematical formula or by using a sample. These grains are usually 5–100 milliseconds long and are spliced together in order to form a sound. Altering the order of slices or modifying the individual properties of each slice can change the overall sound.

Wavetable synthesis is based on the playback of sampled waveforms. Wavetable synthesis offers a few key benefits, such as the capability to sweep through the wavetable at any speed without affecting the pitch, and isolating and looping specific points of the wavetable.

For modern-day examples of both granular and wavetable synthesis, check out the Native Instruments Reaktor virtual synth.

As stated, graintable synthesis is a combination of these two forms of synthesis and works in the following way:

1. The oscillators of the Malström play sampled sounds that have been pre-processed in a complex manner and cut into individual grains. From this point on, these converted samples are now called graintables.

2. These graintables are made up of periodic sets of waveforms that, when combined, play back the original sounds.

Figure 11.1 The Malström is a virtual synth unlike any other, software or hardware.

3. At this point, the graintable is treated in the same way as a wavetable. You have the ability to sweep through the graintable and single out any nuance of the graintable that you would like to manipulate. For example, you could extract a vowel out of a voice graintable. Additionally, the graintable can be manipulated further by incorporating the ability to "shift" the frequency region or "formant" without altering the pitch, which is a granular synthesis quality.

Tour the Malström

Now that you have learned the fundamentals of graintable synthesis, load an instance of the Malström and take a tour of the interface. Before you begin this section, start a new Reason song and load an instance of reMix and the Malström.

The Oscillator Section

The Malström has two oscillators from which to generate sound (see Figure 11.2). The Malström's oscillators are meant to perform two tasks:

■ Play the loaded graintable

■ Generate a pitch

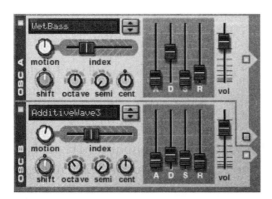

Figure 11.2 The Malström has two built-in oscillators.

Upon first creating an instance of the Malström, a default patch will load and can be heard by playing your keyboard. This is a good, solid sound to begin touring the Malström, but you can click on the Patch Browser located in the upper-left corner of the Malström interface and load patches from the Reason Factory Sound Bank. As was the case with the Subtractor, Malström patches are organized by their intended use, including the following:

- Bass

- FX

- Mono synths

- Pads

- Percussion

- Poly synths

- Rhythmic

Of course, none of these presets is set in stone, so to speak. You can modify a poly synth patch to be used as a pad, or a mono synth patch to be used as a bass synth. You just have to learn your way around the Malström and understand how each part of the interface works. With that thought in mind, let's continue onwards by touring the individual sections of the Malström with a clean slate. Right-click on the interface and select Initialize Patch. This will reset the Malström and give you a good starting point.

After activating either of the oscillators, the next task is to select a graintable from the display just to the right of the OSC A and OSC B power buttons. You can select a graintable either by using the scroll buttons of the graintable display or by clicking on the display itself. If you click on the display, a pop-up menu will appear, displaying a very long list of available graintables to choose from (see Figure 11.3).

Organization of the Graintables   As you begin to explore the long list of over 80 graintables, it's refreshing to see that Propellerhead has categorized these graintables by type. This makes it much easier when beginning to build a new patch from scratch or when editing a patch.

The graintable list is organized as follows:

- **Bass**—6 graintables

- **FX**—10 graintables

- **Guitar**—5 graintables

- **Misc**—3 graintables

Figure 11.3 The Malström includes many available graintables. Notice that they are categorized by type (for example, Guitar: Acoustic Guitar and FX: Drips).

- **Perc**—5 graintables
- **Synth**—22 graintables
- **Voices**—11 graintables
- **Wave**—10 graintables
- **Wind**—10 graintables

Setting the Oscillator Frequency

Once a graintable has been selected, you can then alter the frequency of the oscillators by using a combination of three parameters (see Figure 11.4).

Figure 11.4 Alter the frequency of the oscillators by using the Octave, Semi, and Cent parameters.

- **Octave**—This parameter alters the frequency of a graintable by octaves and has a range of seven octaves.

- **Semi**—This parameter alters the frequency of a graintable by semitones and has a range of 12 semitones, or one full octave.

- **Cent**—This parameter alters the frequency of a graintable by cents. With a range of one semitone, it is used to make very fine adjustments to a loaded graintable.

Altering the Oscillator Playback

After setting the frequency of a graintable, you can alter the playback of the oscillators by using the Motion, Index, and Shift parameters (see Figure 11.5).

Figure 11.5 The Index, Motion, and Shift controls allow you to tweak the selected graintable to the max.

- **Index**—This slider is used to set the start point for the playback of the graintable. It has a range of 0–127.

- **Motion**—This parameter is used to set the speed at which a graintable is played, according to its motion pattern. Turning the knob to the left slows the motion of the graintable down, whereas turning it to the right speeds it up.

- **Shift**—This parameter alters the timbre or formant spectrum of a graintable. The formant spectrum is the overview that determines the overall character of a graintable. This is done by a procedure known as re-sampling. Using this parameter effectively creates a pitch shift effect on the oscillator.

Motion Pattern   Each graintable in a patch has a preset motion pattern and speed. If you're setting the Motion parameter to any value higher than –63 or hard left, the graintable loops and follows one of two motion patterns:

- **Forward**—The graintable is played from beginning to end, and then loops back to the beginning.

- **Forward/Backward**—The graintable is played from beginning to end, and then from the end to beginning. It then starts over.

As stated before, the Motion parameter can change the speed of the graintable, but not the actual graintable itself.

The Amplitude Envelope

Each of the Malström oscillators has an individual envelope and volume knob to alter its amplitude (see Figure 11.6).

Figure 11.6 The Amp Envelope of each oscillator allows for precise amplitude control.

- **Attack**—When an envelope is triggered, the Attack parameter determines how long it takes for the envelope to reach its maximum value.

- **Decay**—Once the maximum value is reached, the Decay parameter determines how long it stays at the level before the value begins to drop.

- **Sustain**—After the value begins to drop, the Sustain determines the level the falling value should rest at.

- **Release**—Once the value has been set at its rested value, the Release parameter determines how long it will take for the value to return to zero after the keys have been released.

Routing and Output

Once you have set the oscillator parameters, you can then route the output of those signals to a combination of four filter destinations. Looking at Figure 11.7, you can see

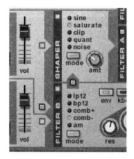

Figure 11.7 The oscillators point to the right, which means that they can be routed to the filter sections. Notice that OSC A points to both filters, which means that the output signal of OSC A can actually be split and routed to two destination filters.

that each oscillator points to the right, with a corresponding "routing" button that looks a lot like the standard power buttons you have been looking at throughout this chapter. To route the oscillators to their corresponding filters, just click on the available routing buttons.

The Output section of the Malström is very simple and has only two adjustable parameters (see Figure 11.8).

Figure 11.8 The output of the Malström can control the amplitude and panning assignment for both oscillators.

- **Spread**—This parameter is used to adjust the panning width of OSC A and B. Turning this knob hard right creates a very wide stereo field, in which OSC A is heard only in the left channel, whereas OSC B is heard in the right.

- **Volume**—This adjusts the overall volume of the Malström.

The Filter Section

As you have read in previous chapters, a filter is used to alter the overall character of a sound. The Filter section of the Malström does this tenfold by including additional filters and parameters that deviate significantly from most other filters (see Figure 11.9).

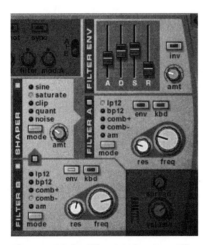

Figure 11.9 The Malström Filter section provides many creative filtering possibilities that differ greatly from those of most other synths.

To activate Filter A or Filter B, click on their power buttons, found in the upper-left corner of each filter. Also, make sure that the appropriate oscillator is assigned to the desired filter.

Filter Types

Before altering the Resonance and Cutoff Frequency parameters, you must choose one of five filter types (see Figure 11.10).

Figure 11.10   Each of the Malström filters offers five filter types.

- **LP12:** This filter allows low frequencies to pass through it, while high frequencies are filtered out. This low pass filter has a roll-off curve of approximately 12 decibels per octave.

- **BP12:** Filters out both the high and low frequencies, leaving the mid frequencies alone to be toyed with. With a roll off curve of 12 decibels per octave, the BP 12 can be used effectively on instrument loops such as a guitar loop or possibly hi-hat heavy percussion loops.

- **Comb +/−:** A comb filter is essentially a series of delays with very short delay times assigned to each delay instance, resulting in a detuned sound. The feedback of these delays is controlled by the Resonance parameter in each filter. The difference between the Comb+ and Comb− is the position of the delay peaks within the spectrum.

- **AM (Amplitude Modulation):** This filter produces a Sine wave, which is then multiplied by the output of OSC A or B. The resulting sound contains additional frequencies that are a result of the sum and difference of the two frequencies. Note that the Resonance knob controls the mix between the two signals. If this sounds familiar, another way to think of this is as a *ring modulator*.

The Filter Controls

Once a filter type has been selected, you can then use the main controls of the filter to alter the character of the Malström patch (see Figure 11.11).

Figure 11.11   The main parameters of the Malström filters.

- **Kbd (keyboard tracking)**—When this parameter is activated, it enables the filter to react differently the higher you play on the keyboard. If this parameter is deactivated, the filter effect will remain constant.

- **Env (envelope)**—When this parameter is activated, the filter will then be modulated by the Filter Envelope.

- **Freq (Cutoff Frequency)**—This parameter has two purposes, depending on which filter type is selected. When LP24, BP12, or Comb+/– is selected, this parameter acts as a cutoff frequency knob that specifies where the filter will function within the frequency spectrum. When the AM Filter Type is selected, the Frequency knob will control the frequency of the ring-modulated signal generated by the AM filter.

- **Res (Resonance)**—This parameter has two purposes depending on which filter type is selected. When LP12, BP12, or Comb+/– is selected, this parameter emphasizes the frequencies set by the Frequency knob. When the AM Filter Type is selected, the Resonance knob regulates the balance between the original and the modulated signal.

The Filter Envelope

The Filter Envelope is used to alter the characteristics of both Filter A and B. The main parameters of the envelope match those of the Oscillator Envelopes, so there is no need to review how Attack, Decay, Sustain, and Release work (see Figure 11.12). The additional parameters for the Filter Envelope are as follows:

Figure 11.12 The Filter Envelope can be used to create long, sweeping effects for pad sounds, or bubble-like sweeps for bass synths.

- **Inv (Inverse)**—This button is used to invert the individual parameters of the Filter Envelope. For example, say you are using the Attack parameter of the Filter Envelope and have assigned a positive value of 80, which produces a very slow attack. Activate the Invert button and the Attack parameter is inverted, which means the attack will be much faster now.

- **Amt (Amount)**—This knob is used to assign the amount of envelope to the filters.

The Shaper

In addition to the obvious auditory goodies that the Filter section provides, take a moment to focus on the small but mighty Shaper. The Shaper is a *waveshaper*, which alters the waveform shape itself. This results in either a more complex, rich sound or a truncated distortion that rivals Industrial Music on a good day.

The Shaper is activated by clicking on its power button, located in the upper-left corner of the Shaper interface. Once activated, you can edit the waveshaping effect by selecting a mode and assigning an amount.

Let's have a look at the different shaping modes. They can be selected by using the Mode button or by just clicking on the name of the desired mode itself (see Figure 11.13).

Figure 11.13 The Shaper is capable of beefing up your synth patches with saturation or creating a synthetic meltdown with ultra distortion.

- **Sine**—Creates a smooth sound.

- **Saturate**—Saturates the original signal, resulting in a rich, lush sound.

- **Clip**—Adds digital distortion to the signal.

- **Quant**—Truncates the signal and can be used to create a grungy 8-bit sound.

- **Noise**—Multiplies the original signal with noise.

Using the Shaper With Filter B   Located at the top of Filter B is a routing button that allows that filter to be sent to the Shaper, creating a very interesting combination of sounds. For example, you can send OSC A to the Shaper, while at the same time split and send OSC A to Filter B. OSC B will also be sent to Filter B, and then routed to the Shaper as well. After both signals are combined and processed by the Shaper, the signal is then sent to Filter A, and sent along to the outputs of the Malström.

The Modulator Section

Located above the Oscillator section is a pair of modulators, which are used to alter the character of the synth sound (see Figure 11.14). If this sounds a little familiar, another way to think of these modulators is as low frequency oscillators, which were discussed in the last two chapters and will be discussed again in the future. However, because the Malström is a synth unlike anything else in Reason, it's safe to say that these

Figure 11.14 The Malström modulator section is actually a pair of LFOs.

modulators go way above and beyond the call of duty when it comes to modulating the oscillators.

The Sounds of Silence As with the Subtractor and Dr. Octo Rex, the Malström modulators do not produce sound on their own. Although they do generate a waveform and frequency, they are assigned to alter the character of OSC A and B.

When an instance of the Malström is created, modulators A and B are active and ready to use. To deactivate either of these, click on their power buttons, which are located at the upper-left corner of each modulator.

Take a look at the source parameters of the Modulator section.

- **Curve**—This parameter is used to select a modulating waveform. The selected waveform is shown in the Curve display window. You can either use the scroll buttons to select different waveforms or click and drag up and down on the display. There are over 30 waveforms to choose from, so it should keep you busy for a long time to come.

- **Rate**—This parameter controls the speed of modulation. Turn the knob to the left to slow the frequency down or to the right to speed it up. Also note that if the Sync button is activated, the rate indicator is measured in note values (that is, 1/4, 1/8, and 1/16).

- **One Shot**—When activated, the One Shot will play the modulation waveform a single time.

- **Sync**—This parameter makes the modulator synchronize with the tempo of your Reason song.

- **A/B Selector**—This parameter is used to select which oscillator the modulator will affect. You can select OSC A, OSC B, or both.

Once a modulation waveform, rate, and source have been selected, you can choose a destination parameter to be modulated. Note that both modulators have different destination parameters, so I will point those out along the way.

Bipolar Parameters The destination parameter knobs are bipolar. This means that when the knob is in the middle position, there is no modulation effect, but turning the knob to the left or right will increase the amount of modulation. To make it even more interesting, when the knob is turned to the left, the waveform of the modulator is inverted.

- **Pitch (Mod A)**—Modulates the pitch parameter of OSC A, B, or both.

- **Index (Mod A)**—Modulates the index start position of OSC A, B, or both.

- **Shift (Mod A)**—Modulates the harmonic content of OSC A, B, or both.

- **Motion (Mod B)**—Modulates the motion speed of OSC A, B, or both.

- **Level (Mod B)**—Modulates the output amplitude of OSC A, B, or both.

- **Filter (Mod B)**—Modulates the cutoff filter of OSC A, B, or both.

- **Mod:A (Mod B)**—Alters the amount of modulation from Mod A.

The Play Parameters

The parameters covered in this section affect the overall sound of the Malström based on the way that you play the synth (see Figure 11.15).

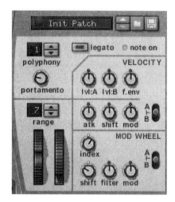

Figure 11.15 The Malström Play parameters can give your synth performance more expression.

Polyphony

Polyphony assigns the number of voices that can be played at one time. The Malström has a polyphony range of 1 to 16 voices, which is not a lot by comparison to the Subtractor or NN-19/XT synths. However, it is important to keep in mind that the Malström is a much more CPU-intensive virtual synth, and every voice takes a little more CPU power.

No Low Bandwidth One feature that the Malström is missing is a Low Bandwidth button. There is no explanation why this feature is not included with the Malström, but perhaps the technology behind this synth wonder makes it impossible to support such a feature.

But I have run Malström with no problems on a pair of fairly slow computers. But keep in mind that the slower the computer, the more trouble you might have running the Malström.

Portamento

Portamento creates a sliding effect between played notes. The knob determines the amount of time it will take to slide from one note to another. It can be used with either monophonic or polyphonic patches and is a great tool for creating some interesting effects.

Legato

Legato is a commonly used parameter for playing monophonic patches, such as leads or bass lines. With the legato parameter activated and the polyphony set to 1, press and hold down a note, and then press and hold another note. Notice that the new note has no attack, because the Malström envelopes have not been retriggered.

Velocity Controls

The Malström is a velocity-sensitive synthesizer, as are the other Reason synths. The Velocity controls are used to affect different parameters of the Malström according to how much velocity is applied to individual notes.

- **Level A**—This parameter velocity controls the output of OSC A.

- **Level B**—This parameter velocity controls the output of OSC B.

- **Filter Envelope**—This parameter assigns the velocity control of the Filter Envelope.

- **Attack**—This parameter velocity controls the Attack parameter of OSC A, B, or both.

- **Shift**—This parameter velocity controls the Shift parameter of OSC A, B, or both.

- **Modulation**—This parameter velocity controls the amounts of Modulator A, B, or both.

Pitch Bend Wheel

The Pitch Bend Wheel is an emulation of a standard pitch wheel found on most MIDI keyboards. Simply put, it is used to bend the pitch of the played notes up and down. The Range parameter, located just above the Pitch Bend Wheel, controls the range of the pitch bend by up to +/– two octaves.

Modulation Wheel

The Modulation Wheel is used to control a number of available parameters:

- **Index**—This parameter affects the graintable index of OSC A, B, or both.

- **Shift**—This parameter affects the Shift parameter of OSC A, B, or both.

- **Filter**—This parameter affects the Frequency Filter of Filter A, B, or both.

- **Modulation**—This parameter alters the amount of modulation from Modulator A, B, or both.

CV Connections

Press the Tab key to flip the Device Rack around, and you'll see that the Malström has many connections that can be used to sequence with the Matrix, to modulate other devices, or to be modulated by other devices (see Figure 11.16).

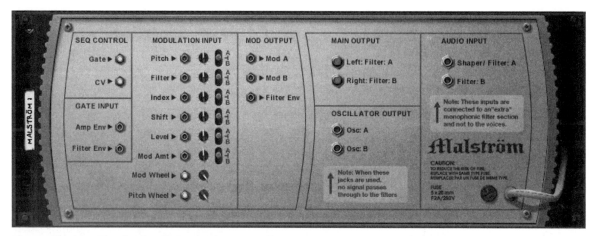

Figure 11.16   The back of the Malström offers many routing possibilities.

Audio Outputs

These connections are used to output the signal from the Malström to reMix. There are a couple of options.

- **Main Outputs**—These are the main audio outputs of the Malström. They are taken from the outputs of the Filter section.

- **Oscillator Outputs**—This second pair of outputs is taken directly from the outputs of OSC A and B. If you connect these outputs to reMix, the main outputs will no longer work.

Audio Input

Another of the many lesser-known, yet equally mind-blowing, features of the Malström is the audio input capabilities. These inputs make it possible to route the audio output of any Reason device into the audio inputs of the Malström, which are then directly fed into Filters A and B. Essentially, this makes the Malström an audio effect that is perfect for laying down some intense filter work on your loops, synths, and samples.

For kicks, try the following exercise:

1. Create a new Reason song.

2. Create instances of reMix, Malström, and the NN-19. Load a sample patch into the NN-19 and arm the sequencer track to receive MIDI.

3. Press the Tab key to flip the interface.

4. Disconnect the NN-19 from reMix by selecting it and choosing Disconnect Device from the Edit pull-down menu.

5. Route the audio outputs of the NN-19 to the audio inputs of the Malström (see Figure 11.17).

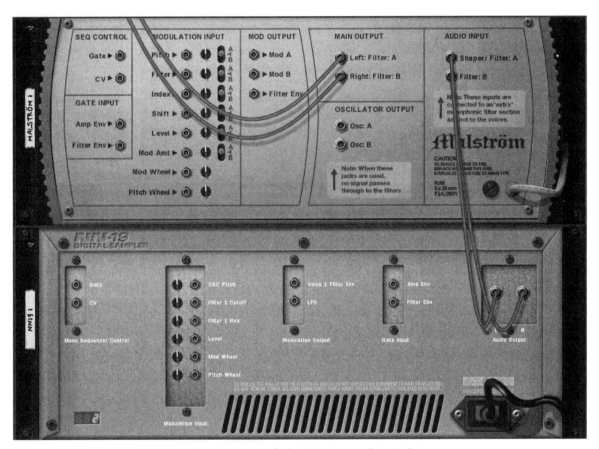

Figure 11.17 Connect the audio outputs of the NN-19 to the Malström.

6. With the NN-19 sequencer track selected and armed to receive MIDI, play a note on your MIDI keyboard, and you will hear the sample patch played through the filters of the Malström.

Sequencer Controls

The Sequencer Control inputs are used to connect the Malström to a pattern-controlled device, such as the Matrix or Redrum.

■ **Gate**—This input is typically connected to the Gate CV output of the Matrix or Redrum in order to receive Note On/Off messages.

■ **CV**—This input is typically connected to the Note CV output of the Matrix in order to receive note information.

> **See Chapter 15**   For more information on using the Matrix, be sure to check out Chapter 15, "The Matrix—Close Up," where you will find some interesting tutorials on how to connect the Matrix to the Subtractor. These tutorials also work great with the Malström.

Gate Input

These inputs are used to receive Gate information from either the Matrix or Redrum in order to trigger the following envelopes:

- Amp Envelope
- Filter Envelope

Modulation Input/Output

To the right of the Sequencer controls and Gate input are the Modulation inputs and outputs. The Modulation inputs can receive modulation output signals from any Reason device. The Curve CV output on the back of the Matrix is a good example of this. The Modulation outputs send out modulation information to any Reason device. A commonly used connection is to connect any of the Modulation outputs of the Malström to the Modulation inputs of the Subtractor.

Take a look at the various inputs.

- **Pitch**—This input is used to affect the pitch of Modulators A, B, or both.
- **Filter**—This input is used to affect the filter frequency of Modulators A, B, or both.
- **Index**—This input is used to affect the index of Modulators A, B, or both.
- **Shift**—This input is used to affect the shift of Modulators A, B, or both.
- **Level**—This input is used to affect the amplitude of Oscillators A, B, or both.
- **Modulation Amount**—This input is used to affect the amount of modulation.
- **Modulation Wheel**—This input is used to affect the amount of Modulation Wheel.
- **Pitch Wheel**—This input is used to affect the amount of pitch.

And now, take a look at the outputs.

- **Mod A**—This connection routes the output of Modulator A to the modulation inputs of any other Reason device. Try connecting it to the FM Amount parameter of the Subtractor.

- **Mod B**—This connection routes the output of Modulator B to the modulation inputs of any Reason device.

- **Filter Envelope**—This connection routes the output of the Filter Envelope to the modulation inputs of any Reason device.

Your First Malström Patch

Now that you have a pretty firm idea of how the Malström works, it's time to dig in and create your first customized Malström patch. This tutorial takes you through a step-by-step process of programming a bass synth patch that will be perfect for any ambient occasion.

Setting Up a Starting Point

Before you program your first Malström patch, it's important to find a good starting point. Writing in a sequence that's appropriate for the kind of patch you are going to create will make the programming process quicker and more efficient. For example, if you were going to create a pad sound, you would typically want to write in a sequence of long, sustained chords, so you could hear the pad sound properly.

If you are planning to program a bass synth patch to be used in techno music, it's a good idea to write in a standard techno bass line in the Reason sequencer. Then set the sequencer to play the bass line over and over again in a loop (see Figure 11.18). Then you can make real-time adjustments to the patch as the sequence is playing and program the patch to complement the style of music you are going to create with the patch.

Programming Your Malström Patch

In this tutorial, you are going to go build a bass patch by working with each section of the Malström interface. Just as in the last chapter, this tutorial serves as a good review tool to help you remember everything that you have learned about the functionality of the Malström.

Programming the Oscillators

Let's start things off simple by working with OSC A, and then add OSC B later. To hear the changes in real time, press Play on the Transport bar. The two-bar loop should start playing continuously.

1. By default, the graintable of OSC A is set to a Sine wave. Notice the organ-like tone that is produced.

2. Use the scroll buttons or click on the graintable box to display a list of available sounds. Choose the Wet Bass graintable.

3. Next, use the Index slider to set the start point of the graintable. Set it to 40, and notice how dramatically the overall tone and timbre of the graintable changes.

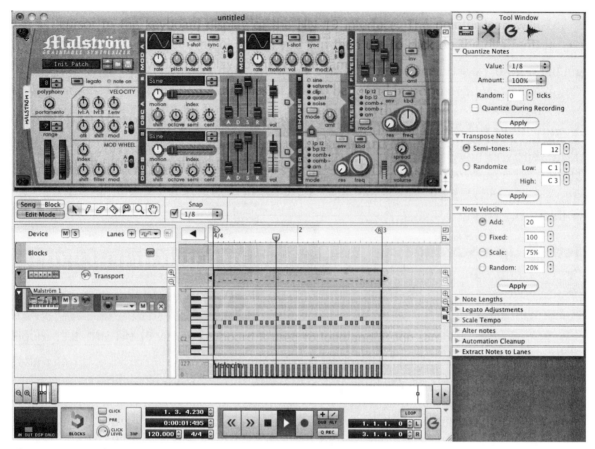

Figure 11.18 I have written a techno styled bass line into the Reason sequencer in order to program a bass synth patch in the Malström.

Let's also make a few adjustments to the Amplitude Envelope of OSC A. Set the parameters to the following values:

■ **Attack**—Set to 0.

■ **Decay**—Set to 65.

■ **Sustain**—Set to 0.

■ **Release**—Set to 14 for a short release.

And now, on to OSC B.

1. Activate OSC B, and set its graintable to Synth: Additive Wave 3.

2. Set the Motion to 7.

3. Set the Octave parameter to 3.

4. Set the index slider to 48.

Let's make a few adjustments to the Amplitude Envelope of OSC B. Set the parameters to the following values:

- **Attack**—Set to 12.

- **Decay**—Set to 25.

- **Sustain**—Set to 16.

- **Release**—Set to 10.

Upon listening to the patch at this point, it lacks uniqueness. You can introduce such a quality by way of the modulators.

Programming the Modulators

As you read earlier in this chapter, the modulators are actually two separate LFOs. In this section of the tutorial, you are going to assign the modulators to manipulate OSC A and B.

1. Activate Mod A and select the Sync button. This will lock the modulation effect up with the tempo of the Reason sequencer.

2. By default, the waveform of Mod A should be set to a Sine wave. Leave it at this setting and set the Rate knob to 1/4, which means that the modulation effect will take place every quarter note.

3. Set the destination of Mod A to OSC A&B by using the A/B selector to the right of the Mod A interface.

4. Assign a negative value of –24 to the Index knob. This should then cause the Shift of OSC A&B to open and close in tempo.

Programming the Filter and Shaper

In this section of the tutorial, you are going to add the Shaper to OSC A to introduce a little distortion to the bass sound.

1. Activate both the Route Oscillator A to Shaper and Activate Shaper buttons.

2. Select the Saturate Shaper mode by using the Mode button or by clicking on the name. You should immediately hear a strong distorted signal applied to OSC A.

3. Set the Shaper Amount knob to 39 to turn down the distortion effect.

Next, you'll route OSC B to Filter B and do some more damage.

1. Activate the Route Oscillator B to Filter B button. Filter B should already be activated and ready to use. Also note that the Env button is already active, which means that the Filter Envelope can be used at this time.

2. Set Filter mode to Comb– by using the Mode button or by clicking on the name.

3. Set the Resonance knob to 70.

4. Set the Frequency Filter knob to 99.

You can also assign OSC A to Filter B by clicking on the Route OSC A to Filter B button. I suggest not activating it for this tutorial because OSC A has a very strong signal of its own.

Additionally, you can route Filter B to the Shaper by clicking on the Route Filter B to Shaper button, which is located just in between Filter B and the Shaper sections. This will add a pleasant distortion to the Filter B, which sounds pretty cool.

To finish with the Filter and Shaper sections, use the Filter Envelope on Filter B. Set the envelope parameters to these values:

■ **Amount**—Set to 32

■ **Attack**—Set to 38

■ **Decay**—Set to 59

■ **Sustain**—Set to 64

■ **Release**—Set to 10

Programming the Play Parameters

You're in the home stretch; you can finish this patch by making a few adjustments to the Play parameters of the Malström, as follows:

■ **Polyphony**—By default the Malström has polyphony of 8, and this is fine for a bass synth sound. You might even want to assign a polyphony of 1 so that you can make this a monophonic synth.

■ **Modulation Wheel**—Set the A/B Selector to its default position. Assign a negative value to the Shift knob in the Mod Wheel section so it will decrease in value as the Modulation Wheel is used. Assign a positive amount to the Index knob in the Mod Wheel section.

■ **Portamento**—Assigning a positive amount of 34 to this parameter will create a sliding effect that sounds great with monophonic bass synths.

After all is said and done, your new bass patch should sound pretty awesome and work well with just about any form of electronic music. Just make sure to click on the Save Patch button to save your work.

For the bold explorers out there, I suggest some free-form experimentation. Sequence a short loop, start it playing, and then use your ears as you switch graintables and adjust the Motion, Shift, Index, Shaper, Modulation, and Filter parameters. You will quickly find that there are no upper (or outer) limits to what weird and wonderful sounds you can create.

12 Thor—Close Up

When it comes to going above and beyond in order to please the hardcore synth fan, Reason's centerpiece to the Device Rack is Thor (see Figure 12.1). And like the mythical God of Thunder, Thor has more than enough "junk in the trunk" to give your songs that extra kick of dynamics with filters, effects, and, yes, a built-in step sequencer. In other words, you're going to love this synth.

Polysonic—Many Synths

At first sight, you will certainly notice that Propellerhead has yet again coined a new phrase to describe this synthetic wonder, which is *polysonic*. If you ask them, I'm sure that they've got a great PR sort of way to tell you how they came to call it such. But to me, polysonic suggests that Thor is not just one, but rather a palette of different types of synthesis, mixed together in order to create truly unique sounds and textures. These forms of synthesis include the following:

- Subtractive

- Wavetable

- Phase Modulation

- Frequency Modulation (FM)

- Multi Oscillation

- Noise

In addition, Thor also sports an impressive step sequencer, real-time effects and filters, and an impressive Modulation Bus, all of which can be routed in a variety of ways. So in essence, this makes Thor a semi-modular synthesizer.

Easy Does It   I'm sure that upon your first look at Thor, you're probably thinking, "How am I going to figure this all out?" Well, the good news is that you've already read about most of the components that make up Thor. For example, the Subtractor is all about subtractive synthesis, whereas the Malström shares a

315

similarity or two with Wavetable. So worry not brave readers, Thor is a piece of cake to navigate, as you will see throughout this chapter. However, if you haven't read Chapters 10 or 11 yet, it might be a good idea to do that first before proceeding.

Figure 12.1 Thor is one of the hottest synths you'll find within Reason. It supports several types of synthesis.

Take a Tour of Thor

You're now ready to push on and start exploring Thor, so I'm going to break it down and tackle each of the following sections step-by-step.

- **The Controller**—This is the first thing you see when you create an instance of Thor.

- **The Programmer**—This is where you tweak to your heart's content.

- **The Modulation Bus**—From here, you can create simple or complex modulation curves to control Thor's parameters in real-time.

- **The Step Sequencer**—This is where you can create different patterns, such as melodies or modulation sources.

This section also covers the CV connections on the back of Thor. Then in the chapter's final section you'll apply what you have learned by building a few different patches.

The Controller

Upon first loading an instance of Thor, you'll immediately see the Controller panel, which displays and controls its play parameters (see Figure 12.2). Obviously, this is just an abbreviated look for Thor, because it's a very complex synth. It's just simply a way to load patches easily and begin playing with the real-time parameters, such as portamento and pitch.

Figure 12.2 When you create an instance of Thor, the first thing you'll see is the Controller panel.

Because you've seen a few of these common parameters already in past chapters of this book, I'll just briefly list them, as there's no need for in-depth discussion.

- **Patch Browser**—This works exactly as you have already read.

- **Pitch Wheel**—No mystery here, and there is also a range dialog box above, which governs the amount of pitch (+/– 2 octaves)

- **Modulation Wheel**—Although this is a common parameter, you'll find that there are several sources that can be routed to this wheel, making it quite versatile.

- **Master Volume**—This knob adjusts the overall amplitude of Thor.

Now, let's dig into the more complicated parameters of Thor, starting with the Keyboard modes. Although most of these parameters may seem a little common, like portamento, Thor introduces some additional features that set it apart from anything you've learned about up to this point.

Thor includes two kinds of polyphony, as you can see from Figure 12.2.

- **Polyphony**—This is the standard polyphony that you've already read about in previous chapters. Thor supports a polyphony count of 0–32 voices.

- **Release Polyphony**—This is a unique type of polyphony that deals with the decay of your patches. Simply put, Release Polyphony manages the amount of notes that are allowed to decay naturally after you release a note on your keyboard. It has a maximum value of 32, just like the regular polyphony. When set to its lowest value of 0, any notes played after released notes will simply cut those released notes.

Just keep in mind that the greater the polyphony count, the more CPU you use.

In addition to the polyphony are the play modes, which can be selected by clicking on them with your mouse or by using the Mode button. Let's discuss these in detail.

- **Mono Legato**—This is a simple monophonic mode that does not retrigger the envelope.

- **Mono Retrig**—This monophonic mode does exactly the opposite, as it will trigger the envelope regardless if another note is already held down.

- **Polyphonic**—When this is selected, Thor will play notes according to the amount of polyphony and release polyphony assigned to it.

Moving onto the right, portamento creates a sliding effect between played notes. The knob determines the amount of time it will take to slide from one note to another. It can be used with either monophonic or polyphonic patches and is a great tool for creating some interesting effects. There are three modes:

- **Off**—No portamento effect.

- **On**—The portamento effect will happen no matter what notes you play on the keyboard.

- **Auto**—When this mode is selected, you'll hear the effect only when more than one note is played. However, if the mono modes are selected, portamento will affect the legato notes.

The Trigger section dictates how Thor will be played:

- **MIDI**—Selecting this will tell Thor to respond only when receiving note information via MIDI.

- **Step Sequencer**—Selecting this will tell Thor to respond when receiving note information from the Step Sequencer.

- **Both**—You can select both MIDI and Step Sequencer options to have Thor respond to either option.

To the right of the Trigger section are the Virtual controls, which consist of two knobs and two buttons (see Figure 12.3). This is a feature unique to Thor, as these knobs and buttons can be assigned to several parameters and can also be easily automated.

All of the assignments are handled by the Modulation Bus, which you'll be getting into later in this chapter. Note that you can easily label the different knobs and buttons simply by double-clicking on their corresponding labels.

Figure 12.3 The Virtual controls can be assigned to many parameters. As you can see here in this figure, the knobs are assigned to the Comb Filter/Frequency while the buttons are assigned to the Delay and Chorus effects.

In addition, the functions that you assign to the buttons can be assigned to MIDI notes in order to turn them off and on much more easily. For example, you could route them to the Delay and Chorus power switches and use MIDI notes to turn the effects off and on during a performance, thereby making the performance all the more dynamic. I'll show you how to do this later.

The Programmer

The programmer is where the real magic of Thor comes into play, because there are so many different creative possibilities (see Figure 12.4). I could spend much more time than a book allows, but I'm going to leave that part to you. First things first, let's take a tour through this interface to better understand how everything works.

Figure 12.4 The Programmer of Thor offers up a healthy dose of synthesis.

Because this is a "semi-modular" synth, I'm going to refer to each of these highlighted segments as "modules," as that is in fact what they are. Each of these modules is routed or can be routed in a variety of different configurations to produce very different and complex sounds. To make things simple, I'm going to section off and explain each of the following modules.

- **The Oscillators**
- **The Mixer**
- **The Filters**
- **The Shaper**
- **The Amplifier**
- **The LFOs**
- **The Envelopes**
- **The Global Parameters**

> **Space Saving**   As you have already read about a lot of the principals of synthesis, such as the definition of an oscillator, envelope, I'm going to jump straight into touring the actual functions and features here in order to save time and get you working in Thor quickly.

The Oscillators

Thor has a total of three slots for oscillator modules and each includes six types of oscillators. Any of these oscillators can be selected by clicking on the pop-up menu arrow at the top-left corner of each slot:

- Analog
- Wavetable
- Phase Modulation
- FM Pair
- Multi Oscillator
- Noise

You also have the option to select Off to bypass a slot.

There are several common parameters that these oscillators share, so let's get them out of the way right off the bat.

- **OCT**—The Octave knob sets the oscillator tuning to one of 10 possible octaves.

- **Semi**—This alters the pitch in semitone increments.

- **Tune**—This is a fine tuning knob that adjusts in cents.

- **KBD**—The Keyboard Track knob tells Thor how to interpret the pitch of each incoming MIDI message.

- **Waveform Selectors**—Each oscillator can produce one of several different waveforms.

- **Sync**—Each of the oscillator modules can be synced (more on this later).

The Analog Oscillator. This module is the most common type of oscillator (see Figure 12.5). It is very similar in sound and style to that found in the Subtractor. There are four waveforms to select from: Sawtooth, Pulse, Triangle, and Sine.

Figure 12.5 The Analog Oscillator is the first line of defense when it comes to just about any soft synth.

You'll also notice that there is a Pulse Width knob (labeled PW), which affects just the pulse waveform.

The Wavetable Oscillator. This module is fashioned after the classic wavetable synths of the 80s, such as the Waldorf PPG and Korg Wavestation (see Figure 12.6). Wavetables are compilations of different waveforms that are combined to create different waveforms.

Figure 12.6 The Wavetable Oscillator provides 32 different wavetables.

There are 32 wavetables to choose from here, ranging from the simplest (Basic Analog), to the more complex (Sax), to the actual original wavetables found in the classic PPG synth. This module also includes some exclusive parameters.

- **Position**—This knob determines at which point to sweep through the selected wavetable. You'll find that this alters the timbre of the wavetable drastically.

- **X-Fade**—The X-Fade is used to smooth the transition between waveforms found within a wavetable.

Phase Modulation Oscillator. This module is quite unique, in that it uses different waveforms to emulate the sound of a filter (see Figure 12.7). By activating two waveforms and tweaking them with the modulation knob (labeled PD) this module can create a filter sweep.

Figure 12.7   The Phase Modulation Oscillator takes after the classic CZ synths by Casio.

The first waveform selector includes:

- **Sawtooth**

- **Square**

- **Pulse**

- **Pulse and Sine**

- **Sine and Flat**

- **Saw x Sine** (combined)

- **Sine x Sine** (combined)

- **Sine x Pulse** (combined)

The second waveform selector offers the first five waveforms.

FM Pair Oscillator. The FM Pair Oscillator (see Figure 12.8) produces a unique sound through the usage of Frequency Modulation (FM). As you will recall from Chapter 10, FM is a form of synthesis that combines an oscillator called the *carrier* with another oscillator called the *modulator*. When combined, these two oscillators can produce a variety of different signals by making use of the various parameters. So when you think about it, there are two oscillators at work here in this single module.

Figure 12.8   The FM Pair Oscillator is a module that uses FM to generate strange, bell like signals.

There are 32 waveforms available between each oscillator as well as an FM Amount knob, which is used to intensify the FM effect.

Multi Oscillator. The Multi Oscillator (see Figure 12.9) is a module that creates huge, wide sounds by stacking several oscillators of the same waveform type. This module has all the same waveforms as the Analog module, but with additional parameters.

Figure 12.9 The Multi Oscillator is capable of producing very large sounds by stacking on several oscillators of the same waveform and altering their tuning.

- **Amount (AMT)**—This knob controls the amount of detune between the multiple oscillators.

- **Detune Mode**—There are eight modes or starting points, where the AMT knob will intensify the detune effect. For example, there is an octave mode, which stacks a lower and higher note an octave apart. The AMT knob can then be used to create strange but interesting detune effects.

Noise Oscillator. Thor's Noise Oscillator is a much different sounding module than any I've heard in a long time (see Figure 12.10). It offers several types of noise, most of which can then be manipulated by a modulating knob called the Bandwidth or BW to the right of the different noise waveforms. Noise is particularly useful when creating percussion sounds, such as cymbals or snare drums.

Figure 12.10 When it's percussion patches you're building in Thor, a noise oscillator is a must.

- **Band**—This oscillator produces a pure noise that can be changed to a pure tone by using the BW knob.

- **Sample and Hold (S&H)**—This is a random type of noise, which sounds a lot like bit crushing, where a pure signal is broken down and degraded bit by bit.

- **Static**—This is an emulation of static noise that you might hear on a car radio.

- **Color**—This type of noise is associated with a color type based on its characteristics.

- **White**—This mode produces a pure white noise, which cannot be altered by the BW knob.

Additional Oscillator Parameters. In addition to the three oscillators, this section includes a couple of routing possibilities to help shape the overall sound.

- **Sync buttons**—Used to sync the outputs of Oscillator 2 and 3 to Oscillator 1. This creates a unified sound of pitch and base frequency. A good way to demonstrate this is to create an Analog Oscillator in the top slot, and then load a Wavetable Oscillator into the slot below. Set the Octave knob on the Wavetable Oscillator to a lower value and then make adjustments with the Position knob. As you make changes to the position, this will drastically affect the timbre of the sound, because both oscillators are working independently of each other. Now, activate the Sync button and the two oscillators will function in unison.

- **The BW slider**—Works in combination with the Sync buttons, as they adjust the sync bandwidth. This can create much more pronounced synced sound the higher the value.

- **The AM slider**—Creates a ring modulation effect between Oscillators 1 and 2. Simply adjust the slider and then make changes to the pitch settings of either Oscillator 1 or 2 to hear the effect.

The Mixer

The mixer is used to mix the amplitudes of the three oscillators (see Figure 12.11). It's fairly straightforward and easy to use. There are just a couple of key features to point out here.

- **Balance 1-2**—This knob is used to adjust the balance between oscillators 1 and 2.

- **Sliders**—These sliders adjust the volume of all three oscillators. The first sliders adjust the combined volume of oscillators 1 and 2. The second slider adjusts just oscillator 3.

Figure 12.11   The mixer module is used to adjust the mix of the three Thor oscillators.

The Filters

Thor includes two modules for loading filters to modify your oscillators and a third one to modify the character of the entire patch (see Figure 12.12). Additionally, these filters can be routed and used in a variety of creative ways. For example, oscillator 1 and 3 can be routed to Filter 1 while oscillator 2 can be routed to Filter 2. Another possibility is to send all of your oscillators to both filters simultaneously and mix them all.

Figure 12.12   Thor includes two primary filter modules and a third global filter.

Before you learn about the different filters, it's a good idea to first learn about their common parameters.

- **Frequency/Resonance (FREQ/RES)**—No filter would be complete without these vital parameters. However, these parameters are a little less obvious when discussing the Formant Filter, which I'll do in a few.

- **Keyboard Tracking (KBD)**—This knob determines how the Filter Frequency reacts to notes played on your keyboard.

- **Envelope (ENV)**—This knob determines how the Filter Frequency reacts to the Filter Envelope.

- **Velocity**—This knob determines how the Filter Frequency reacts to velocity.

- **Invert (INV)**—This button inverts how the Filter Frequency reacts to the Filter Envelope.

- **Drive**—Each filter includes an input gain, which can be used to overdrive the filter effect. Note that the drive reacts differently with the Low Pass Ladder Filter.

Routing the Filters   Looking back at Figure 12.12, you'll notice the 1, 2, and 3 buttons to the immediate left of the primary filters. These are used to assign three oscillators to one or both of the available filter modules. Simply click on them with your mouse to activate them, load a filter, and you're good to go. Just make sure that you click on the Filter 2 to Amplifier button to route Filter 2 to the Amp or you won't hear it.

Low Pass Ladder Filter. The Low Pass Ladder Filter is fashioned after classic filter modules commonly found on Moog modular synths (see Figure 12.13). There are five filter modes in addition to a built-in "Shaper" that reshapes the waveform with distortion.

Figure 12.13 The Low Pass Ladder Filter can be thought of as the "classic" filter in Thor, as it emulates the filters found in popular analog synths.

As you've read about these filter slopes in detail in previous chapters, I'll just point out the "bonus features" of the Low Pass Ladder.

The Self Oscillation button at the top-right corner is used to create a feedback loop of high-pitched, bell like tones that can be further enhanced by making use of the built-in shaper and the 24dB slopes. A word of warning though, a self-oscillating filter can get very loud and easily clip your mix, not to mention damage your hearing.

Self-Oscillating Pitch   You can use the KBD knob to assign a pitch to the self-oscillating filter. Just turn it up to its maximum value and it will produce 12 semitones per octave.

There are two types of 24dB slopes and each one routes the Shaper differently. Type I will place the Shaper before the feedback loop. Type II will place the Shaper after the feedback loop.

State Variable Filter. The State Variable Filter differs greatly from the Low Pass Ladder, because it offers filtering possibilities other than just the lower frequencies (see Figure 12.14). Instead, the State Variable includes Band Pass, High Pass, as well as a unique Notch/Peak mode that combines a low pass and high pass filter. The filter frequency is then routed to the LP/HP knob that mixes between the two filters.

Sounds a little complicated I know, but with a little practice, it will certainly find its way into your Thor patches soon.

Figure 12.14 The State Variable filter is very similar to filters that you have already looked at in previous chapters. It's also very similar to the filters found on Oberheim synths.

Comb Filter. The Comb Filter is a bit simpler than the previous two filters that you've looked at (see Figure 12.15). As you will recall from Chapter 11, a comb filter is essentially a series of delays with very short delay times assigned to each delay instance, resulting in a detuned sound. The feedback of these delays is controlled by the Resonance parameter in each filter. The difference between the Comb+ and Comb– is the position of the delay peaks within the spectrum.

Figure 12.15 Thor's Comb Filter is a series of delays that can produce massive, metallic-like sweeps.

Formant Filter. The Formant Filter is probably one of the coolest modules I've used in Reason (see Figure 12.16). It's not your traditional filter module, because its primary function is to produce vowel sounds by making use of the XY pad to emulate the vowels through filter formant.

Aside from the traditional parameters in the Formant Filter, the Gender knob offers the ability to alter the timbre of the filter in order to emulate a male voice versus a female voice. Additionally, the ENV, VEL, and KBD knobs are controlled by the X slider (horizontal).

Figure 12.16 Want to create male or female voices in Thor? Look no further than the Formant Filter.

Best Formant Example There are quite a few "choir" patches available in Thor, but one of the best examples of the Formant Filter has got to be the "I Am Thor" patch, which is one of the default patches when an instance of Thor is created.

The Shaper

The Shaper is Thor's on-board distortion (see Figure 12.17). Its primary function is to alter the waveshape of the oscillators by adding a bit of saturation, or a heavy digital distortion. It's split up into three parameters.

■ **On/Off**—Turns the Shaper on and off.

Figure 12.17 The Shaper is Thor's distortion effect.

- **Modes**—There are nine modes of waveshaping, including Soft/Hard Clip, **Saturate**, Sine, Unipulse, Peak, Rectify, and Wrap.

- **Drive**—This knob adjusts the amount of waveshaping.

> **Routing the Shaper** Looking back at Figure 12.17, you'll see two buttons below the Shaper—one pointing to the left, and one to the right. These buttons determine how the Shaper is routed through Thor. Activating the button that points to the left sends the Shaper output to Filter 2. Clicking on the button that points to the right sends the output of the Shaper to the Amplifier.

The Amplifier

After you have mixed, filtered, and shaped your oscillators, it's onto the Amplifier. There are three main parameters to be aware of here.

- **Gain**—This knob adjusts the overall volume.

- **Velocity (VEL)**—This knob determines how much velocity affects the gain.

- **Pan**—This knob places the oscillators in the stereo field.

The LFO

The LFO is used to modulate the oscillators by introducing the waveform of another inaudible oscillator operating at a very low frequency. Additionally, this is a polyphonic LFO, which means that every note played will have its own LFO effect. The LFO can generate 18 waveforms from its spin controls that can be applied by making use of the following parameters.

- **Rate**—This sets the speed of the LFO in hertz (Hz). Note that if Tempo Sync is selected, the Rate knob will adjust in note values.

- **Delay**—This introduces a delay prior to the LFO effect.

- **Keyboard (KBD) Follow**—This knob sets how much the Rate is controlled by the notes played on the keyboard.

- **Key Sync**—This resets the LFO each time a note is played.

LFO 2 Thor actually includes two LFOs, the second of which is included with the Global Parameters.

The Envelopes

Thor includes three envelopes that all perform different tasks for your patches (see Figure 12.18). All of them include the standard ADSR parameters (Attack, Decay, Sustain, Release), but they also include a few extra bells and whistles. Let's cover each one.

Figure 12.18 The Envelope Section is used to alter the Filter, Amplifier, and Modulation.

The Filter/Amp Envelopes. These envelopes are used to alter the character of Thor's filter and amplifier over a determined period of time. Aside from the standard parameters, they both include a Gate Trig parameter. On the surface, this parameter is meant to be used as a power button of sorts, as it activates the envelopes. But, the Gate Trig can also be accessed by way of the Modulation Bus, which you're going to read about later in this chapter.

The Mod Envelope. The Mod Envelope functions a bit differently than the other envelopes. For one, the Mod Envelope does not have a default assignment. That has to be handled by the Modulation Bus. It also has a different type of envelope (Attack, Decay, Release, no Sustain), and it includes additional parameters.

- **Delay**—This slider introduces a delay before the envelope takes effect. The range is 0ms to 10.3 seconds.

- **Loop**—This loops the envelope as long as a note is held on your keyboard.

- **Tempo Sync**—When activated, this button will sync up all the Mod Envelope parameters to the tempo of the song. Each parameter will be adjustable in note values.

The Global Parameters

The Global Parameters of Thor affect the entire synth by introducing effects, filters, and a second LFO (see Figure 12.19). Let's go ahead and burn through these modules.

Figure 12.19 The Global Parameters are used as the synthetic icing on the cake for your Thor patches.

The Effects. In addition to the Shaper, which you looked at earlier in this chapter, Thor includes a Delay and Chorus effect to give your patches a little extra zing. You can read much more about these types of effects in Chapter 17. So for now, assume that you know what a Delay and Chorus do and push ahead and read about their parameters.

The Delay parameters include:

- **Time**—This knob adjusts the amount of time between delay repeats.

- **Feedback**—This knob determines the amount of delay repeats.

- **Rate**—This knob determines the rate at which the repeats are modulated.

- **Amount (AMT)**—This knob determines how intense the modulation is.

- **Dry/Wet**—This knob adjusts the amount between the unprocessed (dry) and processed (wet) signal. In this case, if the signal is completely wet, you hear only the delay repeats.

The Chorus parameters include:

- **Delay**—This is very similar to the Time knob in the delay. However, as this is a chorus effect, the Delay parameter introduces a very short time in the effect.

- **Feedback**—This performs the same as the Delay effect.

- **Rate**—Same as Delay.

- **Amount (AMT)**—Same as Delay.

- **Dry/Wet**—This knob adjusts the amount between the unprocessed (dry) and processed (wet) signal.

The Filter. This is the third Filter module available in Thor. However, this filter affects the entire synth, rather than just the oscillators. Because I have already discussed the different filters available, I won't repeat myself here. The best advice I can give is to try the different filter types to see which one fits your patch.

The Global Envelope. The Global Envelope is a bit more complicated than the others previously discussed, because it includes more parameters and must be assigned via the Modulation Bus. Aside from the standard ADSR parameters, the Global Envelope includes:

- **Delay**—This slider determines the delay time before the envelope kicks in.

- **Loop**—Activating this will cause the envelope to loop once triggered.

- **Hold**—This creates a hold before the Decay parameter begins.

- **Tempo Sync**—This sets the parameters of the envelope to the tempo of your song.

- **Gate Trigger**—This activates the Global Envelope.

LFO 2. This LFO is much like the one you toured earlier in this chapter as it has most of the same parameters (sans the KBD Follow). However, unlike LFO 1, this LFO is not polyphonic. Also, it must be assigned to a parameter via the Modulation Bus, which you're about to learn about now.

The Modulation Bus

Once you have crafted your Thor patch using its many oscillators, filters, and effects, you'll soon want to take your patches to the left next level, which is handled by the Modulation Bus (see Figure 12.20). This is where you can add enhancements and modifications to your patch to make them ideal for live performance, or just to make them sound more creative and spontaneous in your sequences.

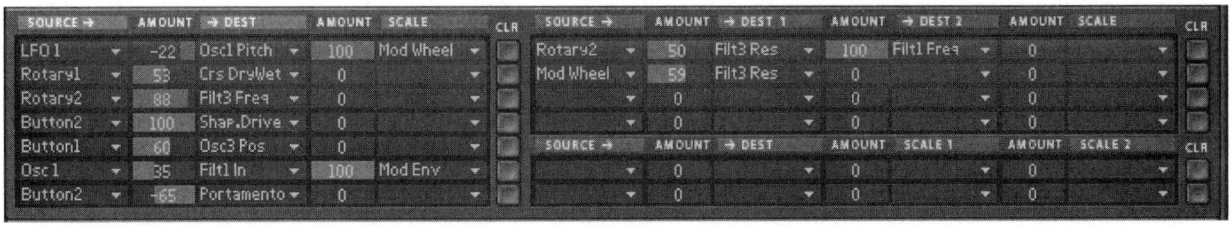

Figure 12.20 The Modulation Bus offers one of the most user-friendly interfaces for spicing up your Thor patches.

Before I can get in-depth with the Modulation Bus, first consider its main parameters.

■ **Source**—Sources can be pretty much anything you want them to be inside of Thor. Click on the first source of any Modulation Bus and you'll find that everything from audio inputs, to LFOs, to Oscillators can be used as modulation sources.

■ **Destination**—Once a source has been selected, you must select what that source is going to modulate, which is the Destination. Additionally, all destinations have an Amount slider that determines the intensity and direction of modulation for the destination.

■ **Scale**—The Scale parameter is used to govern the modulation amount. For example, let's say you set up a simple modulation where the source (LFO 1) is routed to the destination (OSC 1 pitch). If you play a note, you'll hear LFO 1 modulate OSC 1, which will create a pitch-based vibrato. You'll probably not want to hear the note played that way all the time, so you can assign the modulation to an additional parameter that will control or scale the effect, such as a Modulation Wheel. Once this parameter has been selected, you can then use its Amount slider to determine the intensity and direction of the scale effect.

It's a lot to take in at one time, but I have created a couple of examples for you in order to help make more sense out of this. The Modulation Bus offers three types of Modulation Busses.

■ There are seven Source > Destination > Scale busses.

■ There are four Source > Destination 1 > Destination 2 > Scale busses.

■ There are two Source > Destination > Scale 1 > Scale 2 busses.

Clear Your Modulations   To the immediate right of every Modulation Bus, there is a Clear button labeled CLR. Press this button to reset the bus.

Modulation Sources

At this point, it would be a good idea to list all of the possible modulation sources for the Voice section (oscillators, envelopes, LFO, Filter 1/2, and the Shaper), as well as the Global section (envelope, Filter 3, LFO 2, and so on). Click on the Modulation Source pop-up menu to begin (see Figure 12.21).

■ **Voice Key**—This assigns modulation according to notes, which is divided into four possible parameters: Note (Full Range), Note 2 (Octave), Velocity, and Gate.

■ **Osc 1/2/3**—This assigns any of Thor's oscillators as a modulation source.

■ **Filter 1/2**—This assigns the audio output of Filter 1 or 2 as modulation sources.

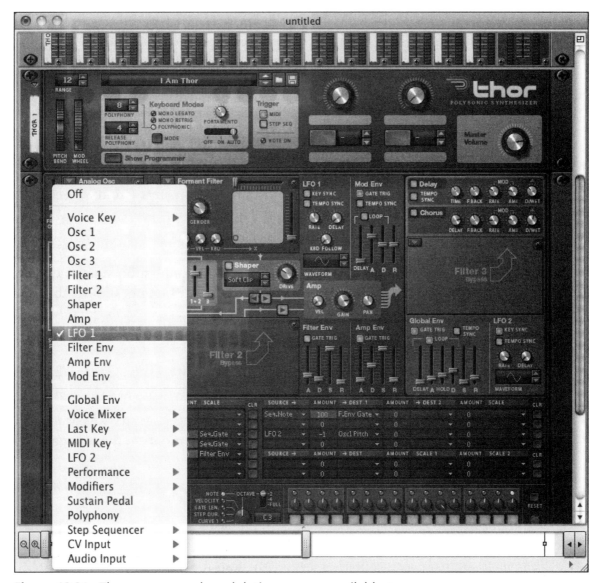

Figure 12.21 There are several modulation sources available to you.

- **Shaper**—This assigns the audio output of the Shaper as a modulation source.

- **Amp**—This assigns the audio output of the Amp as a modulation source.

- **LFO 1**—This assigns LFO as a modulation source. Perfect for creating a vibrato or tremolo effect.

- **Filter/Amp/Mod Envelopes**—This assigns either of these envelopes as modulation sources.

And now, on to the Global Modulation parameters.

- **Global Envelope**—This assigns the global envelope as modulation source.

- **Voice Mixer**—This assigns the left and right mixer inputs as modulation sources.

- **Last Key**—This applied modulation based on the last monophonic note played, either via the built-in step sequencer or MIDI. You can select either Note, Velocity, or Gate to be your source of modulation.

- **MIDI Key**—This behaves similarly to Last Key, however this modulation is heard on notes globally. As with the Last Key, you have a choice of Note, Velocity, and Gate.

- **LFO 2**—This assigns LFO 2 as a modulation source.

- **Performance Parameters**—This assigns performance parameters (Mod Wheel/Pitch Wheel, Breath, After Touch, and Expression) as modulation sources.

- **Modifiers**—This assigns the Rotary knobs and buttons as modulation sources.

- **Sustain Pedal**—This assigns a sustain pedal to be your modulation source. If you don't have one yet, go to your local music shop and pick one up. It's worth it.

- **Polyphony**—This sets polyphony as a modulation source. You can use this to create different envelope attacks depending on how many notes you play at one time.

- **Step Sequencer**—This assigns one of eight parameters (Gate, Note, Curve 1/2, Gate Length, and Step Duration) as a modulation source.

- **CV Inputs 1-4**—This allows you to use other Reason devices (Matrix, Redrum, Dr. Octo Rex) as modulation sources via any or all of the CV inputs in the rear panel of Thor.

- **Audio Inputs 1-4**—This allows you to use the audio outputs of other Reason devices as modulation sources.

Modulation Destinations

As you can imagine, there are also quite a few modulation destinations (see Figure 12.22).

- **OSC 1**—This assigns the parameters of OSC 1 (Pitch, Frequency, Pulse Width, and OSC 2 AM) as modulation destinations.

- **OSC 2/3**—Same as OSC 1 without the AM.

- **Filter 1/2**—This assigns the parameters of either Filter 1 or 2 (Audio Input, Frequency, Frequency (FM), Res, Drive, Gender, LP/HP Mix) as modulation destinations.

- **Shaper Drive**—This assigns the Shaper drive as a modulation destination.

- **Amp**—This assigns the velocity, pan, and input of the Amp as modulation destinations.

- **Mix**—This assigns the parameters of the Mix section (OSC 1+2 Level/Balance, OSC 3 level) as modulation destinations.

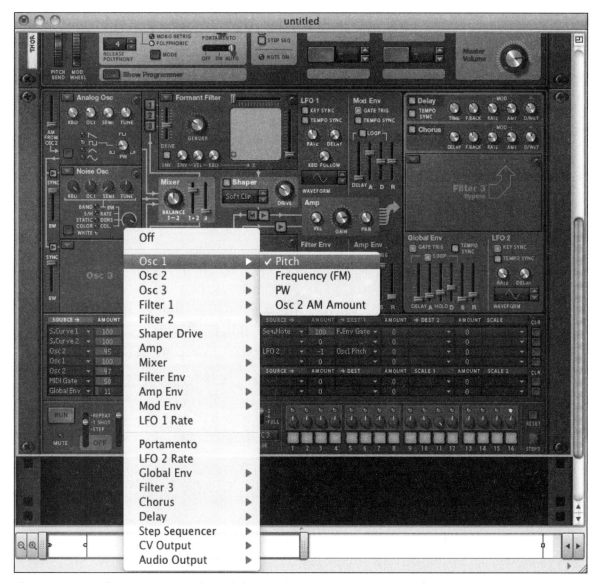

Figure 12.22 There are several modulation destinations to choose from.

- **Filter/Amp/Mod Envelopes**—This assigns the parameters of either envelope as modulation destinations.

- **LFO 1 Rate**—This assigns the LFO 1 Rate as a modulation destination.

And here are the Global Destinations.

- **Portamento**—This sets the portamento time as a modulation destination.

- **LFO 2 Rate**—This sets the rate of LFO 2 as a modulation destination.

- **Global Envelope**—This assigns any of the Global Envelope parameters as a modulation destination.

- **Filter 3**—This assigns several Filter 3 parameters (Left/Right Inputs, Freq, Freq (FM), Resonance) as modulation destinations.

- **Chorus**—This assigns almost any of the Chorus parameters (Dry/Wet, Delay, ModRate, Mod Amount, Feedback) as modulation destinations.

- **Delay**—This assigns almost any of the Delay parameters (Dry/Wet, Time, Mod Rate, Mod Amount, and Feedback) as modulation destinations.

- **Step Sequencer**—This assigns any of five-step sequencer parameters (Trig, Rate, Transpose, Velocity, and Gate Length) as modulation destinations.

- **CV Outputs 1-4**—These set any of the four CV outputs as destinations.

- **Audio Outputs**—These assign any of the four audio outputs as destinations.

Some Modulation Examples

Now that you have a good idea on how the Modulation Bus works, let's put that knowledge to the test by going through a few modulation exercises. Remember, this is something that takes a bit of practice, so these exercises are going to be pretty basic.

This first example is going to be a well-known effect, which is to have the Modulation Wheel open and close a filter. Be sure to initialize your patch before beginning by selecting Edit > Initialize Patch.

1. In the Filter 1 slot, load the Formant Filter.

2. In the Modulation Bus, navigate to the upper-left corner and select Performance > ModWheel as your source.

3. Assign an amount of 100.

4. Now select your destination by selecting Filter 1 > Y.

Play a note and try out the Modulation Wheel. The formant filter will respond by creating a vowel sound that will open and close. You can also try assigning an amount of –100 to get the exact opposite effect.

Now, you'll create a tremolo effect and use the Rotary knob to control the effect. You can continue using the same patch from the previous example.

1. In the second Modulation Bus slot, select LFO 1 as your source.

2. Set the modulation amount to 100.

3. Select Amp > Gain as your destination.

At this point, you should be able to clearly hear the effect. You can enhance this effect even more by using different waveforms in LFO 1 and changing the rate amount.

Now, let's make it a bit more of a performance effect by routing it to Rotary 1 knob.

1. Set the scale amount to 100.

2. Select Modifiers > Rotary 1.

Play a note now and use the first Rotary knob in the Thor Play Parameters. This will now control the tremolo effect.

The Step Sequencer

As a synth, Thor is one commanding creation of software. And as if it couldn't get better, Thor's Step Sequencer offers up a selection of powerful features and musical creativity that can be used as a source of either melodies or modulation (see Figure 12.23). There are up to 16 steps in total that can be sequenced with a variety of data including Note, Velocity, and Gate. All in all, this thing really packs a punch.

Figure 12.23 Thor's Step Sequencer can be used to create melody line or modulation patterns.

Similar Sequencing...Kind of   If you've been reading this book from cover to cover, this is certainly not the first time you've seen a step sequencer, as Redrum has a first rate sequencer of its own, as well as the Matrix (see Chapter 15 for more info). However, you'll find that this step sequencer includes a few more tricks up its sleeves than either of the aforementioned sequencers, so read on carefully.

The Basics

Before you can get to sequencing Thor, you should probably take a couple of minutes to familiarize yourself with the basic layout of the Step Sequencer to better understand it.

- **Run**—This button is used to start/stop the Step Sequencer.

- **Mute**—This LED lights up whenever Thor is muted in the sequencer. However, the LED will not light up if Thor is muted from reMix.

Next up are the Run modes, which include:

- **Off**—The sequencer does not play.

- **Step**—The sequence advances one step at a time each time the Run button is pressed.

- **One Shot**—The sequence plays through one time and then stops.

- **Repeat**—The sequence plays continuously until the Run button is pressed again.

Once a Run Mode has been selected, one of five sequence directions can be selected.

- **Forward**—The sequence simply plays from left to right and then jumps back to the left.

- **Reverse**—This does exactly the opposite by playing from right to left and then jumping back to the right.

- **Pendulum 1**—This direction plays the sequence from left to right, repeats the last step, and then plays right to left. It will then repeat the first step and start over again.

- **Pendulum 2**—This direction plays the sequence from left to right and then right to left continuously.

- **Random**—This direction plays the sequence steps in random order.

Moving onto the right, the Rate dialog box controls the speed of the Step Sequencer. This can be set to either Hertz or note values (if the Sync button is activated). You can change the value of this dialog box by clicking and dragging up or down with on the knob.

As mentioned earlier in this section, there are up to 16 steps that can be filled to the brim with sequencing data, and that data is determined by the Edit controls, which are just to the left of the sequencer steps. Note that as you select these controls and assign values to them in the sequence (by using the knobs of each step), the Value dialog box will display either the numeric or note value (either length or number) of each step.

- **Note**—This allows you to enter in note data on a step-by-step basis. Note that there is an additional switch to the right of this parameter that governs the note range of the sequence. You can select two octaves, four octaves, or full range.

- **Velocity**—This sets the velocity of each sequenced step.

- **Gate Length**—This sets the length of each sequenced step.

- **Step Duration**—This sets the length of each step in the sequence. For example, the first step can be a quarter note, the next can be an eighth. The possibilities are endless.

- **Curve 1/2**—These set the value of curve data on a step by step basis. As you'll recall from earlier in the chapter, these curves are assigned through the Modulation Bus.

Write a Quick Sequence

Now, let's put your new knowledge to the test and write in a quick first sequence.

1. Start by selecting a Thor patch that would work well for sequencing, such as a bass or lead patch.

2. Next, go ahead and turn off a few sequencer steps in order to create an interesting rhythm. Try turning off steps 2, 7, 11, and 15 (see Figure 12.24).

Figure 12.24   Turn off steps to create a more rhythmically interesting sequence.

Go ahead and press the Run button to hear the sequence. Keep in mind that you'll want to have the play mode set to Repeat. At this point, it would be a good idea to enter some notes into the sequence. Try the following notes.

- Step 1—C#2

- Step 3—C4

- Step 4—C3

- Step 5—G4

- Step 6—C5

- Step 8—C3

- Step 9—C3

- Step 10—C3

- Step 12—C#4

- Step 13—F4

- Step 14—D#2

- Step 16—D#2

Reset   If you listen back to your sequence and you want to start over, you can simply press the Reset button at the far right of the Step Sequencer. Just note that this resets everything (note value, gate length, curve date, and so on), so proceed with caution.

You've written out a pretty interesting melodic line, so from this point on, you should try to spice it up a bit by making use of the additional Edit parameters. For example, you could select Gate Length and write in a more interesting gate pattern that makes use of staccato note lengths versus legato. You could also try altering the velocity of different notes to create a dynamic impact. The sky's the limit really, so let your hair down and experiment.

CV/Audio Connections

Press the Tab key to flip the Device Rack around, and you'll see that Thor has many connections that can be used to sequence with the Matrix, RPG-8, modulate other devices, or be modulated by other devices (see Figure 12.25). In addition, Thor includes several audio I/Os for pushing the creative limits of soft synthesis.

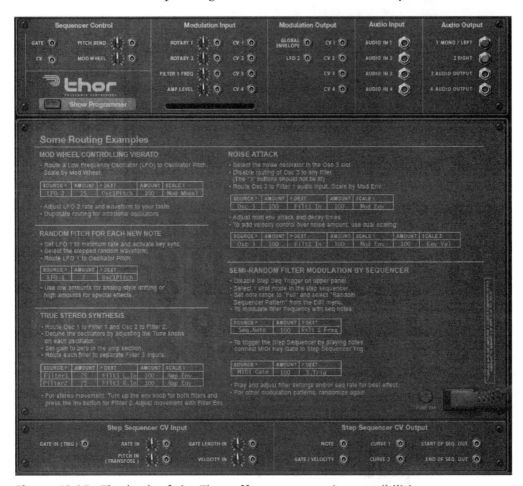

Figure 12.25 The back of the Thor offers many routing possibilities.

> **Thor's Cheat Sheet**   Have a quick look on the back of the Thor interface and you'll notice that the programmers have provided a neat cheat sheet of sorts, because it lists several modulation and routing possibilities. This can be a real helper when you are just starting down the road of modular synthesis.

Audio Outputs

These connections are used to output the signal from Thor to reMix. There are a couple of options.

- **1 Mono/Left-Right**—These are the main outputs of Thor. Note that if you build a mono patch with Thor, use output one to retain the proper effect.

- **Outputs 3/4**—These are the additional audio outputs, which can be assigned from the Modulation Bus.

Audio Input

As you learned in the previous chapter, audio inputs on a soft synth are hot, and Thor's got four of them. You can literally route just about any Reason device output to these inputs and then assign them to Thor's various modulation inputs via the Modulation Bus.

Let's try an interesting experiment:

1. Create a new Reason song.

2. Create instances of reMix, Thor, and Redrum.

3. Select the Percutron patch for Thor. This is a percussion pitch-based patch that makes use of the Step Sequencer.

4. On Redrum, write a hi-hat pattern in its sequencer that has lots of dynamics.

5. Press the Tab key to flip the interface.

6. Disconnect the hi-hat output of Redrum and re-route it to Audio Input 1 of Thor (see Figure 12.26).

Figure 12.26 Connect the hi-hat output of Redrum to Audio Input 1 of Thor.

7. Press the Tab key to flip the interface again.

8. Use Thor's Modulation Bus to route Audio Input one as the source to Oscillator 1's Pitch or FM amount (see Figure 12.27).

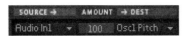

Figure 12.27 Once you create this modulation, the hi-hat output of Redrum will modulate Oscillator 1's pitch of Thor.

At this point, you can run the step sequencers of both Reason devices and you should now hear the hi-hat pattern modulating the pitch or FM of Oscillator 1 of Thor.

Modulation Input/Output

Moving on to the left, you'll see that Thor offers up a lot of possible CV I/O connections for modulation (see Figure 12.28). This can lead some serious modulating bliss if you play your cards right. For example, you could use LFO 2 to modulate in sync with the CV input of another Reason device. Consider, for example the Damage Control CV input of Scream 4, which would cause the amount of distortion to rise and fall in time with the tempo of your song. Or, you could also use the LFO CV output of Dr. Octo Rex to modulate the Filter 1 Frequency 1 CV input of Thor. And the list goes on and on and on.

Figure 12.28 The Modulation CV Inputs and Outputs offer a wide variety of modulating possibilities.

First, let's start with the Modulation Outputs:

■ **Global Envelope**—This connection routes the output of the Thor Global Envelope to any CV input.

■ **LFO 2**—This connection routes the output of LFO 2 to any CV input.

■ **CV 1-4**—These modulation outputs are assignable through the Modulation Bus and can route the CV output of just about any Thor parameter to the CV input of your choosing.

And now, look at the Modulation inputs. Note that these have Amount knobs that intensify or decrease the effect.

■ **Rotary 1/2**—These modulation inputs are used to route the CV outputs of any Reason device to the Rotary knobs on the front of the Thor interface. Remember that these knobs can be assigned to just about any Thor parameter.

■ **Filter 1 Freq**—This modulation input controls the filter frequency knob of Filter 1.

■ **Amp Level**—The modulation input alters the Amp Envelope on the front of the Thor interface.

■ **CV 1-4**—These inputs allow you to send modulation data to just about any Thor parameter via the Modulation Bus.

Additional CV Inputs Keeping in line with the other Reason synths that you've already read about, Thor also includes a pair of CV inputs for the Modulation Wheel and Pitch Wheel parameters. Additionally, there are Sequencer Control inputs for the Gate and CV, which are used to link up to an instance of the Matrix sequencer.

Step Sequencer CV Inputs/Outputs

Scroll down to the bottom of the Thor interface and you'll see that the Step Sequencer also has its own set of CV inputs and outputs (see Figure 12.29). Every parameter that you alter in a Thor sequence (Note, Gate, Velocity, and so on) can be used as a CV output. Conversely, you can use the CV outputs of other Reason devices, such as the Matrix sequencer, to control most of the vital inputs of the Thor sequence.

Figure 12.29 The Step Sequencer has its own assortment of CV ins and outs.

■ **Gate In (Trig)**—This CV input triggers the Gate Input of the Step Sequencer. A good way to check this out is to route the Slice Gate Output of Dr. Octo Rex to this input. Load up a REX file and let the fun begin.

■ **Rate In**—This CV input controls the rate of the Step Sequencer. Try connecting the Curve CV output of the Matrix sequencer to this.

■ **Pitch In (Transpose)**—This input alters the pitch of the Step Sequencer. Try connecting the LFO output of any other Reason device to this input.

- **Gate Length In**—This input alters the gate, or note length, of the sequencer steps.

- **Velocity In**—This input alters the Velocity of the sequencer steps. Both this and the Gate Length inputs are perfect for the Matrix or perhaps Redrum.

And now, take a look at the outputs.

- **Note**—This outputs the note data from the Step Sequencer to any device.

- **Gate/Velocity**—These output gate and velocity data to any device. They might serve as an interesting way to drive the Amp Envelope of another device such as Dr. Octo Rex or the Malström.

- **Curve One/Two**—These output data from the Curve parameters found in the Modulation Bus.

- **Start of Sequence Out**—This outputs a start message when the step sequencer starts.

- **End of Sequence Out**—This outputs an end message when the step sequencer stops.

Building Thor Patches

By now, you're more than ready to start programming away, so let's go ahead and build some Thor patches to get you going. Throughout this section, I'll help you program a bass and a pad patch.

Before beginning each of these tutorials, be sure to reset Thor by selecting Initialize Patch from the Edit pull-down menu.

Programming a Bass Patch

Bass patches can be a great starting point when you are learning how to program synths, as they are somewhat simple to build. And yet, with Thor and its diverse feature set, any bass patch has the chance to become something unique and creative.

Let's begin by selecting the right kind of oscillator for this patch. As this is a bass patch, let's keep it simple and use just Oscillator 1. Click on the Osc 1 pop-up menu and select Multi Oscillator. Once selected, press any key on your keyboard and you'll hear a rather uninteresting "vanilla" sound playback. So without further ado, make the following changes.

- **Waveform**—Set to Soft Sawtooth.

- **Detune**—Set the Detune mode to Interval and set the Amount knob to 24.

- **OCT**—Set to 3 to create a really low, solid sub-oscillator sound.

Next, you'll use a Low Pass Ladder Filter to add presence and overdrive to the bass patch. Make the following adjustments.

- **Drive**—Set 127.

- **Freq**—Set to 21.6kHz.

- **Filter Type**—Set to 24 Type I. This is really more a matter of taste, but this filter type adds much more punch. Also, make sure the Self Osc button is turned off.

Play a couple of notes now and you'll definitely hear a difference in the low range, especially if you have a subwoofer in your studio. Let's wrap this up by adding a Comb Filter in the Filter 3 slot. Once you do this, set it to the following values.

- **Freq**—Set to 2.69kHz.

- **Res**—Set to 95.

- **Drive**—Set to 78.

Last, but not least, go ahead and set the Play parameters to the following values.

- **Polyphony/Release Polyphony**—Set these both to 1.

- **Keyboard mode**—Set to Mono Retrig.

- **Portamento**—Turn it on and set the portamento time to 8.

At the end, your bass patch should look a lot like Figure 12.30.

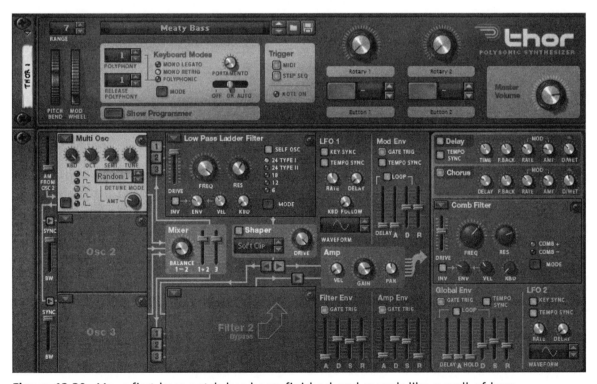

Figure 12.30 Your first bass patch has been finished and sounds like a wall of bass.

Programming a Pad

With all the programming potential of Thor, it would be a crime not to program a pad sound. Because this is a somewhat complicated patch to program, I have placed it on the Course website (go to www.courseptr.com and click on the Downloads button) for you to download to double-check your work, or to just play with it on your own.

First things first, make sure that you initialize Thor. And away you go!

Programming the Play Parameters

To start things off, punch in the following values into the Play Parameters.

- **Pitch Bend**—Set this to 12.

- **Polyphony/Release Polyphony**—Set both of these to 8. You can choose a greater value if you want, but just remember that you'll eat up that much more CPU.

- **Portamento**—Turn this on and set the knob to 30.

Programming the Oscillators

At this point, it's time to start breathing a little more life into this patch by activating and routing the oscillators. Make the following adjustments to Oscillator 1.

- **Oscillator Type**—Select Phase Mod Osc.

- **Second**—Set the second waveform to Sine x Pulse.

- **PM**—Set this to 74.

Now, let's move onto Oscillator 2, which is going to be an FM Oscillator.

- **OCT**—Set this to 5.

- **MOD**—Set this parameter to 2.

- **FM**—Set this to 91.

Let's finish this off by activating and programming Oscillator 3, which is a Multi Osc.

- **OCT**—Set this to 5.

- **Waveform**—Set this to a square wave.

- **Detune Mode**—Set this to Random.

- **AMT**—Set this to 21.

At this point, you should only hear Oscillator 1, as you haven't routed Osc 2 or 3 yet, so set Oscillator 2 and 3 to Filter 2 by clicking on their corresponding numeric buttons next to Filter 2.

Programming the Filters and Mixer

In this patch, you'll be using all three filters, but for the time being, let's start with the two primary filters. By default, Thor provides a Low Pass Ladder Filter, and you're going to continue using that here. Make the following parameter adjustments to it.

- **Mode**—Set this to 24 Type II and also activate Self Oscillation.

- **Drive**—Set this to 102. Also, activate the INV parameter.

- **FREQ**—Set this to 317Hz.

- **RES**—Set to 101.

- **VEL**—Set this to 103. This will cause the filter to open differently depending on how hard the notes are played.

Now, let's set up Filter 2, which is going to be a Formant Filter.

- **Drive**—Set this to 49.

- **Gender**—Set this to 48.

- **X**—Set this slider to 43.

- **Y**—Set this slider to 68.

- **VEL**—Set this to 108.

Playing the patch at this point, it has some interesting characteristics, but it's way out of balance. Let's fix that by setting the Mixer to the following values.

- **Balance 1-2**—Set this to 24, which will emphasize Osc 1 over 2.

- **1+2 Level**—Set this slider to −5dB.

- **3**—Set this slider to −9dB. This will make Oscillators 1 and 2 the dominant element in this patch.

Finally, under the Shaper are the direction buttons. Click on the left direction button to send Oscillator 1 to Filter 2. And then, click on the direction button from Filter 2 to the Amplifier.

Save Frequently   Make sure to save your patch frequently to ensure you don't lose any of your valuable work.

Programming the Amp, LFO, and Amp Envelope

You're almost done with the primary ingredients to this patch. Now it's time to program the Amp, LFO and Amp Envelope to start bringing it "Pad" status.

There's not much to do with the Amp, except to set the Pan to –42. This will sound a little out of balance, but it will make more sense when you look at the Modulation Bus.

Make the following changes to LFO 1.

- **Key Sync/Tempo Syn**—Activate both of these.

- **Rate**—Set this to 2/4.

- **KBD FOLLOW**—Set this knob to 57.

- **Waveform**—Set this parameter to a square wave.

Finally, let's create a nice slow attack by setting the Attack slider on the Amp Envelope to 4.22s.

Programming the Global Parameters

You're getting pretty close to synthetic pad bliss, but you need to make a few adjustments to the Global Parameters to spice it up a bit, at which point you'll round it off by using the Modulation Bus.

First, let's start with the effects. There's really no reason to use the Chorus, as the patch is already thick enough, so let's add some Delay. Activate this effect and set it to the following values.

- **Tempo Syn**—Activate this and set the Time knob to 6/16.

- **Feedback**—Set this to 50.

- **Rate**—Set this to .54Hz.

- **Amount**—Set this to 25.

- **Dry/Wet**—Set this knob to 40.

Next up, you're going to introduce a third filter to this patch. Select the Comb Filter and make the following parameter adjustments.

- **Drive**—Set this slider to 60 and activate the INV button.

- **FREQ**—Set this to 91.7Hz.

- **RES**—Set this to 61.

Finally, the last of the Global Parameter adjustments are quick and easy.

- **Global Envelope**—Set the Hold parameter to 30s.

- **LFO 2**—Activate the Key and Tempo Sync and set the Rate knob to 3/8.

Setting the Modulation Bus

Last but not least are the Modulation Bus parameters. This last section introduces some modulation to LFO 1 and 2.

Make the following parameter settings to the first Modulation Bus.

- **Source**—Set this to LFO 1.

- **Amount**—Set this to 63.

- **Destination**—Set this to Osc 2 FM.

- **Scale Amount**—Set this to 100.

- **Scale**—Set this to the Modulation Wheel.

Play a note and use the Mod Wheel. At this point, you should hear the FM amount change dramatically.

Now, make the following parameter adjustments to the second Modulation Bus.

- **Source**—Set this to LFO 2.

- **Amount**—Set this to 100.

- **Destination**—Set this to Amplifier Pan.

Play your patch now and you will hear a pad sound that morphs over time, and also offers a healthy dose of ambience.

As you have read throughout this chapter, Thor is a synth's synth when it comes to programming, playing, and above all creativity. Now that you have a clear understanding of this wonder, take some time to program your own patches.

13 NN-19—Close Up

Introduced with Reason in version 1.0, the NN-19 (see Figure 13.1) is a software sampler that looks and functions a lot like the classic Akai hardware samplers of the past decade. If you are new to the concept of sampling and samplers, the NN-19 is a perfect tool for learning all about this interesting technology.

Yes, It Samples Now! In past versions of Reason, the NN-19 and its big brother NN-XT could not be classified as samplers. By musical instrument standards, a *sampler* is a piece of hardware capable of recording and playing back selected bits of digital audio.

Such is not the case with Reason 5, as both the NN-19 and NN-XT can sample, edit, and play back audio.

Basic Sample-Creation Principles

A great advantage to using software samplers is that they support a number of audio file formats, unlike their hardware counterparts (for example, Akai and EMU), which are format-specific. The NN-19 supports several digital audio formats, including:

- NN-19 sample patches (.smp)
- WAVE (.wav)
- AIFF (.aif)
- SoundFonts (.sf2)
- REX files and individual REX slices (.rex2, .rex, and .rcy)

Using Single Samples

Using a single sample with the NN-19 is accomplished by loading a sample into its interface. This sample is then *mapped*, or spread out over the entire length of the virtual keyboard of the NN-19 interface. Once a sample is loaded into the NN-19, you can arm its sequencer track and press a key on your MIDI controller keyboard to trigger

Figure 13.1 The NN-19 emulates a hardware sampler, but with a few tricks and treats to fuel creativity.

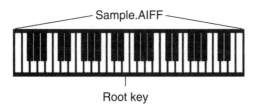

Figure 13.2 In this diagram, a single sample has been loaded into the NN-19 sampler and automatically mapped out over the entire keyboard. By doing this, the loaded sample will trigger no matter which key is pressed on your MIDI keyboard.

the sample. Additionally, the loaded sample's original pitch (or *key*) is automatically assigned to the C3 key (see Figure 13.2).

The next sections show how to accomplish this by first importing a standard AIFF or WAV file, and then loading an individual REX slice. Begin each exercise by selecting Initialize Patch from the Edit pull-down menu to wipe the slate clean before you start working with the NN-19.

Basic Sampling

As mentioned earlier in this chapter, the NN-19 has the ability to sample audio via your computer's audio interface. The recorded sample can then be edited and saved within an NN-19 patch. You were introduced to sampling back in Chapter 7, but here's a quick refresher course.

1. Click on the Start Sampling button, which is located to the right of the Load Sample button.

2. NN-19 will immediately begin to record up to 30 seconds of audio, which will be represented in the waveform display window.

At this point, you can click on the Stop Sampling button, which will automatically load the newly recorded sample into the NN-19. You can also click the Edit button, which will launch the Sample Editor window (see Figure 13.3).

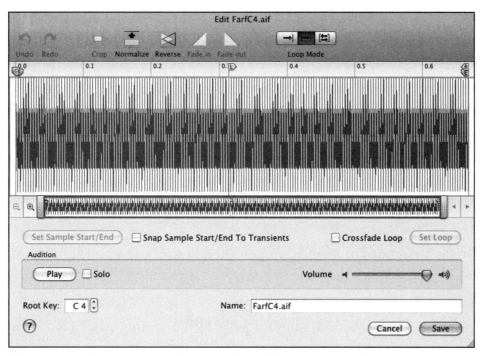

Figure 13.3 The Sample Editor window allows you to edit your newly recorded sample with simple, yet powerful, tools.

If all else fails and you want to record again while you're currently sampling, you can click on the Restart Sampling button.

This is just a brief explanation of sampling to get your started. You'll delve more deeply into sampling towards the end of the chapter.

Loading AIFF and WAV Files

Loading AIFF and WAV files into the NN-19 is done almost exactly the same way as loading REX slices.

1. Create a new NN-19 and click on the Sample Browser button (located above the upper-left corner of the big blue keyboard display) to open the browser window.

2. Click on the Reason Factory Sound Bank to display the contents.

3. Double-click on the folder called Other Samples to open it.

4. Double-click on the folder called Chords-Phrases-Pads-Stabs to open it.

5. You will see a long list of available AIFF files. Double-click any one of them to import it into the NN-19.

Loading REX Slices

As mentioned earlier, the NN-19 can import and use REX files. This can be done from the standard patch-browsing interface in the upper-left corner. Once imported, the REX file is mapped out chromatically on the NN-19 interface starting at the C1 key.

The NN-19 can also import individual REX file slices. This is a great feature because it can lead to several creative possibilities. For example, by importing individual slices from different REX files, you can build your own custom drum kit and save it as an NN-19 patch, or possibly a kit of different sound effects taken from different REX files. It really is up to you and your creativity!

In order to import a REX slice, you must use the Browse Sample tools, found in the upper-middle portion of the NN-19 interface (see Figure 13.4). Click on the folder icon to launch the sample browser window, which is identical to the Patch Browser window. Let's get in a little practice importing a REX slice.

Figure 13.4 Use the Browse Sample button and its scroll buttons to import individual samples.

1. Use the sample browser window to find the Reason Factory Sound Bank.

2. Open the Reason Factory Sound Bank and navigate to (and open) the Dr:rex Drum Loops folder. Open the first folder in the list, called Abstract Hip Hop.

3. Double-click the first REX file, SoleSide. The sample browser window will then display all of the 17 individual slices within the SoleSide REX file (see Figure 13.5). Notice that, just like the Patch Browser window, you have the Autoplay option in the lower-right corner to audition each slice.

4. Select the first slice and double-click on it to load it into the NN-19 interface (into note #C3). If you have a MIDI keyboard, arm the NN-19 sequencer track and play the C3 key on your keyboard to hear it play back.

5. You can now create a few more key zones and add more REX slices or other AIFF/WAV files to create your first drum kit. When you're finished, save it as an NN-19 patch (an .smp file).

Although single samples are incredibly easy to work with, they have a serious drawback. A single-sampled note sounds natural only within a very limited range. For example, if you load one piano sample into the NN-19 and play the root note (C3), that note will sound fine. Now try playing that sample a half-octave from the root note; you will hear digital noise in the playback, and you'll notice that the sample is playing faster or slower depending on where you are playing in relation to the root note.

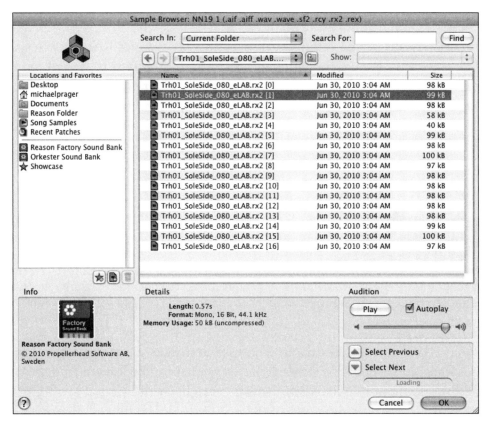

Figure 13.5 The sample browser window is used to locate and load individual audio samples into the NN-19.

Another way to demonstrate this effect is to use a sample of a person talking. When you play this sample above its root note, the person's voice will sound too fast, just like a tape machine that is playing faster than normal. You will get the opposite effect when playing the same sample below its root note.

The whole point of using a sampler is to make your performance sound just like the real instrument you are attempting to emulate. This is accomplished using a technique called multisampling, discussed next.

Deleting Samples   To delete a loaded sample, select the sample by clicking on it in the virtual keyboard and selecting Delete Sample from the Edit pull-down menu.

Multisampling

Multisampling is a process in which several samples of a specific instrument are loaded into assigned parts of the sampler keyboard. The resulting sound is usually an accurate representation of the instrument you are attempting to emulate. There are many multi-sampled NN-19 patches included with Reason, but this can also be done on your own.

To begin the process of multisampling, you must first divide the sampler's virtual keyboard into sections. This is accomplished by using key zones. As shown in Figure 13.6, *key zones* are assignable portions of the virtual keyboard that contain a defined range of notes. For example, a key zone can have a specified low note of C3, and a specified high note of E3, giving you a five-note range. Additionally, a sample that has a root note within this range (C3 for instance) can then be loaded into this zone and played, and it will sound very natural.

Figure 13.6   In this diagram, the sampler keyboard has been split into specified sections, known as key zones. Once these zones are created, individual samples can be loaded into each zone.

Creating a key zone is very simple. You simply choose Split Key Zone from the Edit pull-down menu of Reason, at which point a marker is placed on the keyboard display of the NN-19. This marker can be moved to the left or right in the virtual keyboard. After the zone has been created, you can then load a sample into it by clicking on the Sample Browser button, located just above the virtual keyboard. Once the sample is loaded, you can then create and select another zone to load another sample. Because only one key zone can be active at a time, it's no problem if these samples have been loaded onto the same note (like the default C3). You can always change the root note of the sample after the sample has been loaded. Click in the area above the keyboard to select the key zone that contains the sample you want to move. The key zone you have selected will be highlighted bright blue. The note on which the sample currently resides will be shaded in. Click on this note, and then turn the Root Key knob to select the root note for your sample. You can then do the same thing with other samples in other key zones. You can also adjust the key zone split points whenever you want by selecting a key zone and either clicking and dragging its end markers or by adjusting the Low Key and High Key knobs.

Deleting Key Zones   If you need to delete a key zone, just select it in the virtual keyboard. Then choose Delete Key Zone from the Edit pull-down menu.

Hands-On Multisampling   At the end of this chapter, you'll find a step-by-step tutorial showing how to multisample an acoustic guitar.

Another Use for Multisampling   Another way to use multisampling is to load multiple sample loops to the virtual keyboard. This will enable you to play different sampled loops at the same tempo within one sampler (see Figure 13.7). This is done by creating numerous key zones and setting each of them up with a range of one note. For example, C3 to C3 would be the range of one key zone, and C#3 to C#3 would be the range of the next key zone.

Loop 02.aiff   Loop 04.aiff

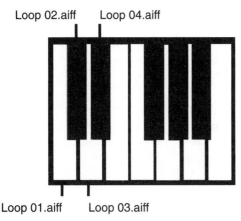

Loop 01.aiff   Loop 03.aiff

Figure 13.7   When using multiple sampled loops, you can create numerous key zones and load a loop into each one.

A Guided Tour of the NN-19
It's time to begin an in-depth tour of the NN-19. Toward the end of this chapter, you can further enhance your NN-19 education by following the step-by-step tutorial for creating your own sample patches.

Loading Patches
At the top-left corner of the NN-19 interface is the patch-browsing interface. This functions in exactly the same way as all of the other Reason devices.

Auditioning Patches   Reason allows you to audition patches either before loading them into the NN-19 or after. When you select an NN-19 patch from the Patch Browser window, Reason will load those samples into the browser so you can audition the patch before actually loading it into the NN-19.

Once a patch has been loaded into the NN-19 interface, you will want to audition it before using it in your song. This can be done by using a MIDI keyboard or by using the Key Editor in the Reason sequencer.

There is a third way to accomplish this, using your computer keyboard and mouse. Hold the Alt key down (or Option key on the Mac) and navigate your cursor to the keyboard display of the NN-19 interface. The pointer icon will change to a speaker symbol, which you can then use to click on the different keys of the keyboard display to trigger the samples.

The NN-19 Virtual Keyboard Display

In the center of the NN-19 interface, the virtual keyboard is where all of the preferences are set for the loaded samples (see Figure 13.8).

Figure 13.8 The NN-19 virtual keyboard is used to load and assign samples.

Once a sample has been loaded into the NN-19, it can then be selected and given specific parameters. You can see how this works by loading up a basic NN-19 patch and looking at the individual parameters. For this tour, use a basic patch, such as the Didgeridoo patch, which can be found in the Mallet and Ethnic folder of the NN-19 folder.

Selecting and Editing Key Zones

In the upper-left and upper-right corners of the virtual keyboard are the scroll tools to help you navigate to the right and left sides of the keyboard. Use these tools to navigate to the highest key zone so it can be selected. Once you locate it, click on the key zone to display its information just below the virtual keyboard. To get the hang of this, you may want to click around on the other key zones as well and view their information just below the virtual keyboard.

Select a Key Zone via MIDI   Another way to select a key zone is to activate the Select Key Zone Via MIDI button, located just above the virtual keyboard. Once this is selected and the NN-19 sequencer track is armed to receive MIDI, you can use a MIDI keyboard to select the different key zones of any loaded patch.

The following key zone parameters can be edited:

- **Low Key**—Sets the lowest possible note in a selected key zone. Note that it cannot have a value greater than its high key value.

- **High Key**—Sets the highest possible note in a selected key zone. Note that it cannot have a value less than its low key value.

- **Sample**—If you are using a patch with multiple samples and key zones, you can use this knob to select a sample for a particular key zone.

- **Root Key**—Displays the root or original pitch of the loaded sample. Use the Root Key knob to move the original pitch up or down the keyboard.

- **Tune**—This knob is used to correct the pitch of a sample and has a range of +/– 50 semitones.

- **Level**—Sets the amplitude for a selected sample.

- **Loop**—Sets the loop mode for the sample. You can select Off (no looping), FW (constant looping between two points), and FW-BW (plays loop from start to end, and then end to start).

Setting Loop Points   A *loop point* occurs when a sample is prepared to continuously loop from left to right in order to give the illusion that the sample is sustaining. Loop points are commonly used on sample patches such as pianos or guitars to make the patch act more like the actual instrument. Another use for loop points are with drum loops that need to repeat cleanly without pops and clicks.

These loop points are created in the Edit Sample window of Reason. NN-19 will then use the loop points when the Loop mode is activated in the virtual keyboard.

Selecting Key Zones and Soloing Samples

Located just above the key zone display are two additional parameters:

- **Select Key Zone Via MIDI**—When activated, this parameter links the key zone display to your MIDI keyboard. Whenever you press a key on your MIDI keyboard, the relevant key zone will display in the Key Zone Editor.

- **Solo Sample**—This parameter will solo a sample within a key zone and hear it mapped throughout the virtual keyboard. This is used primarily to make sure that the root note is set correctly. Note that Select Keyzone Via MIDI must be disabled prior to activating this parameter.

The NN-19 Synth Parameters

Once you have loaded your samples into the NN-19 interface, you can begin to manipulate, twist, and contort them to your heart's content by using the synth parameters. As shown in Figure 13.9, the synth parameters of the NN-19 bear a striking similarity to those in the Subtractor and Dr. Octo Rex. If you are familiar with these aforementioned Reason devices, the NN-19 synth parameters should be a walk in the park.

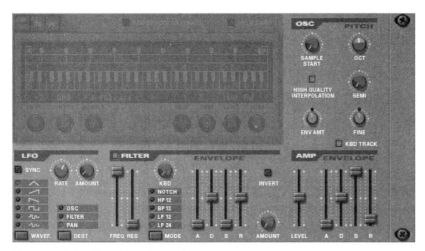

Figure 13.9 The NN-19 synth parameters.

These Parameters Are Global   It's important to note that all of the parameters in the NN-19 are *global*, meaning that they affect the playback of the entire loaded sampler. Those of you who want to edit the individual parameters of each sample will be glad to know that the NN-19's big brother, the NN-XT, can handle it easily. When you've finished this chapter, move to Chapter 14, "NN-XT—Close Up," to learn how individual manipulation is done.

The Oscillator Section

Although the name suggests that the NN-19 has an oscillator, that's not quite true. Yes, the NN-19 does make sounds, but not with the help of an oscillator, like the one found in the Subtractor. A sampler produces sounds by using digital audio as its catalyst, rather than using oscillation (see Figure 13.10). The NN-19 Oscillator is used to tune the sample and set its octave, as well as set its start time. In addition, the Oscillator Envelope Amount control (ENV AMT knob) determines to what degree the sample pitch will be affected by the Filter Envelope. Setting a positive

Figure 13.10 The NN-19 Oscillator section is used to specify when a sample starts and is also used to tune the sample.

or negative value determines whether the Filter Envelope parameters will raise or lower the pitch of the sample. You can get some pretty radical effects with this knob!

The Sample Start knob alters the starting position of a loaded sample. As you increase the value of the Sample Start knob, the start position moves farther and farther toward the end of the sampled sound. This can be used, for example, to remove unwanted silence before a sample or to trigger a specific part of a sample, rather than the whole sample itself.

To make a little more sense out of this parameter, see Figure 13.11. I prepared a sequence using the Pizzicato string sample patch found in the NN-19 sample directory. On the left side of this figure, you can see the waveform of the sequence playing but the Sample Start knob is set to 0. The waveform on the right side of the figure shows the same sequence with the Sample Start knob set to 50, or 10:00. Notice how much more abruptly the sample played back.

Sample Start via Velocity   For added effect, the Sample Start feature is linked to the Velocity section of the NN-19 Play parameters. By using the Velocity section to control your Sample Start, it is possible to achieve a wide variation of dynamics with percussive samples.

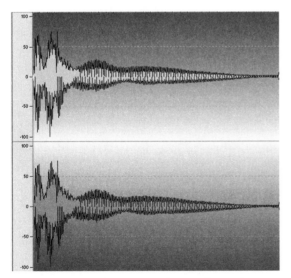 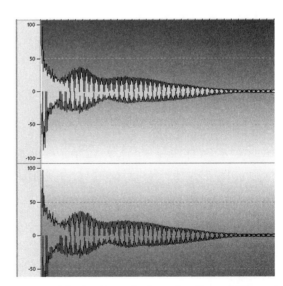

Figure 13.11   These waveforms show the same sequence with the Sample Start knob at different positions.

Below the Sample Start knob is the High Quality Interpolation button. When active, this function optimizes the sound quality of the loaded samples by using more complex interpolation algorithms to calculate the sample playback. To review more detailed information about how the High Quality Interpolation button works, see the note called "Algorithms? Interpolation?" in Chapter 7, "Redrum—Close Up," for more information.

To the right of the Sample Start knob are the NN-19 pitch controls. These manipulate the pitch of your sample patches using any of the three main parameters:

- **Oct**—Shifts the sample pitch by octaves. It has an 8-octave range with a default setting of 4.

- **Semi**—Shifts the sample pitch by up to 12 semitones, equaling one octave.

- **Fine**—Shifts the sample pitch by 100ths of a semitone and allows for very precise pitch adjustments. This knob has a range of –50 to 50.

Located in the lower-right corner of the main pitch parameters are two additional controls that can be used with them:

- **KBD.Track button.** This specifies whether the sample patch you have loaded contains variable pitches or a constant pitch. For example, a violin has many pitches, so you would want to make sure that the keyboard tracking button is active. But if you are using a sample that is not pitch specific, such as a snare drum, you can turn this button off, and the pitch of the snare drum will remain constant, no matter what key you play on your keyboard.

- **Env Amt knob.** This links the pitch of your sample patches to the Filter Envelope, which is discussed later in this chapter. When assigned a positive amount, the pitch of the sample will raise according to the settings of the F.Envelope parameters. When assigned a negative amount, the pitch will lower according to the same parameters. You're going to have a little fun with this knob later on.

The Filter Section

The NN-19 Filter section is used to shape the timbre of the loaded samples (see Figure 13.12). Its functionality is akin to the filter sections of Dr. Octo Rex and Subtractor because it is a multimode filter with five available filters.

Figure 13.12 The NN-19 Filter section. You can select the different filter modes by clicking on the Mode button at the bottom of the filter or by just clicking on the desired filter mode.

■ **Notch**—This filter can be thought of as the opposite of a Band Pass filter. It will reject the mid-frequencies, yet allow the high frequencies and low frequencies to pass through. Although not the most dramatic filter effect, it still has a place in the mix for making minor changes to a sample.

■ **HP 12**—This High Pass filter is the opposite of the Low Pass filters; it will filter out the low frequencies, yet allow the high frequencies pass through. It has a roll-off curve of 12 decibels per octave.

■ **BP 12**—This Band Pass filter filters out both the high and low frequencies, leaving the mid frequencies alone to be toyed with. With a roll-off curve of 12 decibels per octave, the BP 12 can be used effectively on instrument loops such as a guitar loop or possibly hi-hat heavy percussion loops.

■ **LP 12**—This 12dB Low Pass filter is similar to the 24dB low pass, but the roll-off curve is not as strong because it has a range of 12 decibels per octave. This makes the LP 12 a perfect solution for creating a filter sweep that is low but not low enough to blow up your speakers.

■ **LP 24**—This 24dB Low Pass filter allows low frequencies to pass through, yet filters out the high frequencies. To top it off, this low pass filter has an intense roll-off curve (approximately 24 decibels per octave), which produces a greater emphasis on the low frequencies.

To the left of the mode buttons are the controls for the Resonance and Filter Frequency parameters.

The Filter Frequency, or *cutoff filter* as it is also called, is used to specify where the filter will function within the frequency spectrum. It is a very popular parameter used to create the sweeping effect heard so often in electronic music. When the frequency is used to alter a filter, it opens and closes the filter within a specific frequency range. In order to better understand what the Filter Frequency does, try the following exercise.

1. Load a "pad" patch from the Reason Factory Sound Bank. A good one for this example is the Big Strings patch, located in the Strings folder.

2. The Filter is already activated. Make sure the filter mode is set to LP 12 and that the Resonance slider is set to 0. Also make sure the Filter Frequency slider is set to its maximum setting of 127.

3. Arm the NN-19 sequencer track to receive MIDI, and play a sustained chord with your left hand. With your right hand, click on the Filter Frequency, and slowly drag the control down so you can hear the filter close as it decreases in value. Once the Filter Frequency is set to 0, all of the high frequencies are filtered out. Try this same exercise with other filter modes, such as the Notch or Band Pass, to hear the effect.

The Resonance slider is used in combination with the Filter Frequency parameter. It emphasizes the frequencies set by the Filter slider, which thins the sound out, but also increases the sweep effect mentioned earlier. In order to better understand how the Resonance slider works with the Filter Frequency, try the following exercise.

1. Using the same sample patch as before, set the filter mode to LP 12, and set both the Filter Frequency and Resonance sliders to 0.

2. Arm the NN-19 sequencer track to receive MIDI, and play a chord over and over again with your left hand. With your right hand, click and drag the Resonance slider until it reaches its maximum value of 127. Release the mouse and listen to the emphasis on the lower frequencies. Now click and drag the Resonance slider back down to a value of 70.

3. While playing a sustained chord with your left hand, slowly click and drag the Filter Frequency slider all the way up to 127 and then back down again until it reaches a value of 52. This should create a grand sweeping sound because the higher frequencies of the sample patch have now been re-introduced into the mix.

4. Try this with other filter modes to hear the different filter sweeps you can create when using the Filter Frequency and Resonance sliders together.

Located above the filter modes, the Filter Keyboard Track knob (labeled KBD) is used to compensate for the loss of high frequencies as you play higher notes on the keyboard, bringing those higher notes to the forefront in a mix. To demonstrate how this works, try the following exercise.

1. Using the same sample patch as before, set the filter mode to LP 12; set the Resonance to 86 and the Filter Frequency to 60. Also make sure that the Filter Keyboard Track knob is set to 0.

2. Play a sustained chord and include some high notes. Notice that the low notes are very loud and present in the mix.

3. Increase the amount of Keyboard Track knob by clicking and dragging on the knob until it reaches 70, or 12:00. Play the chord again; the high notes should now be much more present in the mix.

4. Increase the Keyboard Track knob to its maximum setting and play the chord again. This time, the high notes should be the dominant voices in the chord. This is not an ideal setting because you do not want to lose the low frequencies, so it is important to find that happy medium.

The Envelope Section

To the right of the Filter section are the NN-19 envelope generators (see Figure 13.13). An envelope generator is used to modify specific synth parameters,

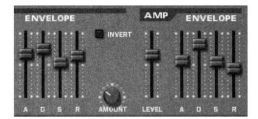

Figure 13.13 The NN-19 Envelope section includes two envelope generators.

including pitch, volume, and filter frequencies. By using an envelope creatively, you can control how these parameters are to be modified over a specific amount of time. The NN-19 includes two envelope generators. One is assigned to the Filter section, whereas the other is assigned to Amplitude.

As you read in Chapter 10, "Subtractor—Close Up," an envelope generator has four basic parameters; Attack, Decay, Sustain, and Release (collectively called ADSR).

This list very briefly recaps what these parameters do:

- **Attack**—When a sound's envelope is triggered, the Attack parameter determines the length of time before the envelope reaches its maximum value.

- **Decay**—Once the maximum value is reached, the Decay parameter determines the length of time until the value begins to drop.

- **Sustain**—After the value begins to drop, Sustain determines the level at which the falling value rests.

- **Release**—Once the value has been set at its rested value, the Release parameter determines how long it will take until the value will fade out after releasing the key.

Now that you have reviewed these parameters, let's discuss what each of the envelope generators does.

The Filter Envelope modifies the Filter Frequency and Sample Pitch. When used in combination with the Filter Frequency and Resonance sliders, the Filter Envelope can create long, sustained filter sweeps and percussive filter-powered stab sounds. To the right of the Filter Envelope are two additional parameters that can be used in combination with it.

- The Invert button is used to invert the functions of the individual envelope parameters. For example, you are using the Attack parameter and have assigned a positive value of 74 to it, which produces a very slow attack. Activate the Invert button and the attack parameter is inverted, which means the attack will be much faster. Essentially, the Invert button reverses the effect of the envelope parameters.

■ The Amount knob determines how much the filter will be affected by the envelope. Increasing the value of this parameter directly affects the set value of the Filter Frequency, which in turn affects the Filter Envelope, which results in some very intense filter combinations to use.

To demonstrate the capabilities of the Filter Envelope, try the following exercise. Make sure that your NN-19 sequencer track is selected.

1. Use the Patch Browser window to locate and load a good patch to work with. I suggest the Bright Piano patch in the Piano folder of the Reason Factory Sound Bank. Once it is loaded, notice the filter settings of this patch.

2. Use your mouse to increase the value of the Attack parameter. Play a chord on your keyboard and notice the sweeping effect it produces.

3. Now decrease the value of the Decay parameter. Play a chord, and notice how the filter abruptly closes as soon as the Attack reaches its maximum value. Also notice how there is still a long sustain after the filter closes.

4. Set both the Decay and Sustain parameters to their maximum values. Now set the Release to 0, play a chord on your keyboard, and then release the notes. Notice how quickly the envelope closes.

The Amplitude Envelope (AMP ENVELOPE) is used to shape the volume characteristics of the sample. This is useful for creating very long sustained patches (such as pads), or medium to short sustained patches (such as bass guitars or drums). The same types of parameters are available here (Attack, Decay, Sustain, and Release). The included level knob to the left of the Amplitude Envelope is used as a Master Level for the NN-19.

To experiment with the Amplitude Envelope, try using the previous exercise as a road map to guide you through the different envelope parameters.

The LFO Section

No synth would be complete without an LFO, or Low Frequency Oscillator (see Figure 13.14). Like a standard oscillator, LFOs can generate a waveform and frequency, but there are two distinct differences between them.

Figure 13.14 The NN-19 LFO section is used to adjust the Low Frequency Oscillator.

- An LFO is capable of generating waveforms with a low frequency, hence the name LFO.

- An LFO's purpose is to modulate a parameter, such as a filter or another oscillator. This means that the LFO itself is never actually heard, just its effect on other synth parameters.

The Waveform Selector (WAVF) is used to choose a desired waveform for modulating one of three available parameters. Because the NN-19 Waveform Selector functions exactly as the one found on the Subtractor, this section briefly recaps the available waveforms.

- **Triangle**—Creates a smooth up and down vibrato.

- **Inverted Sawtooth**—Creates a cycled ramp up effect.

- **Sawtooth**—Creates a cycled ramp down effect.

- **Square**—This waveform makes abrupt changes between two values.

- **Random**—Creates a random stepped modulation. Also known as sample and hold.

- **Soft Random**—Exactly as the previous waveform but with a smoother modulation curve.

Once you have selected a waveform, you then need to specify which parameter the LFO will modulate. This is done using the LFO Destination (DEST) button. There are three parameters available to modulate.

- **Osc**—This assigns the LFO to modulate the sample pitch of the NN-19.

- **Filter**—This assigns the LFO to modulate the Filter Frequency. This is great for creating tempo-controlled filter sweeps.

- **Pan**—This assigns the LFO to modulate the panning position of the samples. By using this, you can create a tempo-controlled stereo vibrato effect.

Located just above the Waveform Selector, the Sync button assigns the frequency of the LFO to synchronize to the song tempo. Once activated, the Rate knob then assigns one of 16 possible time divisions to the LFO. If the Sync button is not active, the Rate knob has a range of 0–127.

After the Sync and Rate are sorted out, the Amount knob is then used to assign a specific amount of LFO to the desired destination (Osc, Filter, or Pan). There is a lot of room to work with when using this parameter. How much you use depends on how much you think the sample needs to be modulated.

Read the Tutorial   Near the end of this chapter, you will find a step-by-step tutorial for creating your own NN-19 patch from scratch. Also included in this tutorial is a section devoted to editing the patch using the featured sections just covered. Be sure to check it out!

The NN-19 Play Parameters

After using the NN-19 synth parameters to shape and mold your samples, the play parameters are fantastic for giving your samples some character (see Figure 13.15). These parameters are meant to be used during a live performance; they modify your samples on the go.

Figure 13.15   The NN-19 Play parameters are best used during a live performance.

Low Bandwidth

The Low Bandwidth (LOW BW) button will remove some of the high frequencies of the loaded NN-19 patch. This is a play parameter that should be used on slower computers with less RAM because it will help conserve your computer resources.

Voice Spread

Located just below the Patch Name window, Voice Spread (SPREAD) is used to create a stereo effect by placing the separate voices of the loaded samples in different parts of the stereo field. The intensity of this effect is controlled by the knob, and then panned according to one of the three pan modes.

- **Key Mode**—As you start from the low part of the keyboard and work your way up, the panning position will change gradually as you move from left to right.

- **Key 2 Mode**—This functions in the same way as the previous key mode, except the panning will shift from left to right every eight steps on the keyboard and then repeat.

- **Jump Mode**—Panning will alternate from left to right for each note played. This function is not note specific, so you can play the same note in succession and the panning position will still change.

Polyphony and Portamento

Polyphony assigns the number of voices that can be simultaneously played. The NN-19 has a wide range of polyphony, from 1 to 99 voices, offering a wide range of creative possibilities. For example, when set at 1, the NN-19 becomes a monophonic instrument, which is perfect for use with a flute or clarinet sample because they are monophonic instruments.

Portamento is a parameter that creates a slide effect between the notes you play. The Portamento knob assigns the amount of time needed to slide from one note to another. When used in combination with Polyphony, the Portamento feature can be used to create a sliding monophonic synth, much like the retro classic Moog or ARP synths, or a slide effect ideal for a chord progression. Near the end of this chapter, you will work through an in-depth tutorial using these parameters.

Retrig and Legato

Retrig is thought of as the "normal" setting for the NN-19 because it is the commonly used parameter for playing polyphonic patches. The NN-19 envelopes are triggered when you press and hold down a note, and then they are retriggered when another note is played.

Retrig can be used with monophonic patches as well. Try pressing a note and holding it while pressing a new key. Release the new key, and the first note will retrigger.

Legato is a commonly used parameter for playing monophonic patches. With the polyphony set to 1, press and hold down a note, and then press and hold another note. Notice that the new note has no attack, because the NN-19's envelope has not been retriggered. If you add some portamento to this patch, you will get a retro vintage mono synth glide sound. Note that the NN-19 envelope *will* retrigger if you release all of the keys and play a new one.

It is also possible to use legato with a polyphonic patch. Set the polyphony of a patch to a low number of voices, such as three. Hold down a three-note chord, and then play another note. Notice that the new note will be played with a legato effect (no attack), but it will cease to play the highest note of the chord you are playing because it is "stealing" that note in order to play the new note.

The Controller Section

The NN-19 is capable of receiving three commonly used MIDI controller messages, and then sending those messages to three available parameters:

- **A.Touch**—Also known as *channel pressure*. You can hold a note down and apply a little more pressure to the key to send additional MIDI data, if your keyboard supports this feature.

- **Expr**—This is an external piece of gear that works a lot like a sustain pedal on a piano. If your MIDI keyboard has an input for an expressional pedal, you can buy one at your local music instrument shop, plug it in, and use it to send MIDI data to the NN-19.

- **Breath**—This is also an external piece of gear that is found on electronic wind instruments, or EWI. This is used to give your patches a woodwind effect by emulating the attack of a woodwind instrument.

If you have any of these external devices, you can use them to send MIDI data to any or all of these three parameters:

- **F.Freq**—When set to a positive value, the additional MIDI data will increase the Filter Frequency parameter. A negative value has the opposite effect.

- **LFO**—When set to a positive value, the additional MIDI data will increase the LFO amount knob. A negative value has the opposite effect.

- **Amp**—When set to a positive value, the additional MIDI data will increase the amplitude of the NN-19. A negative value has the opposite effect.

Pitch and Modulation

The Pitch Bend Wheel is an emulation of a standard pitch wheel found on most MIDI keyboards (see Figure 13.16). Simply put, it is used to bend the pitch of the played notes up and down. The Range parameter, just above the Pitch Bend Wheel, controls the range of pitch by up to +/– two octaves.

Figure 13.16 The Pitch and Modulation Wheels and corresponding parameters.

The Modulation Wheel is used to control a number of available parameters. Undeniably one of the most useful and expressive play parameters, the Modulation Wheel can be used to give your sequences a very realistic and emotional performance.

The Modulation Wheel can control the following parameters:

■ **F.Freq**—When set to a positive value, the Modulation Wheel increases the Filter Frequency parameter. A negative value has the opposite effect.

■ **F.Res**—When set to a positive value, the Modulation Wheel increases the resonance. A negative value has the opposite effect.

■ **F.Decay**—This knob controls the Decay parameter of the Filter Envelope. When set to a positive value, the Modulation Wheel increases the amount of decay. A negative value has the opposite effect.

■ **Amp**—When set to a positive value, the Modulation Wheel increases the amplitude of the NN-19. A negative value has the opposite effect. It's very cool for creating a crescendo with your sample patch.

■ **LFO**—When set to a positive value, the Modulation Wheel increases the LFO amount knob. A negative value has the opposite effect.

Velocity Control

The Velocity section of the play parameters gives you control over multiple parameters according to how hard the notes are played. This is a feature not commonly found on hardware synths and samplers (see Figure 13.17).

Figure 13.17 The Velocity controls can make your samples sound livelier and add expression by making specific parameters sensitive to varying velocities.

The Velocity controls can modify the following parameters:

■ **F.Env**—When set to a positive value, different velocities control the Amount knob of the Filter Envelope. A negative value has the opposite effect.

■ **F.Decay**—When set to a positive value, different velocities control the Decay parameter of the Filter Envelope. A negative value has the opposite effect.

■ **Amp**—When set to a positive value, the velocity controls the amount of volume. A negative value has the opposite effect.

- **A.Attack**—When set to positive value, the velocity controls the Attack parameter of the Amplitude Envelope. A negative value has the opposite effect.

- **S.Start**—When set to a positive value, the velocity modifies the starting time for the sample patch. A negative value has the opposite effect.

Sampling Audio with the NN-19

When you get right down to it, sampling audio with the NN-19, or any of Reason's other instruments that include this feature (NN-XT, Redrum, and Kong) is a smooth ride indeed. Propellerhead has created a simple, yet effective way to sample your instruments by providing effective tools that make the whole process more creative and spontaneous. Take it from a guy who sampled a lot with hardware samplers in the 90s; this is a great feature!

You'll learn throughout this section of the chapter how easy it really is to sample within the Reason environment.

Setting Up to Sample

The first thing you'll want to do is set up an audio source to sample. This requires the use of the audio input on your selected audio interface for Reason. For this tutorial, I am using an Apogee One audio interface and plugging my guitar directly into its line level input. This produces a very simple, yet solid sounding audio source for the purposes of sampling.

After you have selected what you intend to sample and have made the proper connections to your audio interface, it's time to activate an audio input and get a good audio level. Navigate to the Hardware Interface device on the Device Rack, and locate the Sampling Input section (see Figure 13.18).

- **Sample Monitoring**—This button will activate the sample monitoring function, which allows you to monitor your audio source before, during, and after you sample your audio.

- **Auto**—When active, this button will automatically cause Reason to monitor your audio source only as you begin to sample. Once you're done sampling, the monitoring will be automatically disabled.

- **Level**—This knob sets the input level you'll use to sample your audio source. While it's important to record a good, solid signal into whichever of Reason's sampling devices you use, be sure not to overdo it. As discussed before, digital clipping is a bad thing.

Figure 13.18 The Sampling Input section of the Hardware Interface device is where you set up to monitor your audio source.

Another point of interest with this device is the Big Meter display, which can be used to display the ins and outs of Reason in a much larger format. Clicking on the bottom button of any of Reason's inputs or outputs will activate and display the Big Meter (see Figure 13.19).

- **Meter Mode**—This button toggles between the different meter displays. You can select between Volume Units (VU), Peak Program (PPM), and Peak. Additionally, you can select a combination of VU and Peak or PPM and Peak.

- **Peak Hold**—This determines how long the peak (loudest) signal is displayed within the Big Meter. You can select either Five Seconds or Infinite.

- **VU Offset**—This knob determines at which point to display the offset, or red peak indicators within the Big Meter.

- **Channel**—This knob is used to select which of Reason's inputs and outputs to display in the Big Meter.

- **Reset**—This button is used to reset the clip indicators within the Big Meter display.

Figure 13.19 The Big Meter is used to view the volume of any Reason input or output channel.

Sampling in Mono or Stereo   By default, Reason will sample your audio as a stereo file, regardless of whether it's a true stereo audio signal or not. You can change this setting by disconnecting one of the Sampling Inputs from its corresponding Audio Input on the Hardware Interface.

Press the Tab key to view the back of the Device Rack and disconnect Sampling Input Right from Audio Input 2. Press the Tab key again to begin sampling your audio source in mono (see Figure 13.20).

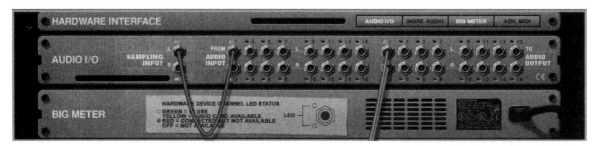

Figure 13.20 Disconnecting one of the Sampling Inputs from the Audio Inputs on the Hardware Device allows you to sample your mono audio source as a true mono recording.

Recording Your Sample

At this point, you're ready to record your first sample into the NN-19. Assuming that you've properly set up your audio source, try the following exercise.

1. Navigate to the NN-19 and click on the Sampling button.

2. NN-19 should now begin to sample and will display your audio in the Waveform display window (see Figure 13.21).

3. If you are recording a piano or guitar chord, be sure to let the note sustain as long as possible while you're sampling it.

4. Once you've finished sampling, click the Edit button to launch the Edit Sample window.

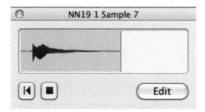

Figure 13.21 The Waveform display window shows your audio sample as it's being recorded in real-time.

Editing Your Sample

Once you've sampled your audio, Reason provides a powerful sample editor that can help you perform all of the edits needed to make your sample sound and perform its best (see Figure 13.22).

Navigating the Edit Sample Window

Before you can start to edit your samples, you should get to know the various features and points of interest throughout the Edit Sample window.

■ **Undo/Redo**—Use these to undo and redo various edits in the Edit Sample window.

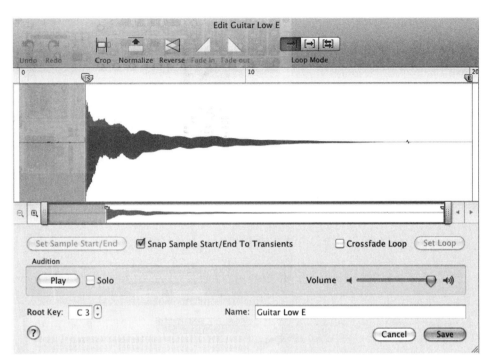

Figure 13.22 The sample editor is any sampling artist's tool of choice. Not only can it perform basic edits, but it can also be used to set up loop points and fades.

- **Crop**—This button will crop the unwanted sample date before and after the start and end points.

- **Normalize**—This is used to find the loudest point in the sample, amplify it, and then amplify the rest of the sample accordingly.

- **Reverse**—Use this to reserve the playback of the sample.

- **Fade In/Out**—Use these buttons to set a fade in or fade out on your sample.

- **Loop Mode**—These buttons set the loop type when using loop points. You can select "no loop," "loop forward," or "loop forward and backward".

- **Waveform Display**—This is where the sample is displayed in either mono or stereo and then edited by the tools above and below it.

- **Set Sample Start/End**—Use this button to set the start and end points of your sample by clicking and dragging across the waveform to select a specific part of it.

- **Snap Sample Start/End To Transients**—When selected, this will cause the start and end locators to snap to different transients in the sample as you adjust their positions.

- **Crossfade Loop**—Use this to set a crossfade in the loop. This will help to remove any unwanted pops or clicks that may occur when setting loop points.

- **Set Loop**—Use this button to set the loop points of your sample by clicking and dragging across the waveform to select a specific part of the waveform and then clicking Set Loop.

- **Audition**—These tools allow you to preview your sample. Press the Play button to play the sample. Use the Solo check box to solo the sample while your song is playing. Use the Volume slider to adjust the volume of the sample.

- **Root Key**—This dialog box is used to set the "original" root key of the sample. For example, if you sampled a Low E string on a guitar, the root key of that sample would be E1.

- **Name**—Use this dialog box to name your sample.

Where Are the Samples Stored?   All of the samples created with the sampling function of Reason are self-contained within your song file. Additionally, the samples are displayed in the Song Sample List in the Tool Window (see Figure 13.23).

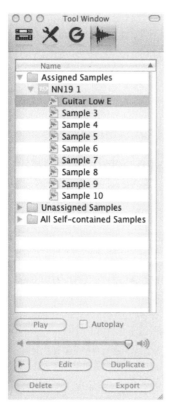

Figure 13.23 Whenever you create a sample in your Reason song, you can find the sample in the Sample List tab of the Tool Window.

Cropping Your Sample

The first edit you should perform to your sample is to crop it, so that the empty data before and after the start and end points are discarded. Have a look at Figure 13.24 and you'll see that the image on the left is before cropping the sample, whereas the image on the right has been cropped and as a result, the sample is considerably shorter.

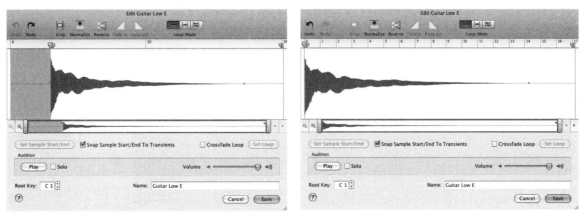

Figure 13.24 The before and after effect of cropping your samples.

Setting Your Loop Points

Now that the sample has been cropped, it's time to set up your loop points, so that the sample can sustain infinitely. This will help make the sample sound natural should you decide to trigger the sample and hold the key down for a long period of time.

1. Select a section of the sample that has steady amplitude by clicking and dragging across the waveform (see Figure 13.25).

2. Once your selection is highlighted, you can click on the Set Loop button and this will place the Left and Right locators to the beginning and end of the selection (see Figure 13.26). At this point, the Loop Forward mode will automatically be selected.

3. Click on the Play button to audition the sample with the loop points. If it sounds a little unsteady in amplitude or has pops and clicks, you can select the Crossfade Loop function and this will help smooth out the transition between the loop start and loop end.

The final touch you'll want to put on your sample is to assign it a Root Key and finally name it. As I've been using a Low E string as the sample throughout this section, the appropriate Root Key would be E1, and looking at previous figures throughout this section, you can see that I've named this sample "Guitar Low E".

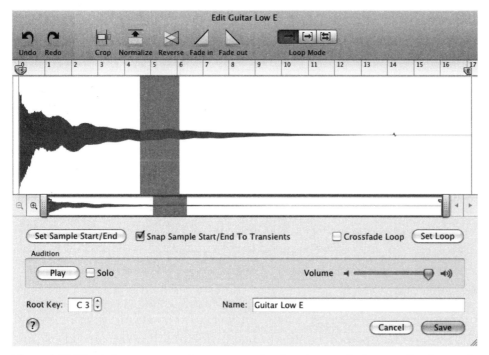

Figure 13.25 Select a part of your sample that is steady in amplitude so that when the loop occurs, the volume won't suddenly jump and sound unnatural.

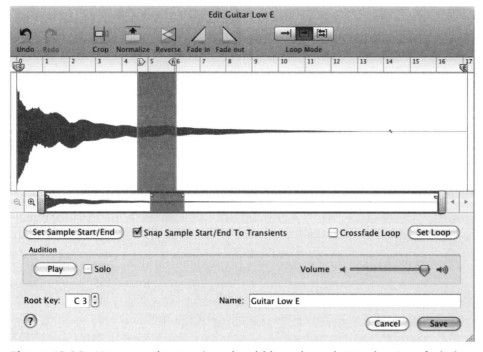

Figure 13.26 Now your loop points should be selected. Use the Crossfade loop function to help smooth out the transition between the start and end of the loop.

Once this is done, you can click the Save button and you've just created your first sample. Not quite as easy as pie, but certainly a lot easier than it used to be with hardware-based samplers.

This Is Just the Beginning   Don't let this be the end of your sampling experience in Reason. There are tons of samples in your home that you probably don't know about. For example, I've sampled all kinds of household goods to achieve some eclectic percussion samples. The sound of a can of aerosol spray can easily become a hi-hat, whereas one of those large water cooler bottles can be made into a kick drum or toms. And for the centerpiece, the sound of crushing a soda can is perfect as a snare drum.

These are just some examples, but I'm sure you're getting the point here. Sampling is in itself a true expression of creativity just waiting to be discovered by the budding samplist, so keep on it!

Creating Your First NN-19 Sample Patch

Now that you have learned all there is to learn about the functionality of the NN-19, it's time to put your knowledge to the test and create your first sample patch from scratch. In this section, you'll use a few samples of single guitar notes. You will then proceed to map these notes over the NN-19 key zones. You will top it off by using the filters and envelopes to end up with a unique guitar sound that can then be saved as an NN-19 patch.

Get the Samples   Before you begin this tutorial, take a quick trip to the Course Technology website (go to www.courseptr.com and click on Downloads) to download the sound files needed. They are in a ZIP compressed file that can be automatically opened from Windows XP or Mac OSX.

Once you download and decompress the Guitar Samples folder, place it in the Reason application folder on your computer's hard drive. Note that these samples have been specifically designed for this tutorial, meaning that the individual guitar samples have been processed with loop points and assigned a root note. There is no need to process these in another audio-editing program.

These Samples Are Copyright Safe   After going through the steps of this tutorial and creating your first NN-19 sampler patch, you might get the urge to use these samples in a song you're working on. This is perfectly fine to do because these samples are *copyright safe*. These samples were not taken from a sample collection. They were created *specifically* for this tutorial, so you are encouraged to use these guitar samples freely in any songs you write with Reason and the NN-19 or NN-XT sampler.

Setting the Key Zones

Before you can begin to import the guitar samples, you must first create a few key zones so that the samples will reside in their proper mapped locations. This is an acoustic guitar, which has six natural tones (E, A, D, G, B, and E). To make the upper register of the acoustic guitar sound more realistic, I have also added a high A and a high D to the Guitar Samples folder. So here are the key zone assignments these samples are going to use:

- **Low E**—Will be mapped out over the lowest portion of the map and have an assigned range of C1 to G#1.

- **Low A**—Will have an assigned range of A1 to C#2.

- **Low D**—Will have an assigned range of D2 to F#2.

- **Low G**—Will have an assigned range of G2 to A#2.

- **Low B**—Will have an assigned range of B2 to D#3.

- **High E**—Will have an assigned range of E3 to G#3.

- **High A**—Will have an assigned range of A3 to C#4.

- **High D**—Will be mapped out over the highest portion of the map and have an assigned range of D4 to G8.

This means that you will need to have eight key zones, so let's get cracking!

Starting from Scratch   Make sure you're starting this tutorial on the right foot by initializing the NN-19. This way, the NN-19's memory is cleared, and you are ready to press on. From the Edit pull-down menu, choose Initialize Patch, and that's it.

Start by creating the key zone for the Low E sample:

1.   Choose Edit > Split Key Zone. This will split the map in half and create a marker point that looks a lot like the left and right locators in the Reason sequencer (see Figure 13.27).

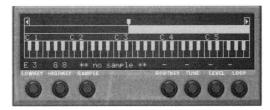

Figure 13.27 You've just split the key zone.

2. Select the left key zone, and look below the virtual keyboard. You will see that the low key is set to C2, and the high key has been set to D#3 (see Figure 13.28). Click and drag the high key knob down until it reads G#1.

Figure 13.28 The high note of the first key zone must be set to G#1.

3. Once this is accomplished, click on the folder icon, located above the virtual keyboard. This will bring up the Sample Browser window. Locate the Guitar Samples folder, which should be located in your Reason program folder. Once you have it open, select the Low E.wav file and click Open to import that sample into your first key zone.

4. Look in the key zone display, and you will see all of the sample details. Notice that the root key has been automatically set to E1 and that the Loop mode has been set to FW.

5. Next, you need to create another key zone. Select the empty key zone on the right. Now, choose Split Key Zone from the Edit pull-down menu again. Select your new key zone. Adjust the low key to A1 and the high key to C#2.

6. Click on the folder icon, and locate the Low A.wav file. Import it into the new key zone.

7. Repeat the same steps until you have eight separate key zones with the proper sample imported into each zone. When you are finished, your map should look like Figure 13.29.

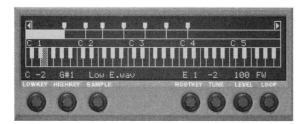

Figure 13.29 The key zones have now been created, and there is a guitar sample loaded into each zone.

After you have inserted your samples, make sure to increase the polyphony to a higher value than its default setting of 6. For this tutorial, try a value of 12.

If your NN-19 sequencer track is armed to receive MIDI, try plunking a few keys to hear how the guitar samples sound. Try holding down some chords to hear the richness of an open E major (the notes are E1, B1, E2, G#2, B2, and E3).

Before you proceed, make sure to save your newly created acoustic guitar patch by clicking on the Save button in the upper-left corner of the NN-19 interface. Be sure to save it in the Reason program folder and call it "Acoustic Guitar".

Editing Your Sample Patch

Now that your patch has been created, it's time to make your patch unique by using the NN-19 filters, envelopes, and play parameters. This is where the real fun begins.

Write in Some Chords   Before you begin editing your guitar patch, take a few minutes to create a loop of guitar chords. That way, you can play the loop over and over again while making adjustments to the individual NN-19 parameters without having to play a chord on your MIDI keyboard. It makes it a lot more fun to tweak!

If you are not a guitar player, try this chord progression:

- **E major**—E1, B1, E2, G#2, B2, and E3
- **A major**—A1, E2, A2, C#3, and E3
- **G major**—G1. B1, D2, G2, B2, and G3
- **D major**—D2, A2, D3, and F#3

You are going to create a guitar pad sound, so I suggest creating an eight-bar sequence in the Reason sequencer. Each of these chords should be two bars in length.

Using the Amp and Envelope

Because you are going to create a pad patch, the first place to start making adjustments is to the Amp and its Envelope parameters. Set the Amp slider to 82; this will prevent the NN-19 from clipping when you make adjustments to the filter and LFO.

Make the following parameter adjustments to the Envelope:

1. Set the Attack to a high value. 70 is a good place to start; this will create a very slow attack on the pad patch.

2. Set the Decay to an even higher value, such as 105.

3. Set the Sustain to a mid-to-high value, such as 70.

4. Set the Release to a slightly smaller value than the Attack, such as 54. This will allow the pad patch to really sustain and ring out.

Press Play and listen to the guitar chord progression as it plays through these adjustments you've just made. The chords should sound very long and dreamy, making it a perfect place to start adding a filter.

Using the Filter and Envelope

The first or second parameter any good synth-o-holic will want to start editing is the Filter section. In this part of the tutorial, you are going to use the filter to complement the full sound of the guitar samples when played in a chord by making it into a pad sound.

You are going to use a Band Pass filter so that you can still hear the original guitar sample, while introducing a sweep filter effect to the mix. Select the BP 12 filter mode and make sure the Keyboard Tracking knob is set to 0.

Next, you need to create a sweeping filter effect, and the first step towards making this happen is using the Filter Frequency and Resonance sliders. Set the Filter Frequency slider to a low-to-mid value, such as 48. Now set the Resonance slider to a much greater value, such as 100. Press Play on the sequencer, and listen to the sweeping effect that has been created. Notice that the original timbres of the acoustic guitar samples are still present, but now a dreamy filter sweep has been added.

To further enhance the filter sweep, make the following adjustments to the Filter Envelope:

1. Set the Attack to a very high value, such as 84. This will cause the filter sweep to begin playing the lower frequencies, and then introduce the higher frequencies as it progresses.

2. Set the Decay to an even higher value, such as 95.

3. Set the Sustain to a mid-to-high value, such as 66.

4. Set the Release to a high value that's less than or equal to the Attack parameter, such as 81.

Now increase the intensity of the filter by setting the Filter Amount knob to 42. Press Play, and listen to how the filter sweep has dramatically changed with the help of the Filter Envelope.

Before you go any further, make sure that you save your newly created patch. Click on the Save icon in the upper-left corner of the NN-19 and give your new patch a name, such as AcGuitar Pad, for example.

Using the LFO

It's time to add a little LFO and create a tempo-controlled filter sweep. Start by making sure that the Sync button is active and that the Amount knob is set to a low value, such as 24.

Next, select a waveform for your LFO to use. For this tutorial, try a square or random waveform. If you decide to use the square waveform, note the abrupt changes between the two values.

After you have selected your waveform, make sure to select the proper destination assignment for the LFO. Set the destination to Filter, and this will send the LFO effect to the Filter section. Just for kicks, you might try assigning the LFO to Pan in order to create a tempo synced panning effect.

Last, but not least, you must select a proper time division for your Rate knob. Because this is a pad sound, you might begin experimenting with a low division setting to complement the slow ominous sound of the pad patch.

Press Play to hear your new Acoustic Guitar Pad patch!

Additional Parameters

After you have adjusted the parameters of the Filter and Envelopes, you can further enhance your new pad patch by adding in a few of the Play parameters.

You can use the Spread knob to create a very realistic stereophonic effect with your pad. Try setting the Spread knob to a high value and experimenting with the different types of spread available to you (Key, Key 2, and Jump). Press Play, and you will hear your pad in a stereo field, which sounds awesome.

Although the Portamento knob is typically used for mono synth instruments, it can also be used for pad sounds. Try setting the Portamento knob to a low-to-middle setting, such as 67. Press Play, and notice how the chords slide into each other as the progression plays.

As soon as you have made your final tweaks and adjustments, be sure to save your work.

Throughout this chapter, I have shown you the ins and outs of the NN-19 sampler. Although it might be considered a very basic sampler, it is easy to use in creative ways.

But if you find yourself begging for more, go to the next chapter and meet the NN-19's big brother, the NN-XT.

14 NN-XT—Close Up

The NN-XT is the sampler that picks up where the NN-19 leaves off. For people who have created Reason Song files with earlier versions of Reason previous to the addition of the NN-XT, it is a good thing that the NN-19 remains in the program for the sake of compatibility. However, after using the NN-19 as a learning tool, you will probably want to move up to the NN-XT. It's a big step toward more functionality, compatibility, and of course creativity (see Figure 14.1).

What Makes the NN-XT Different?

Aside from the extreme graphic facelift, there are many other differences between the NN-XT and NN-19:

- **Multilayered sampling**—The NN-XT can trigger samples according to their assigned velocity.

- **More outputs**—The NN-XT has eight stereo outputs, or up to 16 mono outputs, with the use of the panning assignments.

- **More sample formats**—The NN-XT can import a wider range of sample formats.

- **More control**—The NN-XT allows individual control over each sample in a patch.

A Guided Tour of the NN-XT

It's time to begin your guided in-depth tour of the NN-XT. Toward the end of this chapter, you can further enhance your NN-XT education by following the step-by-step tutorial for creating your own multilayered sample patches and learn how to expand your sample library by using Reload.

The NN-XT Main Display Panel

When you first create an instance of the NN-XT, Reason does not automatically expand the device's entire interface; this is because it takes up a lot of room and might seem a little intimidating to the novice sampling artist (see Figure 14.2). Rather, the NN-XT main display panel is the first part of the device that you will see. The main display includes all of the global controls of the NN-XT.

Figure 14.1 The NN-XT is a two-panel Reason device. The main panel handles the global controls. The Remote Editor controls the individual parameters of the loaded sample patches.

Figure 14.2 When the NN-XT is created, you will first see the compact version.

Loading Patches

As with all of the Reason devices, the Patch Browser is available to locate and load patches, scroll through them, and save them. Because you already know how to browse for patches, you're ready to consider the various formats the NN-XT can import.

■ **.sxt**—This is the standard NN-XT patch format extension name.

- **.smp**—This is the standard NN-19 patch format extension name.

- **.sf2**—This is the common file extension name for Sound Fonts. Unlike the NN-19, the NN-XT can import an entire Sound Font patch instead of just single Sound Font files.

- **.rcy, .rex, and .rx2**—These are the commonly known file extensions for REX files. As with the NN-19, when the NN-XT imports a REX file, it chromatically maps the individual REX slices, starting from the C1 note.

Additionally, the NN-XT can also sample audio, just like Redrum, Kong, and the NN-19 and can be accessed from the Remote Editor, which you'll read about soon. You can refer back to Chapter 13 for more information and tutorials on sampling.

Just below the Patch Browser window is the High Quality Interpolation button and the Note On indicator, which lights up whenever a MIDI message is received.

Global Controls

To the right of the Patch Browser are the global controls for your loaded patches.

- **Filter Controls**—These knobs are used to control the Freq and Res parameters of the Filter found on the NN-XT Remote Editor. Note that the Filter must be turned on before you can use these knobs.

- **Amp Envelope Controls**—These knobs are used to control the Attack, Decay, and Release of the Amp Envelope on the Remote Editor.

- **Modulation Envelope**—This knob is used to control the Decay parameter of the Modulation Envelope in the Remote Editor.

- **Master Volume**—Controls the amplitude level for the NN-XT.

Pitch and Modulation

Located to the far left of the main display, the Pitch and Modulation controls are common to just about every Reason synth.

- **Pitch Bend Wheel**—This wheel is used to bend the pitch of the sample up and down. The potential range of the pitch bend effect is determined by its corresponding controls found in the Remote Editor.

- **Modulation Wheel**—This wheel is used to control and modify a number of parameters, such as Filter Frequency, Resonance, and Level. When used effectively, modulation is a key tool for adding expression to your sampled instruments. Note that the Modulation Wheel is called the Wheel or simply "W."

External Control

To the right of the Modulation Wheel is the External Control Wheel. The External Control Wheel can receive three MIDI controller messages, and then send that data to any of its assigned parameters in the NN-XT Remote Editor.

- Aftertouch

- Expression

- Breath

Additionally, the External Control Wheel can be used to send these three MIDI controller messages to the Reason sequencer, should your MIDI keyboard not support these parameters.

Also note that the External Control Wheel is labeled "X" in the main display, just as the Modulation Wheel is labeled "W." These controls will be discussed in greater detail later in this chapter.

The NN-XT Remote Editor

As previously stated, when an NN-XT is first created in the Reason Device Rack, its main display is the only visible element. Just below the main display is the collapsed Remote Editor. Click on the arrow icon located on the lower-left corner of the NN-XT to expand the Remote Editor (see Figure 14.3).

At first sight, the Remote Editor looks very complex. But as you read through the guided tour of this beauty, you will soon see that the Remote Editor is quite possibly one of the most well thought out and versatile devices in Reason.

There are several sections to the Remote Editor. Here's a rundown of what this section covers:

- **Synth parameters**—The parameters in this section are used to edit and manipulate your sample patches using filters, envelopes, and two LFOs.

- **Group parameters**—These parameters are used to enhance the performance or playing style of the NN-XT. They are very similar to the Play parameters of the NN-19.

- **Key Map display**—This area is used to map samples across the NN-XT. Any sample information you need to know can be found in this section.

- **Sample parameters**—These parameters are used to set the key zones, root keys, play modes, and more for each sample loaded into the key map.

Group
Parameters

Key Map
Display

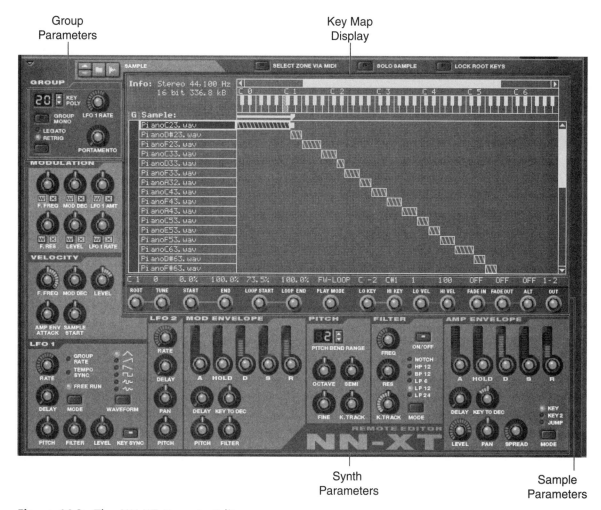

Synth
Parameters

Sample
Parameters

Figure 14.3 The NN-XT Remote Editor.

These Parameters Are Not Global   While touring through the Remote Editor, it's important to remember that, with the exception of the Group parameters, all of the remaining parameters you will be using are not global. When you select a single sample from the key map and make any change to the pitch, filter, or modulation, you are affecting just that single sample zone, not the rest of the sample patch.

However, if you want to make global changes to the entire sample patch, you can do so in several ways. Here's one:

1. Use the Patch Browser to load a sample patch into the NN-XT. Then choose Edit > Select All Zones.

2. Click on one of the samples in the key map. Then hold the Shift button down and click on the additional samples.

3. Click the group of samples you want to make changes to in the Group column. This will select all of the samples in that particular group. If there are additional groups, you need to hold the Shift key down and select the next groups as well.

The Synth Parameters

The NN-XT synth parameters are used to edit and manipulate the characteristics of your samples with ease and precision. To make it easier to understand, I break these parameters into the following groups:

- Modulation

- Velocity

- Pitch

- Filter

- Envelopes

- LFOs

The Modulation Section. The Modulation section of the NN-XT is one of the most versatile of its kind (see Figure 14.4). There are six parameters that can be used on an individual basis or grouped together. Additionally, these parameters can be assigned to either the Modulation Wheel by selecting the "W" button under each knob, or the External Control Wheel by selecting the "X" button under each knob. Better yet, the parameters can be assigned to both wheels simultaneously by selecting both the "W" and "X" buttons.

Figure 14.4 The NN-XT Modulation section is used to assign modulation to different parameters.

Take a look at what each of these parameters does:

- **F.Freq**—This parameter assigns the Filter Frequency parameters to the Modulation section. When assigned a positive value, the filter will open as the

Modulation Wheel's value is increased. Assigning a negative value has the opposite effect.

■ **Mod Dec**—This parameter assigns the Decay parameter of the Modulation Envelope to either the Modulation or External Control Wheel.

■ **LFO 1 Amt**—This parameter determines the amount of modulation of LFO 1 that is affected by the Modulation Wheel.

■ **F.Res**—This parameter assigns the Filter Resonance parameter to the Modulation section.

■ **Level**—This parameter assigns the Level or amplitude of a single or several zones to the Modulation section.

■ **LFO 1 Rate**—This parameters assigns the rate of LFO 1 to the Modulation section.

The Velocity Section. The Velocity section is used to modify a combination of five parameters according to the velocity of notes played by a MIDI keyboard (see Figure 14.5).

Figure 14.5 The NN-XT Velocity section is used to assign velocity to different parameters.

■ **Filter Envelope**—When set to a positive value, different velocities control the Amount knob of the Filter Envelope. A negative value has the opposite effect.

■ **Filter Decay**—When set to a positive value, different velocities control the Decay parameter of the Filter Envelope. A negative value has the opposite effect.

■ **Amplitude**—When set to a positive value, the velocity controls the amount of volume. A negative value has the opposite effect.

■ **Amplitude Attack**—When set to a positive value, the velocity controls the Attack parameter of the Amplitude Envelope. A negative value has the opposite effect.

■ **Sample Start**—When set to a positive value, the velocity modifies the starting time for the sample patch. A negative value has the opposite effect.

The Pitch Section. The Pitch Bend Range is used to assign a bend range to the Pitch Bend Wheel of the main display (see Figure 14.6). By default, a value of two semitones is selected whenever a NN-XT is created in the Reason Device Rack because this is the standard pitch bend range found on most hardware synths. However, the Pitch Bend Range has a potential range of 24 semitones, or two octaves. To increase or decrease the bend value, you can click on its scroll buttons, or simply click and drag on the display itself.

Figure 14.6 The NN-XT Pitch section is used to make tuning adjustments to the samples.

Below the Pitch Bend Range are three parameters used to modify the pitch of individual samples within a patch. Take a look at what each of these parameters does:

- **Octave**—This parameter shifts the pitch of a selected sample in octave increments. The range of the Octave knob is +/– five octaves.

- **Semi**—This parameter shifts the pitch of a selected sample by semitone increments. The range of the Semi knob is +/– 13 semitones, or two octaves.

- **Fine**—This parameter is used to make minimal adjustments to selected samples by cent increments. The range of the Fine knob is +/– 50 cents, or half a semitone.

The Keyboard Track knob is a parameter used to control the keyboard tracking of the NN-XT pitch. It's a fairly unique and unusual parameter that is best explained when having a patch loaded ready to listen to the resulting effect.

Load up a bass patch from the Reason Factory Sound Bank, and try the following exercise.

1. Select all of the samples in the patch by choosing Edit > Select All Zones.

2. Navigate to the Keyboard Track knob and turn it all the way down by clicking and dragging with your mouse.

3. Arm the NN-XT sequencer track so you can play your MIDI keyboard to hear the effect. All the keys should now be the same pitch.

4. Now turn the Keyboard Track knob all the way up. Play the C3 note on your MIDI keyboard, followed by C#3 and D3. You should hear the same pitch played in different octaves. Experimenting with the Keyboard Track knob (especially with more subtle settings) can result in some interesting musical scales that you may find inspiring. This can work especially well with tuned ethnic percussion and metallic sounds. It can also allow you to play some ear-grabbing passages that would be very difficult with standard tuning.

The Filter Section. As with most of the other Reason devices, the Filter uses a combination of resonance and cutoff frequencies to shape the sound and timbre of a sample (see Figure 14.7). Take a look at the available parameters.

Figure 14.7 The NN-XT Filter section can be used to alter the timbre of individual samples or an entire selection of samples.

To activate the Filter, just click the On/Off button located at the top-right corner of the Filter section. Once activated, you can also use the Filter controls in the NN-XT main display.

After activating the Filter section, you can then select one of six filter modes by clicking on the Mode button or by clicking on the filter's name. Here's a brief run down of the available filter modes and the additional parameters.

- **Notch**—Rejects the mid-frequencies while allowing the high frequencies and low frequencies to pass.

- **HP 12**—Filters out the low frequencies while allowing the high frequencies to pass through with a roll-off curve of 12dB per octave.

- **BP 12**—Filters out both the high and low frequencies, while allowing the mid-frequencies to pass with a roll-off curve of 12dB per octave.

- **LP 6**—Unique to the NN-XT, the LP 6 is a Low Pass filter that filters out the high frequencies while allowing the low frequencies to pass with a gentle roll-off curve of 6dB per octave. The LP 6's effect can be heard only when changing the value of the Frequency Filter knob because it has no resonance.

- **LP 12**—Filters out the high frequencies while allowing the low frequencies to pass with a roll-off curve of 12dB per octave.

- **LP 24**—Filters out the high frequencies while allowing the low frequencies to pass with a steep roll-off curve of 24dB per octave.

The Filter Frequency, or *cutoff filter* as it is also called, is used to specify where the filter will function within the frequency spectrum. Once the Filter section is activated, just click on the Filter Frequency knob and drag your mouse up or down to increase or decrease the cutoff effect.

The Resonance knob is used in combination with the Filter Frequency. It emphasizes the frequencies set by the Filter knob, which thins the sound out but also increases the sweep effect.

The Keyboard Track knob is used to compensate for the loss of high frequencies as you play higher notes on the keyboard. It can be used to bring the higher played notes to the forefront in a mix.

The Envelopes. An envelope generator is used to modify specific synth parameters, including pitch, volume, and filter frequencies. By using an envelope creatively, you can control how these parameters are to be modified over a specific amount of time. The NN-XT includes two envelope generators. One is assigned to Modulation, and the other is assigned to Amplitude (see Figure 14.8).

Figure 14.8 The NN-XT has envelopes for Modulation and Amplitude.

Here are the standard envelope parameters:

- **Attack**—When an envelope is triggered, the Attack parameter determines how much time passes before the envelope reaches its maximum value.

- **Hold**—Unique to the NN-XT, this parameter is used to determine how long the envelope remains at its maximum potential.

- **Decay**—Once the maximum value is reached and held for a determined Hold time, the Decay parameter determines how much time passes before the value begins to drop.

- **Sustain**—After the value begins to drop, the Sustain determines at which level the falling value should rest.

- **Release**—Once the value has been set at its rested value, the Release parameter determines how long it will take until the value will begin to drop to 0.

- **Delay**—This parameter determines the amount of delay between playing the note and hearing the effect of the envelope. The Delay knob has a range of 0–10 seconds.

- **Key to Decay**—This creates an offset of the Decay parameter, which is determined by where you play on your MIDI keyboard. If assigned a positive value, the Decay parameter will increase. The opposite effect occurs when assigned a negative value.

The Modulation Envelope is used to alter specific parameters over time. Aside from the common parameters that are found on both the Mod and Amp Envelopes, the Modulation Envelope also contains a few additional parameters:

- **Pitch**—This parameter causes the envelope to control the pitch of the notes played. If assigned a positive value, the pitch bends up. The opposite effect occurs when assigned a negative value.

- **Filter**—This parameter causes the envelope to modulate the Filter Frequency. When assigned a positive value, the value of the Filter Frequency increases. The opposite effect occurs when assigned a negative value.

The Amplitude Envelope is used to alter the volume of a patch over time. Aside from the common parameters shared by both the Mod and Amp Envelopes, the Amplitude Envelope also has a few additional parameters:

- **Level**—Controls the volume level of a selected zone in the key zone map. This parameter can also control the volume of an entire patch by selecting all of the zones.

- **Pan**—Controls the panning of a selected zone in the key zone map. This parameter can also control the panning assignment of an entire patch by selecting all of the zones.

- **Spread**—This parameter creates a stereo effect by placing single notes played in various places within the stereo field. The knob determines the amount of Spread whereas the type of Spread is determined by the Spread modes, which are located just to the right. For a detailed explanation of these different modes, please refer to Chapter 13, " NN-19—Close Up," where they are discussed in detail.

■ **Mode**—Also called Spread mode or Pan mode, this parameter has three settings, which are Key, Key2, and Jump. Key pans gradually from left to right across the entire range of the keyboard. Key2 pans from left to right and back again over a span of eight keys, and Jump alternates the pan left or right each time a note is played.

The LFOs. The NN-XT includes two independent *Low Frequency Oscillators*, or LFOs (see Figure 14.9). As discussed in previous chapters, LFOs do not actually produce audible sound on their own. Rather, an LFO is used to modulate the main oscillators of a synthesizer. The NN-XT's LFOs are designed to modulate the samples themselves.

Figure 14.9 The NN-XT has two separate LFOs.

If you look at both of the LFOs, you'll notice that they share common knobs, but there are some key differences between LFOs 1 and 2.

■ Although LFO 1 supports a number of waveforms, LFO 2 supports only the triangle waveform.

■ LFO 1 can modulate the NN-XT filter, whereas LFO 2 modulates the pan.

■ LFO 2's play mode is *always* set to Key Sync. This means that the waveform of LFO 2 will always trigger whenever a note is pressed on your keyboard.

The Rate knob determines the frequency of the LFO. To increase the modulation rate, turn the knob to the right. For a slower modulation, turn the knob to the left.

It is important to note that LFO 1 has three Rate modes, as follows:

■ **Group Rate**—When this mode is selected, the rate of LFO 1 is controlled by the LFO 1 Rate knob in the Group parameters of the Remote Editor. This ensures that all of the zones in the NN-XT modulate at the same rate.

■ **Tempo Sync**—When this mode is selected, the rate of the LFO is controlled by the tempo of the Reason sequencer. If you activate this mode and then begin to make changes to the Rate knob, a tooltip displays the different time divisions.

- **Free Run**—When this mode is selected, the LFO runs continuously at the rate set by the Rate knob. If the Key Sync is activated, the LFO triggers every time a note is played. Also note that LFO 2 *always* runs in the Free Run mode.

The Delay knob is used to set a delay between playing the note on your keyboard and hearing it. Both LFO 1 and LFO 2 Delay knobs have the same capability and range of 0–10 seconds.

Although LFO 2 always uses the triangle waveform, LFO 1 has six waveform choices for modulation. These modes can be selected by clicking on the Waveform Mode button or by just clicking on the desired waveform.

- **Triangle**—Creates a smooth up and down vibrato.

- **Inverted Sawtooth**—Creates a cycled ramp up effect.

- **Sawtooth**—Creates a cycled ramp down effect.

- **Square**—Makes abrupt changes between two values.

- **Random**—Creates a random stepped modulation. Also known as sample and hold.

- **Soft Random**—Exactly like the previous waveform but has a smoother modulation curve.

After a rate, delay, and waveform mode have been selected, it's time to choose a modulation destination. Although LFO 1 and LFO 2 contain different destinations, I have placed them all in a single list to discuss them.

- **Pitch**—This parameter modulates the pitch of the loaded sample patch. It is commonly used for trills and vibrato, but that is just a couple of the many sound design possibilities. The Pitch knob has a range of –2400 to 2400 cents (up to four octaves) and is available in both LFO 1 and LFO 2.

- **Filter**—This parameter modulates the Filter Frequency. It is a great tool for creating a filter sweep that can open upward (when set to positive) or downward (when set to negative). Note that this parameter is available only on LFO 1.

- **Level**—This knob is used to modulate the output level of the NN-XT for creating a tremolo effect. Note that this is available only with LFO 1.

- **Pan**—This parameter is used to modulate the panning of a single or multiple zones. It is a great effect to use on orchestral percussion, such as xylophones or glockenspiels. When turned to the left, the panning effect will move from left to right in the stereo field. When the knob is turned to the right, the panning effect will move from right to left in the stereo field. Note that this parameter is available with LFO 2.

The Group Parameters

Located in the upper-left corner of the NN-XT interface, the Group parameters apply to all of the zones within a selected group (see Figure 14.10).

Figure 14.10   The NN-XT Group parameters apply to all tones within a selected group.

Polyphony. *Polyphony* determines how many notes can be played simultaneously from the NN-XT. When set to a value of 1, the NN-XT becomes a monophonic instrument, which is perfect for playing lead synth lines or mimicking monophonic instruments, such as a flute or clarinet. When set to a greater polyphonic value, the NN-XT becomes the perfect device for mimicking instruments that are capable of producing many voices at one time, such as a piano, guitar, or a choir.

The NN-XT has a Polyphony range of 1–99 voices, so that should give you plenty of room to work with.

Legato and Retrig. *Legato* is the play mode of choice for monophonic sounds. While in Legato mode, play a note and hold it. Now play another note, and you will notice that the NN-XT will not retrigger the envelope but rather just change the pitch. If you combine this with a good portion of portamento, you can create a fantastic sliding synth sound.

Legato will also work with polyphonic patches. Set the Polyphony to 3, and play a three-note chord on your MIDI keyboard. Now press and hold another note, and you will hear that the new note will be played legato style, but it steals one of the original notes of the chord.

Retrig is thought of as the "normal" preference for polyphonic patches. While in Retrig mode, the NN-XT envelopes are triggered every time a note is played on your MIDI keyboard, which differs greatly from the legato effect.

Retrig can also be used with monophonic patches. Press a note, hold it, and then play another note and release it. Notice that the NN-XT will now retrigger the sample of the first note, unlike the Legato mode.

Group Mono. The Group Mono is used in combination with notes that are grouped together in a patch. Once grouped and selected, activating the Group Mono function will bypass the Polyphony value and treat the grouped notes as monophonic. However, this function does not work with the Legato or Retrig play modes.

A real-world example of this would be the open hi-hat, closed hi-hat scenario. When you play an open hi-hat, you'd want the sound to be cut if you play the closed hi-hat sound. This is easily accomplished with Group Mono by simply selecting both closed and open hi-hat samples, grouping them, and then activating Group Mono. Now play an open hi-hat, let it ring out, and then play a closed hi-hat sample. The open hat should immediately cut out.

LFO 1 Rate. The LFO 1 Rate knob is used to control the frequency of modulation within the LFO 1. This knob is active only when the Group Rate mode is selected in the LFO section of the synth parameters.

Portamento. Portamento is used to create a sliding effect between played notes. The knob determines the amount of time it will take to slide from one note to another. It can be used with either monophonic or polyphonic patches and is a great tool for creating some interesting effects. Try loading a polyphonic patch, such as a string section or piano. Set the portamento to a value of 45 and play some chords. You will hear a slight sliding effect that makes the patch sound a little funny, but try adding some delay and reverb. After a while, you'll have an ambient masterpiece on your hands.

The Key Map Display

Occupying the majority of the Remote Editor, the Key Map display is where all the action happens when it comes to importing, grouping, and creating sample patches (see Figure 14.11). There are a few similarities to the NN-19 as you will see, but the NN-XT

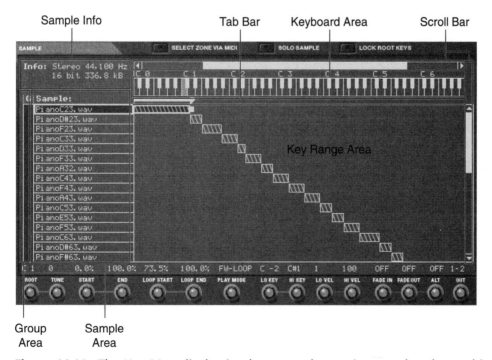

Figure 14.11 The Key Map display is where samples are imported and sorted in a very easy-to-understand interface.

key map is a much more diverse and mature interface that is intuitive and shouldn't take too long to master.

The Key Map display is split into seven areas:

- **Info**—The Info area is used to display the sampling rate, bit depth, and file size of a selected sample.

- **Sample Info**—The Sample area is used to list the filenames of the loaded samples in a patch.

- **Group**—The Group area does not display information. Rather, it is used to select a compilation of sample zones that are assigned to a group.

- **Keyboard**—The Keyboard area is used to display key ranges, audition loaded samples, and set root keys.

- **Tab Bar**—The Tab Bar is located just below the Keyboard area and is used to display the key range of a selected sample zone. It is here that you can resize a sample zone's key range.

- **Key Range**—The Key Range area is used to display the sample zones within a patch. Zones can be moved and resized in this area.

- **Scroll Bars**—There are vertical and horizontal scroll bars that allow you to view any key range (vertical) or position on the keyboard (horizontal) .

Aside from the Info area and scroll bars, which are pretty self explanatory, let's have an in-depth look at these areas.

The Sample Area. All the files that are used to create a sample patch for the NN-XT are displayed in the Sample area as a list. The Sample area can also be used as a tool to load samples into a zone. To get better acquainted with the Sample area, try this quick exercise.

1. If you have a patch loaded into the NN-XT, clear it by choosing Edit > Initialize Patch. This will give you a clean slate to work with.

2. Next, you need to add a zone to your key map so you can load a sample. Choose Edit > Add Zone to create an empty zone into which a sample can now be loaded. Notice that in the Sample area, the newly created zone is labeled No Sample.

3. To load a sample into the zone, you can click on the Load Sample button at the upper-left corner of the Remote Editor or double-click on the No Sample label to open the Sample Browser window. At this point, you can select a sample and load it into your new zone. Additionally, you can record a sample straight into the NN-XT by clicking on the Start Sample button.

The Group Area. After you have created a number of zones and loaded samples into them, you can compile these zones into a group. Once you do this, a number of zones can be selected and modified at one time, making it a big time saver.

To create a group, try this quick exercise:

1. Using the previous exercise as an example, create several zones and load samples into them.

2. Once you have created a number of zones, select them all by either choosing Select All from the Edit pull-down menu or using Ctrl+A (or Apple+A on the Mac).

3. Choose the Group Selected Zones option from the Edit pull-down menu. This will place all the zones into one group.

The Keyboard Area. The Keyboard area is a graphical representation of the virtual keyboard within the NN-XT. It is here that key ranges can be viewed, root notes can be set, and loaded samples can be auditioned without the use of a MIDI keyboard.

The *key range* refers to the lowest and highest key that will trigger a loaded sample. For example, let's suppose that you've imported a snare drum sample into a newly created zone in the key map. As a snare drum is a sample that does not have a specific pitch, you will not need more than one or two keys on your keyboard to trigger the sample. By using a key range, you can specify that the snare sample will be heard only by pressing the D1 or D#1 notes on a MIDI keyboard.

A *root note* specifies the original frequency at which a sample was recorded. If you record a piano played at Middle C, C3 is its root note. It is very important to specify a sample's root note, because you want to make sure that the recorded sample retains its realism and natural timbre.

Later in the Show   In the next main section of this chapter, called "The Sample Parameters," you will read about root notes in more detail. You will also get an opportunity to work with root notes again in a tutorial that helps you create your first NN-XT patch.

It is very easy to audition loaded samples in the NN-XT by using your computer keyboard and mouse. If you are on the PC, just hold the Alt key and click on a key in the virtual keyboard. Notice that the mouse icon becomes a Speaker icon as you press the Alt key. This can also be done on the Mac by using the Option key.

The Tab Bar. The Tab Bar is one of several ways to adjust the key range of a zone. Start by selecting a sample zone in the key map. Once selected, the zone's Tab Bar will display the zone's key range and supply boundary handles to make adjustments. Just drag the handles to the left and right to make adjustments to the key range.

The Tab Bar can also be used to adjust the key range of several zones at one time and shift the positions of several zones at once. In order for this to work, the zones must share at least one common key range value.

Key Range Area. The Key Range area is used to adjust the key range of a selected zone and also to shift the position of a zone up and down the Keyboard area. The main difference between the key range and the Tab Bar is that the key range will make adjustments on an individual basis. If there are two zones that share the same key ranges, adjustments to the key range are still made individually.

Zones can also be shifted in the Key Range area on a singular or multiple basis if they are both selected.

The Sample Parameters

Located in the bottom portion of the Key Map display, the Sample parameters are used to edit any selected zone in the key map (see Figure 14.12). Whereas the synth parameters are used to alter the timbre and tone of a selected zone, the Sample parameters are used to set up loop points, root notes, route outputs, and generally help you do some pretty creative things with your samples.

Figure 14.12 The Sample parameters include 15 ways to edit your samples and enhance your sample performance.

Root Notes and Tune. The Root knob is used to adjust the original pitch of a loaded sample. When a sample is loaded into the NN-XT, it is necessary to assign a root as the original frequency of the recorded sample. For example, if you recorded a piano's C3 note and then imported it into the NN-XT, you will need to tell the NN-XT that the original pitch of the sample was C3. This is done with the Root knob.

Once a sample is imported into the key map, you can click and drag on the Root knob until you reach the desired root note. Another way to change the root note is to hold the Ctrl key (Apple key for Mac users) on your computer keyboard and click on the root note you want.

Lock It Down   Once you have set a root note, activate the Lock Root Keys button at the top of the Key Map display. Once active, you can still make adjustments to the root note with the Root knob, but if you want to shift the position of the sample zone, the root note will remain in place.

The Tune knob is used to make fine adjustments to your samples. It is used to make sure that the pitch of the samples matches the tunings of your other imported samples as well. For example, if you import a piano sample with a root note of C3 and then import another sample with a root note of E3, you might need to make fine-tuning adjustments to ensure that the piano samples will play in tune with each other as you make the transition from C3 to E3.

The Tune knob has a range of +/– half a semitone.

If you are not sure what the root note of your sample is or which way to tune it, Reason has a solution to help you out. Reason can automatically detect the root note of any imported sample with a perceivable pitch. Here's how it works:

1.   Select the zone of the sample whose root note you want to detect.

2.   Choose Edit > Set Root Notes from Pitch Detection. Within a second, Reason will detect and assign a root note to your sample and will also make any fine-tuning adjustments.

Sample Start and End. The Sample Start knob is used to offset the start position of a loaded sample in the NN-XT. This function can be used for many purposes, such as

■   Removing unwanted noise at the beginning of a sample.

■   Creating different versions of one sample. For example, if you have a sample of a person speaking the phrase "one, two, three, four," you could use the Sample Start and End knobs to isolate each word and map it on its own key without having to perform this task in an audio-editing program.

■   Creating very realistic and dynamic performances perfect for percussion and drum samples, using the Sample Start knob along with the Sample Start Velocity Amount knob (S.Start) in the Velocity section.

The Sample End knob is used to offset the end position of a loaded sample in the NN-XT. This is useful for removing unwanted sample portions from the end of a sample, such as noise or hiss.

To make changes to the Sample Start and End knobs, you can click and drag up or down with your mouse to move the offsets by percentages. If you want to make very fine changes to these knobs, hold the Shift key down while making adjustments to the start and end knobs.

Loop Start and End. In sampling terms, a loop is used to prolong the *sustain* of a note that is held down on your MIDI keyboard. For example, if you play a piano sample and hold the key down, notice that like a real piano, the note sustains as long as you hold it (see Figure 14.13). This is accomplished by finding a portion of the sample that can be looped continuously to sound like a sustain. Figure 14.13 shows a loop point

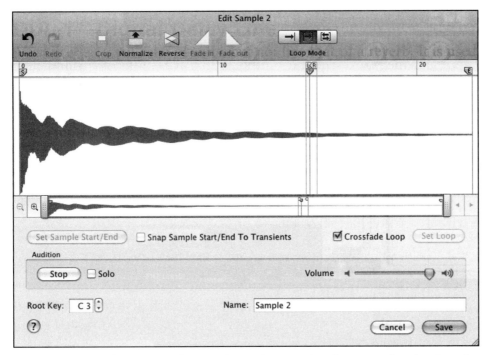

Figure 14.13 A loop is used to prolong the sustain of a note that is played on your keyboard.

that will occur toward the end of the sample. This loop point was created for this guitar sample using the NN-XT Sample Editor. The loop that has been created occurs in an area where the loop start and end differ very slightly in amplitude. By creating a loop there, the loop is not noticeable and sounds very natural when used.

All of the samples in the Reason Factory Sound Bank and Orkester Sound Bank have already been assigned loop points, and you will find that this is the case for any sample collection that is commercially available.

The Loop Start knob shifts the offset of the loop starting point to the right in a sample. The Loop End knob shifts the offset of the loop end point to the left in a sample.

Play Mode. After a pair of loop points has been established, the Play Mode knob determines how the loop will be played. The Play Mode knob offers five choices:

- **FW**—The sample will play through once, without looping.

- **FW-LOOP**—The sample will play from the sample start to the loop end, and then it will jump back to the loop start and proceed to loop continuously between the loop points until the note is released.

- **FW-BW**—The sample will play from the sample start to the loop end. At this point, the sample will then play backward from the loop end to the loop start and finally play from the loop start to the loop end. This process will loop continuously until the note is released.

- **FW-SUS**—The sample will play from the sample start to the loop end, and then it will jump back to the loop start and proceed to loop continuously between the two loop points. After the note is released, the sample will play to the absolute end of the sample that reaches beyond the loop boundaries.

- **BW**—The sample will play backward once, without looping.

Low Key and High Key. These knobs are used to assign boundaries to the loaded samples. The *low key* assigns the lowest note that a sample can be played at, whereas the *high key* does exactly the opposite. You'll get a better idea of how this works later in the chapter when you will build your own sample patch.

Low Velocity and High Velocity. These knobs are used to assign velocity ranges to the loaded samples. *Low velocity* assigns the lowest velocity at which a sample can be played, whereas *high velocity* does the opposite.

Understanding these knobs and how they work is essential when creating a multilayered sample patch. For example, you can create sample zones and assign them all to the same key but give them different velocities. Here's an example of how you would velocity map four snare drum samples to the D1 note. Please note that this will include all of the other sample parameters that you have read about up to this point.

- **Snare 1.aif**—Root D1, Tune 0, Start 0%, End 100%, Play Mode FW, Low Key D1, Hi Key D1, Lo Vel 1, Hi Vel 32

- **Snare 2.aif**—Root D1, Tune 0, Start 0%, End 100%, Play Mode FW, Low Key D1, Hi Key D1, Lo Vel 33, Hi Vel 64

- **Snare 3.aif**—Root D1, Tune 0, Start 0%, End 100%, Play Mode FW, Low Key D1, Hi Key D1, Lo Vel 65, Hi Vel 99

- **Snare 1.aif**—Root D1, Tune 0, Start 0%, End 100%, Play Mode FW, Low Key D1, Hi Key D1, Lo Vel 100, Hi Vel 127

Fade In and Fade Out. These knobs are for assigning velocity crossfades to overlapping zones. As discussed in the Key Map display section, it is possible to have two zones that share the same range, root note, and velocity. The Fade In and Fade Out knobs can be used to smooth the transition between these two samples, making for an interesting dynamic effect.

The Fade In knob is used to create a velocity threshold that will trigger a sample when that threshold is reached via velocity. Once the threshold is reached, the sample will fade in, rather than abruptly trigger.

The Fade Out knob performs the same function, except when the threshold is reached the sample will fade out.

Here's an example of how to use these knobs:

1. Create two zones and load a sample into each one. Set the low velocity of both zones to 1 and their high velocities to 127.

2. Use the Fade Out knob on the first zone and set it to 40. This will tell the NN-XT to play that zone at its full level when the velocity is played under 40. Once the velocity has reached 40 and over, the sample will fade out.

3. Use the Fade In knob on the second zone and set it to 80. This will tell the NN-XT to play that zone with a fade in effect when the velocity equals 80. After the played velocity has surpassed 80, the sample will then play at its full level.

Alternate. To give your sample performance a realistic sound, the Alternate knob is used to semi-randomly trigger different sample zones during playback. For example, if you have a sample of a guitar chord playing with a down stroke and a sample of that same chord playing with an upstroke, you can use the Alternate knob to create a pattern where the NN-XT will determine when to alternate between the two samples.

Here's how you set up the Alternate function:

1. Create two zones and load a sample into each.

2. Select both zones.

3. Set the Alt knob to the On position. The NN-XT will then determine when to alternate between the two samples.

Output. The Output knob is used to assign your sample zones to one of eight stereo pairs of outputs. This comes in handy when you work with a sample patch that has many samples loaded in it. Each of these samples can be routed to any of these outputs by selecting the zone that the sample is loaded on and using the Output knob.

Route the Outputs   Before you reassign all of the samples in your patch to different outputs, press the Tab key to flip the Device Rack around and route the additional outputs of the NN-XT to reMix (see Figure 14.14). This will help avoid any confusion you might encounter when you want to listen to all of the samples in your patch.

Here's an example of how you would use the Output knob:

1. Use the Patch Browser to locate the Perc Set A.sxt patch in the Percussion folder of the Orkester Sound Bank. Load it, and you will see that there are many sampled instruments here, including bass drum, snare, toms, castanets, cowbell, and a gong.

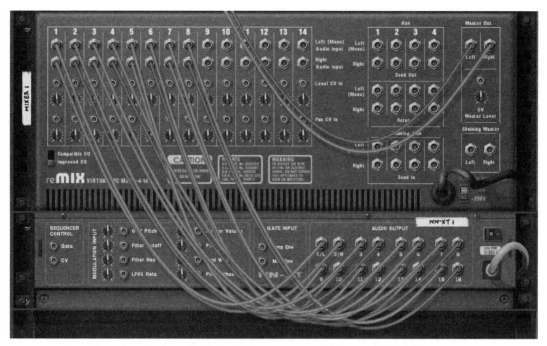

Figure 14.14 Route all of the outputs of the NN-XT to reMix before assigning your samples to different outputs.

2. Select all three bass drums by clicking on its Group column. Notice that the output is set to 1-2, which are the main outputs of the NN-XT.

3. Select the snare samples by clicking on the appropriate Group column. Set the output of the snare samples to 3-4.

4. Select the Tom samples by clicking on the appropriate Group column. Set the output to 5-6.

5. Repeat this for all of the other grouped samples until they all have their own outputs.

Note that you can pan each sound mono out of outputs 1–16, and then patch them into the reMix and pan them wherever you want within the stereo field. For instance, sample #1 could be assigned to Out 1-2 and panned all the way left in the Amp Envelope section. This way it would actually only be coming through Out 1, and then sample #2 could also be assigned to Out 1-2 and panned all the way to the right, thus only coming through Out 2. Repeat this process until all the outputs are assigned. Actually, if you use 16 individual outs in this way, you will need two reMix devices because reMix only has 14 channels, and it would come up two channels short. That's okay. There's plenty of reMix to go around!

Creating a Multilayered NN-XT Patch

Now that you have all the ins and outs of the NN-XT down, it's time to put your knowledge to work and create your first NN-XT sample patch. In this tutorial, you are going to build a patch step-by-step by using guitar samples created specifically for this tutorial.

Unlike the sample patch that you created in Chapter 13, this guitar patch has different elements to it:

- The samples are multilayered. There is a mezzo forte, forte, and double forte for each single note.

- There are samples of major chords played with an up stroke and down stroke.

- There are FX samples, including a string slap and string slide sounds.

Before You Begin Before you begin this tutorial, take a moment to download the necessary samples from the Course Technology website at www.courseptr. com. Because there are more samples used this time around, it might take some time to download the archived file (it's around 11MB).

After completing the download, you will need to unzip the archive file using either WinZip or Stuff-It Expander. Once the archive is expanded, place the NN-XT Guitar Samples folder into the Reason Program folder on your Mac or PC.

Importing Single Note Samples

Let's start the tutorial by working with the single note samples. Make sure you are working with a blank NN-XT and that there are no samples loaded into it. You can do so by choosing Initialize Patch from the Edit pull-down menu.

1. Click on the Load Sample button. This will bring up the Sample Browser. Navigate to the NN-XT Guitar Samples folder, open it, and double-click on the Single Notes folder to display the list of single note samples.

2. Locate the Low E samples, as these will be your starting place. There are three Low E samples available with three different dynamic levels.

3. Highlight the Low E mf.wav file first, and click on the Open button to import it into the key zone area of the NN-XT.

4. As these samples have already been prepared for you, all you have to do is set the key range and velocity for each sample. Begin by setting the key range of the Low E mf.wav file, which is Lo Key D1, High Key G#1.

5. Now set the velocity of the Low E sample as Lo Vel 1, Hi Vel 69. Notice as you do this, the zone that contains the sample is no longer solid shaded as before. Rather, a series of diagonal lines appears through the zone. This symbolizes that a velocity has been assigned to this zone.

6. Now, click anywhere in the key zone area to deselect the first Low E sample. Click on the Load Sample button again and import the Low E f.wav file.

7. Set the key range of the second Low E sample to the same values as the first sample. Set the velocity of this sample as Lo Vel 70, Hi Vel 99.

8. Click anywhere in the key zone area to deselect the first Low E sample. Click on the Load Sample button again and import the Low E ff.wav file.

9. Set the key range of the second Low E sample to the same values as the first and second samples. Set the velocity of this sample as Lo Vel 100, Hi Vel 127. You should now have three samples with different velocities stacked vertically, as shown in Figure 14.15.

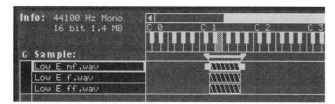

Figure 14.15 The three Low E samples have been imported and set up with different velocities.

10. Arm the sequencer track and use your MIDI keyboard to trigger the samples at different velocities. Notice the differences in dynamics between the three samples.

Save for a Rainy Day   A reminder: You should save your patch periodically as you go through this tutorial. Click on the Save Patch button and save the patch in the NN-XT Guitar Samples folder. You can choose your own name of course, but keep it simple so you can easily find it.

At this point, the first three single note samples have been imported into the NN-XT and have been assigned different velocities. It's time to move on to the next batch of guitar samples, so here is a list for each sample of the remaining strings.

■ **Low A mf.wav**—Lo Key A1, Hi Key C#2, Lo Vel 1, Hi Vel 69

■ **Low A f.wav**—Lo Key A1, Hi Key C#2, Lo Vel 70, Hi Vel 99

- **Low A ff.wav**—Low Key A1, Hi Key C#2, Lo Vel 100, Hi 127

- **Low D mf.wav**—Lo Key D2, Hi Key F#2, Lo Vel 1, Hi Vel 69

- **Low D f.wav**—Lo Key D2, Hi Key F#2, Lo Vel 70, Hi Vel 99

- **Low D ff.wav**—Low Key D2, Hi Key F#2, Lo Vel 100, Hi 127

- **Low G mf.wav**—Lo Key G2, Hi Key A#2, Lo Vel 1, Hi Vel 69

- **Low G f.wav**—Lo Key G2, Hi Key A#2, Lo Vel 70, Hi Vel 99

- **Low G ff.wav**—Low Key G2, Hi Key A#2, Lo Vel 100, Hi 127

- **Low B mf.wav**—Lo Key B2, Hi Key D#3, Lo Vel 1, Hi Vel 69

- **Low B f.wav**—Lo Key B2, Hi Key D#3, Lo Vel 70, Hi Vel 99

- **Low B ff.wav**—Low Key B2, Hi Key D#3, Lo Vel 100, Hi 127

- **High E mf.wav**—Lo Key E3, Hi Key G#3, Lo Vel 1, Hi Vel 69

- **High E f.wav**—Lo Key E3, Hi Key G#3, Lo Vel 70, Hi Vel 99

- **High E ff.wav**—Low Key E3, Hi Key G#3, Lo Vel 100, Hi 127

- **High A mf.wav**—Lo Key A3, Hi Key C#4, Lo Vel 1, Hi Vel 69

- **High A f.wav**—Lo Key A3, Hi Key C#4, Lo Vel 70, Hi Vel 99

- **High A ff.wav**—Low Key A3, Hi Key C#4, Lo Vel 100, Hi 127

- **High D mf.wav**—Lo Key D4, Hi Key A4, Lo Vel 1, Hi Vel 69

- **High D f.wav**—Lo Key D4, Hi Key A4, Lo Vel 70, Hi Vel 99

- **High D f.wav**—Lo Key D4, Hi Key C#2, Lo Vel 70, Hi Vel 99

When you're finished, you should have a key map chock full of samples like the one in Figure 14.16. As a finishing touch, select all of the notes, and then choose Group

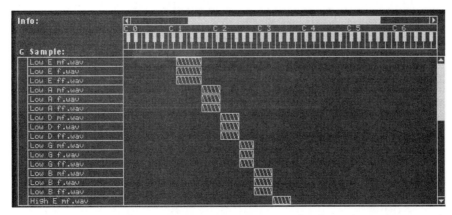

Figure 14.16 All of the single-note guitar samples have been imported and configured.

Selected Zones from the Edit pull-down menu. Also make sure that you have assigned a high amount of polyphony to the patch, such as 12.

Importing Chord Samples

Now that the single notes have been imported and set up, it's time to import the chord samples. All the chords that were recorded for this tutorial are major triad chords and were recorded with up strokes and down strokes, providing an opportunity to use the Alternate feature.

1. Click on the Load Sample button. This will bring up the Sample Browser window.

2. Select the E Major Down.wav audio file and import the sample.

3. Because these chord samples were not assigned a root note, the NN-XT will assign the root note to C3 by default. Change the root note to E5, which can be done using the Root knob in the Sample Parameter area.

4. Now that the sample has been assigned the correct root note, you will need to assign the correct key range. Use the Lo Key knob to set the lowest note of the key range to D5. Use the Hi Key knob and set the highest note of the key range to F#5. This will give your E major chords a few extra notes to play.

5. Click in the empty part of the key map to deselect the newly created zone and click on the Load Sample button again. The Sample Browser window should still be pointed at the Chords folder. Import the E Major Up.wav audio file and the NN-XT will create a zone and import the sample as before.

6. Following Steps 1–5 , make the root key E5, the lowest note D5, and the highest note F#5.

7. At this point, you can preview the samples when played together by using the Alt key on your PC, or the Apple Key on your Mac and clicking in the correct key range, which is D5–F#5. It should sound a little strange because there are clearly different timbres and textures resulting from the way both samples were recorded.

8. Select both sample zones and turn on the Alternate function by using the Alt knob in the Sample Parameters area. Preview the samples again. The NN-XT should now alternate between the two samples.

Now that the E major sample has been imported and properly set up, you can proceed to do the same with the other chord samples. Use this list as a guide for setting up the correct root notes and key ranges.

- **G Major Up/Down**—Root Key G5, Lo Key G5, Hi Key G#5, set the Alt to On

- **A Major Up/Down**—Root Key A5, Lo Key A5, Hi Key B5, set the Alt to On

- **C Major Up/Down**—Root Key C6, Lo Key C6, Hi Key C#6, set the Alt to On

- **D Major Up/Down**—Root Key D6, Lo Key D6, Hi Key D#6, set the Alt to On

After you import and configure each sample, select all of the chord samples and choose Group Selected Zones from the Edit pull-down menu. This will group all of the chord samples together so that they can be edited and selected at one time.

Importing FX Samples

The single notes and chords are finished, so now it's time to top it off with a couple of guitar effect samples. I have included two types of effects that are commonly used when playing acoustic guitar:

- A string slide down the neck of the guitar on the Low E and A strings

- A slap of the guitar strings against the guitar frets

Unlike the chord samples you just imported and configured, these effects are going to be mapped at the C0 key. Use this list as a guide for setting up the correct root notes and key ranges.

- **Low E String Slide.wav**—Root Key E0, Lo Key D0, Hi Key G#0

- **Low A String Slide.wav**—Root Key A0, Lo Key A0, Hi Key C1

- **String Slap.wav**—Root Key C#1, Lo Key C#1, Hi Key C#1

Keeping It Real   The Reason sequencer is an excellent tool for making your samples sound and act like the actual instrument. Let's use the acoustic guitar patch that you just created as an example. When a player strums a chord on an acoustic guitar, the strings are stroked down or up. This means that the attack of each string is heard individually because all six strings cannot be played simultaneously.

By using the Snap pull-down menu in the Reason sequencer, you can create a realistic guitar performance by making a few tiny adjustments.

Here's how to make the guitar patch sound like the real thing:

1. Plan out a chord progression that would be suited for an acoustic guitar. For example, E major to A major to G major to D major.

2. After planning the chord progression, determine the correct notes for each chord. For example, E major would traditionally be played using the notes E1, B1, E2, G#2, B2, and E3.

3. Using the Reason sequencer, switch to edit mode and set the Snap value to Bar.

4. Write an E major chord using the notes listed in Step 2. Make sure that the notes are a full measure long (see Figure 14.17).

Figure 14.17 The E major chord has been written in as whole notes.

5. Once this is done, press Play to hear how the guitar chord sounds. The actual sounds of the acoustic guitar are fine, but the attack of the chord sounds very unreal.

6. Now, set the Snap to a much finer resolution of 1/64.

7. Using your mouse, select the second note of the chord (B1) and move it to the right by a 64th note.

8. Select the next note (E2) and move it to the right by two 64th notes.

9. Continue to do this to the other remaining notes in the chord until you see each note of the chord on its own beat in the measure (see Figure 14.18).

10. Press Play and listen to the chord. It now sounds like the actual strumming of an acoustic guitar.

Whew! That's a lot of sampling information. If you've made it through these last two chapters, it would be fair to say that you probably know more about sampling now

Figure 14.18 Each one of the notes in the chord has been moved to the right in 64th-note increments.

than many seasoned professionals! But don't let that stop you from continuing your sampling education. Try your hand at sampling drums, pianos, basses, voices, or a few unique noises from a creaky bedroom door to see how you can twist and turn those samples into music with the NN-XT!

15 The Matrix—Close Up

T his chapter takes an in-depth look at the Matrix Pattern sequencer, shown in Figure 15.1. The Matrix is a pattern-based sequencer that can be used to write lead lines for the various Reason devices. As you might have guessed, it is not a sound module itself. Rather, it is a device that controls Reason's other sound-generating devices.

Essentially, the Matrix Pattern sequencer generates three kinds of data:

- **Note**—This is pitch-based data that is assigned from within the Pattern window of the Matrix.

- **Gate**—This data is used to send Note On, Note Off, and Velocity data to the Reason device it is routed to.

- **Curve**—This data is used to send controller information to different modulation parameters of any Reason device.

The Matrix is capable of producing 32-step pattern sequences with many note resolutions. Once patterns are written, they can be stored in the Pattern section of the Matrix interface. Note though that written patterns are saved within a Reason song and cannot be stored individually for later use in another song.

Endless Routes The possibilities for using the Matrix within Reason are just about endless. Create any Reason device and press the Tab key to flip the Device Rack around, and you will find an input of some kind that can be used with the Matrix. For example, you can use the Matrix to alter the panning and volume of any channel in reMix. Or you can use the Matrix to alter the individual parameters of any real-time effect.

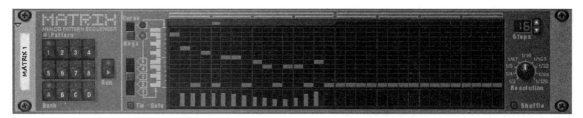

Figure 15.1 The Matrix Pattern sequencer is used to sequence any Reason device, such as the Subtractor and Malström.

Exploring the Matrix Pattern Sequencer's Features

Now that you have a basic understanding of what the Matrix does, it's time to consider its individual functions and features.

The Pattern Section and Run Buttons   As you read through this chapter, you will see many similarities between the Matrix Pattern section and the pattern section of Redrum, most notably, the Run button. The controls are the same in the pattern sections of both devices, so please refer to Chapter 7, "Redrum—Close Up," to review.

Edit Mode

At the top-left corner of the Matrix interface is the Edit Mode selector. This selector switches between the two available edit modes—Key and Curve.

- **Key Edit**—When this edit mode is selected, the Matrix Pattern window displays note information and Note On, Note Off, and Velocity values for each note. This is the view that you use to write a sequenced pattern.

- **Curve Edit**—When this edit mode is selected, the Matrix Pattern window displays curve information and displays the Note On, Note Off, or Velocity values for each note. Curve Edit allows you to create patterns that can control various parameters on any of the Reason devices.

Bipolar or Unipolar Curves   If you press the Tab key to view the back of the Matrix, you will see a switch in the middle of the interface that offers two curve types—bipolar and unipolar.

A *unipolar curve* has values starting from zero, which is the lowest setting. It is the default curve setting when an instance of the Matrix is created. See Figure 15.2 for a better look at a unipolar curve.

A *bipolar curve* is divided in the middle, where the middle value equals zero. When you begin to draw in a bipolar curve, it looks much different than

---

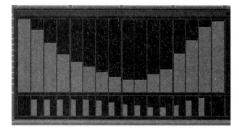

Figure 15.2 A unipolar curve's values begin at its lowest numeric value of zero.

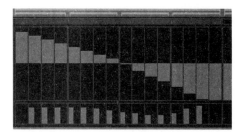

Figure 15.3 The bipolar curve setting allows the Matrix to control device parameters containing positive and negative values, such as the pan controls for reMix, or possibly the OSC phase controls for the Subtractor.

the unipolar curve because both positive and negative values can be drawn in (see Figure 15.3). This presents a number of possibilities for using the bipolar curve to control other Reason device parameters that contain positive and negative values.

Octaves and Ties

Just below the Edit Mode switch are the Octave switch and the Tie button.

- Octave—This switch is used to view and edit notes within a five-octave range. When an instance of the Matrix is created, the Octave switch is set to 3 by default, which is approximately Middle C.

- Tie—When activated, this Tie button makes it possible to increase the length of your sequenced notes by tying them together. For example, tying two 16th notes together in order to create an 8th note. This button is covered in the Subtractor tutorial section later in this chapter.

The Matrix Pattern Window

The centerpiece of the Matrix device is the Pattern window. This is where your notes, velocities, and curve patterns are drawn, edited, and stored into the Pattern Selector within a saved Reason song. All three types of output information are viewable here—Note, Gate, and Curve.

The Pattern window is split into two sections. The majority of the window is dedicated to drawing in note and curve patterns, whereas the lower portion of the interface is used to draw in the Note On, Note Off, and Velocity of the sequence (see Figure 15.4).

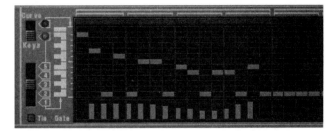

Figure 15.4 The Matrix Pattern window is used to draw and edit sequences for all three types of output information.

Steps, Resolution, and Shuffle

To the right of the Matrix Pattern window are three important controls that assign the number of steps, note value, and shuffle feel to your Matrix sequences (see Figure 15.5).

Figure 15.5 The Steps, Resolution, and Shuffle controls.

- **Steps**—This parameter assigns the number of steps to your Matrix sequences. It has a range from 1–32 steps, offering a wide variety for creating patterns based on common and odd time signatures. This parameter is set at 16 by default whenever an instance of the Matrix is created.

- **Resolution**—This parameter is used to assign the overall note value of your pattern sequences. There are many note values to choose from. For example, you can use quarter notes (1/4) to draw in a slower pattern, or something much faster, like 32nd notes (1/32). This parameter is set to 16th notes by default whenever an instance of the Matrix is created. This means that every note in your pattern is going to be a 16th note in length. You can alter these note lengths by using the Tie button, which you'll learn about later in this chapter.

- **Shuffle**—When activated, this button gives your Matrix sequences a shuffle or swing feeling that's useful with many styles of music, including Rap and R&B

music, or music with a jazzy feel. The Pattern Shuffle knob in the Transport panel determines the strength of the shuffle.

Different Steps—Different Time Signatures   Being a musician of many musical influences, I enjoy a lot of music that focuses on odd time signatures, such as 3/4, 5/4, 6/8, and 7/8. Although I certainly have nothing against good old "four on the floor" time signatures like 4/4 and 2/4, a little variety never hurts.

If you're like me, you'll be excited to know that the Matrix is fully capable of producing oddly timed sequences. You just have to do a little math to determine the correct number of steps to assign to it.

Here is a list of step numbers to accommodate different time signatures:

- **3/4**—12 or 24 steps
- **5/4**—20 steps
- **6/8**—12 or 24 steps
- **7/8**—14 or 28 steps

Matrix Outputs

Press the Tab key to flip the Device Rack and you'll find the CV outputs of the Matrix (see Figure 15.6). Although each of these outputs appears to have a specific destination in mind, you'll find there is more than one possibility for each when you're using them creatively.

Figure 15.6 The CV outputs on the back of the Matrix.

- **Curve CV**—This CV output is used in combination with the curve pattern data created within the Matrix Pattern window. This output can be routed to just about any type of modulation input on a Reason device. For example, it could be routed to the Modulation inputs of the Subtractor or Malström, or to the Panning controls of reMix.

- **Note CV**—This CV output is used in combination with the note pattern data created in the Matrix Pattern window. This output can also be routed to just about any modulation input; however, it is best served by being used with the CV input of a Reason device, like the Subtractor or NN-19.

■ **Gate CV**—This CV output is used in combination with the Note On, Note Off, or Velocity pattern data created in the Matrix Pattern window. This output is best served by being connected to the Gate input of any Reason device, such as the NN-19 or Malström. Another possible connection is the Level input of reMix.

Matrix Tutorials

Now that you understand the interface and parameters of the Matrix, it's time to kick things into high gear and learn how to use the Matrix with the Subtractor. Although there are many different Reason devices, the same basic routing and sequencing theory applies to each device, so you can take the information within this tutorial section and apply it to the Malström, NN-19, and the NN-XT. You can also use this information with Dr. Octo Rex and Redrum, because they both have CV inputs on their rear panels. After that, the chapter then shows you how to use the Matrix with other Reason devices in ways that you might not have thought possible.

Using the Matrix with the Subtractor

This tutorial shows you how to connect the Matrix to the Subtractor. Once connected, you'll use the combination together to create a melody or lead line. To top it off, you'll see how to use the Matrix creatively with the Subtractor by connecting it in different combinations.

Making the Connection

The first thing you have to do is make a basic connection from the Subtractor to the Matrix. This section shows you how Reason can do this automatically as well as how to make a connection manually between the two devices.

Before getting started, take a minute to start a new Reason song and create a reMix and Subtractor.

1. Click once on the Subtractor to select it. Then choose Matrix Pattern Sequencer from the Create pull-down menu.

2. An instance of the Matrix should now appear under the Subtractor. Press Tab to swing the Device Rack around. The Matrix outputs should already be connected to the Subtractor (see Figure 15.7).

3. Press the Tab key to flip the Device Rack again.

In the next part of the tutorial, you disconnect the Matrix from the Subtractor so that you can get a clear understanding of how to make the connection manually. Before you begin, click once on the Matrix (to highlight it) and choose Disconnect Device from the Edit pull-down menu. This gives you a clean slate to start with and allows you to make

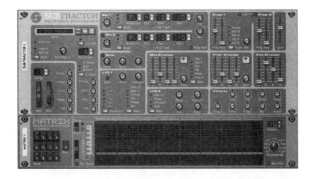

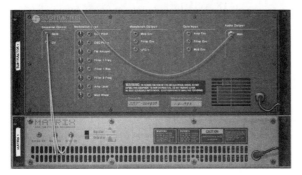

Figure 15.7 In the upper figure, the Matrix has been created and placed just below the Subtractor. In the lower figure, you are looking at the back of the Device Rack, and you can see that two of the three Matrix outputs are connected to the Subtractor Sequencer Control inputs.

all the disconnections at once, rather than one by one as you would by clicking on cables on the rear of the device.

1. Press the Tab key to flip the Device Rack. The Matrix should be disconnected from the Subtractor (see Figure 15.8).

2. Click and drag on the Gate CV output on the Matrix and connect it to the Gate input in the top-left side of the Subtractor (see Figure 15.9).

3. Now, click and drag on the output of the Note CV output of the Matrix and connect it to the CV input of the Subtractor (see Figure 15.10).

4. Press the Tab key to flip the Device Rack.

Sequencing the Subtractor with the Matrix

After connecting the Matrix to the Subtractor, you'll probably want to begin sequencing right away. It's extremely easy to do and will only take a minute to learn.

Let's keep it simple and create a 16-step sequence with a resolution of 1/16. This means that there are 16 steps total in this pattern, and a single 16th note represents one step. At this time, make sure that the Edit Mode selector is set to Key Edit mode.

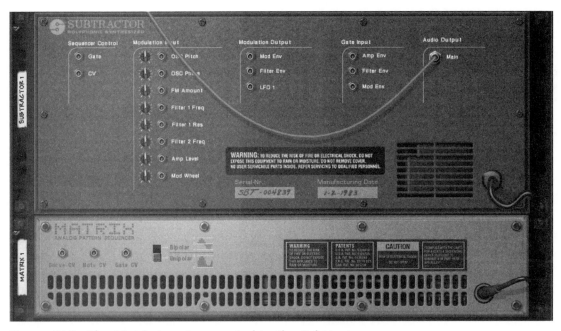

Figure 15.8   The Matrix is not connected to the Subtractor.

Figure 15.9   First connect the Gate CV output of the Matrix to the Gate input of the Subtractor.

Figure 15.10 Now, the Note CV output is connected to the CV input.

Before you begin, look at the Pattern window. Notice that there are already notes and velocity drawn in along the low C note and default velocity respectively (see Figure 15.11). This is done by default whenever an instance of the Matrix is created. This means that the Subtractor can already begin to play sequenced notes from the Matrix.

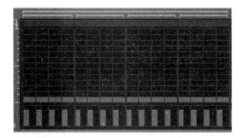

Figure 15.11 Looking at the Matrix, you can see that there are notes and velocities already drawn in.

To vary the dynamics (or remove notes from the pattern), use your mouse to click in the velocity section of the Pattern window, just below the note for which you would like to assign a different velocity. For example, if you want to change the velocity of the first note (or remove the note altogether from the pattern), click in the Gate section of the first note in order to assign values to it (see Figure 15.12). This will assign a Note On/Off and Velocity value to the note.

Figure 15.12 Click in the gate portion of the Pattern window in order to assign a velocity value to its corresponding note.

Press Play and you should now hear the Subtractor play the C note with whatever values you assigned to it. At this point, you can go ahead and write values for each of the 16 steps in this sequence. It should be noted here that although the Matrix default setting is for a 16-step sequence, you could choose any number of steps between 1 and 32 by adjusting the Steps parameter located in the upper right of the Matrix.

Now let's write in some proper notes. Once again, the rule of thumb here is to keep it simple, because you'll have plenty of time later to channel some techno heaven out of the Matrix. So draw in a C Major arpeggio line (the notes are C-E-G) consisting primarily of 16th notes. Use your mouse to select the notes for the sequence. When you're finished, it should look like Figure 15.13.

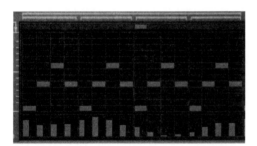

Figure 15.13 A 16th note arpeggio is easy to create with the Pattern window. For some variation in the sound of the sequence, you can use different velocities by clicking on the Note On, Note Off, and Velocity values for each corresponding note.

Now press Play on your Transport panel (or press Run on the Matrix) and you should hear your 16th note arpeggio line play back in all its techno glory. That's pretty much all there is to writing in a Matrix pattern, but let's try a couple of variations.

Listening to just 16th notes in a run can get extremely boring after a while, because it is just begging for some variation. This can be achieved by using the Tie button to tie a couple of 16th notes together to create an 8th note. Here's how to do it.

First, press the Tie button in the lower-left corner of the Matrix interface. Next, using your mouse, navigate to the gate portion of the Pattern window and click on

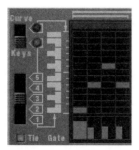

Figure 15.14 Activate the Tie function and click in the gate portion of the Pattern window under the note you want to hear played back as an 8th note.

the first note. Notice that the Gate bar, which was once thin, is now much thicker (see Figure 15.14). Press Play and you should now hear those two 16th notes played together as a single 8th note.

Tie Keyboard Shortcut   A handy shortcut for accessing the Tie function is to hold down the Shift key while clicking on the velocities of the notes you want to tie together. Clicking (without holding down the Shift key) on the velocities of notes that have already been tied will untie them.

Shift It Up, Shift It Down, Shift Them Notes All Around   As you might recall from Chapter 7, the Redrum is also a pattern-based sequencer. It's therefore safe to assume that these two pattern-based sequencers share a lot of functions that can be used to achieve different effects with the patterns.

Click on the Matrix to select it. Then click on the Edit pull-down menu, and you'll see a list of the different options. Because most of these options were mentioned in Chapter 7, I won't go into each one unless there are any differences.

- **Cut Pattern**
- **Copy Pattern**
- **Paste Pattern**
- **Clear Pattern**
- **Shift Pattern Left**
- **Shift Pattern Right**
- **Shift Pattern Up**—This option transposes the pattern up one half step.
- **Shift Pattern Down**—This option transposes the pattern down one half step.

- **Randomize Pattern**—This option randomly generates Note, Gate, and Curve pattern data.

- **Alter Pattern**

When you finish writing in your sequence patterns, you can create another pattern by selecting A2 or you can choose Copy Pattern to Track from the Edit pull-down menu. This will copy the Matrix pattern to its sequencer track between the locator points, which can then be moved to a sequencer track belonging to another Reason device.

Monophonic Only   Although you probably have figured this out already, the Matrix cannot be used to sequence chord patterns. Its sole purpose is to create monophonic synth lines and curve patterns to control the parameters of other Reason devices. If you want to create chord progressions for the Subtractor, Thor, Malström, and NN-19/XT, you should do so within the Reason sequencer. See Chapter 5, "The Reason Sequencer—Close Up," for more information.

Creative Connections with the Subtractor

Now that you've read about the basics of using the Matrix with the Subtractor, you're ready to consider a few creative connections that you can make between the two devices.

This first example uses the Curve CV to control the pitch of the Subtractor.

1. Press Play to start the sequencer. Press the Tab key to flip the Device Rack.

2. Disconnect the Note CV output from the CV input of the Subtractor. The Subtractor should now begin playing a 16th-note sequence comprised of single notes.

3. Connect the Curve CV output of the Matrix to the OSC Pitch input on the Subtractor (see Figure 15.15).

4. Press the Tab key.

5. Switch the Edit mode from Key to Curve Edit (see Figure 15.16).

6. Use the Selector tool to draw in a Curve pattern (see Figure 15.17).

7. Press Play and the Matrix will use the Curve pattern to affect the OSC pitch of the Subtractor. At this point, you can make additional adjustments to the Curve pattern until you get a sequence of notes that you like. With a little practice, you'll be channeling those old Atari 2600 video game sounds in no time.

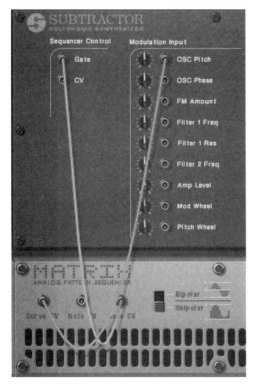

Figure 15.15 Connect the Curve CV output of the Matrix to the OSC Pitch input on the Subtractor.

Figure 15.16 Switch the Edit mode from Key to Curve Edit.

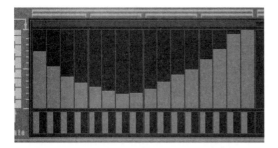

Figure 15.17 Draw in a Curve pattern with the Selector tool.

You can also route the Note CV output of the Matrix to any additional modulation inputs on the Subtractor. For example, try routing the Note CV output to the FM Amount input on the Subtractor. Additionally, you can increase or decrease the amount of input to this parameter by using the knob to the left of the input. Also

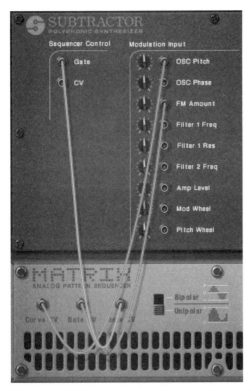

Figure 15.18 Try connecting the Note CV output of the Matrix to any of the modulation inputs on the back of the Subtractor. This example has connected the Note CV output to the FM Amount input.

note that you must use a Subtractor patch that uses the FM function (see Figure 15.18). One patch you can choose in order to hear a good FM effect is Attack Bass, located in the Bass folder within the Subtractor Patches folder in the Reason Factory Sound Bank.

Creative Connections with the Matrix

If there is one thing that can be said about Reason, it's that it excels at creative solutions. The Matrix is a prime example; it offers a great variety of interesting possibilities and creative connections. In fact, this section shows you some connections that will have you thinking, "No Way!"

Using One Matrix with Two Devices

Although I have very few gripes about the Subtractor, it would really be great to see some sort of panning control within the interface to automate the panning between the left and right channels. But, with a little research and experimentation, I found that using the Matrix with the Subtractor *and* reMix makes this possible.

Try the following exercise. Get ready by starting a new Reason song and creating an instance of reMix, the Subtractor, and the Matrix.

1. Using your mouse, write a quick sequence into the Matrix in order to trigger the sounds of the Subtractor (see Figure 15.19).

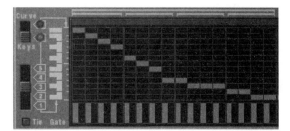

Figure 15.19 Write a quick sequence into the Matrix. Remember to assign gate to your sequence so that you will hear it play back.

2. Press the Tab key to flip the Device Rack.

3. Switch the Curve mode from unipolar to bipolar.

4. Next, click and drag a virtual cable from the Curve CV output of the Matrix to the Pan CV input of reMix channel 1 (see Figure 15.20).

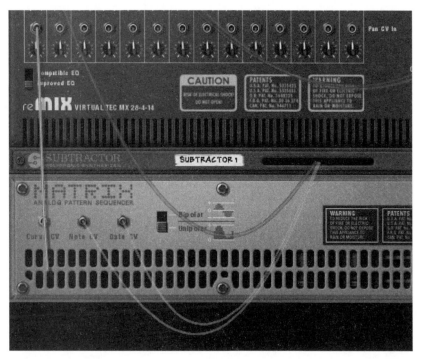

Figure 15.20 Connect a virtual cable from the Curve CV output of the Matrix to the Pan CV input of reMix channel 1. This will make it possible to have the Matrix control the panning assignment of reMix channel 1 by way of the Matrix Curve Edit.

5. Press the Tab key to flip the Device Rack.

6. Switch the Edit mode on the Matrix from Key to Curve.

7. Draw in a curve pattern using your mouse (see Figure 15.21).

Figure 15.21   Draw in a curve pattern. By switching to the bipolar curve mode, you can draw in curve values that will affect the left and right channels.

8. Press Play to start the Matrix sequencer. You should now hear the sequence panning from left to right.

Using the Matrix with Real-Time Effects

Although the next chapter discusses real-time effects in more detail, I can't resist showing you how to use the Matrix with a few choice effects.

Using the Matrix with Chorus/Flanger. Although Chorus/Flanger might more commonly be used to add a lush, thick, dreamy ambience to a sound, this section intentionally misuses this effect for purposes of freaking out. In this tutorial, you will connect the Matrix to a Subtractor that is using an instance of CF-101Chorus/Flanger as an insert effect. Before you begin, start a new Reason song and create instances of the following Reason devices in this order:

1. reMix.

2. Subtractor.

3. CF-101 Chorus/Flanger. This will make Reason automatically route the output of the Subtractor to the input of the Chorus/Flanger. The Chorus/Flanger's outputs will then automatically be routed to a channel on reMix.

4. The Matrix. Reason will automatically route its Note CV and Gate CV outputs to the CV and Gate CV inputs of the Subtractor, which is exactly what you want.

Now you have everything you need in your Device Rack, so let's go.

1. On the rear of the Device Rack, click and drag a virtual cable from the Curve CV output of the Matrix to the Delay input of Chorus/Flanger (see Figure 15.22). If

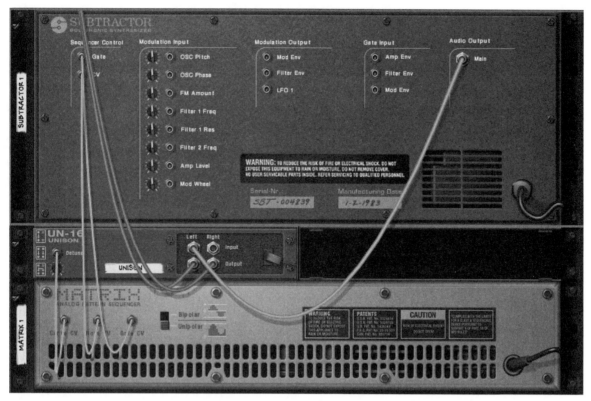

Figure 15.22   The Matrix is ready to alter the Delay Time parameter of Chorus/Flanger.

you press Play on the Transport panel or Run on the Matrix, you can already hear your sequence play back because the Matrix loads with note and velocity data already in place. Stop playback for the moment.

2. On the back of the Matrix, switch the Curve mode from unipolar to bipolar.

3. Press the Tab key to flip the Device Rack.

4. Switch the Edit mode on the Matrix from Key to Curve mode.

5. Write in a whacked-out random curve pattern that looks something like Figure 15.23.

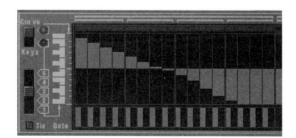

Figure 15.23   Draw in a curve pattern something like this.

6. Turn the Feedback knob on the Chorus/Flanger all the way to the left (counter-clockwise) and fasten your seatbelt.

7. Press Play on your Transport panel or Run on the Matrix. You should now hear your Subtractor sequence playing back as well as the not-so-subtle effect of the delay time of Chorus/Flanger rapidly changing along with your Matrix Curve CV output. While the sequence is playing, try experimenting with the controls on the Chorus/Flanger, especially with the Feedback control and the LFO Rate control.

Note that you can leave your crazy curve data in place and switch the Edit mode on the Matrix back to Key mode and draw in any notes you like, all live and on the fly while your sequence is playing.

Using the Matrix with the Envelope Controlled Filter. This next tutorial has you double your pleasure by using two instances of the Matrix along with another really great real-time effect called the ECF-42. For this exercise, you don't have to start over with a new song. You can continue to use the Reason song you created in the last exercise and make a few adjustments to it along the way.

First, get rid of Chorus/Flanger in order to use the ECF-42 instead. Click on Chorus/Flanger once and choose Cut Device from the Edit pull-down menu.

Now, click on the Subtractor once and choose ECF-42 Envelope Controlled Filter from the Create pull-down menu. This will create an instance of the ECF-42 under the Subtractor. If you press the Tab key to flip the Device Rack around, you will also see that the Subtractor's output has been automatically routed to the ECF-42.

Make the following parameter adjustments to the ECF-42 interface.

■ **Resonance**—Set to 100

■ **Envelope Amount**—Set between 50–60

■ **Velocity**—Set to 42

■ **Filter Mode**—Set to BP12 to use as a band pass filter

■ **Decay**—Set to 100

■ **Sustain**—Set to 24

■ **Release**—Set to 0

No adjustment is necessary for the FREQ and Envelope Attack controls. Draw in a curve pattern like the one in Figure 15.23, and you're ready to begin.

1. Press the Tab key to flip the Device Rack.

2. Connect the Curve CV output of the Matrix to the Frequency CV input on the ECF-42.

3. Click on the Matrix to select it and choose Matrix Pattern Sequencer from the Create pull-down menu to create another instance of it (see Figure 15.24).

Figure 15.24   After creating a second instance of the Matrix, connect the Curve CV output to the Env Gate CV input of the ECF-42.

4. Click and drag a virtual cable from the Curve CV output of the second Matrix to the Envelope Gate input of the ECF-42.

5. Change the Curve mode of the second Matrix from unipolar to bipolar.

6. Press the Tab key to flip the Device Rack.

The second instance of the Matrix has now been created, and you are just about ready to draw in a curve pattern that will affect the Envelope section of the ECF-42. However, you need to make a few adjustments to the second Matrix.

1. Change the number of steps from 16 to 4.

2. Change the resolution from 1/16 to 1/8.

Now, switch the Edit mode on the second Matrix from Key to Curve and draw in a curve pattern similar to Figure 15.25.

Press Play and now both Matrix sequencers should begin playing in perfect sync. Notice the really cool filter effect that you have just created with the ECF-42.

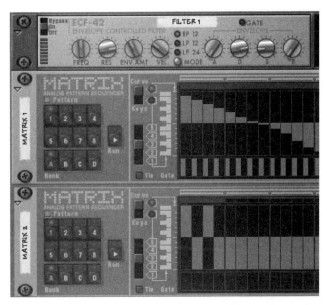

Figure 15.25 Now that the connections have been made and the parameters have been adjusted, draw in a simple curve pattern that will affect the Envelope section of the ECF-42.

Automating the Matrix

Once you have compiled a set of different pattern sequences for your song, you need to program them into your Reason song. This requires writing automation data into the Pattern section of the Matrix. By doing this, you can program when the Matrix will play different patterns within your song. Writing this automation is simple.

There are two ways to automate the Pattern section of the Matrix:

■ **Live Automation**—This kind of data is recorded in real-time while the song plays back.

■ **Drawn Automation**—This kind of data is drawn in using the Pencil tool while in the Edit mode with the Pattern lane.

To see how automation works, you can do a little live automation by trying the following exercise. Before you start, take a minute to start a new Reason song and load it with an instance of the Matrix.

Note that this exercise is meant to teach you about automation, not to actually produce a sound.

1. Make sure that the Matrix is armed for recording by checking the Record Enable Parameter Automation button of the Matrix sequencer track. If it's already red, you're good to go.

2. Press Record and Play in the Transport panel to have the Reason sequencer start recording data.

3. As the Matrix track is recording, select different patterns and banks. At the same time, look at the Transport panel, and you will see the bright red LED of the Automation Override section.

4. When you're finished recording, click on the Stop button. At this point, a purple framed box should appear around the Pattern section of the Matrix, which indicates that automation data has been recorded here (see Figure 15.26). Also, notice that performance data has been written into the Matrix sequencer track. This also indicates that data has been written in here.

Figure 15.26 There is now automation data recorded on the Pattern section of the Matrix.

Automation in Detail   You have briefly read about automation in this chapter, but you can learn more about it in Chapter 20, aptly called "Automation."

At first, some users might find the Matrix to be a little awkward or at least unfamiliar and, therefore, intimidating. But if you desire more pattern-driven elements in your songs, the Matrix may quickly become a very welcome device in your Reason studio.

This pretty much finishes up the dinner course of your Reason tour. You should now be ready to move onto the dessert course by getting into the real-time effects.

16 The RPG-8—Close-Up

I f you've used Reason for as long as I have, this is probably going to be one of your favorite chapters, because you're going to take a good look at one of the few things that Reason has always needed and finally has, the RPG-8 Arpeggiator (see Figure 16.1).

For those of you not familiar with an arpeggiator, it's a module used to make a synthesizer play a specific pattern of notes called *arpeggios*, which you can do by simply pressing one note or chord shape on your keyboard. Once the arpeggiator starts to generate the arpeggios, they can be recorded onto a sequencer track or used in a live environment.

Setting Up the RPG-8

First thing's first. Let's go through the steps to create an instance of the RPG-8 and use it with one of the Reason synths. Try the following exercise:

1. Start a new Reason song and create an instance of reMix and the Malström.

2. Select the Malström and create an instance of the RPG-8 by selecting Create > RPG-8 Monophonic Arpeggiator. This will place it under the Malström (see Figure 16.2).

3. Hold down a basic chord on your keyboard and you should now see and hear the RPG-8 in action. Press the Tab key to swing the Reason Device Rack around. You will see that the CV outputs of the RPG-8 have been connected to the Sequencer Control inputs of the Malström (see Figure 16.3).

Best in Show for Arpeggio   Obviously, not all Malström patches were meant to arpeggiate, so take a minute to find a patch that best suits the RPG-8, because you're going to be using this setup for the rest of the chapter. I suggest looking in the Mono Synths folder in the Reason Factory Sound Bank.

Figure 16.1 Reason has given us yet another creative tool essential to the creation of dance music, the RPG-8 Arpeggiator.

Figure 16.2 The RPG-8 has been created and is ready to start arpeggiating.

A Guided Tour of the RPG-8

Assuming that you have your Malström and RPG-8 appropriately grooving, let's go ahead and have a closer look at the RPG-8.

Looking back at Figure 16.1, you can see that the RPG-8 is split into three sections:

- MIDI to CV
- Arpeggiator
- The Pattern Editor

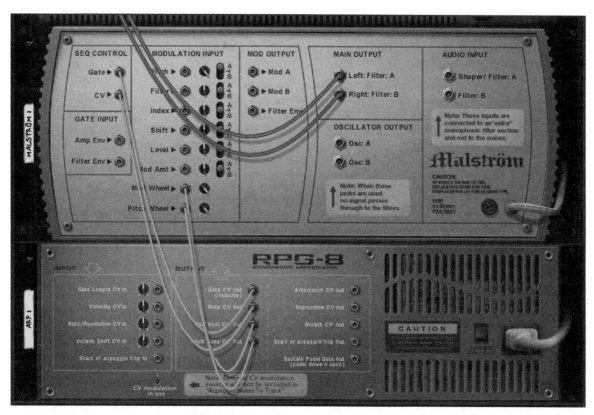

Figure 16.3 The RPG-8 is appropriately connected to the SEQ CONTROL inputs of the Malström. Also, take a minute to look at all of the other routing possibilities of the RPG-8. You'll read about these later in the chapter.

I'm going to break these down and take you through them one at a time.

MIDI to CV

The MIDI to CV section is used to alter the control voltage output of the RPG-8 (see Figure 16.4). Obviously when I talk about control voltage in the Reason environment (as was the case with the Matrix), I am referring to the emulation of a control voltage

Figure 16.4 The MIDI to CV section is used to determine the velocity of the notes generated by the RPG-8 and to select an octave step that best suits the arpeggio pattern.

arpeggiator, and not an actual control voltage piece of hardware. But as you begin to dig into this device, you'll find that Propellerhead went to great lengths to make this device come pretty close to the real thing.

So, let's have a look at the parameters in this section.

Velocity

The Velocity knob is used to determine the fixed note velocity that the RPG-8 will play back once triggered. You can use the knob to adjust the fixed note velocity by clicking on it and dragging your mouse up and down. Once a value has been set, play a note or chord on your MIDI keyboard and the RPG-8 will play the notes at that fixed velocity, no matter how hard or soft you play the notes. Setting this knob to its maximum value will allow you to trigger the RPG-8 at the same velocity that you play a note or chord on your keyboard. Also note that when the knob is at maximum, the "Man" LED will light up.

Hold On/Off

This button is used to trigger the RPG-8 even after releasing a note or chord on your keyboard. Activate it by clicking on it, and then hold down a note or chord. Release the notes and the RPG-8 will continue to run until you either click on the Hold button again, or press Stop on the Reason Transport. Additionally, if you play another note while the RPG-8 is running, it will add that note to the arpeggio, rather than starting over.

There are also a couple of FYI features here as well:

- If the Arpeggiator section is turned off, but the Hold is active, it will act like a sustain pedal in that it will hold and sustain any notes you play on your keyboard.

- You can also turn Hold on and off using a Sustain pedal, which no MIDI setup should be without. If your keyboard controller has a "Sustain Input" on the back or side, you can simply buy a pedal from your local music store, plug it in, and have it control the Hold button. This should come in handy for live performances.

Octave Shift

The Octave Shift section is simply used to transpose the arpeggiated notes up or down in octaves. You can shift up or down by three octaves.

The Arpeggiator Section

The Arpeggiator section is used to determine how and at what rate the arpeggiator will play back (see Figure 16.5). At the top of this section is the power button that used to activate the arpeggiator section, but as you read in the last section, the RPG-8 can still be used even when this section is turned off.

Figure 16.5 The Arpeggiator section is used to alter the speed and type of arpeggios the RPG-8 will trigger.

The Mode Switch

The Mode switch determines the arpeggio patterns or direction that the RPG-8 will play back once triggered.

- **Up**—The RPG-8 will play the arpeggio from the lowest note to the highest note.

- **Up+Down**—The RPG-8 will play from the lowest to the highest note, and then back down to the lowest note.

- **Down**—The RPG-8 will play from the highest note to the lowest note.

- **Random**—The notes you hold down on the MIDI keyboard will be arpeggiated randomly.

- **Manual**—The notes will arpeggiate according to the order of the notes that you play.

The Octave and Insert Buttons

The Octave and Insert buttons determine the range and addition of repeated notes into the arpeggio. Let's first go through a rundown of the Octave buttons:

- **1 Octave**—The RPG-8 will arpeggiate only with the notes you play.

- **2 Octaves**—The RPG-8 will arpeggiate within a two octave range. For example, if you hold down a C chord, the RPG-8 will play an arpeggio in the octave of the notes you held and the same notes an octave higher.

- **3 Octaves**—Same as 2 Octaves, but with the addition of another octave.

- **4 Octaves**—Same as 3 Octaves, but with the addition of another octave.

The Insert buttons are used to insert additional repeated notes into the arpeggio pattern. This makes for a much more interesting performance of the RPG-8.

- **Off**—The Insert function is off.

- **Low**—The RPG-8 will repeat the lowest note between every second note in the arpeggio pattern.

- **Hi**—The RPG-8 will repeat the highest note between every second note in the arpeggio pattern.

- **3-1**—The RPG-8 will play three notes forward, then step back one note, and then play three notes forward.

- **4-2**—The RPG-8 will play four notes forward, then step back two notes, and then play four notes forward.

Rate, Gate, and Repeat

The Rate sets the rate of the arpeggio and contains the following parameters:

- **Sync/Free**—These buttons determine the rate of arpeggio in values of either notes or Hertz. When Sync is selected, the RPG-8 will synchronize to the tempo of the Reason sequencer. When Free is selected, the RPG-8 will arpeggiate in free time.

- **Rate**—This knob will set the rate of arpeggio. When Sync is selected, the Rate knob will make changes according to note values. When Free is selected, the Rate knob will make changes according to Hertz.

Just to the right, the Gate Length knob determines the length of arpeggiated notes. At its minimal setting, the Gate Length is a great tool to create a staccato effect to any arpeggios, making it a great texture for a rhythm track. At its maximum setting, the Gate Length knob does nothing, because the gate is always open. The trick in using this effectively is to have your arpeggio playing along with the song and then using the Gate Length knob to find its best placement.

Last, the Single Note Repeat button is used to determine how the RPG-8 handles single notes played from your keyboard. When activated, the RP8-8 will repeat a single note if the 1 Octave value is selected in the Octave Range Parameters, if a greater octave value is selected, the RPG-8 will arpeggiate the single note across several octaves. When Single Note Repeat is not active, holding a single note will not trigger the RPG-8.

Shuffle Your Arpeggios   Just to the right of the Single Note Repeat button is the Shuffle button, which introduces a Shuffle feel into the arpeggiated pattern playing back from the RPG-8. The amount of shuffle is determined by the Global Shuffle knob, which is found on the ReGroove Mixer in the Reason sequencer (see Figure 16.6).

The Pattern Editor

The Pattern Editor of the RPG-8 is a creative way for you to edit the rhythms of your arpeggio pattern to help make them sound a bit more interesting (see Figure 16.7). From here, you can utilize 16 steps to give you the rhythm you desire and the Pattern Editor will lock to the tempo of your song, as long as the Sync option is selected.

Figure 16.6   The Global Shuffle knob will determine the overall amount of shuffle introduced in any pattern-driven Reason devices, including the RPG-8, Thor, Matrix, and Redrum.

Figure 16.7   The Pattern Editor is used to edit the rhythm of your arpeggio patterns. The note values are represented from left to right with 16 steps, and the pitches are represented vertically between C1–C7.

Editing Notes   It's important to point out here that the Pattern Editor does *not* edit the pitch of your arpeggio patterns. Rather, just the rhythms. The editor simply acts as a visual representation of your arpeggiated pattern.

To begin, activate the Pattern Editor by clicking on the Pattern button in the upper-left corner of the editor. Now, hold down a chord and you will now see the Pattern Editor in action. If you activate the Hold function and play a chord, this will allow you to experiment with the editor as I take you through its functionality.

In the upper-right corner are the Step buttons, which are used to increase or decrease the amount of steps in an arpeggiated pattern. By default, all 16 steps are active but you can decrease this amount by simply clicking on the minus button and this will reduce the amount of steps in the pattern. However, the pattern itself will still be in perfect sync, provided the sync function is turned on.

As you begin to experiment with the step buttons, you'll notice that this only allows you to edit in a linear fashion, from left to right or vice versa. If you want to get more creative with the rhythms, you can turn off and on steps by simply clicking on their appropriate buttons (see Figure 16.8). It's a lot like the rhythm programmer in Redrum.

Figure 16.8 Activating different steps in the arpeggiator is as simple as turning them off and on along the editor timeline.

Once a pattern is playing back, you'll have a few editing parameters to choose from, courtesy of the Edit pull-down menu.

- **Alter Pattern**—Selecting this parameter alters the activated steps of the arpeggio pattern. For example, if you have three active steps in the editor, Alter Pattern simply changes the placement of those three patterns. It does not add or subtract steps.

- **Randomize Pattern**—This parameter also alters the arpeggio pattern in a similar way to Alter Pattern. However, selecting Randomize Pattern randomly activates or deactivates steps, to create entirely different arpeggio patterns.

- **Invert Pattern**—This parameter inverts the pattern, which simply means that activated steps are turned off, whereas deactivated steps turn on.

- **Shift Pattern Left/Right**—These parameters simply move the steps of your pattern to the right or left one step at a time.

Automating the Pattern Editor

I've said it before throughout the course of this book, and I'll say it again, just about every parameter of Reason can be automated and this includes the Pattern Editor. On the surface, automating the editor is as simple as right-clicking on the steps and selecting Edit Automation, at which point, a neon green frame will appear along the steps of the editor and you can click on the Record button in the Transport panel and make your changes as the song plays back. However, to the Reason sequencer, each automation event represents every possible combination of the 16 steps buttons, which comes out to a bewildering 65,535 possible combinations (do you really need to know the math for this?) That said, it's incredibly difficult to draw in automation for the Pattern Editor, so it's a much better idea to record your automation in real-time.

So, let's try a quick automation exercise to show you how this is done. Before starting, be sure to activate the Hold function.

1. Get ready by turning on all the editor step buttons.

2. Right-click on the step buttons and select Edit Automation. This will draw the aforementioned green neon frame around the steps.

3. Now, turn off the steps that you don't want in your pattern, at which point you'll see the Automation Override LED light up.

4. Press Record on the Transport and you'll be off and running.

5. Play a chord on your keyboard and the RPG-8 should start playing back the arpeggiated pattern with the rhythm you created.

6. At this point, turn off and on different steps and you'll see that automation data drawn in real-time along the sequencer timeline.

7. Press Stop. You've now recorded your automation into the RPG-8.

Sending Arpeggiator Patterns to the Sequencer

Once your sustained chords have been recorded onto the RPG-8 sequencer track, you can either leave them as is, or you can also have the RPG-8 generate a sequencer clip that contains the individual notes that the RPG-8 played with the sustained chords. This way, you can send those arpeggiator patterns to other Reason synths to double up the arpeggio effect. Assuming that you have a recorded performance on the RPG-8 sequencer track, follow these steps:

1. Right-click on the RPG-8 and select Arpeggio Notes to Track (Figure 16.9).

2. The RPG-8 will create a clip of the individual notes and place it on a new lane in the RPG-8 sequencer track (Figure 16.10).

3. You can now move the newly created clip to any other Reason device's sequencer track. Looking at Figure 16.11, you can see that I've created an instance of Subtractor and moved the new clip to its sequencer track.

Clip Shortcut   A quicker way of generating a sequencer clip is to simply select any Reason sequencer track, and then select Arpeggio Notes to Track. The RPG-8 will then place the new clip on the selected sequencer track.

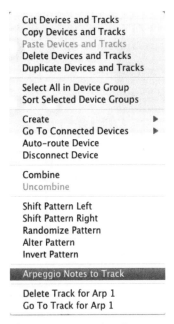

Cut Devices and Tracks
Copy Devices and Tracks
Paste Devices and Tracks
Delete Devices and Tracks
Duplicate Devices and Tracks

Select All in Device Group
Sort Selected Device Groups

Create   ▶
Go To Connected Devices   ▶
Auto-route Device
Disconnect Device

Combine
Uncombine

Shift Pattern Left
Shift Pattern Right
Randomize Pattern
Alter Pattern
Invert Pattern

Arpeggio Notes to Track

Delete Track for Arp 1
Go To Track for Arp 1

Figure 16.9 Selecting Arpeggio Notes to Track will create a clip of the individual RPG-8 notes. You can also select this option from the Edit pull-down menu.

Figure 16.10 There is now a new clip of notes in a new lane on the RPG-8 sequencer track.

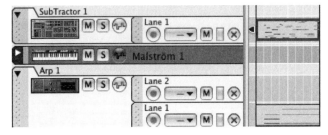

Figure 16.11 You can now move the newly created clip to another Reason synth. In this example, I've moved it to an instance of Subtractor.

The RPG-8 CV Connections

Press the Tab key and you'll see several different CV inputs and outputs that can be used to trigger either the RPG-8 or other Reason devices (see Figure 16.12). Let's go through these, starting with the CV inputs.

■ **Gate Length**—This input alters the Gate Length parameter of the RPG-8. You might try connecting the Mod A/B output of the Malström to this CV input and assign an interesting waveform from the Malström to create some interesting gate values.

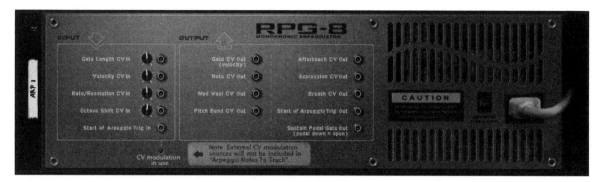

Figure 16.12 The RPG-8 has plenty of CV I/O for creative routing possibilities.

- **Velocity**—For this CV input, you might try using the Curve CV output of the Matrix to vary the velocity of the arpeggio.

- **Rate/Resolution**—An interesting idea here would be to use the Gate CV output of Redrum or Dr. Octo Rex and have it trigger the different Rate values of the RPG-8.

- **Octave Shift**—Again, this would be a great opportunity to try out the Curve output from the Matrix.

- **Start of Arpeggio Trig In**—This is an interesting way to trigger the RPG-8 with the Gate CV output of another Reason device, such as the Gate CV output of Redrum.

And now, let's finish this chapter by having a look at the CV outputs of the RPG-8:

- **Gate**—This CV output transmits gate and velocity values by way of the Velocity knob in the front of the interface. It's typically connected to the Gate CV input of another Reason synth, like the Subtractor or Malström.

- **Note**—This CV output transmits pitch data to other Reason synths.

- **Mod Wheel/Pitch Bend**—These CV output transmit modulation and pitch bend data to their corresponding CV inputs on other Reason synths.

- **Aftertouch/Expression/Breath**—These CV outputs transmit performance controller data based on Aftertouch, Expression, and Breath control.

- **Start of Arpeggio Trig Out**—This CV output transmits a gate signal whenever the arpeggio pattern starts over.

- **Sustain Pedal Gate Out**—This CV output can be used to trigger synth envelopes via a sustain pedal.

As you can see, the RPG-8 is capable of so much creative potential; you'll have a hard time putting it down when you're working with Reason. Now let's move on and explore the effects of Reason.

17 Effects—Close Up

No virtual studio is complete without a horde of virtual effects, and Reason 5.0 is no exception. There are 12 unbelievable real-time virtual effect processors here that are sure to be just what the doctor ordered when a healthy dose of audio spice is needed for your tracks.

This chapter digs into each one of these hotties and shows you how they can be used effectively and creatively. Please note that in addition to the 12 effects discussed in this chapter, Propellerhead has also included a suite of mastering processors, which are discussed in Chapter 18, "The MClass Mastering Suite—Close Up."

Effects Common Features

As you look more closely at these real-time effects, you will notice that they all share a few common parameters.

Each real-time effect includes an input meter, located on the left side of each graphic interface. This meter shows the level of an incoming audio signal.

Each effect also comes with a Power/Bypass switch that has three modes:

- **Bypass**—When this mode is selected, the input signal passes through the effect module without being processed. It is a good way to compare "clean versus processed" audio signals.

- **On**—When this mode is selected, the input signal passes through the effect and is processed.

- **Off**—When this mode is selected, the effect is turned off. No audio whatsoever will pass through this effect device.

All of the real-time effects support stereo ins and outs and can be used as sends or inserts. However, some of these effects were programmed to be used as insert effects only or send effects only. To help you tell the difference, each effect has a signal flow graph that demonstrates how the effect handles mono and stereo signals. To see a device's graph, press the Tab key to flip the Device Rack around.

There are five signal flow charts used to describe the signal flow through the different effects:

Chart A—This can be used as a mono-in, mono-out device.

Chart B—This can be used as a mono-in, stereo-out device. This means that the effect will create a stereo effect, or it can also be used as a mono effect and panned.

Chart C—Connecting both inputs and outputs in stereo makes this device a dual mono effect because both left and right signals will be processed independently.

Chart D—The left and right signals are summed, or combined, before being processed, which does not make it a true stereo signal. However, the effect itself is a stereo effect.

Chart E—This is a true stereo processor because the effect uses both left and right signals in order to generate a new signal. This process can be found in the RV7000 Reverb, which is discussed later in this chapter.

The remainder of this chapter is a guided tour through each of Reason's real-time effects, with the exception of the MClass Mastering Suite.

RV-7 Digital Reverb

Reverberation is probably one of the most important effects needed to create ambience and space in your Reason songs. The RV-7 Digital Reverb is the first of two real-time reverbs available in Reason 5.0 (see Figure 17.1) and is sure to help you add new life to your pads and snare drums.

Figure 17.1 The RV-7 Digital Reverb is one of two reverb effects in Reason.

The RV-7 offers several presets, including:

- **Hall**—Simulates the characteristics of a standard sized hall.

- **Large Hall**—Simulates the characteristics of a large hall.

- **Hall 2**—Sounds very similar to Hall 1, but with a brighter attack.

- **Large Room**—Simulates the characteristics of a large room with hard early reflections.

- **Medium Room**—Simulates the characteristics of a medium sized room with semi-hard walls.

- **Small Room**—Simulates the characteristics of a much smaller room; suitable for drums.

- **Gated**—A reverb that is fed through a gate with a quick release.

- **Low Density**—A thin sounding, low CPU-consumption reverb.

- **Stereo Echoes**—An echo reverberation that pans left and right.

- **Pan Room**—Similar to Stereo Echoes, but with softer attacks.

Save Your CPU—Use Low Density Reverbs are without a doubt the most CPU-intensive of all real-time effects. With so many variables and algorithms needing to be calculated in real-time, using several reverbs like the RV-7 in one Reason song can overload your computer's processor. If you plan to use several instances of the RV-7 within one Reason song, choose the Low Density preset because it was designed to use less processing power than the others.

Once you have selected the preset you want to work with, you can then begin to edit the preset with these available parameters:

- **Size**—This knob adjusts the size of the room. Decreasing this parameter causes the room size to shrink. Increasing the parameter has the opposite result. Also note that this knob is used to adjust the delay time when using the Stereo Echoes or Pan Room presets.

- **Decay**—This parameter adjusts the length of the reverb's decay. Also note that Decay is not used in the Gated preset.

- **Damp**—This parameter is used to adjust the equalization of the reverb effect. Increasing this parameter cuts the high frequencies, making for a warm and smooth effect.

- **Dry/Wet**—This parameter determines the balance between a processed, or *wet*, signal and an unprocessed, or *dry*, signal. When using the RV-7 as a send or aux effect, this knob should be set to its maximum. When used as an insert effect, it should be set in the middle, or 12:00 position, so you can hear both wet and dry signals at once.

The Matrix Pattern sequencer can be used to control the Decay parameter of the RV-7. Just route the Curve CV output of the Matrix to the Decay input on the back of the RV-7. Switch the Matrix from Note to Curve mode, select a note value, and create a curve for your RV-7 Decay.

DDL-1—Digital Delay Line

A *delay* effect is an echo of sorts, but not like that of a reverb. It is used to repeat synths phrases, thicken up pads, syncopate drum sounds, and introduce a funky tempo feeling to your songs. One of the best examples of this to be found in popular music is the guitar part for "Run Like Hell" by Pink Floyd. The whole rhythm of the song is based solely on a guitar part played through a delay in tempo with the song. Delay is simply one of those effects you cannot live without. It's an effect that can be used on any instrument, even the less conventional ones, like bass synths. The DDL-1 (see Figure 17.2) is a delay that does it all and, what's more, is incredibly easy to understand and use.

Figure 17.2 The DDL-1 Digital Delay is used to repeat synth phrases and syncopate drum sounds.

Take a look at the available parameters:

- **Delay Time**—The window to the far left of the DDL-1 displays the currently selected delay time in either note-valued steps or in milliseconds. You can have a maximum of 16 steps or 2000 milliseconds (approximately two seconds).

- **Unit**—This button is used to select either steps or milliseconds for the DDL-1. If you select steps, the delay effect synchronizes with the Reason sequencer. If you select milliseconds, the delay effect is in *free time,* meaning that it is not tempo related.

- **Step Length**—This button is used to select the note value of the DDL-1 when it is set to steps. You can select between 16th notes (1/16) or 8th note triplets (1/8T).

- **Feedback**—This knob sets the number of delay repeats.

- **Pan**—This knob pans the delay effect within the stereo field.

- **Wet/Dry**—This knob determines the balance between a processed, or *wet,* signal and an unprocessed, or *dry,* signal. When using the DDL-1 as a send or aux effect, this knob should be set to its maximum. When used as an insert effect, it should be set in the middle, or 12:00 position, so you can hear both wet and dry signals at once.

The Matrix Pattern sequencer can be used to control the DDL-1 via CV input. Just connect the Curve CV, Note CV, or Gate CV outputs of the Matrix to one of these two parameters on the back of the DDL-1:

- **Pan**—Once connected, the Matrix can pan your delay effect in step mode. Increasing the amount of input on the back panel of the DDL-1 can intensify this effect.

- Feedback—Once connected, the Matrix can control the amount of feedback in step mode. Increasing the amount of input on the back panel of the DDL-1 can intensify this effect.

D-11 Foldback Distortion

The D-11 is a fantastic-sounding digital distortion (see Figure 17.3). It is a perfect and easy solution for adding a little more growl to your Subtractor bass lines or for going full-on industrial with Redrum.

Figure 17.3 The D-11 Foldback Distortion is one of two distortion effects available in Reason.

Controlled by just two parameters, the D-11 is a basic real-time effect that can be used as an insert or auxiliary send.

- **Amount**—This knob assigns the amount of distortion to be used.

- **Foldback**—This knob is used to add character to the shape of the distortion. At its minimum setting, the Foldback knob sounds dark and flat. At its maximum setting, the Foldback becomes the audio equivalent of nuclear meltdown by introducing a sharp and jarring effect into the mix.

The Matrix can control the Amount parameter of the D-11. Just route the Curve CV output of the Matrix to the Amount input on the back of the D-11 and you're set.

ECF-42 Envelope Controlled Filter

The ECF-42 is a combination filter/envelope generator that can be used to create pattern-controlled filter and envelope effects with any Reason device (see Figure 17.4). This effect should be used as an insert because it is more of a niche effect used for specific sounds rather than a universal effect such as a reverb or delay.

Figure 17.4 The ECF-42 Envelope Controlled Filter is used to create tempo-based sweeping filter effects.

Let's have a look at the filter parameters of the ECF-42:

- **Mode**—This button is used to switch between the different filter modes (BP 12, LP 12, and LP 24). Also note that you can simply click on the name of the filter mode to select it.

- **Freq**—This knob controls the Filter Frequency of the ECF-42. When using the ECF-42 in its static or filter-only mode, this knob controls the overall frequency of the audio. When used in combination with the envelope generator, this knob is used as a start and end frequency for the created filter sweep effect.

- **Res**—This knob controls the resonance of the filter.

- **Envelope Amount**—This parameter is used to specify how much the filter frequency will be affected by the triggered envelope.

- **Velocity**—This parameter is used to specify how much the gate velocity affects the envelope.

The envelope parameters of the ECF-42 are available only when triggered by another Reason device, such as Matrix or Dr. Octo Rex (see the Tip entitled "Triggering the Envelope" for more info). Once the envelope is triggered by another Reason device, you can use any of these standard envelope parameters:

- Attack

- Decay

- Sustain

- Release

Triggering the Envelope   Unlike most of the other real-time effects in Reason, the ECF-42 does not function completely as an independent effect and requires an additional Reason device to trigger the envelope. This is done very easily by routing the gate output of any Reason device that has a gate output on the back, such as Redrum, Dr. Octo Rex, or the Matrix.

Here's how to set it up with a Dr. Octo Rex:

1. In any Reason song, create a Dr. Octo Rex and load it up with any available REX file. Click the Copy Loop To Track button to send it to the sequencer.

2. Click on the Dr. Octo Rex to select it, and then select the ECF-42 Envelope Controlled Filter from the Create pull-down menu. Reason will automatically set the ECF-42 up as an insert effect for Dr. Octo Rex.

3. Press the Tab key to flip the Device Rack.

4. Route the Gate Output of Dr. Octo Rex to the Env Gate input on the back of the ECF-42.

5. Press the Tab key again and press Play.

You should now see the Gate LED on the ECF-42 light up because it is receiving gate information from Dr. Octo Rex. At this point, you can use the Envelope parameters.

The Matrix can control the Frequency, Decay, and Resonance parameters of the ECF-42. Just route any of the CV outputs of the Matrix to any of the three available ECF-42 parameters, and you're set.

CF-101 Chorus/Flanger

The CF-101 is a combination chorus/flanger effect device (see Figure 17.5). A chorus/flanger effect is commonly used to add depth and ambience to a sound by introducing a short delay to the fed audio signal. That delayed signal is then mixed with the original dry signal, creating a much larger sound than before. The size and broadness of the delayed signal is determined by the set delay time, feedback, and LFO modulation.

Figure 17.5 The CF-101 Chorus/Flanger is used to thicken up your pads and leads.

A Chorus/Flanger Line To really understand the magic of a chorus or flanger effect, you should hear these beauties in action. Some of the best examples can be found in classic rock tunes of the 70s and 80s. For example, the vocal track from "In The Air Tonight" by Phil Collins is drenched in chorus, whereas "Never Let Me Down Again" by Depeche Mode or "Barracuda" by Heart are examples of flanging at its best.

Sure, they may be "moldy golden oldies" to some, but you can really benefit from exploring the groundbreaking work found in these tunes.

Let's have a look at the CF-101 parameters:

- **Delay**—This knob sets the delay time needed to create the chorus/flanger. For best results, use short delay times to create a flanger effect and medium-to-long delay times for the chorus.

- **Feedback**—This knob controls the amount of effect being fed back into the input, which gives character to the effect.

- **LFO Rate**—This knob controls the modulation rate of the LFO. Increasing this parameter speeds up the frequency of oscillation.

- **LFO Sync**—This button synchronizes the LFO Rate to the tempo of the Reason sequencer. Note that when this button is activated, the LFO Rate knob displays note values rather than the standard numeric value.

- **LFO Modulation Amount**—This knob is used to assign a depth to the LFO modulation.

- **Send Mode**—This button is used to properly integrate the CF-101 with the other Reason devices. When activated, the CF-101 is in Send mode, which means that the device outputs only the modulated signal, making it possible to use the Aux send knob to mix in the additional dry signal. When not active, the CF-101 is used as an insert effect, where the device outputs a mix of the dry and wet signal.

Aside from parameters on the front of the device, the Matrix Pattern sequencer can also modify the CF-101. Press the Tab key to flip the Device Rack, and you will find two CV inputs, one for the Delay parameter and one for the LFO Rate parameter.

Just route the Curve, Note, or Gate CV outputs of the Matrix to either of these parameters and experiment.

PH-90 Phaser

The PH-90 is a sweeping effect perfect for use with guitar samples, Rhodes piano patches, or pads (see Figure 17.6). At times, it can be confused with the likes of a standard chorus/flanger effect, but a phaser is a much different monster once you look under the hood.

Figure 17.6 The PH-90 Phaser is a perfect effect for guitar samples.

A phaser shifts portions of an audio signal out of phase and then sends that effected signal back to the original signal, causing narrow bands (called *notches*) of the frequency spectrum to be filtered out. The aforementioned *sweeping effect* happens when these notches are adjusted.

The PH-90 has four adjustable notches in the frequency spectrum that can be modified by way of seven parameters:

- **Frequency**—This knob assigns the frequency of the first notch. Once this is set, the remaining three notches move in parallel within the frequency spectrum.

- **Split**—This knob changes the distance between each notch. This alters the character of the overall effect.

- **Width**—This knob adjusts the width of the notches. Increasing this parameter creates a very deep effect, while also making the overall sound hollow.

- **LFO Rate**—This knob controls the modulation rate of the LFO. Increasing this parameter speeds up the frequency of oscillation.

- **LFO Sync**—This button synchronizes the LFO Rate to the tempo of the Reason sequencer. Note that when this button is activated, the LFO Rate knob displays note values rather than the standard numeric value.

- **LFO Frequency Modulation**—This knob assigns the depth of LFO modulation.

- **Feedback**—This knob is used to alter the tone of the phaser, much in the same way as a resonance knob on a filter.

The Matrix Pattern sequencer can also modify the PH-90. Press the Tab key to flip the Device Rack, and you will find two CV inputs, one for the LFO Frequency and one for the LFO Rate parameter.

Just route the Curve, Note, or Gate CV outputs of the Matrix to either of these parameters and experiment.

Here's an exercise to demonstrate how to use the PH-90 with Dr. Octo Rex. Be sure to create a new song and load it with a reMix and Dr. Octo Rex. Also, load a REX file and send it to its sequencer track:

1. Select the Dr. Octo Rex by clicking on it once, and then select PH-90 Phaser from the Create pull-down menu. This will automatically connect the PH-90 to the Dr. Octo Rex to be used as an insert effect.

2. Press Play and you will hear the PH-90 in action. By default, it already sounds great, but would probably sound even better if it was synced up to the tempo of the Reason song.

3. Press the Sync button to synchronize the PH-90 effect with the song tempo. Then adjust the Rate knob until it reads 4/4, which means that the phasing effect will recycle every bar.

4. Adjust the Split knob to 0 and notice the extra sweep that has been introduced to the low end.

5. Adjust the Width knob to its maximum setting, and you will notice that the high and low frequencies are accented, but not the mid-frequencies, which makes the overall sound hollow.

6. Finally, experiment with setting the Feedback knob to add a singing tone to the mix.

460 Reason 5 Power!: The Comprehensive Guide

UN-16 Unison

The UN-16 Unison can be thought of as a simple and straightforward chorus effect (see Figure 17.7). By using the available parameters, it produces a set number of voices that are each slightly delayed and detuned by way of low-frequency noise. This produces a very thick stereo-friendly chorus that can be used on vocal samples, guitar/drum loops, and so on.

Figure 17.7 The UN-16 Unison Module is a basic chorus effect.

Take a look at the UN-16 parameters:

- **Voice Count**—This assigns the number of voices to be produced. You can select between four, eight, or 16 individual voices.

- **Detune**—This knob increases/decreases the detuning of the individual voices.

- **Dry/Wet**—This knob determines the balance between a processed, or wet, signal and an unprocessed, or dry, signal. When using the UN-16 as a send or aux effect, this knob should be set to its maximum. When used as an insert effect, it should be set in the middle, or 12:00 position, so you can hear both wet and dry signals at once.

The Matrix Pattern sequencer can control the detune parameter of the UN-16. Just connect the Curve CV output of the Matrix to the Detune input on the back of the UN-16.

PEQ-2 Two Band Parametric EQ

The PEQ-2 is a two band parametric EQ that allows very precise control over the equalization curve of any Reason device (see Figure 17.8). Its features and sound quality far surpass those found in the EQ controls of reMix, making it a perfect solution for advanced mixing.

Figure 17.8 The PEQ-2 two band parametric EQ is a fantastic parametric EQ for adjusting the frequency bands of any Reason device.

The two bands of equalization, EQ A and EQ B, are controlled independently within the interface of the PEQ-2. EQ A is always active and ready to use when an instance of the PEQ-2 is created within a Reason song. In order to use EQ B, you must first activate it by clicking the B button, found in the lower-center portion of the interface. Once activated, its individual parameters are at your disposal.

The graphical display in the left portion of the PEQ-2 is used to show the frequency response curve as it is being created by the EQ parameters. This is a fantastic visual aid that helps you sculpt your EQ curve.

Let's have a look at the parameters of the PEQ-2:

- **Frequency**—This knob assigns the center of the EQ curve. When setting this parameter, you should first increase the Gain parameter to hear the effect. The range is 31Hz to 16Hz.

- **Q**—This knob determines the frequency width of the EQ curve around the set center frequency.

- **Gain**—This knob boosts and cuts the gain of the EQ curve.

The Matrix can control Frequency A and B by connecting the Curve CV, Note CV, or Gate CV outputs of the Matrix to the Frequency 1 or 2 inputs on the back of the PEQ-2.

Using the PEQ-2 as an Insert Effect   The PEQ-2 is best used as an insert or mastering effect. If you recall, an *insert effect* is when the dry signal of a Reason device is completely sent to the effect. The effect then processes this signal and sends it back to an input of reMix.

To review how to create and use an insert effect, try the following exercise:

1. Create a Reason device, such as a Dr. Octo Rex or Subtractor. Once created, it will appear on the channel strip of reMix.

2. Click on the interface of the created Reason device to select it.

3. Select the PEQ-2 from the Create pull-down menu. This will create an instance under the selected Reason device.

4. Press the Tab key to flip the Device Rack around. You will see that the outputs of the Reason device have been automatically routed to the inputs of the PEQ-2. Also notice that the PEQ-2's outputs have been routed to the channel strip of reMix.

COMP-01 Auto Make Up Gain Compressor

The COMP-01 is real-time compressor that is typically used to level out audio signals that are too loud in the mix and are in danger of digital clipping. The COMP-01 is a great solution to combat this problem and can be used as an insert effect or send effect (see Figure 17.9).

Figure 17.9 The COMP-01 auto make up gain compressor will level out any signal with too much amplitude.

- **Ratio**—This knob sets the gain reduction of the audio signal according to the set threshold.

- **Threshold**—This knob sets the level that dictates when the compressor effect will kick in. Any audio signal that meets this set level or goes above it will be compressed, whereas signals that fall below this level are not affected.

- **Attack**—This knob adjusts the attack of the compression effect.

- **Release**—This knob adjusts the length of time needed before the audio signal is unaffected by the COMP-01, once its level has fallen under the threshold. At its lowest setting, a short release will cause a pumping sound, which is good for kick drums. At its mid to high settings, the release will become long and sustained, which is good for pads or pianos.

- **Gain Meter**—This meter displays the amount of gain reduction and increase in decibels.

In order to use the COMP-01 as an insert effect (which is its intended use), refer back to the tutorial found in the PEQ-2 section of this chapter.

The BV512 Vocoder/Equalizer

One of the coolest effects in Reason 5.0 is the BV512 vocoder (see Figure 17.10). This effect is commonly used to create robotic voices in dance and performance music. Another popular use of a vocoder is to create a "choir of synthetic voices" as heard in songs by Moby and New Order. Possibly the single most famous use of a vocoder in popular music is the opening of the 80s hit "Mr. Roboto" by Styx. A beautiful and very artistic use of vocoder can be found in another 80s track, "O Superman" by Laurie Anderson.

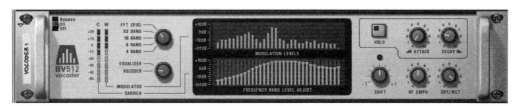

Figure 17.10 The BV512 vocoder/equalizer is an amazing vocoder that can also be used as an equalizer.

What Is a Vocoder?

A vocoder is an effect that uses two separate sources of input to create a new audio signal by applying the frequency bands of one signal to the other. These two separate audio sources are known as the *carrier* and the *modulator*.

The carrier is ideally an audio source that is constantly generating sound. A good example of this is a string pad playing from the Subtractor in a sequence that is looped continuously.

The modulator is typically an audio source such as a spoken voice or vocal track. Another typically used modulator is a drum loop for creating rhythmically enhanced sounds.

Once you have these two elements, they are then routed to their appropriate vocoder inputs. The modulator is divided into a set number of bands (4, 8, 16, 32, or 512) by using band pass filters. These separate bands are then sent to an envelope follower (a device that continuously monitors and analyzes the signal levels).

Meanwhile, the carrier is processed with the same number of bands as the modulator. The same frequency ranges used in the modulator's band pass filters are also applied to the carrier. By doing this, the carrier will have the same frequency characteristics as the modulator. This means that if the modulator gets louder or more dynamic in shape, the carrier will follow and emulate this as well.

The Vocoder in Action   If you want to hear good audio examples of vocoding, listen to just about any CD by Laurie Anderson ("O Superman"), Daft Punk ("Around the World"), Air ("Remember"), or Zapp and Roger ("More Bounce to the Ounce").

Take a look at the basic parameters of the BV512:

- **Level Meters**—These meters display the signal level of the carrier and the modulator.

- **Band Switch**—This switches between the number of filter bands (4, 8, 16, 32, or 512).

- **Equalizer/Vocoder Switch**—This switches the BV512 between Vocoder mode and Equalizer mode. Note that when using the BV512 in Equalizer mode, the modulator input is not used.

- **Modulation Level Display**—This displays the overall spectrum of the modulation signal.

- **Frequency Band Level Adjust**—This adjusts the levels of the individual filter bands. When using this section in Vocoder mode, each band adjusts the sound and shape of the vocoder. When using this section in Equalizer mode, each band adjusts the amplitude of the individual frequencies in the EQ curve. After making adjustments to the individual bands, you can use the Reset Band Levels option from the Edit pull-down menu.

- **Hold Button**—When activated, this button freezes the current filter settings. The modulator signal no longer affects the carrier in this mode. Pressing it again releases the filter settings.

- **Attack**—This parameter affects the overall attack of the frequency bands. Increasing the attack amount can create some very cool pad sounds. Note that when the BV512 is in Equalizer mode, this parameter is not available.

- **Decay**—This parameter affects the overall decay of the frequency bands. As with the Attack, this parameter is not available when the BV512 is used as an equalizer.

- **Shift**—This parameter shifts the carrier signal filters up and down, creating a sweeping effect.

- **High Frequency Emphasis**—This knob increases the high frequencies in the carrier signal.

- **Dry/Wet**—This knob mixes between the unprocessed (or dry) signal, and the processed (or wet) signal.

The BV512 as an Equalizer

The BV512 can also be used as a graphic equalizer. Capable of supporting up to 512 bands of equalization, the BV512 is perfect for enhancing individual devices in a Reason song or can even be used as a mastering equalizer.

Follow these steps to learn how to use the BV512 as a mastering equalizer:

1. Press the Tab key to flip the Device Rack around.

2. Click on the AUDIO IN device to select it.

3. Select the BV512 Vocoder device from the Create pull-down menu. This will place the BV512 between the AUDIO IN and reMix.

4. Route the outputs of reMix into the carrier inputs on the BV512.

5. Route the outputs of the BV512 to inputs 1 and 2 of the AUDIO IN device.

6. Press the Tab key again to flip the Device Rack around.

7. Set the Equalizer/Vocoder switch to Equalizer. Also, set the Band Switch to 512 for the best quality equalization (read the Note entitled "FFT Vocoding and Equalizing").

At this point, you can load some Reason devices, sequence them, and play them through the BV512 as a mastering EQ.

FFT Vocoding and Equalizing   As you know, the BV512 supports up to 512 bands of EQ, but what does this really mean? If you use the band switch to change between 32 bands and 512 bands of EQ, there is no visual difference in the interface of the BV512, but there is a noticeable auditory difference, thanks to FFT.

FFT (*Fast Fourier Transform*) refers to a very detailed and precise form of analysis and processing in which waveforms are represented as a sum of sines and cosines (math geeks rejoice!).

To the rest of us, this means that using the BV512 as a vocoder or as an EQ in 512FFT mode produces very precise and detailed control over the shaping of the effect. One thing to keep in mind is that when you are making adjustments to the BV512 in 512FFT mode, a majority of the available bands in the interface will control the high frequencies rather than the low frequencies.

Basic Vocoding Tutorial

Let's apply what you have just learned about vocoding by going through a basic vocoding tutorial. In this section, you will open a Reason song that I have prepared that consists of an NN-19 (the modulator) playing a single sample, a Subtractor (the carrier) playing chords, and the BV512 vocoder. Through a step-by-step method, you will learn how to route the carrier and modulator to the BV512, adjust the frequency band, and create a unique signal that you can edit further by using the synth parameters of the Subtractor.

Before You Get Started   Before you start this tutorial, take a minute to visit the Course Technology website (www.courseptr.com), where you will find a Reason song called Vocoder Tutorial. This song file is a *published* song, which means that all of the elements specifically created for this tutorial are self-contained within the song file.

You'll learn more about published songs in Chapter 22, "Mixing and Publishing Your Reason Songs."

---

1. Open the Vocoder Tutorial song. You will see reMix, the DDL-1 delay, a Subtractor, the NN-19, and the BV512 at the bottom. The NN-19 has a loaded sample of my voice, and the Subtractor has the Bowy patch loaded. Also notice that there is a sequence written for both the Subtractor and the NN-19, but if you press Play, you won't hear anything, because the audio has not yet been routed.

2. Press the Tab key to flip the Device Rack and notice that there are no audio signals routed to reMix. This gives you a perfect starting point to begin routing your carrier and modulator.

3. Route the output of the Subtractor to the carrier input left of the BV512 (see Figure 17.11).

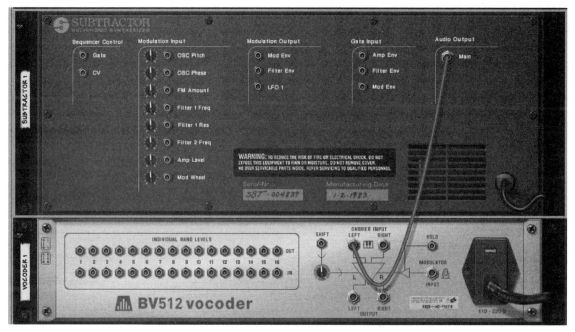

Figure 17.11   First the carrier . . .

4. Route the left output of the NN-19 to the modulator input on the BV512 (see Figure 17.12).

5. Route just the left output of the BV512 to the channel 1 left input of reMix; this is a mono signal.

6. Press Play on the Transport panel. You should now hear the BV512 in action. It should be a strong signal that is very bass-heavy and slightly distorted. This means that some adjustments will need to be made to the frequency band level section of the BV512.

7. Because this is your first time using the BV512, switch to the 16-band display using the Band switch, and make some adjustments to the lower frequency bands (see Figure 17.13).

This should give you a pretty good idea of how the BV512 works. You can experiment further by changing the band range of the BV512, making further adjustments to the synth parameters of the Subtractor, or replacing the Subtractor with the Malström for a whole new sound.

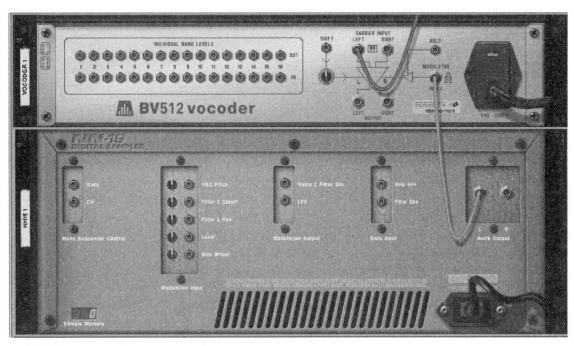

Figure 17.12 Then the modulator.

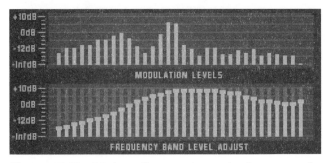

Figure 17.13 Make adjustments to the frequency band level to ensure that you will not digitally distort your signal.

Using Dr. Octo Rex as the Modulator   Another interesting application for the BV512 is to use a drum loop as the source of modulation. This creates a very interesting rhythmically driven audio signal. Try the following exercise:

1. Create an instance of Dr. Octo Rex, and load a 16th-note patterned REX file. (For example, something from the Abstract Hip-Hop folder in the Reason Factory Sound Bank should work well.)

2. Press the To Track button on the Dr. Octo Rex interface to load the REX file into the Reason sequencer.

3. Press the Tab key to flip the Device Rack. Disconnect the NN-19 from the BV512.

4. Disconnect Dr. Octo Rex from channel 2 of reMix. Connect the left output of Dr. Octo Rex to the modulator input of the BV512.

Now press Play and you will hear the rhythmic bliss of vocoding in action. Try to add some delay to the signal, or use some of the synth parameters of either Dr. Octo Rex or the Subtractor for a whole new sound.

Automation

All of the parameters in the BV512 can be automated in the same way as any Reason device. If you would rather draw in your automation data than record it in real time, the only hoop you have to jump through in order to begin automating is to create a sequencer track.

You can see how by working through the following exercise. Before you begin, start a new Reason song and create an instance of reMix, an NN-19, and a BV512.

1. Right-click on the BV512 and select Create Track for Vocoder 1. This will create a sequencer track that is automatically routed to the BV512.

2. Right-click on the vocoder track and select Parameter Automation.

3. A window will pop up giving you a list of parameters to select. Select the ones you want and click OK.

4. The Reason sequencer will now display these parameters as lanes on the vocoder sequencer track. Switch to the Edit mode and draw your automation moves.

For more on automation, check out Chapter 20, "Automation."

CV Connections

As if it couldn't get any better, the BV512 offers many individual inputs and outputs on the back of the device that allow for some very interesting routing possibilities (see Figure 17.14).

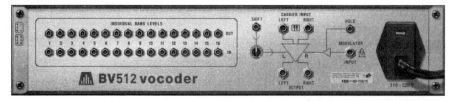

Figure 17.14 The BV512 offers many routing possibilities by providing a wide assortment of ins and outs.

- **Frequency Band Outputs**—These CV outputs use the amplitude of an individual frequency band to control the parameter inputs of other Reason devices. For example, you could use the output of band 8 and route it to the FM Amount input of the Subtractor.

- **Frequency Band Inputs**—These CV inputs can be controlled by the Matrix to alter the amplitude of each frequency band in the BV512. Note that once you make a connection from the Matrix to a specific frequency band, the Matrix exclusively controls that band's amplitude.

- **Shift**—This input controls the Shift parameter on the front of the device and can be used to create fantastic sweeping effects.

- **Hold**—This input is to operate the Hold parameter and can be used to create a step-driven vocoder effect. Perfect for creating percussive vocoder stabs on vocals and pads. Note that you must use the Gate CV output of the Matrix to make this input work.

Scream 4 Sound Destruction Unit

Aside from the comical Wes Craven-esque name (programmers always have a good sense of humor), the appropriately titled Scream 4 is the digital distortion that takes vocals, drums, and synth patches to a whole new level (see Figure 17.15). Divided into three sections (Damage, Cut, and Body), Scream 4 can shape, mold, and destroy any audio signal it comes into contact with.

Figure 17.15 Scream 4 is the kind of distortion that non-Reason users can only dream of.

Another welcome addition to Scream 4 and the upcoming RV7000 (discussed later in this chapter) is the ability to load, edit, and save customized presets. Scream 4 already comes with a lot of great sounding presets, but it never hurts to make your own.

For those of you who were looking for a distortion box with more to offer than the D-11, this *is* it!

The Damage Section

Let's have a look at the various parameters of Scream 4. This section starts by looking at the parameters and presets for the Damage section (see Figure 17.16).

- **Damage button**—Turns the Damage section on and off.

- **Damage control**—This knob is used to assign an amount of input gain to Scream 4. The higher the value, the more distortion there is.

- **Damage type**—This knob lets you select the type of distortion.

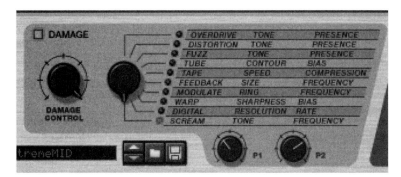

Figure 17.16   The Damage section of Scream 4 is used to select the type of distortion and edit its characteristics.

- **P1/P2 knobs**—These knobs work differently with each Damage type. These types are covered next.

There are 10 Damage types available with Scream 4:

- **Overdrive**—This is a standard analog-type distortion that responds well to variable dynamics. When selected, the P1 knob is used as a tone control. The P2 knob controls the presence, which increases the mid to high frequencies before it's passed through the distortion effect.

- **Distortion**—This is similar to the Overdrive preset, but it is capable of creating a much thicker distortion effect. Note that the P1 and P2 knobs work the same here as they do with the Overdrive preset.

- **Fuzz**—This preset is a heavy distortion that is strong even at low damage control settings. Note that the P1 and P2 knob work the same as they do with the Overdrive preset.

- **Tube**—This preset simulates a classic tube distortion (à la Led Zeppelin or Jimi Hendrix). When using this preset, the P1 knob acts as a contour, or high pass filter. The P2 knob controls the bias, or balance, of the tube distortion. When set to a 12:00 position, the Bias is very balanced in shape. When set to its maximum resolution, the Bias knob will create an uneven balance to the distortion, which sounds very close to a tube-driven amplifier.

- **Tape**—This preset is a simulation of tape saturation, which can add compression and punch to the distortion. The P1 knob acts as a tape speed, which helps to preserve the higher frequencies when set to high speeds. The P2 knob controls the compression ratio.

- **Feedback**—This preset is a combination of heavy distortion and looped feedback. Feedback is created when a sound source is fed back to itself. A good example is an electric guitar or microphone that is placed too close to its amplifier or speaker. The Damage Control knob assigns the amount of gain to the feedback loop, whereas the P1 and P2 knobs control the size and "howl," or frequency, of the feedback respectively.

■ **Modulate**—This preset creates a distortion that resonates by combining two copies of itself before it is fed through a distortion. The P1 knob controls the resonance ring, whereas the P2 knob controls the filter frequency.

■ **Warp**—This preset creates a strong, stinging distortion by multiplying its incoming signal with itself. The P1 knob controls the sharpness of the distortion, whereas the P2 knob controls the bias, or balance, of the distortion.

■ **Digital**—This preset is meant to be used as a low fidelity, gritty distortion. The P1 knob is used to alter the bit depth from the highest resolution possible to a down-and-dirty single bit of resolution. The P2 knob alters the sampling rate of the distortion and ranges from clean and pristine to crunchy and static.

■ **Scream**—This preset is similar to the Fuzz preset, but it includes a band pass filter including high resonance and gain before distorting. The P1 knob controls the tone of the distortion, whereas the P2 knob controls the filter frequency.

The Cut Section

The Cut section of Scream 4 acts as EQ controls, allowing for many creative possibilities in carving and shaping an interesting EQ curve for your distortion (see Figure 17.17).

Figure 17.17 The Cut section is a simple yet effective three-band EQ.

Click on the Cut button to activate the EQ. At this point, you can adjust the low, mid, and high bands of equalization to your liking. At any time, you can reset any of the three bands by holding down the Ctrl key on your PC or Apple key on your Mac and clicking on the band slider to reset it to its default position.

The Body Section

The Body section of Scream 4 is used to create different effects, such as speaker cabinet simulations and auto-wahs (for us guitarists), by placing the signal in different

Figure 17.18 The Body section places the signal in a resonant body, which makes it possible to simulate speaker cabinets and other effects.

simulated enclosures (see Figure 17.18). There are five body types that can be selected and then edited by resonance and scale parameters.

- **Body button**—This button switches the Body section on and off.

- **Body type**—This knob switches between one of five available body types.

- **Body resonance**—This knob creates a resonance effect for the selected body type.

- **Body scale**—This knob controls the size of the selected body. Please note that this knob is inverted and that turning the knob clockwise creates a smaller size, whereas counter-clockwise increases the size.

- **Auto**—This knob controls the amount of the Envelope Follower (see the following Note, called "The Envelope Follower").

The Envelope Follower   The Envelope Follower is used to change the body scale according to the incoming dynamic level. The louder the incoming sound, the more the scale parameter is increased. This creates what is commonly known as an "auto-wah" effect, which is set by the Auto knob.

To demonstrate the versatility of this effect, try the following exercise. Before you begin, start a new Reason song and create an instance of reMix.

1. Create a Dr. Octo Rex and load a REX file from either the Abstract Hip-Hop folder or the Techno folder in the Reason Factory Sound Bank. Press the To Track button to load the Dr. Octo Rex pattern into the Reason sequencer.

2. Create a Scream 4 and route it to be used as an insert effect.

3. Activate the Body section, select Body Type B, and turn the Auto knob clockwise.

4. Adjust the Reso knob.

5. Press Play, and notice how the Body Scale opens up with the various dynamics of the REX loop.

Screaming Mix   Aside from using Scream 4 as a send or insert for your individual Reason devices, Scream 4 can also be used as a mastering effect. By using the Tape preset in the Damage section, you can introduce a warm and welcome tape saturation that will give your mix the kick it needs.

To use Scream 4 as a mastering effect, try the following exercise. Before you begin, open any Reason demo song located in the Demo Songs folder in the Reason Program folder.

1. Press the Tab key to flip the Device Rack.

2. Click once on the AUDIO IN device, and select Scream 4 from the Create pull-down menu. This will place an instance of Scream 4 in between the AUDIO IN and reMix devices.

3. Disconnect the Master outputs of reMix and re-route them to the inputs of Scream 4.

4. Connect the outputs of Scream 4 to the Hardware Interface device.

5. Press the Tab key again to flip the Device Rack.

6. With the EQ and Body sections disabled, set your Damage Control knob to a low setting.

7. Set your Damage type to Tape.

8. Set your P1 and P2 knobs to the 12:00 position.

At this point, you can begin to play back your Reason song and make adjustments to the Damage parameters. Use the P1 knob for brightness and the P2 knob for more compression.

The CV Connections

Using CV outputs can enable the Matrix to control any of four Scream 4 parameters.

- **Damage control**—Changes the amount of distortion.

- **P1 knob**—Increases or decreases the P1 parameter. Note that the Damage type determines what this parameter affects.

- **P2 knob**—Increases or decreases the P2 parameter. Note that the Damage type determines what this parameter affects.

- **Scale**—Increases or decreases the size of the selected body.

Additionally, Scream 4 includes an Auto CV output, which can be routed to the CV input of another Reason device. For example, Scream 4 could be routed to a modulation parameter of the Subtractor or Malström.

RV7000 Advanced Reverb

The RV7000 is a true stereo professional reverb effect that sounds too good to be true (see Figure 17.19). It has nine reverb and echo algorithms that can be used along with an included EQ and Gate for molding and shaping your reverb in ways that just can't be done by most hardware and software reverbs.

Figure 17.19 The RV7000 advanced reverb is one of the best software-based reverbs you'll ever hear.

The Main Panel

The RV7000 is a two-part effect unit, much the same way that the NN-XT is a two-part sampler. When you first load the RV7000, the part of the device you will see is the main panel, which controls the global parameters of the device (see Figure 17.20).

Figure 17.20 The RV7000 main panel.

Notice that the RV7000 has a Patch Browser in the left corner of the main panel. This makes it possible to load, edit, and save customized patches for the device.

Take a look at the global parameters:

- **EQ Enable**—This button switches the EQ section off and on.

- **Gate Enable**—This button switches the Gate section off and on.

- **Decay**—This knob controls the rate of decay within a reverb or the amount of feedback within an echo algorithm.

- **High Frequency Damp**—This knob assigns an amount of decay time for the high frequencies in the reverb. Increasing this amount makes the reverb sound warm and dull.

- **HI EQ**—This knob controls the high shelving EQ. Increase the value of this parameter to boost the high frequencies in the reverb.

- **Dry/Wet**—This knob mixes between the unprocessed dry signal and the processed wet signal.

The Remote Programmer

The Remote Programmer is where all of the individual edits of the RV7000 are completed (see Figure 17.21). To activate the Remote Programmer, click on the arrow button next to the virtual cable slot. The RV7000 will then perform a little animation and load up right below the main panel.

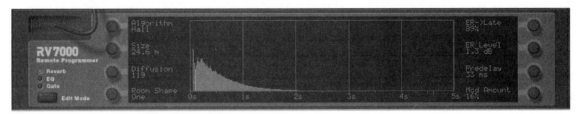

Figure 17.21 The RV7000 Remote Programmer.

Once the Remote Programmer is open, you can select between one of nine algorithms. To see each of these algorithms, use the knob located on the top left of the remote programmer to scroll through them. Each of the algorithms emulates a specific type of reverb or echo and offers a number of editable parameters.

- **Small Space**—Emulates a small room.

- **Room**—Emulates a standard sized room with adjustable shape and wall composition.

- **Hall**—Emulates a standard hall.

- **Arena**—Emulates the characteristics of a large arena.

- **Plate**—A classic plate reverb.

- **Spring**—Emulates a spring-driven reverb, which can be found on the back of most old Fender guitar amps.

- **Echo**—Creates a tempo synced echo.

- **Multi Tap**—Creates a tempo synced multi-tapped delay.

- **Reverse**—A well-known backward effect in which the dry signal comes after the reverb.

As you will notice, each one of these algorithms has its own set of attributes and parameters that can be altered. That said, let's run down the list of each one.

The first algorithm is the Small Space:

- **Size**—Assigns a size to the space.

- **Modulated Rate**—Sets the rate of modulation of the space, which helps to even out the character of the reverb. Works alongside the Mod Amount parameter.

- **Room Shape**—Selects one of four room shapes.

- **Low Frequency Damp**—Controls the rate of decay for the low frequencies.

- **Wall Irregularities**—Adjusts the positioning of the walls within a small space.

- **Predelay**—Adjusts the amount of predelay, which is the delay between the source signal and the starting point of the reverb.

- **Modulation Amount**—Assigns the amount of modulation to the reverb.

The next algorithm is the Room. Note that the Hall algorithm has the same parameters but much larger size settings.

- **Size**—Assigns a size to the space.

- **Diffusion**—Clarifies the *bounce*, or reflection, of the reverb.

- **Room Shape**—Selects one of four room shapes.

- **ER Late**—This parameter sets the time between the "early reflections" and tail end of the reverb.

- **ER Level**—Adjusts the level of the early reflections.

- **Predelay**—Adjusts the amount of predelay, which is the delay between the source signal and the starting point of the reverb.

- **Modulation Amount**—Assigns the amount of modulation to the reverb.

The Arena algorithm is used to emulate the reverberations of a full-sized area. This particular algorithm is unique in that it controls the left, right, and center reflections that are present in an arena setting.

- **Size**—Assigns a size to the space.

- **Diffusion**—Clarifies the *bounce*, or reflection, of the reverb.

- **Left Delay**—Sets the predelay time for the left side of the reverb.

- **Right Delay**—Sets the predelay time for the right side of the reverb.

- **Stereo Level**—Adjusts the level both the left and right channels of the reverb.

- **Mono Delay**—Sets the predelay time for the center of the reverb.

- **Mono Level**—Adjusts the level of the center of the reverb.

There are only two adjustable parameters for the Plate algorithm.

■ **LF Damp**—Controls the rate of decay for the low frequencies.

■ **Predelay**—Adjusts the amount of predelay, which is the delay between the source signal and the starting point of the reverb.

The Spring reverb algorithm emulates the behaviors of the actual spring found on the back of old guitar amps.

■ **Length**—Sets the length of the spring.

■ **Diffusion**—Clarifies the bounce, or reflection, of the reverb.

■ **Dispersion Freq**—Controls the amount of dispersion of the different frequencies created by the initial reflection. Works in combination with the Dispersion Amount.

■ **Low Frequency Damp**—Controls the rate of decay for the low frequencies.

■ **Stereo On/Off**—Determines whether the reverb is mono or stereo.

■ **Predelay**—Adjusts the amount of predelay, which is the delay between the source signal and the starting point of the reverb.

■ **Dispersion Amount**—Controls the amount of the dispersion effect.

The Echo algorithm is an echo or delay-like effect, which can be tempo-synced.

■ **Echo Time**—This parameter adjusts the time between each echo. Note that when Tempo Sync is not active, this parameter has a range of 10–2000 milliseconds (up to two seconds). When Tempo Sync is active, this parameter is set in note values, such as 1/8 or 1/16.

■ **Diffusion**—Clarifies the bounce and number of reflections of the echo. Works in combination with the Spread parameter.

■ **Tempo Sync**—Turns the tempo sync off and on.

■ **LF Damp**—Controls the rate of decay for the low frequencies.

■ **Spread**—Adjusts the space of the additional reflections set by the Diffusion parameter.

■ **Predelay**—Introduces an additional delay before the first echo.

The Multi Tap algorithm produces four separate delays, each with its own adjustable parameters. The settings of this algorithm differ greatly from the others, as each tap is assigned its own set of parameters.

The four individual Tap settings can be selected with the Edit Select knob in the upper-right corner of the Remote Programmer. There are a few common parameters used in taps 1–4, including

- **Tempo Sync**—Turns the tempo sync off and on.

- **Diffusion**—Clarifies the bounce and number of reflections of the echoes.

- **LF Damp**—Controls the rate of decay for the low frequencies in the echoes.

- **Tap Delay**—Adjusts the delay time of each tap. Note that when Tempo Sync is not active, this parameter has a range of 10–2000 milliseconds (about two seconds). When Tempo Sync is active, this parameter is set in note values, such as 1/8 and 1/16.

- **Tap Level**—Adjusts the amplitude of each tap.

- **Tap Pan**—Adjusts the panning assignment for each tap.

When Repeat Tap is selected, this parameter adjusts the time between each repeat of the entire set of tap delays.

One of the grooviest algorithms in the RV7000, the Reverse, mimics the backward effect that you hear so often in ambient electronic music.

- **Length**—Adjusts the time between when the source signal is processed and then played back. Note that when Tempo Sync is not active, this parameter has a range of 10–4000 milliseconds (about four seconds). When Tempo Sync is active, this parameter is set in note values, such as 1/8 and 1/16.

- **Density**—Used to control the thickness of the reverse effect.

- **Rev Dry/Wet**—Mixes between the dry unprocessed signal and the wet processed signal.

- **Tempo Sync**—Turns the tempo sync off and on.

The CV Connections
You can connect the Matrix CV outputs to one of three CV inputs on the back of the RV7000 to control the three parameters in step time:

- **Decay**—Controls reverb decay or echo/delay feedback.

- **HF Damp**—Controls the HF Damp parameter on the RV7000 main display.

- **Gate Trig**—This CV input is used to trigger the Gate section of the RV7000.

The Spider Audio Merger & Splitter

First introduced in Reason 2.5, the Spider Audio Merger & Splitter is not an actual real-time effect (see Figure 17.22). However, it is a utility that serves two basic functions:

■ Merges up to four separate audio inputs into a single output.

■ Splits one audio input into four separate outputs.

Figure 17.22 The Spider Audio Merger & Splitter can be used to split a single audio signal to four outputs. It can also be used to merge four audio signals into one.

Press the Tab to flip the Device Rack around. You will see that the Spider is split into two sections (see Figure 17.23). On the left is the Merge section, and the Splitter is on the right. The next two sections show you how to use the merging and splitting capabilities of the Spider.

Figure 17.23 There are two separate sections to the Spider: the Merge section and the Split section.

Using the Spider to Merge Audio

Merging audio with the Spider may not seem like such a hot idea the first time you think about it. But as this tutorial progresses, you might find yourself coming up with some interesting routing ideas that you may not have thought possible.

First, the basic idea: You can route the outputs of any Reason device to any of the four stereo inputs on the Spider. For example, you could route the outputs of the Malström, the stereo outputs of Redrum, the outputs of Dr. Octo Rex, and the outputs of two Subtractor synths to the Spider inputs (see Figure 17.24). These signals are then merged

Figure 17.24 The Merge section can accept the outputs of four stereo devices, or up to eight mono devices.

internally and routed to the stereo outputs of the Spider, which can be sent off to reMix, a stereo compressor, and so on.

Additionally, the Merge section of the Spider has a couple of rules when it comes to using mono signals from Reason devices, such as the Subtractor, or individual outputs from Redrum or the NN-XT.

■ When you route the mono output of a Reason device to the left mono input of the Spider and don't connect anything to its corresponding right input, the Spider will output the signal to its left and right outputs.

■ When you route the mono output of a Reason device to the right mono input of the Spider and don't connect anything to its corresponding left input, the Spider will output the signal to its right channel only.

Let's look at an example of how to use the Merge section effectively by routing Dr. Octo Rex and Redrum to the Spider in order to send them all to a single insert effect.

1. Create a new Reason song and load it with reMix, Redrum, and Dr. Octo Rex. Additionally, write a pattern for Redrum and load a REX file into Dr. Octo Rex. Send it to its sequencer track.

2. Create a Spider Audio Merger & Splitter at the bottom of the Device Rack.

3. Create a COMP-01 Compressor next to the Spider. Press the Tab key to flip the Device Rack around. Notice that the output of the Dr. Octo Rex device has automatically routed itself to the COMP-01 in order to use it as an insert effect.

4. Disconnect Redrum from reMix and Dr. Octo Rex from the COMP-01. At this point, if you press Play, you won't hear any signal.

5. Route the left output of Redrum to any of the left inputs of the Spider's Merge section. The right output of Redrum should automatically route itself to the Spider's right input as well.

6. Route the left output of Dr. Octo Rex to any of the left inputs of the Spider's Merge section. The right output of Redrum should automatically route itself to the Spider's right input as well (see Figure 17.25).

7. Route the left output of the Spider's Merge section to the left input of the COMP-01.

8. Route the left output of the COMP-01 to the channel 1 left input of reMix.

9. Press the Tab key again and then press Play. You should now see and hear the COMP-01 processing both Redrum and Dr. Octo Rex (see Figure 17.26).

Figure 17.25 The outputs of the Redrum and Dr. Octo Rex have now been routed to the inputs of the Spider.

Figure 17.26 The audio outputs from both Redrum and Dr. Octo Rex are now being processed by COMP-01.

Using the Spider to Split Audio

The Splitter section of the Spider performs the exact opposite function of the Merger section. Simply put, its purpose is to split an audio signal into four separate stereo pairs of outputs. This allows you to route the audio signal of one Reason device into many other devices, such as real-time effects.

Try an example:

1.   Start a new Reason song and load it with a reMix and Dr. Octo Rex. Load a REX file and send it to its sequencer track.

2. Press the Tab key.

3. At the bottom of the Device Rack, create a Spider Audio Merger & Splitter.

4. Create a few real-time effects, such as the RV-7, the DDL-1, and the D-11. Notice that Dr. Octo Rex has automatically routed itself to the first effect as an insert.

5. Disconnect all of the Reason devices to start with a clean slate. If you press Play, you should not hear any audio now.

6. Route the left output of Dr. Octo Rex to the left input of the Spider's Splitter section. The right output of Dr. Octo Rex should automatically route itself to the Spider's right input accordingly (see Figure 17.27).

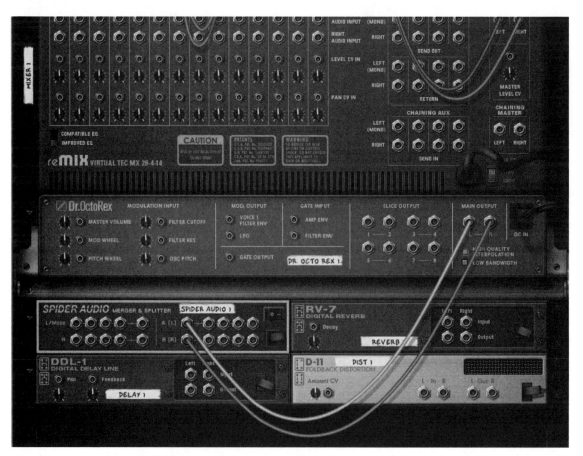

Figure 17.27   After all the devices have been disconnected, route Dr. Octo Rex to the input of the Spider.

7. Route the left output of the first Spider channel to the channel 1 input of reMix. This will give you one dry signal of Dr. Octo Rex.

8. Route the left output of the second Spider channel to the left input of the RV-7 (see Figure 17.28).

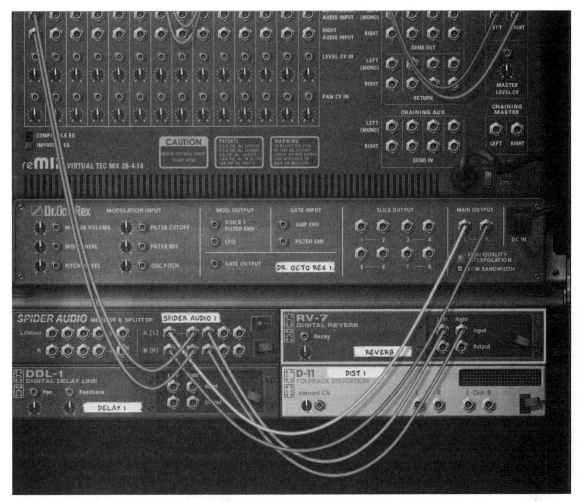

Figure 17.28 Route the second output channel of the Spider to the RV-7.

9. Route the outputs of the RV-7 to channel 2 of reMix.

10. Route the outputs of the third Spider channel to the DDL-1 and route its outputs to channel 3 of reMix.

11. Route the outputs of the fourth Spider channel to the D-11 and route its outputs to channel 4 of reMix.

At this point, you have four channels of reMix playing the same REX loop with different processors (see Figure 17.29).

The Spider CV Merger & Splitter

Along with the Spider Audio Merger & Splitter, Reason 2.5 has a Spider unit that merges and splits CV signals, called the Spider CV Merger & Splitter (see Figure 17.30).

Figure 17.29 The same REX loop is now playing back through four inputs on reMix. Channel 1 is dry, channel 2 is a reverb, channel 3 is delay, and channel 4 is a distortion.

Figure 17.30 The Spider CV Merger & Splitter is used to split and merge CV signals.

The Spider CV Merger & Splitter serves two purposes:

- It merges four separate CV outputs from other Reason devices into one master CV output.

- It splits CV or Gate inputs into several outputs.

Next, take a look at a couple of examples for effectively using the merging and splitting functions of this wonder.

First, try the following exercise to learn how to merge:

1. Start a new Reason song and load it with reMix, Redrum, the ECF-42, and a Spider CV Merger & Splitter.

2. Write in a Redrum pattern using four different drum sounds (such as kick, snare, hi-hat, and cymbal).

3. Press the Tab key.

4. The audio outputs of Redrum have already been routed to the inputs of ECF-42, and routed to reMix.

5. Route the Redrum channel Gate outputs that have pattern data written on them to the inputs on the Merger section of the Spider (see Figure 17.31).

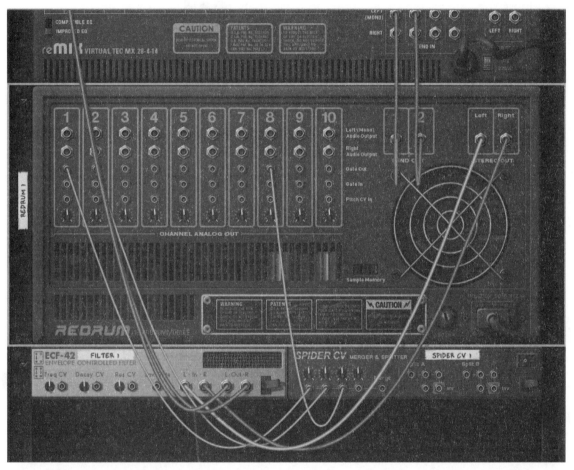

Figure 17.31 The Gate Outputs of Redrum channels 1, 2, and 8 have been routed to the Merging inputs of the Spider.

6. Route the merged output to the Envelope Gate input of the ECF-42.

7. Press the Tab key.

8. Select the Low Pass 24dB filter mode and set the ECF-42 parameters to the following values: Frequency 42, Resonance 91, Envelope Amount 22, Velocity 22, Attack 18, Decay 55, Sustain 43, and Release 127.

9. Press Play. Notice the robotic sounds that Redrum makes now, thanks to a little CV merging.

Now, let's take a stab at splitting. Note that the CV Splitter section of the Spider includes two input points, Point A and Point B.

Split Output 4 Is Inverted   Look at the Split section of the Spider. Notice that the abbreviation INV is displayed next to the bottom-right output (Output 4) of both Split A and B. This means that these outputs send inverted CV data to any CV input they are routed to. Be sure to pay close attention to this in the upcoming tutorial.

Try the following exercise:

1. Start a new Reason song and load it with a reMix, Dr. Octo Rex, and Redrum. Load a REX file and send it to its sequencer track. Write a drum pattern using channel 1 of Redrum, which is a kick drum sound.

2. Press the Tab key.

3. Create a Matrix and place it at the bottom of the Device Rack. Make sure that it is not connected to Dr. Octo Rex or Redrum.

4. Create a Spider CV Merger & Splitter below the Matrix. Route the Curve CV output of the Matrix to Split input A (see Figure 17.32).

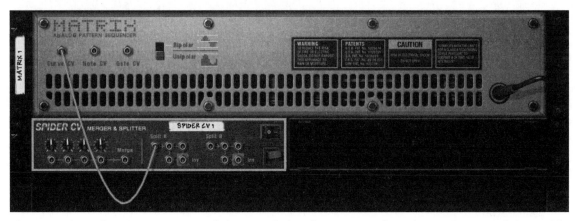

Figure 17.32 The Curve output of the Matrix has been routed to the CV inputs of the Spider's Splitter section.

5. Connect an output of Split A to the Pitch CV input of Redrum's channel 1. Increase the Pitch CV amount of channel 1 to its maximum setting (see Figure 17.33).

6. Route output 4 of Split A to the Filter Cutoff CV input of Dr. Octo Rex. You can also increase the amount of its CV pattern.

7. Press the Tab key.

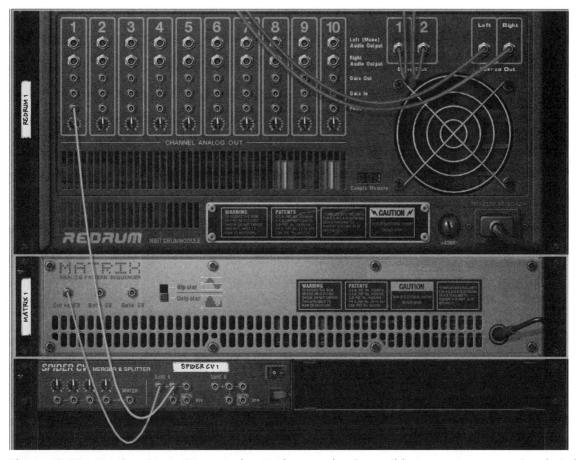

Figure 17.33 Routing Curve CV control to Redrum makes it possible to create some twisted pitch bends to the loaded drum sample.

8. Switch the Matrix from Keys to Curve mode and write in a quick curve pattern (see Figure 17.34).

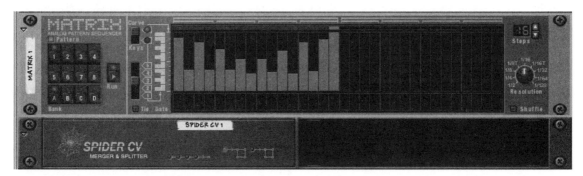

Figure 17.34 Write in a quick Curve pattern to modify the pitch of Redrum and the Filter Cutoff of Dr. Octo Rex.

9. Press Play. You should now hear the kick drum of Redrum pitch shift up or down according to the curve you drew. Also notice that the cutoff filter of

Dr. Octo Rex is modulating as well, but it's inverse to the effect of Redrum. So, if the pitch of Redrum is bending down, the cutoff filter of Dr. Octo Rex should be opening rather than closing.

Judging by the length of this chapter, the amount of possibilities with the effects in Reason should keep you happy and occupied for a long, long time to come. And you haven't even delved into the MClass Mastering Suite of effects yet! (You'll have to wait until Chapter 18 for that!)

18 The MClass Mastering Suite—Close Up

With the MClass devices, Reason 5.0 has four new high-quality effects that can be used anywhere in your song, separately or in any combination. Loaded together as the MClass Mastering Suite Combi (see Figure 18.1), they are ready to put those final touches on your song that can turn a good mix into an outstanding one.

When used for mastering (that is, to process the final output mix), the MClass Mastering Suite Combi should be inserted directly after the Reason hardware interface. The Combi loads with all four of its devices pre-routed internally. Additionally, the MClass Mastering Patches folder, which is located in the Factory Sound Bank, already contains several ready-made patches with names that suggest the effect they will have on your mixes (such as "Dance," "Hard Rock," and "Hip-Hop"). You'll find this incredibly handy if you want that instant gratification effect to complement your mix without having to tweak too much. Don't get me wrong, I'm a stone cold tweaker, but there are times when time and money become major factors when doing jobs and presets become much-needed items.

The MClass Mastering Suite contains an equalizer, a stereo imager, a compressor, and a maximizer (limiter). Feel free to open up an empty rack and create an MClass Mastering Suite Combi as you take a close look at each one of the MClass devices in turn.

The MClass Equalizer

The MClass Equalizer is the most advanced EQ ever to be included in Reason (see Figure 18.2). It boasts a combination of both shelving and parametric types of equalization, and its graphic display provides useful visual feedback while making adjustments to the equalization curve. When used as a mastering EQ, it is just what the doctor ordered for adding that extra bit of sizzle and that perfect bass curve to your final mix. It can be used as a mono or stereo effect, and it should be used as an insert effect.

Let's have a look at the MClass Equalizer parameters:

■ **Graphic Display**—Located to the left of the EQ parameters, the Graphic Display shows a real-time visual representation of the changes to the frequency response curve you make with the EQ controls.

Figure 18.1 Thanks to the MClass Mastering Suite, Reason 5.0 may be all you need to create your finished electronic music product.

Figure 18.2 The MClass Equalizer is the most advanced EQ ever to be included in Reason.

- **Lo Cut**—Cuts frequencies below 30Hz (by 12dB per octave). Helps to clean up the low end of mix, eliminates low frequency "rumble," and helps prevent "topping," whereby the Compressor or Maximizer is activated by subsonic frequencies, which can result in inefficient operation and audible "pumping" in the high end of the mix.

- **Lo Shelf**—Boosts or cuts frequencies below the frequency selected by the Frequency Control, which has a range of 30Hz–600Hz. The Gain Control determines the amount of boost or cut (+/–18dB). The Q Control determines the slope of the shelving curve, with higher values producing steeper curve slopes. Note that High Q settings cause a "bump" in the opposite cut/boost direction at the set frequency, which is visible on the Graphic Display.

- **Param 1 & 2**—Boosts or cuts frequencies around the frequency selected by the Frequency Control. The Gain Control determines the amount of boost or cut of the selected frequency, and the Q Control determines the width of the affected area around the selected frequency. The higher the value, the narrower the affected frequency range.

- **Hi Shelf**—Boosts or cuts frequencies above the frequency selected by the Frequency Control, which has a range of 3kHz–12kHz. The Gain Control determines the amount of boost or cut (+/–18dB). The Q Control determines the slope of the shelving curve, with higher values producing steeper curve slopes. Note that High Q settings cause a "bump" in the opposite cut/boost direction at the set frequency, which is visible on the Graphic Display.

Tune Your Ears for Effects   Let's face it, when you're starting to learn the intricacies of any effect, unless it's a very pronounced effect, like a distortion or flanger, it's difficult to comprehend what exactly is happening. I know that it took a while for me to truly understand and appreciate what a high-quality EQ/compressor/limiter would do for my mix. So here's a suggestion to better understand the concepts discussed here. Load one of your Reason songs, or possibly one of the demo songs, and insert an instance of the MClass suite between the Reason Hardware Interface and reMix. Then, load a preset that best complements the type of music you're playing. At this point, you should begin bypassing all of the effects except for the one you want to experiment and hear on its own. Repeat this with all of the other MClass effects. With a lot of practice, you should be able to hear and comprehend what each MClass effect is doing to the mix of your song, and more importantly, you'll learn how to make those effects work to the best of their abilities.

Tune your ears to the effects of Reason and you'll be on the way to becoming a much better producer.

MClass Stereo Imager

The MClass Stereo Imager is designed to help you achieve a deep, wide, and dazzling stereo image while preserving tight and defined bass in your mix (see Figure 18.3). It should be used as an insert effect, and must be used as a stereo effect (stereo in and

Figure 18.3 The MClass Stereo Imager can help you achieve a high end that really breathes and a low end that hits you where you live.

Figure 18.4 You can isolate and output just the frequency content above or below the X-Over Freq (crossover frequency) through the Separate Out.

stereo out). It will not convert a mono signal to stereo or add a false stereo effect to a mono signal. In addition to the stereo input and output on the rear of the device, there is also the Separate Out (see Figure 18.4), which will output just the Lo Band or the Hi Band, depending on the position of the Separate Out selector switch. The front panel X-Over Freq knob determines the frequency range of either band routed through the Separate Out.

The front panel controls for the MClass Stereo Imager are as follows:

- **Lo Width**—Determines the width of the stereo image for the Lo Band. Turning the knob counter-clockwise makes the stereo image narrower (more "mono"), and clockwise turns make the stereo image wider. When the knob is set in the center position, there is no change from the original signal. The Active LED is lit whenever the Lo Width knob is turned left or right of center, resulting in processing of the signal. For the Lo Band, it is generally more desirable to narrow the stereo image rather than to widen it, because the low frequency content in a mix tends to sound more defined and effective when mixed in the center.

- **Hi Width**—Determines the width of the stereo image for the Hi Band. Turning the knob counter-clockwise makes the stereo image narrower (more "mono"), and turning it clockwise makes the stereo image wider. When the knob is set in the center position, there is no change from the original signal. The Active LED is lit whenever the Hi Width knob is turned left or right of center, resulting in processing of the signal.

- **X-Over Freq**—Controls the crossover frequency between the Hi and Lo Bands. The crossover frequency is selectable between 100Hz and 6kHz. Frequencies below the crossover frequency are affected by the Lo Width setting, and frequencies above the crossover frequency are affected by the Hi Width setting.

- **Solo**—Allows you to monitor the Lo and Hi Bands separate from one another, for reference purposes. During standard operation the Solo mode should remain set to Normal. However, it's worth noting that by setting the Solo switch to Lo and the Separate Out switch to Hi, the MClass Stereo Imager can be used as a basic crossover filter, sending the Lo Band material through the Main Out and the Hi Band material through the Separate Out, allowing each band to be processed separately by other devices.

The MClass Compressor

The MClass Compressor is a single band compressor capable of stereo or mono operation and should be used as an insert effect (see Figure 18.5). Unlike its little brother, the COMP-01 (see Chapter 17, "Effects—Close Up"), the MClass Compressor also has Soft Knee and Adapt Release functions for easily achieving a natural and musical compression, as well as a Sidechain input.

Figure 18.5 The MClass Compressor incorporates high sound quality and professional features to produce a natural and musical compression.

Let's have a look at the MClass Compressor parameters:

- **Input Gain**—Controls the "drive" of the compression. Works together with the Threshold to determine how much compression is applied to the signal.

- **Threshold**—Sets the minimum input signal level at which compression will occur. When the input level is below the Threshold setting, the signal passes through unaffected. Compression begins whenever the input level exceeds the Threshold. The lower the Threshold is set (and the higher the Input Gain is set), the more compression results.

- **Soft Knee**—Without Soft Knee, signals that exceed the Threshold are compressed immediately at the set ratio. At higher compression ratios, this can be rather noticeable and unnatural sounding. Soft Knee smoothes this out by causing the compression to be applied more gradually, resulting in a more natural sound.

- **Ratio**—Determines the amount of gain reduction applied to the signals above the set threshold, and can be set from 1:1 (no reduction) to ∞:1 (infinite).

- **Gain Meter**—Shows the amount of gain reduction.

- **Solo Sidechain**—Allows monitoring of whatever is connected to the rear Sidechain input.

- **Attack**—Determines how quickly compression occurs when signals exceed the threshold. Higher Attack values result in slower compression response, allowing more of the signal to pass through unaffected before the onset of compression. This can be used to preserve the attacks of the sounds.

- **Release**—When the signal level drops below the set threshold, this determines how long it takes before the compressor lets the sound through unaffected. Short Release values can result in intense, "pumping" compressor effects, whereas longer values result in a smoother, more natural change in dynamics.

■ **Adapt Release**—When Adapt Release is activated, the Release knob is used to set the Release time for short peaks, with Release time being automatically increased whenever longer peaks occur.

■ **Output Gain**—Controls the output level of the Compressor and can be raised to compensate for the gain reduction caused by compression.

Understanding the Sidechain

As soon as anything is connected to the Sidechain In of the MClass Compressor, the compressor will no longer react to what is plugged into its main Audio Input (see Figure 18.6). You will still hear the main input signal, and compression will be applied to the main input signal, but this compression is actually triggered by the signal coming in through the Sidechain inputs. The Sidechain signal is never actually heard (unless the Sidechain Solo is activated).

Figure 18.6 Signal going into the Sidechain input triggers the compression, which is applied to the signal going into the main Audio Input.

The following simple exercise serves to demonstrate how the Sidechain works.

1. Start with an empty rack and create an MClass Compressor. It will be auto-routed to inputs one and two of the hardware interface.

2. Create a Malström under the MClass Compressor. It will be auto-routed to the stereo inputs of the compressor. Right-click on the Malström interface and select Init Patch in order to produce a pure sine wave and a perfect reference for this exercise. The Init Patch is rather quiet, so turn the Malström's volume knob up to about 3:00.

3. In the sequencer, set the Left and Right locaters for a two-bar loop. Sequence a three-note chord (somewhere between keys C5 and C6) on each of the first two bars of the Malström track. Make sure each chord sustains through all four beats of its bar (see Figure 18.7).

4. Below the Malström, create a Redrum and load a kick drum into channel 1 of Redrum. Do not connect Redrum's outputs yet.

5. Press Play on the Transport panel and make sure the click is off, because it will make this exercise even more annoying.

6. On the MClass Compressor, turn the Ratio up to 17:1 (very heavy compression) and turn the Threshold down to 9:00 (about −30dB). You will hear the gain reduction (the signal becomes quieter), and you will see this registered on the Gain meter.

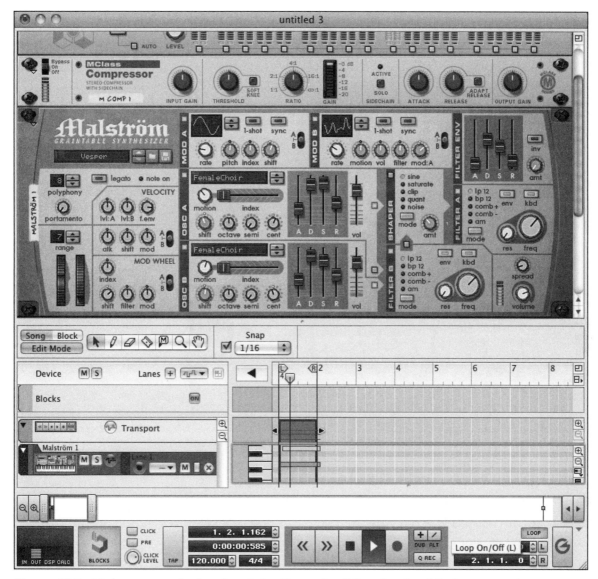

Figure 18.7   Make sure each chord sustains through all four beats of its bar.

7. Flip your rack around and connect Stereo Out L/R of Redrum to Sidechain In L/R of the MClass Compressor. You will immediately hear the Malström signal get much louder because it is no longer triggering the compressor, now that Redrum is plugged into the Sidechain (see Figure 18.8).

8. With Redrum channel 1 selected, click on Step buttons 1, 5, 9, and 13 so that you have a bass drum pattern playing. You will now hear the compressor pumping away, obviously triggered by the bass drum, but applying its compression to the main input signal, which is the Malström. You can monitor the Sidechain Input by clicking the Sidechain Solo button.

9. Press Stop on the Transport panel before your short high-pitched repetitive loop drives you nuts.

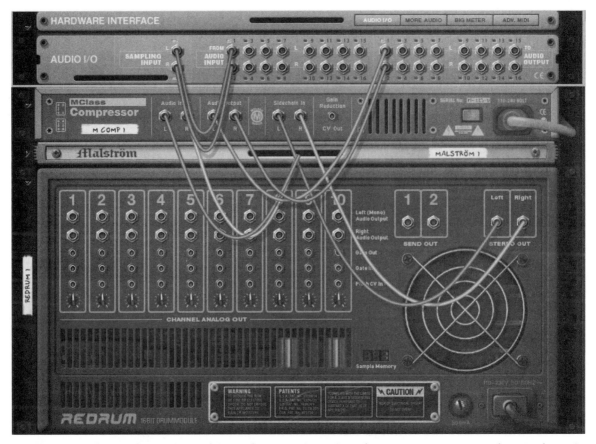

Figure 18.8 The Malström signal is no longer triggering the compressor, now that Redrum is plugged into the Sidechain.

So what can you learn from this exercise, and how can this knowledge apply to your mixes? Well, besides being a fairly clear and simple way to keep straight how the Sidechain functions, it can apply to the mixing process in several ways.

■ **Ducking**—The music in that car dealership ad starts rocking your radio, and when the announcer's voice comes in, the music drops down perfectly, just enough so that the voiceover is clear. Of course, if you were the engineer for this ad, you could fade down the music quickly when the voiceover starts, but a technique known as *ducking* can achieve this more smoothly and automatically. Basically, the main input signal of the compressor would be the background music mix, and the voiceover would be routed both to the Sidechain as well as to another channel on the mixer. That way the background music's gain would be reduced exactly according to the voiceover signal, thus naturally accommodating a clear presentation of the voiceover. Ducking could also be used in a mix to make a solo instrument stand out clearly.

■ **De-essing**—Sometimes you may get a vocal recording that would have been really great if only all the "s" sounds had not been so overly strong and hissy.

This obnoxious hissing, or *sibilance*, on vocals can often be diminished or removed with a process known as *de-essing*. To achieve this, you can split your vocal signal with the Spider Audio Merger and Splitter so that it is routed straight to the MClass Compressor's main input, and also through an equalizer into the Sidechain Input. Find that offending "s" frequency, and crank it up really loud with the EQ while cutting the lower non-offending frequencies, and you will hear the hissing diminish as the main input's compression is activated by the extra-hissy Sidechain Input. Note that when de-essing, you are likely to achieve the most desirable result by keeping your attack and release times on the short side.

■ **Unwanted pumping**—The previous Sidechain exercise demonstrates an extreme case of something that can happen in your mix, even when not using the Sidechain. Often when heavy compression is applied to an entire mix, loud kick drums and bass parts can cause high synth parts or washy, sizzling cymbals to pump in a manner similar to what happened in the exercise. Although a certain amount of this pumping effect can be desirable in some mixes, it can be distracting in others and not necessarily what you might have been trying to achieve. If you really want to squash that drum set or that mix but also want your high synths and cymbals to sizzle "pump-free," you might consider routing some of those sustained high-frequency elements outside the compressor, or compress them separately from heavy rhythmic elements that might affect them in an undesirable way.

Gain Reduction CV Out

Flip the rack around to see the CV Out. This output sends out a control voltage, which is directly related to the amount of gain reduction being applied by the compressor. This control voltage can then be used to modulate parameters of other devices, effectively allowing the compressor to work as an envelope follower.

Do Not Suffocate Your Mix   Compression is an indispensable tool in your mixing arsenal, and the MClass Compressor is a great sounding device and a step forward in compressor quality and functionality for Reason. However, it is not necessary to use it on absolutely everything! If your mix suffers from over-compression, you may find that it no longer breathes or sizzles and that it may actually lack punch. To avoid this problem, at several steps along the way during your mixing process, try bypassing your compressors and see if your mix sounds better or worse without them. You may wish to put on a CD of music in a similar style that you think sounds great for comparison during this process. Of course, more useful than any rules or guidelines are your own two ears and your own creativity!

MClass Maximizer

The MClass Maximizer is actually a special type of limiter known as a *loudness* maximizer, which is used to significantly increase the perceived loudness of a mix without risking hard-clipping distortion (see Figure 18.9). It should be inserted at the very end of the signal chain, between the final mixed output and the Reason hardware interface. Its front panel is detailed as follows:

- **Input Gain**—Use this control (not Output Gain) to set the overall volume of your mix. At high Input Gain settings, the Look Ahead mode or the Soft Clip function should be used in order to avoid the nasty sound of hard-clipping distortion. The range of the Input Gain control is +/–12dB.

- **Limiter On/Off**—Activates or deactivates the limiter section.

- **4ms Look Ahead**—Adds a four millisecond latency (or delay) to the sound coming out of Reason, which the Limiter uses to identify peaks in excess of the specified Output Gain before they occur, therefore allowing the necessary gain reduction to be applied transparently.

- **Attack**—Determines how quickly the limiting effect will be applied. If Look Ahead is activated and the Attack control is set to Fast, the Limiter achieves what is known as "brick wall" limiting, which means that no signal peaks over 0dB will pass.

- **Release**—Determines how long it takes for the Limiter to "open back up" and release its gain reduction after a peak occurs, once again allowing the signal to pass through unaffected.

- **Output Gain**—This control is normally set at 0, because I want my mix to peak as close to zero as possible without going over 0dB. Sounds over 0dB in the digital realm produce a very harsh and undesirable hard clipping distortion, so this control should not be used to boost the level of a mix. Rather, the Input Gain should be turned up if a louder sounding mix is what is desired.

- **Soft Clip**—Provides another form of 0dB brick wall limiting. Rather than attempting to limit the signal transparently, Soft Clip adds a warm, smooth tube-like distortion to the signal. Soft Clip may be used to eliminate the risk of hard-clipping distortion in cases where Look Ahead is either deactivated or being used with Mid or Slow attack settings, or it can be used simply to add some pleasing, subtle distortion to your mix.

- **Soft Clip Amount**—Determines the amount of soft-clipping distortion. If Soft Clip is active, brick wall limiting and some form of distortion will occur in the presence of loud signal. So if Soft Clip is active but the Soft Clip amount is set to zero, the distortion will still occur but will not be the warm, soft pleasing type of distortion but rather more like hard clipping, and probably not the sound you are going for.

- **Output Level Meter**—This meter offers more detail than the one included with reMix. The Peak setting shows a faster response to peaks, whereas the VU setting offers a more accurate average level than Peak mode.

Figure 18.9   The MClass Maximizer will make sure your mix does not get lost in the crowd!

With the recently increased popularity of loudness maximizers and maximizer plug-ins, the trend (especially in electronic music) is to get that mix sounding as loud as physically possible. Of course, when the DJ plays your track at the club, chances are you don't want it to sound way quieter (or "wimpier") than the tracks spinning before and after it. Overcoming this by increasing the perceived loudness of your mix is what the MClass Maximizer was designed for. Be aware, however, that there is something being traded in this process—dynamic range. That means that if your mix is super-squashed (with extreme maximizer or compressor settings), the difference between the loud and soft passages in your song will be diminished. Therefore, if you are trying to achieve a dramatic effect when the really rocking or aggressive part of your song kicks in, and you find that when it starts, it is no louder than the preceding "quiet" section, you may want to ease off the maximizer (or compressor) a bit and see if that reintroduces the "punch" you were looking for.

A Word About Professional Mastering   Using the MClass Mastering Suite Combi to master your song can yield very professional sounding results. However, if you are planning to have your CD professionally mastered by an audio mastering engineer, you should consider exporting two mixes—one with the MClass Mastering Suite on, and one with it bypassed. Audio mastering is an art unto itself, and an audio mastering engineer has devoted quite a lot of time and expertise to the perfection of this art (not to mention a sizeable amount of money to very expensive mastering gear). Additionally, a true audio mastering studio will have a monitoring setup with an accuracy far surpassing the average project studio, and it will contain the finest equipment specific to the art of audio mastering. Once you've added compression, EQ, and loudness maximizing to your final output mix, this processing cannot be removed later. So if you are planning to spend the bucks to have a professional audio mastering engineer master your

CD, feel free to export a mix that you have mastered for demo purposes and perhaps for conveying your intention to the mastering engineer, but give that mastering engineer the option to apply his or her expertise and specialized technology to your project by providing an unmastered mix as well.

As you can see, the MClass Mastering Suite is a powerful new toolbox for your Reason mixes. With practice, your mixes will soon soar to new heights of clarity and overall superb sound quality.

19 The Combinator—Close Up

If there were a single device created for Reason that adds more power to the application than any other, the Combinator would have to be it! In short, the Combinator (see Figure 19.1) allows you to combine multiple devices (all controllable by a single sequencer track), route them any way you like, and save the entire setup as a single patch. As you read through this chapter, you will discover how this seemingly simple concept offers limitless possibilities.

Keep 'Em Combinated

Reason includes numerous Combinator presets, which appear as Combi (.cmb) patches located in the Factory Sound Bank. Becoming familiar with these presets can help you determine which ones will be useful to you as you work on your projects, and should also provide inspiration and direction in creating your own Combi patches.

Combi patches can be divided into two basic types:

- **Effect Combis**—As you might guess, effect Combis are used to process sound, and do not contain any instruments with which to generate sound. The MClass Mastering Suite Combi (discussed in Chapter 18, "The MClass Mastering Suite—Close Up") is an effect Combi.

- **Instrument Combis**—These include sound-generating instrument devices, such as Subtractor, NN-XT, or Redrum, and can also contain effect devices. The only upper limits to the fatness of layered sounds that can be created in this way would be what your computer and your brain can handle!

A Guided Tour of the Combinator

Open a new document and create a Combinator. Take a look at the topmost panel of the Combinator (the part that still shows when the Combinator is folded) and note that, in addition to the usual Select/Browse/Save patch buttons, there is also a Bypass/On/Off switch like that found on Reason effect devices. Also included are input/output level meters, a MIDI note-on indicator, and an External Routing indicator, which will light up if you route audio or modulation output directly from any Combinator device to another device outside of the Combinator. The External Routing

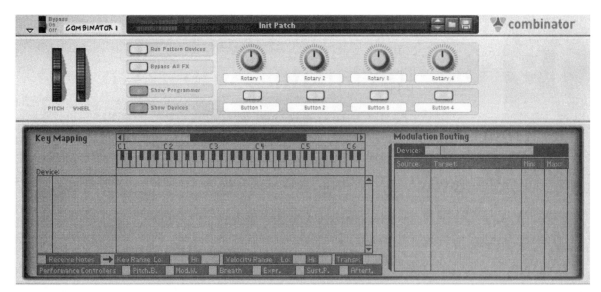

Figure 19.1 The Combinator allows you to create complex multi-device setups, which can be easily saved and loaded into any song.

Figure 19.2 The External Routing indicator alerts you to the presence of external connections, which will not be saved with the Combi patch.

indicator (see Figure 19.2) can be considered a warning indicator because it alerts you to the presence of external connections, which will not be saved with the Combi patch.

The Controller Panel

The Combinator's Controller Panel consists of the following elements:

- **Pitch Wheel**—Sends pitch bend info to all instrument devices contained in a Combi. Bend range is set individually in each instrument device's Range field.

- **Mod Wheel**—Sends modulation data to all instrument devices contained in a Combi. The effect of this modulation data is determined by the individual Mod Wheel assignments made within each instrument device.

- **Run Pattern Devices**—Starts or stops all pattern devices in a Combi, such as a Matrix sequence or a Dr. Octo Rex pattern. This button is automatically activated when you press Play on the Transport panel.

- **Bypass All FX**—Bypasses all effects devices included in a Combi, switching all insert effects to Bypass mode, and switching off all effects connected as send effects to a mixer device. This button will not affect effects already bypassed or turned off.

- **Show Programmer**—Shows or hides the Programmer Panel.

- **Show Devices**—Shows or hides all devices included in a Combi.

- **Rotary Knobs**—Can be assigned to control parameters in any devices included in a Combi. Rotary Knob control assignments are made in the Modulation Routing section of the Programmer Panel. Clicking on the label and typing in a name can customize Rotary Knob labels.

- **Button Controls**—Can be assigned to control any button-controlled parameters in devices included in a Combi. Note that the Button Controls switch between only two values, so if the device parameter you are controlling has more than two possible values (like an On/Off/Bypass switch or an LFO Waveform button), a Combinator Button control will only toggle between two of those values. As with the Rotary knobs, you can assign useful names to your Button Controls by clicking on the labels and typing away.

The Programmer

Now let's press the Show Programmer button and dive into the pretty blue screen, which is really the nerve center of your Combinator. The Programmer may look slightly daunting at first, but it is actually rather straightforward and not at all difficult to master (see Figure 19.3). It controls the following areas of functionality:

- **Key Range**—Controls the lowest and highest note that will trigger any selected instrument device in the Combinator. This parameter cannot be adjusted unless Receive Notes is active for the selected instrument device.

- **Velocity Range**—Controls the lowest and highest velocity that will trigger any selected instrument device in the Combinator. As with the Key Range, the Velocity Range cannot be adjusted unless Receive Notes is active for the selected instrument device.

- **Transpose**—Controls the pitch of a selected device within a Combi patch. The range is +/– 3 octaves.

- **Performance Controllers**—This section indicates which controller messages (pitch bend, modulation, and so on) received by the Combinator are passed along to the combined devices. For example, if you have a Subtractor in your Combi patch and the Pitch and Modulation controllers are selected, whenever you use those controllers via the Combinator, the same messages will be sent along to the combined device. In other words, everything is linked up and will work in combination with each other.

- **Modulation Routing**—Assigns any parameters of the selected device in the Combinator to any of the virtual Rotary or Button controls on the Combinator's Controller Panel. Unlike the Key Range and Velocity Range sections of the Programmer, the Modulation Routing section can control non-instrument devices (such as effects) as well as instrument devices like the NN-XT or the Subtractor.

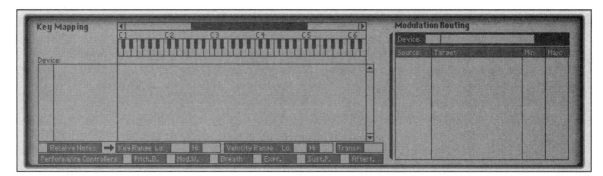

Figure 19.3 The Programmer controls Key Range, Velocity Range, Performance Controllers, Transpose range, and Modulation Routing for devices in a Combi.

Combinator Routing

Make sure that Show Devices is enabled. Then press the Tab key to flip your Device Rack around and take a look at the back of the Combinator (see Figure 19.4).

Figure 19.4 The rear panel of the Combinator, ready for routing.

Audio Connections

■ **Combi Input L/R**—Provides input for the Combinator and is used for effect Combis. In a Mastering Combi, you would likely have the outputs of your main reMix plugged into these inputs.

■ **Combi Output L/R**—Connects with any device outside of the Combinator, usually a mixer, or (in the case of Mastering Combi) the Reason hardware interface.

- **To Devices L/R**—Connects to the input of any device within the Combi. To Devices L/R is internally routed to Combi Input L/R.

- **From Devices L/R**—Connects to the output of a device (the last in a chain of devices or a mixer) within a Combi. From Devices L/R is internally routed to Combi Output L/R.

CV Connections

- **Gate In**—Allows the Combinator to receive Note On, Note Off, and Velocity information from the Gate CV output of another device, typically a Matrix or a Redrum.

- **CV In**—Allows the Combinator to receive Note Pitch information from another device, typically from the Note CV output of a Matrix.

- **Modulation Input**—Allows the Mod Wheel, Pitch Wheel, or any of the four Combinator Rotary controls to be modulated by CV.

- **Programmer CV Inputs**—These inputs are used to route the CV output of any Reason device to a specific parameter of a device loaded in a Combi patch via the Programmer. For example, you can have the filter section of an instance of the Subtractor loaded in a Combi patch modulated via an instance of the Matrix.

Now before you jump headlong into designing your first Combi patch, let's take a moment to look at another Reason device designed for use with the Combinator— the microMIX 6:2 Line Mixer.

microMIX

Want to mix and route some devices in your Combinator, but you don't need all the bells and whistles of reMix? Propellerhead has got you covered. Although reMix can be used in Combinator patches, the microMIX Line Mixer was created specifically for mixing device outputs within a Combi in cases where the more advanced capabilities of reMix may not be required. Although microMIX is tailor-made for use with the Combinator, it can, of course, be used for other applications anywhere in your Reason song, such as submixing large drum kits or for adding a few extra channels when your main reMix is filling up. It should be noted that in the Device Rack, this device is labeled "microMIX," but in the Create menu, it is referred to simply as "Line Mixer 6:2." Go ahead and create an instance of this bad boy so you can follow along.

Each of the six channels in a microMIX (see Figure 19.5) includes an output level control, a pan knob (which can be controlled externally via CV), a mute button, a solo button, one Auxiliary Send Level knob, and a customizable channel label, as well as a three-segment output level meter. Rounding out the front panel is the Master L/R knob, which controls the summed output level of all the channels in the microMIX; and finally you have the Auxiliary Return Level knob, which controls the level of the signal

Figure 19.5 The microMIX was designed with the Combinator in mind.

coming back from whatever effect device has been connected to the Auxiliary Send output of the microMIX.

Now flip your rack around to see the back of the microMIX (see Figure 19.5). The rear connections and controls on the microMIX are as follows:

- **Audio In L/R**—Connects the audio outputs of any audio device to the microMIX. When connecting the output of a mono device, the left input should be used.

- **Pan CV In**—Allows voltage control of the channel pan by other Reason devices.

- **Auxiliary Send**—Connects to the input of an effect device. When connecting to a mono-input device, use the left Auxiliary Send output.

- **Auxiliary Return**—Connects to the output of an effect device.

- **Auxiliary Pre/Post**—Allows you to choose whether the Auxiliary Send signal coming from each channel is sent to the effect device before it goes to the channel fader (Pre) or after the channel fader (Post). Using the Auxiliary Send in the Pre Fader position allows you to send signal to the effect device even if the individual channel output level controls are at zero, which might be especially effective when using a reverse reverb effect, for instance, where it would not be desirable to hear the original input (dry) signal.

- **Master Out L/R**—Self-explanatory and usually connected to the From Devices inputs within a Combi. Outside of a Combi, the Master Out will auto-route to the first available pair of inputs on the hardware interface or to another mixer.

Creating Your First Combi

Now that you have become acquainted with the theory and function of the Combinator, let's dive into some practice and create a Combi patch. If you have not already done so, start with an empty rack, add an instance of reMix, and then create a Combinator. The following performance-oriented tutorial should help you get comfortable with using the various features of the Combinator.

1. Click in the black space at the bottom of the Combinator (called the Holder) and notice the red insertion line (see Figure 19.6). This is where new devices will

be added to the Combinator. Note that the Holder is visible only when the Show Devices button is lit on the Combinator Control Panel. Create a microMIX within the Combinator.

Figure 19.6 The red insertion line (shown in dark grey here) indicates where a new device will be added to the Combinator.

2. Press Tab to flip the rack around and note that Combi Output L/R has been auto-routed to Channel 1 of reMix, and that Master Out L/R of microMIX has been auto-routed to From Devices L/R. Click in the "holder" space under microMIX to show the insertion line, and create an RV 7000 Advanced Reverb. Note that Auxiliary Send of microMIX is routed to the Audio Input L/R of the RV7000 and that the Audio Output L/R of the RV7000 is routed to the Auxiliary Return of microMIX (see Figure 19.7).

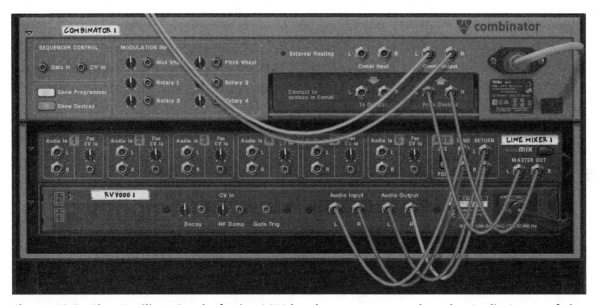

Figure 19.7 The Auxiliary Send of microMIX has been auto-routed to the Audio Input of the RV7000, and the Audio Output of the RV7000 has been auto-routed to the Auxiliary Return of microMIX.

3. Click in the Holder under the RV7000 and create a Malström. It should auto-route to Audio In 1 of microMIX.

4. Under the Malström, create a Matrix. Disconnect the Note CV and Gate CV connections. Then connect the Curve CV output of the Matrix to the Mod Wheel Modulation Input of the Malström (see Figure 19.8).

5. Under the Matrix, create a Subtractor, followed by another Malström.

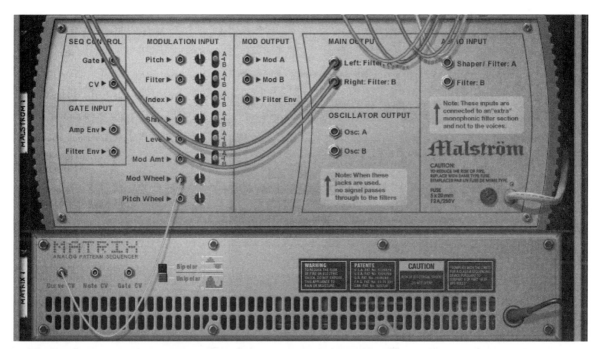

Figure 19.8 Connect the Curve CV output of the Matrix to the Mod Wheel Modulation Input of the Malström.

Now that your ingredients are in place, press Tab to flip the rack around so you can see the front of your devices (see Figure 19.9). Now choose some patches for your synths.

Figure 19.9 The devices are in place and ready to load some synth patches. Note that all of the devices are "folded" in order to fit them in the figure.

1. Open the Patch Browser of the first Malström and choose Redeath Bass from the Bass folder located in the Malström patches folder in the Reason Factory Sound Bank.

2. Open the Subtractor's Patch Browser and select Singing Synth from the MonoSynths folder located in the Subtractor patches folder in the Reason Factory Soundbank.

3. Open the Patch Browser of the second Malström and choose Verbless from the PolySynths folder located in the Malström patches folder in the Reason Factory Sound Bank.

Setting the Key Ranges

On the Combinator, click the Show Programmer button. Look at the Key Mapping section of the Programmer. On the far left, you will see a list of the devices in the Combi. As mentioned previously, the Key Range pertains only to instrument devices. Also, it can be adjusted only when the Receive Notes box is active for the instrument device.

The Key Range can be adjusted in a few different ways. Click on Malström 1 in the Combi Programmer Device List so that it is highlighted. You can click and hold on the Key Range Lo or Hi value fields and move your mouse up or down to adjust the lowest and highest notes that will trigger Malström 1. Alternatively, you can click and drag the markers at either end of the Key Range Bar to the right of Malström 1. You may have to use the scroll arrows above the keyboard display to see the end markers. Finally, you can drag the entire horizontal bar to the left or right, moving the whole key zone at one time.

For this tutorial, you are going to split your keyboard so that the lowest notes trigger your Redeath Bass patch (Malström 1), and the upper keys trigger a layered lead sound. The keyboard I happen to be using in the studio is a Radium61, which has 61 keys, so I have plenty of room for both bass and lead sounds. If you are using a controller with fewer keys, you will want to adjust your split appropriately, in a way that is comfortable to you. The main thing is to make sure Malström 1's key zone covers the lowest notes on your keyboard and comes right up to, but does not overlap, the key zone of your lead sound.

1. With Malström 1 selected in the Programmer Device List, click the right scroll arrow above the keyboard display, and hold it until you see the right end marker of Malström 1's Key Range. By default, the Key Range is set to cover the entire keyboard. Click on the end marker at the far right of Malström 1's horizontal bar and drag it to the left until it reaches G1. You have now set the High Key of Malström 1's key zone to G1 (see Figure 19.10).

2. Select Subtractor 1 in the Programmer Device List. Click the left scroll arrow above the keyboard display and hold it until you can see the left end marker of Subtractor 1's Key Range. Click and drag Subtractor 1's Low Key marker until it reaches G#1.

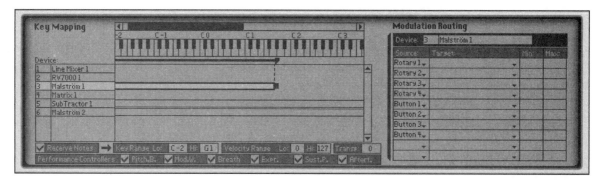

Figure 19.10 Click on the end marker at the far right of Malström 1's horizontal bar and drag it to the left until it reaches G1. You have now set the high key of Malström 1's key zone to G1.

3. Select Malström 2 in the Programmer Device List. Click and hold in the Key Range Lo value field and drag your mouse up until the value reads G#1. This is the same adjustment you made to Subtractor 1, done with an alternative technique. Now you have a perfectly split keyboard (see Figure 19.11).

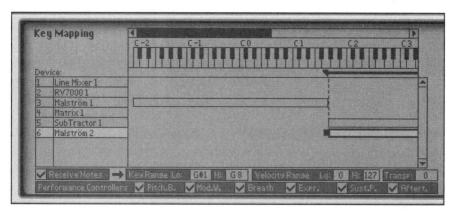

Figure 19.11 Set the Key Range Lo setting of Subtractor 1 and Malström 2 to G#1. The Key Range Hi setting for Malström 1 should already be G1. Now you have a perfectly split keyboard.

Before you continue with the next part of this tutorial, which will be setting the Velocity Range, some minor tweaks are in order. You may have already noticed that some of your signal levels are a bit out of hand, so on microMIX, turn Channel 2 Subtractor down to a value of 92, and turn the microMIX Master level down to 80. You could also reign in the Subtactor's level by inserting a compressor, but for the sake of simplicity, just turn the channel down a bit for now.

Your last little tweak before continuing on will be to add a bit of reverb. Turn up the Channel 2 Subtractor Aux Send to a value of 48 or so. Finally, give the Malström on Channel 3 a larger dose of 'verb by turning up the Channel 3 Aux Send to a value of 86.

Setting the Velocity Range

Okay, now you're ready to set the Velocity Range. Select Malström 2 in the Programmer Device List. Click in the Lo Vel (Low Velocity) field of the Velocity Range and drag your mouse up until you've set a value of 85. Notice the diagonal stripes that have appeared on the horizontal Key Range bar of Malström 2, which will be present any time there is a Velocity Range of less than 127. In this case, Malström 2 will not be triggered at velocities below a value of 85. You may wish to vary this number a bit depending on the feel of your controller keyboard. You want to hear the Subtractor alone when playing soft-to-medium velocities and to hear the additional layer of Malström 2's Verbless patch when striking the keys vigorously. This is a simple example, but hopefully it will stimulate your imagination to consider the many far-out possibilities for multilayered sounds the Combinator offers.

Run Pattern Devices

By now you may be asking, "What did he stick that Matrix in there for, anyway?" Why, just for a little added fun! Set the Matrix to Curve Edit Mode and draw in any old curve pattern that strikes your fancy. It's okay to leave the Steps and Resolution controls on the Matrix at their default settings (16 and 1/16, respectively). On the Combinator Control Panel, click the Run Pattern Devices button. Now play some low bass notes (below G#1) on your controller keyboard, and check out the modulation action on your Malström Redeath Bass sound. Once again, it's worth noting that Run Pattern Devices is also activated automatically when you press Play on the Transport panel, and it is deactivated when you press Stop. Also, you will notice when browsing Combinator patches that Combis containing pattern devices (such as Matrix or Thor) will contain [Run] at the end of their patch name.

Modulation Routing

The Modulation Routing section of the Programmer is where you can decide what the Rotary knobs and Button controls on the Combinator Control Panel will be doing. From a performance standpoint, this is most useful when you can control those Rotary knobs and Button controls with an external MIDI controller. I discuss how to do this (Reason makes it *super* easy) in detail in Chapter 20, "Automation." For now, let's concentrate on assigning the functions of the Rotary knobs and Button controls in the Combinator Programmer.

To assign a function to a Rotary knob or Button control, first highlight the device in the Programmer's Device List, which contains the parameter you would like to control. Then in the Modulation routing Section, select a parameter from the Target drop-down menu located to the right of the Rotary knob or Button control (Source) you are assigning. In this way, Rotary Knob 1, for instance, can control a different parameter for each device in the Device List simultaneously. In fact, it can control three parameters per device. Look at the bottom of the Source column of the Modulation

Routing section and you will notice that there are two Source fields, which are user-definable via a drop-down menu. Let's apply some of these controls to the Combi.

1. Highlight Malström 1 in the Device List. Note that it is now displayed in the Device field in the Modulation Routing section. Assign Rotary Knob 1 to control the Oscillator B Shift of Malström 1 by selecting Oscillator B Shift from the Target drop-down menu to the right of Rotary 1. Set the minimum value to –30 by clicking in the Min field and dragging your mouse down until the desired value has been selected (see Figure 19.12).

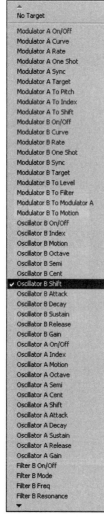
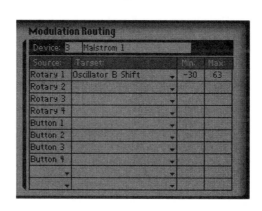

Figure 19.12 Assigning a Rotary knob in the Modulation Routing section of the Combinator Programmer.

2. Find Button 1 in the Source column of the Modulation Routing section. Click in the Target field to the right of Button 1 and select Shaper Mode from the drop-down menu. The Malström has five Shaper Modes, but because the Button controls can only toggle between two values, set the minimum value to zero and

the maximum value to 1. This will toggle between the Sine and Saturate Shaper Modes (Saturate being the default for the Redeath Bass patch).

3. Highlight Line Mixer 1 from the Device List. In the Target field to the right of Rotary 2, select Channel 2 Aux Send from the drop-down menu. Set the maximum value to 99 by clicking in the Max value field and dragging the mouse down until the desired value has been selected. Now the amount of reverb on your Subtractor sound can be controlled with Rotary Knob 2.

If you've made it through the relatively simple Combi patch we've just created together, you should have a good grasp of the basic building blocks you can use to make much more complex and imaginative Combis. The sky's the limit!

Uncombine/Combine

Before you leave your first Combi behind, if you think you might like to play with it later, make sure to save it by clicking on the Save Patch button (located to the right of Patch Browser button), and then try the following:

1. Make sure the Combinator is highlighted (with a light blue border) by clicking on it once, and then select Uncombine from the Edit menu. Alternatively, you right-click (Ctrl-click on the Mac) on the Combinator and select Uncombine from the pop-up menu. Now the Combinator is gone, but the devices it contained still remain, and the routing is intact except that the Master outputs of microMIX are now routed to reMix, as you might expect. Of course, you no longer have any Key Range or Velocity Range information.

2. While holding down the Shift key, click on microMIX, RV7000, and the Malström so that all three devices are highlighted with a light blue border. Now from the Edit menu, click Combine. Now you've got a new three-device Combi.

3. Click on the right or left edge of the Matrix located just below the Combinator and drag it into the Holder until the red insertion line appears (see Figure 19.13), and drop it there. The Matrix is now part of the Combi.

4. Now Shift-click on the remaining Subtractor and Malström so that they are both highlighted. Select Combine from the Edit menu, or right-click (Ctrl-click on the Mac) on either of the two highlighted devices, and select Combine from the pop-up menu. Now you've got a second Combinator.

5. Click on the right or left edge of the bottom Combinator and drag it into the Holder until you see the red insertion line, then let it go. The bottom Combinator has ceased to be, and its devices have been added to the first Combinator.

Figure 19.13 Drag the Matrix into the Combinator Holder.

As you can see, the Combinator is a dynamic part of constructing your Reason songs.

Select Backdrop—More Than One Way to Skin a Combi

The last stop on our Combinator tour is not really musical, but you may find it to be a fun feature. The Combinator is the only Reason device for which you can design and load your own skins. Look inside the Template Documents folder located in your Reason folder, and you will see a folder called Combi Backdrops. It contains a very useful explanatory Read Me file, as well as two Template Backdrop files. One is a JPEG, and can be loaded as a skin for the Combinator. The second file, Template Backdrop.psd, is a Photoshop document that contains everything you need to start designing your own Combi skins (image-editing software not included). If you don't have a program that can read Photoshop files, you can open Template Backdrop.jpg in any bitmap editor and add what you want to it. In either case, save your Backdrop files as JPEGs in the Combi Backdrops folder. Note that any JPEG you use should have a resolution of 754×138 pixels. In your Reason song, you can click on Combinator, and then choose Select Backdrop from the Edit menu. You will then be able to select a Combi Backdrop from among the JPEGs in your Combi Backdrop folder.

In Figure 19.14, you can see what I did with Photoshop and perhaps a little too much time on my hands.

Figure 19.14 Reason allows you to create your own Combi skins. Now you can see what all the buzz is about. Yes, it's the HONEYCOMBINATOR.

With that, you have come to the end of the introductory tour of the Combinator.

20 Automation

One of the great advantages of today's recording technology for any studio, virtual or hardware, is the capability to automate your mix. Automation means the capability to automatically control equipment by recording its movements. A good example of automation is a hardware mixer with motorized faders that are programmed to automatically move with the mix (also known as *flying faders*). Reason's automation can record the movements of nearly any device parameter, and those movements recur as you play back the song.

In this chapter, you'll learn to automate Reason's parameters. It's easy and fun.

Reason is simply one of the easiest programs to automate. Nearly any parameter in the Device Rack can be automated just by creating a device and making sure that it is armed to automate. You can then choose one of two ways to create your automation data.

One method of creation is *live automation*. It involves either using an external MIDI controller that is capable of sending out controller data that's read by the Reason sequencer and recorded as automation data, or using your mouse to move the controls on the Reason Devices in real-time. In either case, you are recording the same data in real-time.

Another method of creation is *drawn automation*. This method involves using the sequencer in Edit mode and drawing in Controller data, which is automation. You might recall that you did this back in Chapter 5, "The Reason Sequencer—Close Up." However, in this chapter, you are going to look at automation with the Pattern lane.

Let's look at both of these methods in detail.

Live Automation

Live automation is generally the first choice of most Reason users because it gives you a real-time, hands-on approach to channeling your creativity.

There are two ways to automate live in Reason:

- Using your mouse
- Using an external MIDI controller

Using the Mouse to Automate

If you do not have an external controller, you can use your mouse as a means of automating your Reason parameters. In this tutorial, you will automate a couple of reMix faders and knobs.

Before beginning, start with an empty rack and create an instance of reMix. Ready? Follow these steps:

1. Choose Edit > Create Track for Mixer 1. Note that the created sequencer track is armed to receive MIDI data (see Figure 20.1).

Figure 20.1 A new sequencer track called Mixer 1 has been created. Note that it's already set up to record automation data.

2. Press the Record button on the Transport panel to start recording.

3. As soon as the sequencer begins to record, select a reMix channel fader to automate and begin to make volume changes to it by clicking and dragging up and down with your mouse (see Figure 20.2). Notice that the Automation Override LED lights up to indicate that automation has been recorded and that a new part is being created on the Mixer 1 sequencer track.

Figure 20.2 Click and drag on any reMix channel fader to automate it while the sequencer is recording.

4. Press the spacebar again to stop recording. Notice the new data that has been written into the sequencer track and that a neon green framed box has been drawn around the reMix channel (see Figure 20.3).

At this point, you can begin to automate any additional reMix parameters.

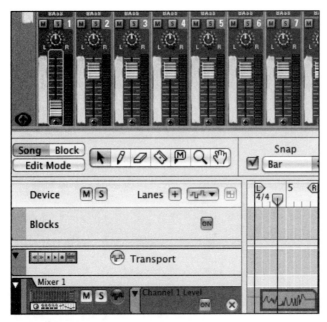

Figure 20.3 After recording your automation, it will be displayed within its sequencer track. Additionally, a framed box has been drawn around the automated parameter.

Clearing Your Automation At some point, you might decide that you want to clear the automation from a particular parameter and start over. You can do this by right-clicking on any automated parameter (or Control-clicking on the Mac) and choosing Clear Automation from the pop-up menu (see Figure 20.4).

Once you select this, the neon green box disappears, the newly created automation part on the sequencer track is gone, and you can now record new automation data.

Figure 20.4 Right-click on any automated parameter and choose Clear Automation to erase its automation data.

Using an External Controller to Automate

The use of an external controller is a great solution for those of you who find using a mouse to automate Reason parameters a bit cumbersome. An external controller can send MIDI controller data to any of the Reason devices, making it perfect for creating volume changes, synth parameter changes, and transport controls.

Reason includes control surface templates for most of the popular controllers on the market today, so chances are that if your controller has MIDI-assignable knobs and/or faders, they will already be pre-assigned to control some of the most common device parameters in Reason.

This tutorial shows you how to automate reMix by using the Axiom 25, which has eight knobs and sliders that send out MIDI controller information (see Figure 20.5). Reason already has built-in controller assignments for the Axiom, so the faders on the Axiom will automatically control channel faders 1 through 7 and the Master fader on reMix, whereas the knobs will control panning for channels 1 through 7 and Aux return 1.

Figure 20.5 The Avid Axiom 25 is a fantastic solution for creating automation data in Reason.

Make sure that you have started a new Reason song, created an instance of reMix, and created a sequencer track for reMix.

Additionally, make sure that you have set up your external controller as a MIDI input device by choosing it from the Keyboards and Control Surfaces page within the Preferences window (see Figure 20.6). This process is explained in detail in Chapter 2, "Installing and Configuring Reason."

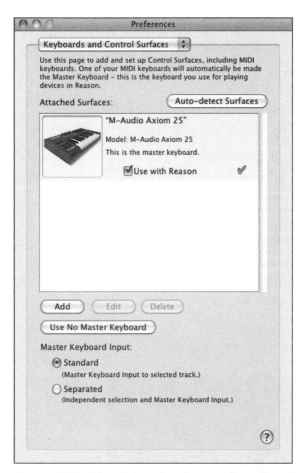

Figure 20.6 The Axiom has been selected as the master keyboard.

1. Press the Record button on the Main Transport. This will make the sequencer start recording.

2. As soon as the sequencer begins to record, begin to make volume changes to channel 1 by using the external controller's slider (see Figure 20.7).

Figure 20.7 In this example, the first slider on the Axiom is set to control channel 1 of reMix.

3. Press the spacebar again to stop recording. The automation data will be written on the reMix sequencer track, and there will be a neon green framed box around the channel 1 fader (see Figure 20.8).

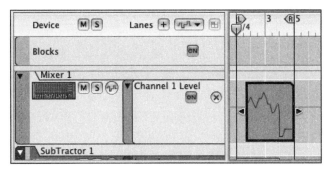

Figure 20.8 The automation data has now been recorded onto the reMix sequencer track.

It's pretty nifty how Reason already has presets that work great with several of the most popular controllers. But what if your controller has no corresponding preset in Reason? Or what if Reason does have preset controller assignments for your controller, but you want to make different assignments to suit your individual needs? Good news—Reason makes this custom assignment so easy you will be surprised.

Once again, make sure that you have set up your external controller as a MIDI input device by choosing it from the Keyboards and Control Surfaces page within the Preferences window.

1. Start with an empty rack. Create a reMix, and then create a Malström. The Malström sequencer track should be armed to receive MIDI input.

2. Right-click (Ctrl-click Mac) on the Filter Env A fader and choose Edit Remote Override Mapping from the pop-up menu.

3. In the Edit Remote Override Mapping window, check the Learn From Control Surface Input box. Move the fader or knob on your control surface with which you would like to control Filter Env A, and you should see the Control Surface Activity display flash. Now click OK.

4. Move that same knob or fader on your control surface, and you will see that the Filter Env A fader also moves. How easy was that!

Another way to do this is to select Remote Override Edit mode from the Options menu, and then click on the device you want to control. All parameters that can be controlled with an external MIDI controller will be marked. Those parameters that have not been assigned to a MIDI controller will be marked with blue arrows, and those that have already been assigned to a MIDI controller will be marked with yellow knob icons. In either case, you can add or change remote control assignments as you did in the preceding tutorial by right-clicking (Ctrl-clicking on the Mac) on a parameter and choosing Edit Remote Override Mapping from the pop-up menu.

Surface Locking

Surface Locking allows you to specify that a MIDI control surface will always control parameters of a Reason device, even if that device is not set to receive MIDI input in the Track List. When a MIDI control surface is locked to a device, it can control the parameters of the device, but it cannot be used to *play* the device. Therefore, the master keyboard cannot be locked to a device because it would no longer be able to play any devices. If you want to lock your master keyboard to a device, you must first choose Use No Master Keyboard from the Keyboards and Control Surfaces page in the Reason Preferences window.

Locking a MIDI control surface to a device is quite easy. Simply right-click (Ctrl-click on the Mac) on the device you want to control and select Lock To (your control surface name) from the pop-up menu. If you do not see this option, it is because either you have no MIDI control surfaces connected to Reason, or because you have only one control surface connected and it has been designated as the master keyboard. Note that you can lock several control surfaces to a single device if you want.

To unlock a device, right-click (Ctrl-click on the Mac) on the device and deselect the Lock To item by clicking on it in the pop-up menu.

Which Controller Is Right for You?   After reading through this tutorial, you might find yourself wanting to get an external controller for your studio. You'll be happy to know that there are many affordable solutions at your local music instrument shop.

In order to select the right controller, you should first decide whether you want to purchase a controller with knobs, faders, or both. They can all be used to automate Reason's device parameters, but you might find controlling reMix's faders with controller knobs a little confusing.

My advice is to purchase an external controller that has both knobs and faders. At around $250 street price, the UC-33e controller from Evolution (see Figure 20.9) is one solution. It is a USB device, so there is no need for additional MIDI inputs to your computer.

There are of course many other external controllers to choose from, but it comes down to a question of how much money you are willing to part with. Visit your local music instrument shop for more information, or possibly try some online resources such as Harmony Central (www.harmony-central.com).

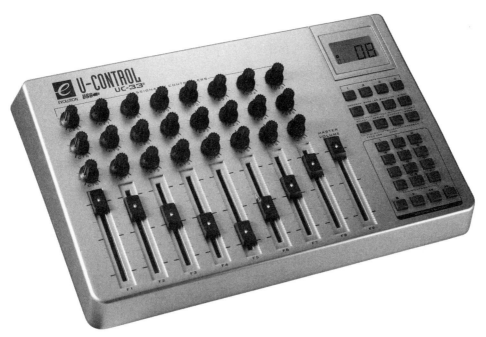

Figure 20.9 The UC-33e by Evolution is an external controller that has both knobs and faders for use with Reason.

Automation Override

Once you have written in your live automation data, you might want to either add more automation data to the same parameter or redo it entirely. There are two ideal ways to do this. One way is to switch to Edit mode and use the editing tools of the Sequencer toolbar to redraw and erase automated parameters. This method is covered later in this chapter.

The other way to edit your live automation data is to use the Automation Override function, which is found in the Transport panel of the sequencer (see Figure 20.10).

Figure 20.10 The Automation Override is used to overwrite already-written automation data.

The Automation Override function makes it possible to replace an entire automation movement or to simply add to an existing one. There is also a Reset button, which is used to make the previous automation active again while still keeping the newly recorded automation up to that point.

You can see for yourself how to use the Automation Override by performing the following exercise. Get ready by starting a new Reason song and creating an instance of reMix and an instance of Subtractor.

1. Start by recording a quick automation of the Subtractor's Modulation Wheel with either your mouse or a MIDI controller. Use the previous tutorials as examples if you are unsure how to do this.

2. Once the automation data has been recorded, press Stop, and you should see it in the Subtractor sequencer track (see Figure 20.11). Press Play to view the automation data playback.

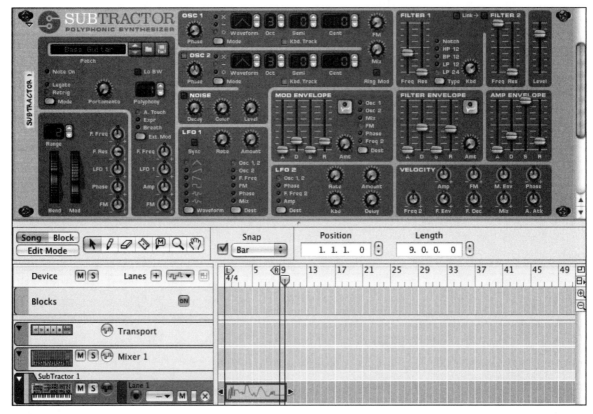

Figure 20.11 The Modulation Wheel has been automated. Note the neon green frame around the Modulation Wheel.

3. Press Stop twice to go back to the beginning of your sequence. Press Record to begin recording a new automation.

4. Record a new automation performance of the Modulation Wheel and take note that the Automation Override indicator is lit up, which means that new automation data is being recorded.

5. About half way through the automated sequence, press the Automation Override button and notice the previously recorded automation has become active again and is controlling the Modulation Wheel.

6. Press Stop and you should see your new and old automation data displayed in the sequencer track. Press Play to verify.

That pretty much covers live automation. Next, you'll take a look at drawn automation.

Drawn Automation

Another way of automating Reason's parameters is by manually drawing the automation into the Reason sequencer. This can appear to be a little tedious at first, but it is very helpful for correcting or modifying any previously written automation data.

Drawing Automation in the Controller Lane

In this tutorial, you will automate the individual parameters of the Subtractor by drawing automation in via the Reason sequencer. Before you begin, start a new Reason song, and then create a reMix and a Subtractor. It's also a good idea to quickly write in a sequence so you can hear the changes as they are being written.

1. Click the Switch to Edit Mode button found in the upper-left corner of the sequencer.

2. Click the Maximize Sequencer Window button. You can stretch and shrink the Note and Velocity lanes to your liking.

3. Click on the Track Parameter Automation button, which will display a pop-up menu of almost every controller that can be displayed and automated (see Figure 20.12).

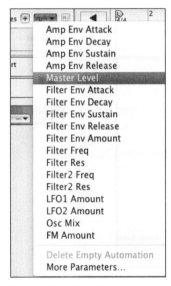

Figure 20.12 Every parameter of the Subtractor is available to automate. If this is your first time, try an easy parameter, such as the Master Level or the Filter Frequency.

4. Choose Master Level and the sequencer will display the Master Level controller (see Figure 20.13).

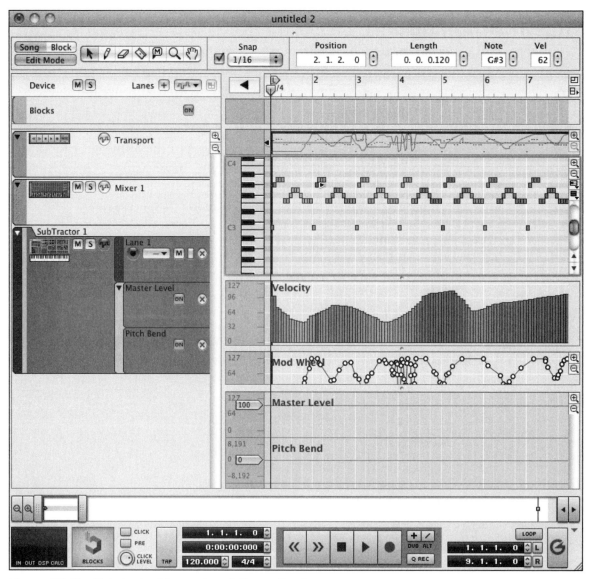

Figure 20.13 This is the Master Level Controller lane.

5. Select the Pencil tool and draw in a part by clicking and dragging as long as you want the automation to occur. Then draw in some automation data (see Figure 20.14).

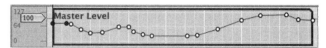

Figure 20.14 Draw in some automation data for the Master Level parameter. Note that you have to draw in a part first before you can draw in the automation. In this example, I drew in a part between the left and right locators.

6. Click on the Restore Sequencer Window button to restore the view of the Device Rack.

7. Click on the Switch to Arrange Mode button.

8. The Subtractor Master Level slider will have a neon green framed box around it. Press Play on your sequencer and you will see the slider move up and down to match the movements of the automation you drew in. You'll also see a new lane on the Subtractor sequencer track.

Keeping It Clean   After your automation has been recorded or drawn in, you may find it to look a little messy from all of the automation points. This is where the Automation Cleanup function found in the Tool Window can come in handy. Simply select the automation data you want to tidy up, and then select Automation Cleanup function found in the Tool Window. Set your desired amount of cleanup, click on the Apply button, and that's that.

Automating the Pattern Lane

The Pattern lane is used to write in automation data for the Pattern section of the Matrix and Redrum, which are pattern-driven devices (see Figure 20.15).

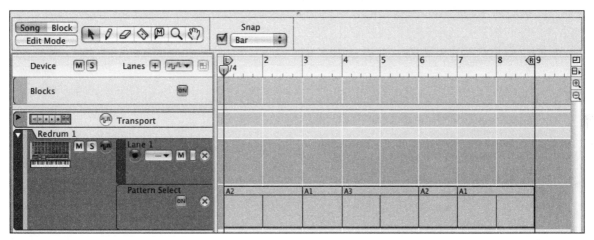

Figure 20.15 The Pattern lane is used to automate the changing of patterns for the Matrix and Redrum.

The next tutorial shows you how to draw in pattern data to automate the Pattern section of Redrum. This can be done from either Arrange or Edit mode, so I'll keep it in the Arrange mode for this example. Before beginning, take a minute to start a new Reason song, and create a reMix and a Redrum. Although it's not necessary, you might also want to load up a Redrum kit and create a few patterns (refer back to Chapter 7, "Redrum—Close Up," for details on this).

1. With the Redrum sequencer track selected, click on the Create Pattern Lane button in the sequencer. This will create a separate lane just below Lane 1.

2. Set the Snap pull-down menu to Bar because this will allow you to write in automation that is one bar in length at a time.

3. Select the Pencil tool and note that the Select Pattern dialog box has appeared near the upper-right corner of the sequencer tool bar. Also note that Pattern A1 appears by default. Draw in a pattern in the Pattern lane at bar 1 (see Figure 20.16).

Figure 20.16 Use the Pencil tool to draw in your first pattern change. Note that the pattern data extends much farther than the first bar.

4. Click on the pattern pop-up menu located in the upper-right corner of the sequencer toolbar and choose A2 (see Figure 20.17).

5. Navigate your mouse to bar 2 in the Pattern lane and click to write in a bar of pattern A2 (see Figure 20.18).

Automating Live Pattern Changes

As you know, nearly any parameter in any Reason device can be automated live, and this definitely includes the Pattern section of the Matrix and Redrum.

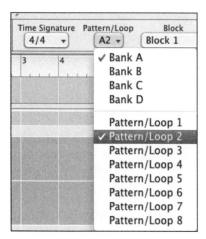

Figure 20.17 The Pattern/Loop pop-up menu is where you select the other available patterns.

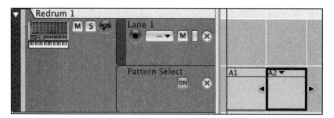

Figure 20.18 Write in a bar of pattern A2.

Try the following exercise:

1. Using the previous tutorial, clear the automation from the Pattern section of Redrum.

2. Select the Selector tool and press the Record button to start recording pattern changes. Pattern A1 should already by playing.

3. While recording, click on Redrum's Pattern A2 button on the downbeat of bar 2. As Pattern A2 begins to play at bar 2, the sequencer track should now reflect that it has recorded a pattern change.

4. Stop the sequencer.

Once the pattern changes have been recorded, you can keep them as is. You can also redo them by drawing them in with the Pattern lane.

A Quick Way to Switch Patterns Select a pattern in the Pattern lane of the sequencer and you'll see a little pull-down menu next to the name of the pattern. Click on this menu to switch the selected pattern to another one (see Figure 20.19).

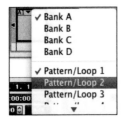

Figure 20.19 If you want to change up a drawn in pattern for a different pattern, just click on the pop-up menu that appears next to the name of the selected pattern in the sequencer.

In this chapter, you learned just about all there is to know about automation within Reason. If you are a seasoned DAW user, you'll probably agree that automating within Reason is much easier than it is with almost any other program out there.

Next, it's on to synchronization!

21 ReWire

You can incorporate the creativity and sounds of Reason into your own virtual studio environment by using a supplied Propellerhead technology known as ReWire. Included with Reason, ReWire gives you the ability to internally synchronize Reason with any other MIDI sequencing/audio recording software that supports it.

Although this is not a new concept to experienced virtual studio musicians, ReWire offers two key benefits that make it a unique technology. With ReWire, you can

- Synchronize two programs with sample-accurate precision.

- Route the virtual outputs of the rewired program into the virtual mixer of the host application. This makes it possible to then internally mix the two programs together within one mixing environment.

Synchronization

Before delving too deeply into the ReWire chapter, you should first have an understanding of what synchronization is and how it works.

Synchronization is the capability to make Reason play at the same time and tempo as another device. Additionally, synchronization makes it possible for Reason and another device to stop, start, and locate different song positions together. This is a great feature if you are a live musician looking to use Reason alongside your rig of drum machines and external hardware sequencers. Although a somewhat simplified definition, it's one that is probably sufficient for most Reason users. Aside from the capabilities offered by ReWire, synchronization is not one of Reason's most versatile features. Reason is meant to be an all-in-one standalone application. But Reason is capable of syncing with other non-ReWire ready programs, as well as external MIDI gear. To find out more, read on.

Different Synchronization Formats There are many synchronization formats found in other DAW applications. Although they serve the same basic purpose, each format has been created in order to cater to the needs of a specific audience.

One of the most common sync-related terms you will hear is *SMPTE timecode*. SMPTE is a sync format developed and implemented by the Society of Motion Picture and Television Engineers for use in video and film. SMPTE timecode has three types or "flavors," that you'll read about in a minute.

Even though you don't learn about most of the different sync formats in this chapter, here is a list of commonly known formats that you might hear about from time to time:

- **LTC (Longitudinal Time Code)**—A timecode format derived from SMPTE that is recorded onto the audio track of a video deck or a multi-track recorder.

- **VITC (Vertical Interval Time Code)**—Another SMPTE-based format in which the timecode is recorded onto a video signal in the first few lines of the picture, which is generally not visible.

- **MTC (MIDI Time Code)**—Another SMPTE-based format in which the time is transmitted via MIDI outputs found on many moderately priced MIDI interfaces or hardware based digital multi-track recorders.

- **Word Clock**—A digital-based timecode used with hardware peripherals that support digital formats, such as AES/EBU, S/DIF, and ADAT lightpipe.

MIDI Clock

The synchronization that Reason supports is called *MIDI Clock*. This form of synchronization functions in much the same way as a metronome—its purpose is to synchronize the two devices by way of sending tempo-controlled information from one device to another. MIDI Clock generates and sends what are called *pulses per quarter note* (PPQN) via a MIDI cable. By default, MIDI Clock generates 24 evenly spaced PPQNs, of which the total number of PPQNs per minute is ultimately decided by the assigned tempo of a song. For example, a song that is playing at 60BPM (beats per minute) sends approximately 1,440 PPQN per minute (or one pulse every 41.67 milliseconds). If you were to double the tempo to 120BPM, MIDI Clock would generate 2,880 PPQN per minute (or one pulse per every 20.83 milliseconds).

There are two basic devices in a MIDI Clock synchronization setup:

- **Master**—This is the device that sends the sync data and acts as the "leader" of the two devices. The master device sends a MIDI Start message to the receiver to initiate sync. It also sends a MIDI End message to stop sync. Additionally, a master device must send a Song Position message to the receiver to have it follow the master from within a specific point in a song.

- **Slave**—This is the device that receives and interprets the sync data from the master and follows it.

How Does ReWire Work?

ReWire is an internal synchronization technology shared between two programs within one computer. However, unlike the complications you may encounter with standard sync setups, you will find that using ReWire is easy and straightforward because there are no specific parameters to adjust when using two programs that support ReWire. You just need a ReWire master and a ReWire slave to make it work.

The ReWire master (a program such as Pro Tools or Logic) sends synchronization information, including transport functions and tempo/time signature information, to the slave program. The ReWire slave then reads this information and reacts in the blink of an eye, thanks to the wonders of sample-accurate timing.

To show you how tight sample-accurate sync is, consider this example. As discussed earlier in this chapter, SMPTE timecode has a standard resolution of 30 frames per second, which mathematically works out to 120th of a second, or 367 samples. The waveform displayed in Figure 21.1 is represented in samples and reads from left to right. At the right side of the figure, you will see that the selected portion of this waveform is positioned at approximately 367 samples. This is precisely how long it would take before SMPTE timecode would lock up and sync.

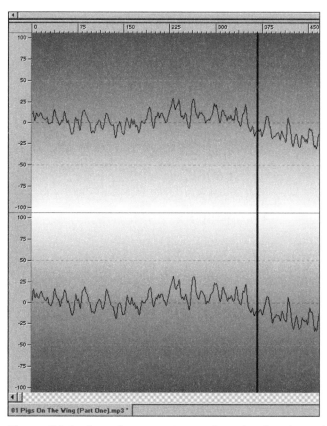

Figure 21.1 Sample accurate synchronization is as tight as it gets.

Sample-accurate timing calls for synchronization to occur within *1-2 samples* after playback of the master device. Look at Figure 21.1 again, and you will see that sample-accurate timing is far superior to any other method of synchronization.

The ReWire slave is the program that reads the synchronization information and follows the lead of the ReWire master. A good example of a ReWire slave program is Reason.

Additionally, the ReWire master receives the virtual audio outputs of the ReWire slave program and routes these signals to its own virtual mixer. In the case of Reason, there are 64 individual outputs that can be routed to its ReWire master application. This function is referred to as *audio streaming*.

Keep an Eye on Your CPU   ReWire is a fantastic technology that will certainly become a permanent fixture in your virtual studio environment for years to come. Keep in mind, though, that running two programs together such as this can lead to CPU overloads and audio dropouts. So, keep an eye on the CPU meter in your ReWire master program.

ReWire Tutorials

Now it's time to learn how to use ReWire with other DAW (digital audio workstation) programs. Throughout the rest of this chapter, you'll find tutorials for using Reason with most of the popular ReWire host applications via ReWire. Before you begin, it should be noted that the order of the steps in these tutorials is very important. The most important thing to remember is that you always start the DAW program (the ReWire master) and then Reason (the ReWire slave) comes second. When you are done recording, you will quit in reverse order—Reason first and the ReWire master second.

Using ReWire with Cubase 4

Steinberg's Cubase VST (Mac/PC) was the first program to integrate ReWire into its applications, so it seems only appropriate to begin with Cubase 4 (see Figure 21.2).

Make sure you are using the built-in song for Reason so you can follow along.

1. Launch Cubase and create a blank project.

2. Navigate to the device's pull-down menu and select Reason ReWire. The ReWire window will pop up (see Figure 21.3).

3. In the ReWire window, you will see that Cubase 4 can activate up to 64 individual channels of ReWire. This can lead to some extremely complex routing, with both virtual effects and synths. Assuming this is your first time using ReWire, this example is simple and just uses Reason's main mix. Activate the first pair of ReWire channels (called Mix L and Mix R) by clicking on the dark green bars located in the middle of the window.

Figure 21.2 Cubase is a DAW built on legacy and functionality that meets the recording needs of any musician.

Figure 21.3 The Reason ReWire window in Cubase is where you select which ReWire outputs will be routed to Cubase 4.

4. Close the ReWire window. Open the Cubase mixer by pressing the F3 key on your keyboard. Notice that a new stereo channel has been opened. Also notice that the track classification logo is different from the logo on your mixer's other tracks (see Figure 21.4).

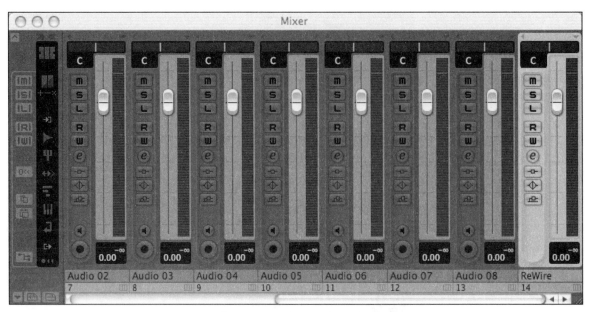

Figure 21.4 Cubase creates a specific ReWire channel on its virtual mixer.

5. Launch Reason. Once it has launched, look at the Audio Out device in the Reason Device Rack. Notice that Reason is now set to ReWire Slave mode, which means that Reason will follow or chase to Cubase. Also notice that the tempo of Reason's built-in song is set to the same tempo as Cubase.

6. Press Play in either Reason or Cubase. Switch over to Cubase. On the mixer, you should now see the active ReWire channels lit up with joy. The Reason mix is playing straight through it, as shown in Figure 21.5.

7. Press Stop.

8. Should you want to quit Cubase and Reason, remember to quit Reason first, followed by Cubase. If you try to quit Cubase first, an alert window will pop up to remind you.

Additionally, Cubase can also trigger the individual instruments and real-time effects of Reason via MIDI through ReWire.

Make sure that you are using the built-in song for Reason so you can follow along.

1. Following the steps in the previous tutorial, activate the ReWire channels in Cubase and launch Reason.

2. In Cubase, create a MIDI track in the Project window. Make sure that the MIDI track is record-enabled by clicking on what looks like a Record button on the track (see Figure 21.6).

3. Click on the Out pull-down menu of the MIDI track, and you will see a long list of routing possibilities, including all of the active devices in Reason. For this

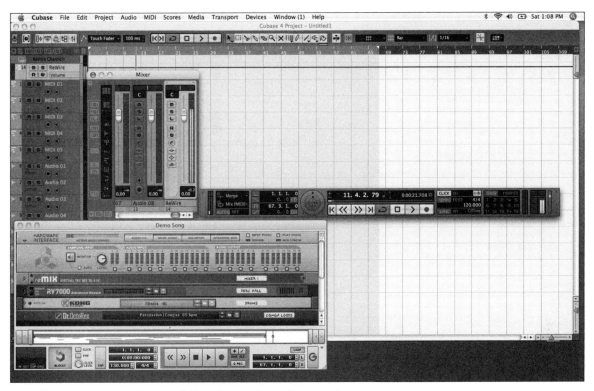

Figure 21.5   Reason is now following Cubase in sample-accurate sync.

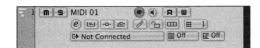

Figure 21.6   Create a MIDI track in Cubase and make sure that it is record-enabled.

example, choose the Reason Drums option. This will give you access to Redrum (see Figure 21.7).

4.   Press the C1 key on your MIDI keyboard. This should trigger the first Redrum channel, which is typically a kick drum.

5.   You can now begin to sequence in Cubase using Redrum as your drum machine.

For More Info   Many DAW applications are covered throughout this chapter. You will be happy to learn that Course Technology's *Power!* series has books dedicated to most of these programs.

For example, if you want to know more about Ableton Live, you can read *Ableton Live 8 Power!* by Jon Margulies. If you want to know more about SONAR, pick up *SONAR 8 Power!* by Scott Garrigus.

Additionally, Course offers a book that's completely dedicated to using Rewire, called *Rewire: Skill Pack* by G.W. Childs.

To see what else is available, visit www.courseptr.com.

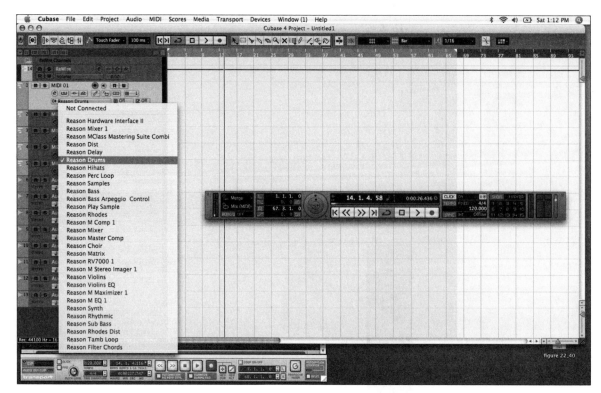

Figure 21.7 Set the output of the MIDI track in Cubase to Reason Drums in order to trigger Redrum.

Two Monitor Heads Are Better Than One   Having two monitors can be really helpful, especially when using two applications synced together via ReWire. If you decide to go the two-monitor route, here are some tips.

First, you need a second monitor that supports a pixel rate equal to or better than the pixel rate of your primary monitor. For example, if your primary monitor can display a 1024×768 pixel resolution, make sure your second monitor does the same. It will save you a lot of eyestrain and headaches when switching back and forth. Also make sure that both monitors support the same color depth.

Secondly, you need a video card that supports dual monitors (or *dual heads*, as they are called). This is more affordable than it used to be, with dual-monitor cards available for around $100. Make sure to get a good brand name, such as Matrox or MSI.

If you're on a newer Apple computer, such as an iMac, you'll find that they already have a second monitor output on the back.

After you have your dual monitor setup, you'll wonder how you ever lived without it.

Using ReWire with Logic Studio (Mac Only)

Logic Studio (Mac only) is without a doubt the most complex of all the MIDI sequencers/audio recording programs (see Figure 21.8). Purchased by Apple Computer in 2002, Logic is the flagship program for Apple's new standard in digital audio, called *CoreAudio* (see Chapter 2, "Installing and Configuring Reason," for more details). Logic is the choice software for musicians who want to stay true to the Mac platform and be able to incorporate different technologies into one lean, mean, music machine.

Figure 21.8 Logic Studio is for those who appreciate every nuance MIDI has to offer.

1. Launch Logic. The New Window will pop up asking you how you would like to start using Logic. Select Empty Project.

2. Once a new project has launched, Logic will then ask you what kind of track to create first. In this case, select one External MIDI track and click Create (see Figure 21.9).

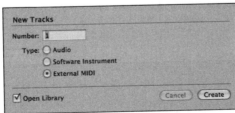

Figure 21.9 Have Logic create an External MIDI track, which will be used to trigger Reason devices later in this tutorial.

3. Navigate your mouse to the bottom of the Project window and select Mixer.

4. Once the mixer has launched, navigate to the Options pull-down menu of the Mixer (not the program, the Mixer) and select Create New Auxiliary Channel Strips.

5. Once selected, a new window will pop up asking you what kind of Aux Channel to create. As this is a basic tutorial, let's keep it simple, so set this window to the following settings: Number: 1, Format: Stereo, Input: RW: Mix L/R, Output: Output 1-2 (see Figure 21.10). Click Create.

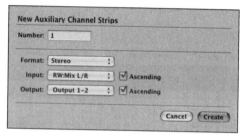

Figure 21.10   Reason ReWire channels are routed to the Auxiliary Channel Strips of Logic Studio.

6. Launch Reason. Assuming that the Demo Song has been opened, press Play and you should now see Logic and Reason rewired together (see Figure 21.11).

Figure 21.11   Reason and Logic are now in ReWire synchronization.

At this point, you have the audio routed correctly, so let's quickly review how to get MIDI working.

1. As you'll recall, you had Logic create an External MIDI track when the program was first launched. Assuming that track is still active, navigate to the right side of the Logic interface, which is the Browser section of the program.

2. Click on the Library option and you should now see three options to choose from on the left side of the browser: GM Device, Other Objects, and Reason.

3. Click on the Reason option and all of the Reason devices that are currently open in the Demo Song. Click on Drums. The External MIDI track should now change to a track with an icon that looks like a cross between audio and MIDI called "Drums" (see Figure 21.12).

Figure 21.12 Routing MIDI to Reason via Logic is a snap with the Browser.

4. Assuming your MIDI keyboard is connected, you should now be able to trigger the Redrum samples via Logic.

Suffice it to say, Logic is a bit more complicated than your run-of-the-mill MIDI sequencer, but many professional musicians rely on its solid feature set and musical potential.

Using ReWire with Digital Performer 5 (Mac Only)

Digital Performer by Mark of the Unicorn (MOTU) is another Mac-only sequencer that has just about everything a budding musician could want (see Figure 21.13). It's the sequencer of choice for many film and television composers as it includes several features that cater to that medium. When I wrote the first version of this book, my one regret was that due to lack of time, I was not able to include a Digital Performer (DP) tutorial, but now I'm happy to include it here.

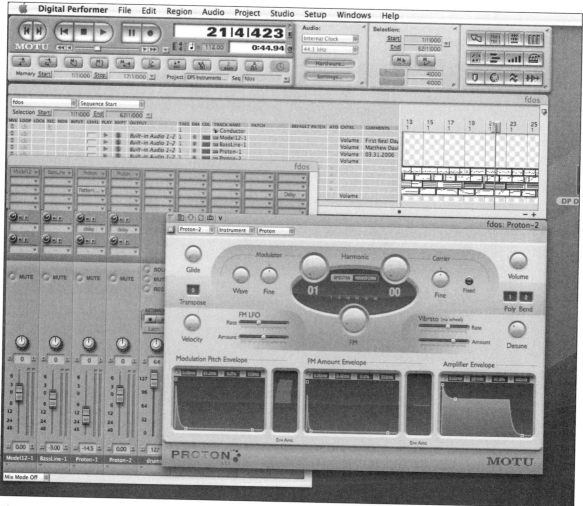

Figure 21.13 MOTU's Digital Performer is a film composer's delight.

1. Launch Digital Performer and start a new empty project.

2. Navigate to the Project pull-down menu and select Add Track > Stereo Audio Track.

3. Once the new track has been created, navigate to the Input column of the Audio Track and select New Stereo Bundle > Reason: Mix L1-R2 (see Figure 21.14).

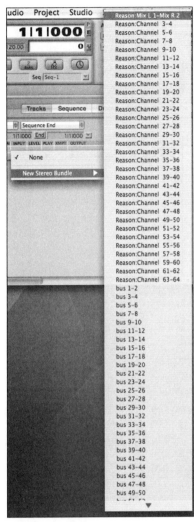

Figure 21.14   Even before you launch Reason, you need to specify it as the input for your audio track in DP.

4.   Next, you need to specify the audio output. Navigate to the Output column of the Audio Track and select New Stereo Bundle > Built In Audio Output. Keep in mind that if you are using an audio card other than the built-in Mac audio card, you'll need to specify that instead.

5.   Once the input and outputs have been selected, you can now see a little speaker icon just to the left of the Input column. This is the Monitor button and you'll need to activate it in order to hear Reason once it's launched.

6.   Launch Reason. Assuming that the Demo Song has loaded, you can now hear and see ReWire in action by clicking the Play button on either program (see Figure 21.15).

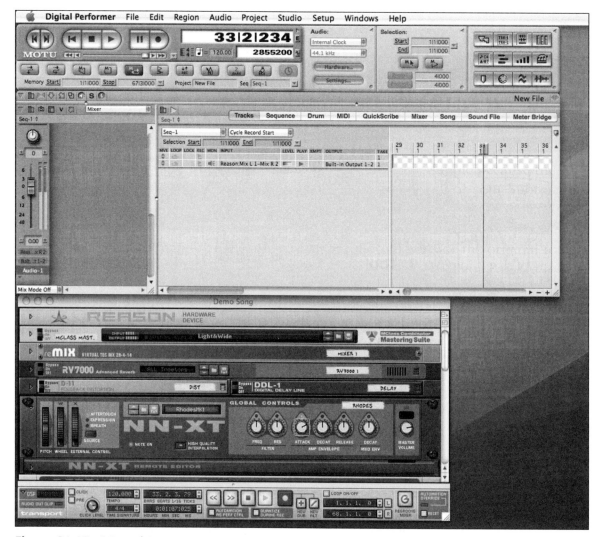

Figure 21.15 DP and Reason are now rewired.

Let's wrap this tutorial up by setting up a MIDI track to trigger Redrum. Assuming that the Demo Song is still open, do the following:

1. Navigate to Project and select Add Track > MIDI Track. This will create a new MIDI track.

2. Looking at the output of this track, you can see that DP went ahead and automatically routed it to the first Reason device, which is the Hardware Interface. Click on the Output column for this track and select Drums (see Figure 21.16).

3. Assuming that you have your MIDI keyboard hooked up correctly, you should now be able to trigger the Redrum samples via Digital Performer.

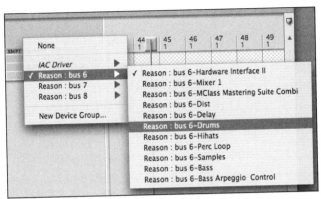

Figure 21.16 Route the output of your MIDI track to Drums.

Using ReWire with Pro Tools

Just about anybody who has delved into this side of music technology has certainly heard of Pro Tools by DigiDesign (Mac/PC). Pro Tools is the first tool of choice for post-production applications, with its basic and straightforward approach to audio recording and editing (see Figure 21.17). Within the last few years, DigiDesign has pursued the consumer market by introducing some great hardware audio interfaces at affordable prices that come included with a light version of the software called Pro Tools LE. There is also a version made for M-Audio hardware called "M-Powered" and another lighter, entry level version called Pro Tools Essentials. These versions, although a bit stripped down, are a formidable solution for audio and MIDI productions.

Figure 21.17 Pro Tools by DigiDesign is an affordable all-in-one solution for digital audio and MIDI.

Here's how to set up ReWire with Pro Tools LE/M-Powered:

1. Launch Pro Tools LE and create a new session.

2. Select Track > New. When the dialog box appears, have Pro Tools create a stereo audio track. After it is created in the Edit view, double-click on it and name the track ReWire Mix, as shown in Figure 21.18.

Figure 21.18 Create a stereo audio track and name it ReWire Mix. If you are familiar with Pro Tools, you will notice that this is indeed a stereo track because it has a pair of meters.

3. Select Window > Mix. This will open up the virtual mixer. You will find the Reason Mix channel strip on the right.

4. On the Insert section of the Reason Mix channel strip, locate the first insert point. Click and hold here to display the available plug-ins for your session. Select the Reason plug-in and Reason will launch automatically.

5. Once Reason is loaded, you will see in the Audio Out device that it is automatically set to ReWire Slave mode. Click Play and Reason will immediately chase to Pro Tools (see Figure 21.19).

6. Should you want to quit Pro Tools LE and Reason, remember to quit Reason first, followed by Pro Tools LE. If you try to quit Pro Tools LE first, an alert window will pop up to remind you.

Once you have successfully synced up Reason and Pro Tools LE, you can send MIDI data to Reason by way of a Pro Tools MIDI track. Just follow these steps to do so:

1. In Pro Tools LE, select Track > New. Repeat Step 2 from the last tutorial, but create a MIDI track rather than an audio track. This will place a MIDI track just below the Reason Mix audio track created in the previous tutorial.

2. Select Window > Mix to bring up the virtual mixer. As shown in Figure 21.20, route the output of the MIDI track to Kong by selecting Drums-channel-3 from the pull-down menu.

Figure 21.19 Pro Tools integrates ReWire into its interface by using Reason, or any other ReWire-ready program, as a plug-in.

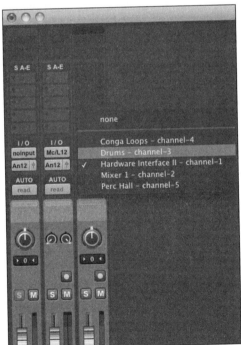

Figure 21.20 Pro Tools LE can route MIDI data to any Reason device. You simply select it from the MIDI Out pull-down menu.

3.   At this point, you can switch back to the Edit view, arm your MIDI track, and sequence in some MIDI data that will now be sent to Redrum.

Although Pro Tools LE is not the most complete MIDI sequencer ever made, adding the power of Reason via ReWire is sure to make your tracks sparkle with creativity.

Using ReWire with SONAR 6 (Windows Only)

There's no doubt that the last few years have been good ones for Cakewalk because SONAR (Windows only) has accumulated a long list of great reviews from the press and its user base (see Figure 21.21). With ReWire, you can integrate the synths and sound modules of Reason with the audio recording and MIDI sequencing capabilities of SONAR 6.

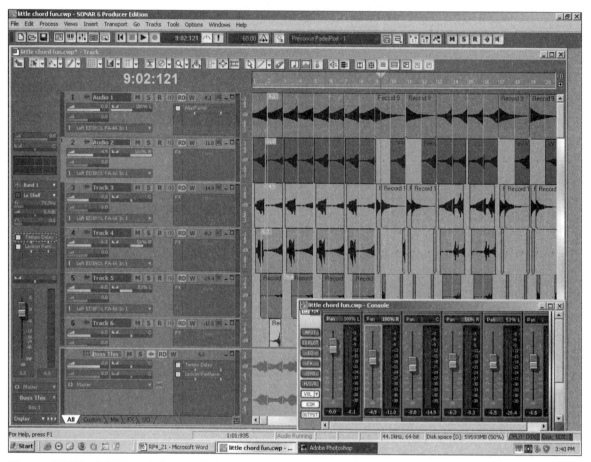

Figure 21.21 SONAR 6 has a killer graphical interface and exceptional audio/MIDI editing features.

Make sure that you are using the built-in song for Reason so you can follow along.

1. Launch SONAR and start a new blank project.

2. Select View > Synth Rack. You can also click on the DXi button, which is located in the Project window. Once you select it, the blank synth rack will open, as shown in Figure 21.22.

3. In the top-left corner of the Synth Rack window, click on the Insert DXi instrument and ReWire devices button. A pull-down menu will then appear with a submenu for DXi synths and one for ReWire devices. Select the Reason option from the ReWire devices submenu (see Figure 21.23).

Figure 21.22 The SONAR DXi synth rack is where you begin to load your ReWire programs.

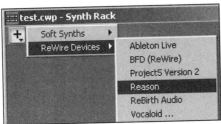

Figure 21.23 Click on the Insert DXi instrument and ReWire devices button and select the Reason option from the ReWire devices submenu.

4. SONAR will then pop up a window asking for synth and ReWire options (see Figure 21.24). If this is your first time performing this task, make sure that you specify SONAR to create a MIDI Source track and a First Synth Output track as well. Click OK.

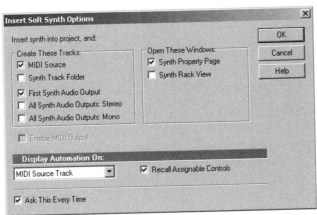

Figure 21.24 The SONAR DXi synth options can be very useful when using virtual synths for the first time because these options take all of the guesswork out of the picture.

5. SONAR will then automatically launch Reason. SONAR will also create a Reason device in the Synth Rack window.

6. Once Reason has loaded the built-in song, press Play and look at the Audio Out device in the Reason Device Rack. Notice that Reason is now set to ReWire

Slave mode, which means that Reason will follow or chase to SONAR. Also notice that the tempo of Reason's built-in song is set to the same tempo as SONAR.

7.   Select View > Console. This will launch the SONAR virtual mixer. If you are still playing the built-in song, you will see the SONAR meters jumping with delight.

8.   Press Stop.

9.   Should you want to quit SONAR and Reason, remember to quit Reason first, followed by SONAR. If you try to quit SONAR first, an alert window will pop up to remind you.

Just as with Cubase, SONAR can trigger the individual Reason devices via MIDI. If you followed the previous tutorial, this can be done in a heartbeat. With ReWire still running in your SONAR project, select the MIDI track that was created when you first launched Reason from the DXi synth rack. Make sure that the output is still set to Reason, and then click on the Channel pull-down menu. As shown in Figure 21.25, you can select any of the Reason devices from this menu, and then proceed to trigger and sequence them from within the SONAR interface.

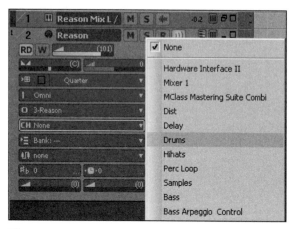

Figure 21.25 Set your MIDI output to Reason, and then use the Channel pull-down menu to select the Reason device you want to trigger and sequence.

Using ReWire with Ableton Live 6

Ableton Live (Mac/PC) is to remixing digital audio what Reason is to synthesis—ultra freaking cool! Don't let the retro, two-dimensional graphical interface fool you (see Figure 21.26); Live 6 is a perfect solution for audio recording and remixing, and Live and Reason together make such a powerful combination for creative electro that it is actually kind of scary!

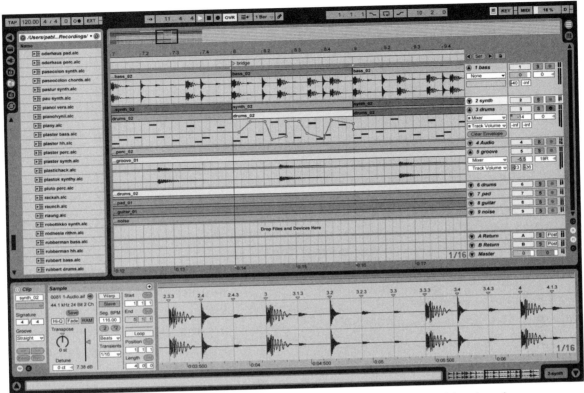

Figure 21.26 Ableton Live 6 bends, twists, and stretches audio like a rubber band.

Make sure that you are using the built-in song for Reason so you can follow along.

1. Launch Ableton Live.

2. Now launch Reason. At the top of the audio device in the Reason Device Rack, you'll see that Reason is automatically set to ReWire Slave mode. Also take notice that the tempo of the Reason built-in song is now set to the default tempo of Live.

3. At this point, you need to activate an audio track in Live and set it to receive the routed audio from Reason. Go to track 1 and locate the Audio From pull down menu. Click on this and you will get a pull-down menu listing all of the input options you have (see Figure 21.27). Choose Reason from the list.

4. Once Reason is selected, select the In option under the Monitor section. This will allow you to listen to the stereo mix of Reason. Press Play and you're good to go.

5. Should you want to quit Live and Reason, remember to quit Reason first, followed by Live. If you try to quit Live first, an alert window will pop up to remind you.

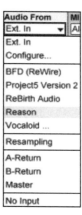

Figure 21.27 Located just below Audio From label on any audio track in Live, you'll find the Input Type box. Although you selected Reason for this example, any ReWire slave program that you own and have installed will appear in this list.

Using Reason with Record

With all the innovations Propellerhead brought to the virtual synth world with Reason, it seemed only a matter of time before they would have a go at the DAW market. In 2009, Propellerhead released Record 1.0, which was a revelation in DAW technology (see Figure 21.28). Not only does Record have the routing capabilities and eye candy like the features of Reason, it also includes a powerful digital recording engine. Unlimited audio tracks, automatic tempo changes with audio, a great selection of real-time effects, and so much more, Record is a great companion to any Reason user.

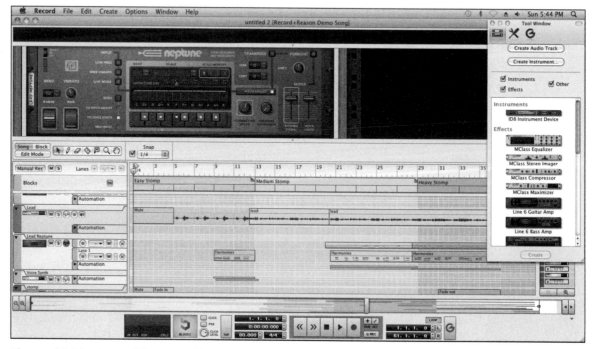

Figure 21.28 Record by Propellerhead is the perfect DAW for Reason, as it includes the looks and functionality of Reason, and also does a great job as a DAW.

As Reason and Record are both Propellerhead products, they work together in a way that differs somewhat from the conventions of ReWire. In this case, Reason songs simply open up within Record. Once Record is launched, just open your Reason song as you would within Reason itself.

Additionally, the synths and effects of Reason become available for Record users. So if you are a fan of the BV512 vocoder, you're in luck, as you'll be able to use the BV512 on your Record audio tracks.

Different Programs, Different Versions   Although this is a chapter dedicated to the technology of ReWire, it simply can't cover every ReWire-ready program on the market nor the various versions of each given program. Fortunately, the Propellerhead website is a good place to find most of the answers to your ReWire questions. Have a look at the Reason support section of www.propellerheads.se, and you'll be sure to find ReWire tutorials that cover software that was not covered in this chapter. You'll also find tutorials covering earlier versions of software, such as Logic 5 or Cubase VST.

ReWire is an essential element in your digital studio. Not only can you get the best of digital audio recording with your ReWire master application, but you can also get the best of virtual synths with Reason.

22 Mixing and Publishing Your Reason Songs

When it comes to finalizing and mixing down your song, Reason offers many options. Aside from the typically found Export Audio function that you will see in just about every digital audio program on the market, Propellerhead has included a very interesting Publish feature that saves your song and allows other Reason users to listen to it on their own computers. This introduces a Reason Community concept that encourages users to interact and exchange ideas.

As with many digital audio workstation programs, such as Pro Tools, Cubase, SONAR, Digital Performer, and Logic, Reason can export many file formats, making it a versatile solution for any digital music junkie (see Figure 22.1).

Reason can do the following:

- Export audio (from an entire song or from a loop)

- Export MIDI files

- Publish Reason songs

The following sections break it down and take an in-depth look at what each export type does.

Exporting Audio

Exporting audio is synonymous with *audio mixdown,* which is simply the process of combining all of the various signals and real-time effects in your Reason song into a single stereo digital audio file. This file can then be used to make an audio CD that can be played in any CD player.

Reason provides a couple of ways to export audio, each of which serves specific functions. Open your File pull-down menu and follow along.

- **Export Song As Audio File**—This option exports your entire Reason song, from start to finish.

Figure 22.1 Choose your export option from the File pull-down menu.

■ **Export Loop As Audio File**—This option exports whatever is contained between the left and right locator points of the Reason sequencer. Although this option might not appear to be immediately useful, the purpose of this function is explained later in this section.

Let's export some audio using both methods.

Export Your Reason Song as an Audio File

In this section, you are going to load a Reason song and learn how to export the entire song as a stereo WAV or AIFF file. Reason offers many choices and options to create the best file possible, so it is important that you understand how the process works.

For this tutorial, I suggest you use the Demo Song (which opens automatically whenever Reason 5 is launched) so you can follow along seamlessly.

1. First, scroll to the right in the Reason sequencer and locate the end marker (see Figure 22.2). Notice that it is set at measure 69 and that the song itself ends at measure 67. Drag the end marker to the left until you reach measure 67 (see Figure 22.3).

2. Next, look at the sequencer tracks and make sure that all of the tracks you want to include in the mix are not muted. For example, if you want to export a mix without the Redrum module, you can simply mute the Redrum track either on its sequencer track or by clicking on its Mute button in reMix. This way, Reason will not include Redrum in the export of the mix.

Figure 22.2 Locate the end marker. In the Demo Song, it is located at measure 69. Note that you will need to move the Right Locator to the left or the right to see the end marker.

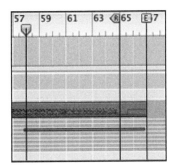

Figure 22.3 In the Demo Song, drag the end marker to the right until it reaches measure 67.

3. Choose File > Export Song As Audio File. A new window will pop up and ask you to name your song and select a location for it (see Figure 22.4). For simplicity's sake, save the mix to the desktop and keep its original name (Demo Song). At this point, you can also select which audio file format to export your mix as—AIFF or WAV. The golden rule is typically "WAV files for Windows and AIFF for Macs." However, with today's computers, this is generally not much of a concern because most programs can support and open both WAV and AIFF files, so it is really up to you. Assuming this is your first time out, perhaps AIFF would be just fine. Click the Save button to continue.

4. Next you are asked to set your export audio settings (see Figure 22.5). In this case, the sample rate has been set to 44100Hz and has been given a bit depth of 16 bits. These are the standard audio settings found on a commercially available audio CD. If your intention is to burn an audio CD right after exporting your Reason songs, these settings are fine. But just for kicks, click on the pull-down menus in this window to see all of the other possible export audio settings (see Figure 22.6). Reason is capable of creating a 24-bit audio file with a sampling rate of 192kHz.

Figure 22.4 Select a place to save your audio file and give it a name.

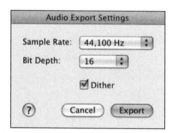

Figure 22.5 Set your audio preferences to export your Reason song.

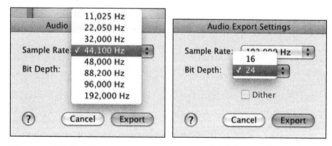

Figure 22.6 Reason can create a 24-bit/192kHz digital audio file, making it the perfect solution to use with a pro-audio application.

If your intention is to take the digital audio file that Reason creates and import it into a high-end mastering program, such as WaveLab or Peak, these settings might be the ticket.

5.   After you have made your settings, click OK. Reason will proceed to mix and export your Reason song into a digital audio file. In Figure 22.7, you will see that Reason counts down the remaining bars to be exported (although at lower

Figure 22.7 Reason counts down the measures as it exports your song.

sample rates and bit depths, this might go by in the blink of an eye on faster computers).

A Word About Dither   Notice in the center of the Audio Export Settings window there is a check box for Dither. You will notice that Reason automatically checks this box whenever a bit depth of 16 bits is selected. This option is available because some of the sounds generated in Reason are 24 bit, and obviously some information has to be removed to mix it down to 16 bits to burn on a standard audio CD. Without dithering, the excess bits are simply *truncated*, or cut off, which can result in a harsher sound or a loss of perceived ambience. Dither aims to smooth out these harsh mathematics by adding a barely percep- tible amount of noise (random bits) at the very bottom of the noise floor in the upper frequencies of the audible range. There is quite a variety of dithering pro- cessors and plug-ins out there, of differing quality. Use your ears to decide how you like the dithering in Reason. Export a song twice at 44.1kHz 16 bit, once with dither, and once without, and see if you hear the difference. If you are actually exporting a mix to bring to a professional audio mastering house, how- ever, you should export at 24 bits, and let them do the dither at the final stage of their process, because their equipment will be processing at 24 bits or higher, and you definitely only want to dither down to 16 bits once.

This has been a super-simplified glimpse at dither and barely scrapes the tip of the iceberg. For more information on this subject, check out some of the excellent explanations written by Bob Katz, author of *Mastering Audio* (2002, Focal Press). In addition to his book, several articles can be viewed at the Digital Domain website (www.digido.com).

Export Your Reason Loop as an Audio File

Reason can also export just portions (or *loops*) of your songs as audio files. It does this by exporting whatever content is between the left and right locators. This is extremely useful for creating high-quality loops that can be used in pro-audio DAW applications, such as Pro Tools, Cubase, SONAR, or Logic.

Why would you want to do this? Although Reason is a great sequencing program, it cannot record audio. There are times when you might find you are working on a piece of music made up of mostly recorded tracks of audio, and you need just a little bit of Reason magic here and there. To do this, you have two options:

■ You can run Reason with your DAW application through ReWire. The problem here is that you'll use a lot of CPU speed that you might need somewhere else.

■ You can create drum loops and synth loops in Reason, export them as audio files, and import them into your DAW application. This is a much better solution because it saves your precious CPU speed. You can even export your tracks separately by soloing and exporting each track one at a time. This way you can have complete control over your mix of the individual Reason tracks in your DAW application.

That said, let's get on with it and create a four-bar digital audio loop in Reason. As in the last tutorial, use the Demo Song once again so you can keep up with the group.

1. Click and drag the left and right locators to measures 17 and 21, respectively (see Figure 22.8). This will give you a four-bar loop to work with.

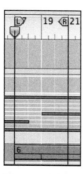

Figure 22.8 Click and drag the left and right locators to measures 17 and 21, respectively.

2. Make sure your Loop button is activated in the Reason Transport panel.

3. Listen to the loop and decide which single instrument you want to export as a digital audio file. This example exports the Dr. Octo Rex track, so press the Solo button on the Conga Loops sequencer track.

4. Now you are set to export your audio loop. Navigate to the File pull-down menu and select Export Loop As Audio File.

5. As with the last tutorial, you need to name the file and select a location for it. You then need to specify your digital audio settings to export your digital audio loop.

Reason Does Not Make MP3s The MP3, or *MPEG Layer 3*, is a digital audio file format that is used primarily to exchange music between friends, family, and, most importantly, fans. It is a popular format because it compresses a high-quality stereo AIFF or WAV file to a much smaller size that can be transferred easily via the web.

Reason does not create MP3 files, although this added functionality would seem to be an obvious step for the Internet/digital music junkie.

But cheer up kids; the good news is that there are *many* MP3 encoding programs available at little or no cost. In fact, Apple's iTunes encodes MP3 files like a champ and is a free program (you may have heard of it!) available for both *Mac OS X* and for *Windows!*

Exporting MIDI

As you read in Chapter 5, "The Reason Sequencer—Close Up," Reason can import any MIDI file to be used within the Reason sequencer. This can lead to some very interesting remixing ideas by routing these various MIDI tracks to some of Reason's virtual synths and sound modules. All you have to do is download some MIDI files of bands you like from the Internet and remix them with the Reason synths. Then you can add new elements to them with REX loops and real-time effects. It's like reinterpreting classic tunes and creating a whole new concept around those songs.

As luck would have it, Reason can also export MIDI files from any opened Reason song. This allows you to import that MIDI file into another program, such as Cubase or SONAR. These MIDI tracks can then be routed to either hardware or software synths for further remixing, so you can record a few tracks of audio.

Let's go over how to export a Reason song as a MIDI file. Open the Demo Song and then follow these steps:

1. Find the end marker, which is located at bar 69. Click and drag the end marker to the end of your Reason song at bar 67.

2. Select File > Export MIDI File.

3. Reason will then ask you to name your MIDI file and where you would like to place it. As shown in Figure 22.9, this example keeps the original name and saves the file to the desktop, where it can be located quickly. Click Save. After you quit Reason, you should see the Demo Song MIDI file on your desktop.

4. At this point, you can save it onto a flash drive and pass it to your friend; but let's suppose that you have another audio/MIDI program on your computer, such as SONAR. Open that program so you can see what the Reason MIDI file looks like.

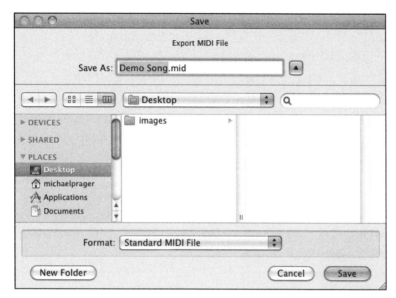

Figure 22.9 Select the name and location for your exported MIDI file.

5. Import the MIDI file into your audio/MIDI program, and you will see all four tracks of the Demo Song displayed as MIDI information (see Figure 22.10). Notice that all of the MIDI tracks still have their original names and that each track is set to MIDI channel 1. Because Reason's sequencer is not channel-dependent like a traditional MIDI sequencer, it sets each MIDI track to channel 1. This is easily correctable in any MIDI sequencing software.

Figure 22.10 The Demo Song imported into Pro Tools. Notice that all of the MIDI tracks still have the same names as they did in Reason.

Publishing a Reason Song

Reason's publishing function is a unique idea because it creates a special Reason song file that can be opened on any computer that has Reason 5 installed. Although that might not sound all that exciting at first, the Publish Song function has a couple of aces up its sleeve.

1. Aside from ReFills, a published song can be self-contained. All extra samples and custom presets can be saved within a published song so that they can be opened and heard from any computer with Reason 5 installed.

2. Published songs are semi-copyright safe. If a user opens a published song, that song cannot be saved with a different filename nor can a user make saved changes to a published song. However, a user can export a published song as an audio file.

How to Identify a Published Song   Look in your Reason program folder and find the Demo Songs folder. Open this folder, and you will see several demo songs that have been prepared by other Reason users.

First, notice that the filename is followed by an .rps extension (Reason Published Song), as opposed to the standard .rns file extension found on new Reason songs that you create and save. This is the first indication that these song files are published songs.

Next, open any of the demo songs and look at the File pull-down menu. As you can see in Figure 22.11, there is no way of saving this published song. That's the second clue that this is a published song.

Figure 22.11 Published Reason songs cannot be saved, as indicated by the Save options being grayed out.

One thing that is great about the Publish feature is that you can export your song as a self-contained song. This simply means that any extra samples, patches, or REX files will be compressed and saved within the song file. That way, any user who opens your published song can listen to it the way you intended it to be heard.

Let's look at how to make a song self-contained. To follow along with this tutorial, you need one of the REX files I have downloaded and made available at the Course Technology site (go to www.courseptr.com and click on the Downloads link). Locate the Chapter 22 Exercises folder, download the folder, and place it on your computer's desktop so you will be able to easily locate it. Unzip the folder.

1. Open the Reason Demo Song.

2. Scroll to the bottom of the Device Rack and create an instance of Dr. Octo Rex.

3. Click on the folder icon of Dr. Octo Rex to open the browser window.

4. Browse to the computer desktop. You should see the Chapter 22 folder. Double-click on it to open it, and you'll see the REX Loops for Chapter 22 folder (see Figure 22.12).

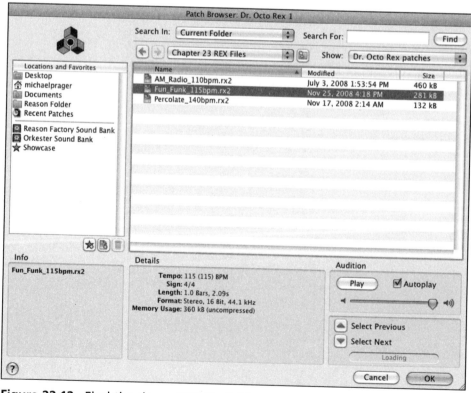

Figure 22.12 Find the demo REX file folder. Double-click on one of the REX files to load it into Dr. Octo Rex.

5. Open any REX file to load it into Dr. Octo Rex.

6. Click on the Copy Loop To Track button in Dr. Octo Rex to place the REX file MIDI notes onto the Reason sequencer.

7. Choose File > Song Self-Contain Settings. This will open the customizable Settings window so you can specify which files will be included in the published Reason song.

8. Look at Figure 22.13 and notice how many files are listed. Included are all of the samples that have been loaded into the Kong and Dr. Octo Rex. Also notice that almost all of these samples cannot be selected, signifying that they are included from the Reason Factory Sound Bank. These files will not be included in your published song.

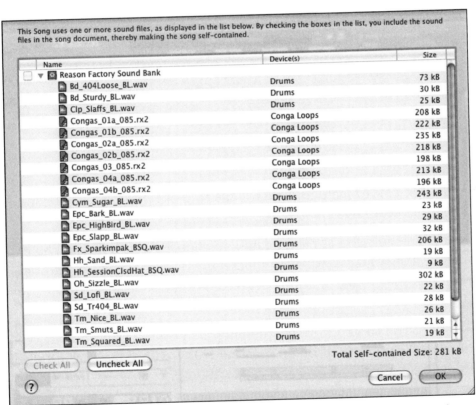

Figure 22.13 The Song Self-Contain Settings window lists all of the samples and REX loops used in a song.

9. Scroll all the way to the bottom of this list, and you will see the only sample that can be selected is the REX file that you just imported into your Reason song (see Figure 22.14). The check box means that you can include this REX file when publishing your Reason song.

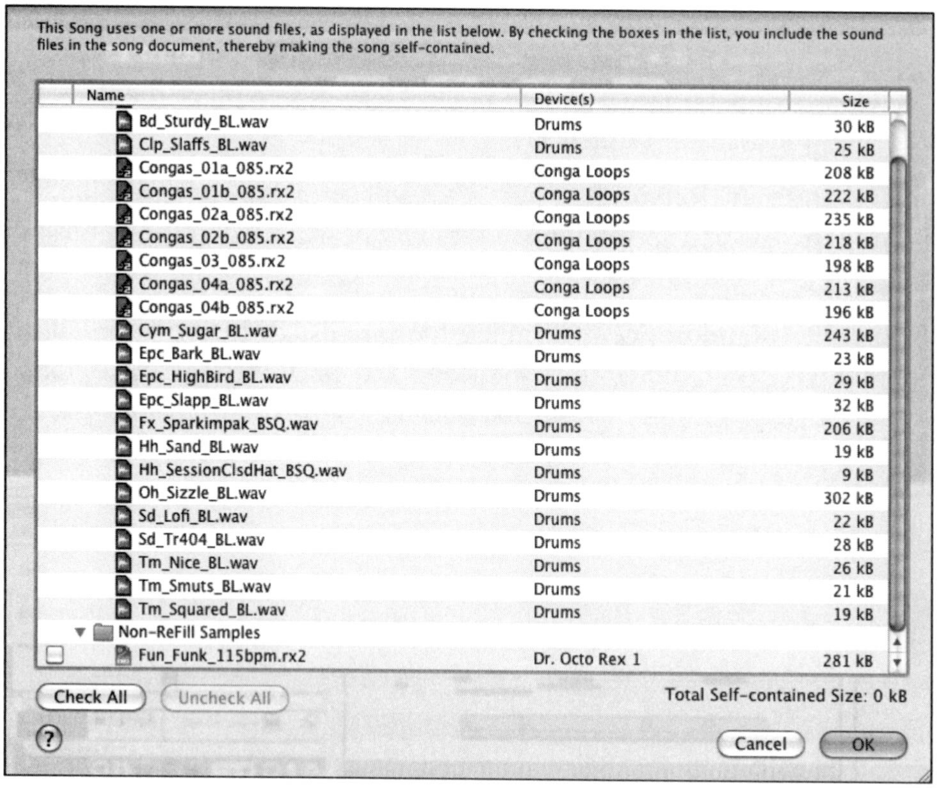

This Song uses one or more sound files, as displayed in the list below. By checking the boxes in the list, you include the sound files in the song document, thereby making the song self-contained.

Name	Device(s)	Size
Bd_Sturdy_BL.wav	Drums	30 kB
Clp_Slaffs_BL.wav	Drums	25 kB
Congas_01a_085.rx2	Conga Loops	208 kB
Congas_01b_085.rx2	Conga Loops	222 kB
Congas_02a_085.rx2	Conga Loops	235 kB
Congas_02b_085.rx2	Conga Loops	218 kB
Congas_03_085.rx2	Conga Loops	198 kB
Congas_04a_085.rx2	Conga Loops	213 kB
Congas_04b_085.rx2	Conga Loops	196 kB
Cym_Sugar_BL.wav	Drums	243 kB
Epc_Bark_BL.wav	Drums	23 kB
Epc_HighBird_BL.wav	Drums	29 kB
Epc_Slapp_BL.wav	Drums	32 kB
Fx_Sparkimpak_BSQ.wav	Drums	206 kB
Hh_Sand_BL.wav	Drums	19 kB
Hh_SessionClsdHat_BSQ.wav	Drums	9 kB
Oh_Sizzle_BL.wav	Drums	302 kB
Sd_Lofi_BL.wav	Drums	22 kB
Sd_Tr404_BL.wav	Drums	28 kB
Tm_Nice_BL.wav	Drums	26 kB
Tm_Smuts_BL.wav	Drums	21 kB
Tm_Squared_BL.wav	Drums	19 kB
▼ 📁 Non-ReFill Samples		
☐ Fun_Funk_115bpm.rx2	Dr. Octo Rex 1	281 kB

Check All   Uncheck All   Total Self-contained Size: 0 kB

?   Cancel   OK

Figure 22.14 The REX file you just imported can be included in the Publishing function because it has a blank check box next to its name.

10. Click on the check box to include the REX file to make your song self-contained. Click OK to continue.

11. Navigate to the File pull-down menu again and choose Publish Song. You can now rename the song and save it to any location you want. For this tutorial, save the published song to the desktop so it is easy to locate. Click Save and quit Reason.

12. On your desktop, you should now see the published song file. If you like, you can burn it to a CD and open it on another computer with Reason 5 installed. The song should load just fine.

Make a Splash

Whether you are saving a Reason Published Song or a Reason Song File, Reason allows you to share a little bit of personality right off the bat as soon as the song is opened. This is thanks to the Song Information feature (see Figure 22.15). The Song Information dialog box (accessible from the File menu) allows you to include information about your song or yourself, including your email address, a link to your website, and (coolest of all) a graphic of your choosing using the Song Splash feature. The graphics file must be saved as a JPEG (.jpg) and must be precisely 256×256 pixels.

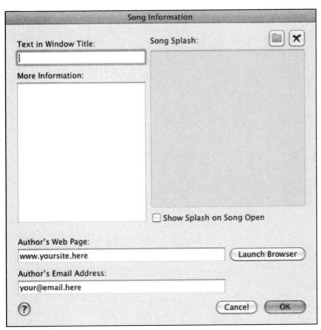

Figure 22.15 The Song Information dialog box is accessible from the Reason File menu.

Before you embark on this little walk-through, make sure you have a 256×256 JPEG (.jpg) prepared and somewhere easy to find in your computer.

1. Open any Reason Song File (.rns file extension). The Demo Song, once again, would be fine, or you can open one of your own creations.

2. From the File menu, click Song Information to open the Song Information dialog box.

3. Add any text you want to appear next to the song title in the Text in Window Title field, plus any additional comments in the More Information field. You will also see fields for your website URL and email address, which you may fill in if you want.

4. In the upper-right corner of the window, click the folder icon to browse for your 256×256 pixel Song Splash JPEG. (The black "X" to the right of this folder is for removing a previously selected Song Splash, but there's no need for that right now.)

5. Select your Song Splash image from the browser and click Open. In the Song Information dialog box, you will now see the image in the Song Splash Window (see Figure 22.16). Underneath the image, make sure that Show Splash on Song Open is checked, and then click OK.

6. Save your song as a Reason Song File or as a Reason Published Song, choosing the Desktop as the save location for easy retrieval. Close the song.

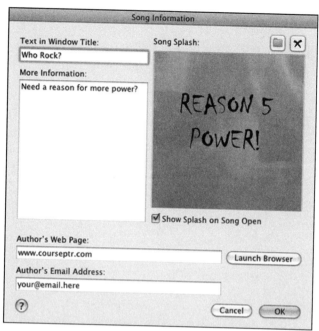

Figure 22.16 Now that the image you have selected is displayed in the Song Splash window, make sure that Show Splash on Song Open is checked.

Figure 22.17 Now your graphic image and information pop up whenever your song is opened.

7. Open the song again and presto! Now anyone who opens your song can enjoy the little extra "splash" of pizzazz you have added (see Figure 22.17).

Get Heard Now!   The Propellerhead website is a fantastic portal to post your published song. Literally hundreds of users a day visit the Propellerhead website to listen to the latest creations and audio innovations of the electronic scene, so why not be a part of the team?

You will need to register your copy of Reason at www.propellerheads.se to obtain a username and password. Once you do, you can upload your Reason songs to the server and, with a little luck, you're on your way to creating your own online fan base!

At this point, you should have created an audio file from your Reason compositions. From here on, what you do with that capability is up to you. Want to burn a CD for your buddies? Want to make MP3s and upload them to your website? These days, the possibilities for distributing your music are almost endless.

Appendix A: ReCycle! 2.1

When it comes to using tempo-based audio loops in music composition, one of the bigger challenges is using the loops in songs of different tempos. Before ReCycle! was available, there were only two ways to do this:

- Map the loop across a set of keys on a hardware sampler and mathematically determine the tempos.

- Compress or stretch the audio loops to fit your tempo in a program such as Pro Tools or Cubase.

In either process, you ran the risk of losing audio quality from the loop, and, what's worse, the pitch of the processed audio loop would be higher or lower than the pitch of the original.

Released in 1994, Propellerhead's ReCycle! solved this problem by providing an original take on making audio loops fit into different tempos (see Figure A.1).

Get the Demo If you don't own ReCycle!, a demo version is available at the Propellerhead website. Go to www.propellerheads.se, find the ReCycle! page, click on Try It!, and you will be taken to a link to download the demo version.

www.propellerheads.se/download

The demo version is fully functional, minus the Save function. The only limitation in this demo version is that you can only work with one of the four provided audio loops. Nevertheless, it should give you a good idea of the potential of this fantastic program!

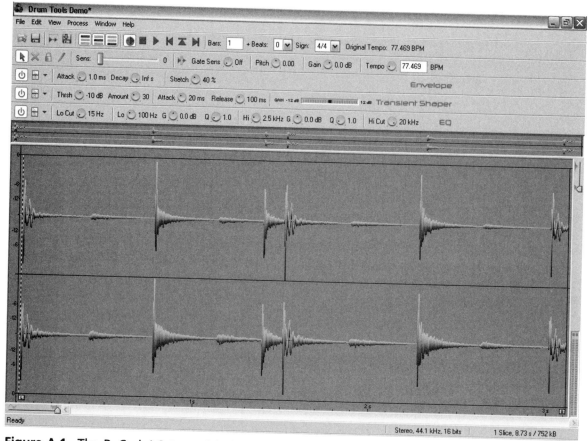

Figure A.1 The ReCycle! 2.1 graphical interface.

Slice and Dice

ReCycle! uses a unique editing process of virtually "slicing" an audio loop in places it determines by use of a sensitivity slider. Once this process is accomplished, ReCycle! can finish the job by performing one of two additional tasks:

■ Transmitting the slices to a hardware sampler by way of SCSI or MIDI.

■ Exporting the slices in a different audio format called REX2 (ReCycle! EXclusive).

The REX2 file is a proprietary format created by Propellerhead Software and is supported by many software applications, such as Reason, Cubase SL/SX, and Logic Audio. Essentially, a REX2 file is a series of slices created by ReCycle!. These slices are transmitted as one audio file that is then imported into software that supports the REX2 format. Once the REX2 file has been imported into a program, it can be used at virtually any tempo by simply adjusting the individual slices to conform to the new tempo.

In musical terms, if you have a drum loop set at 110BPM (beats per measure) and you want to use it in a song that is 120BPM, you can import that loop into ReCycle!, create a REX2 file from it, and import it into your song. Additionally, if you want to change the tempo in your song at a later date, the REX2 file will adjust accordingly to fit that tempo.

Roll Yer Own REX2 Files

Creating your own REX2 files for Reason is less of a challenge than you might think. The following section is a step-by-step tutorial that covers the following:

- Importing an audio loop into ReCycle!

- Slicing up the audio loop

- Editing the loop with ReCycle! effects

- Exporting the loop as a REX2 file

- Importing the REX2 file into Reason using Dr. Octo Rex

Let's get REXing!

1. Start by clicking on the Folder icon located at the top-left side of the ReCycle! interface, or select File > Open. This will open the Open Sound File dialog box (see Figure A.2).

Figure A.2 Use the file browser to locate your audio file for ReCycle!

2. Look at the different file types that ReCycle! can open. All of the standard formats are there, such as WAV and AIFF, but there is the option to open up REX (mono) and REX2 (stereo) files as well. Also notice that there is an Auto Play check box at the bottom-right side of the window, so you can automatically listen to your audio files before importing them. Browse to the ReCycle! folder, and open the file named Drum Tools Demo.

3. As the selected audio file opens, ReCycle! will ask "Do you want to move the left locator to the first slice point?" as shown in Figure A.3. Click on Yes, and ReCycle! will automatically move the left locator to the first slice point, which is located at the beginning of the loop.

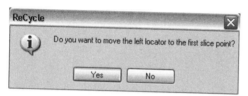

Figure A.3 Click Yes to have ReCycle! automatically move the left locator to the first slice point.

4. ReCycle! will then inform you that you will not be able to hear any effects until you activate the Preview Toggle button (see Figure A.4). As you'll learn about this later, just click OK for now. The audio file will open and is ready to be ReCycled.

Figure A.4 ReCycle! will inform you that you cannot use the effects until the Preview Toggle button is activated. Click OK to continue.

5. Press the spacebar to play the loop, and ReCycle! will proceed to play it over and over again. If you are using the Drum Tools Demo file, you will certainly hear the extra beat that has been purposely thrown in to show you how to use the ReCycle! looping power. Notice the left and right locators, which are similar to those in Reason's sequencer (see Figure A.5).

6. At the top of the ReCycle! interface is the sensitivity slider, which is used to assign slices to the audio loop (see Figure A.6).

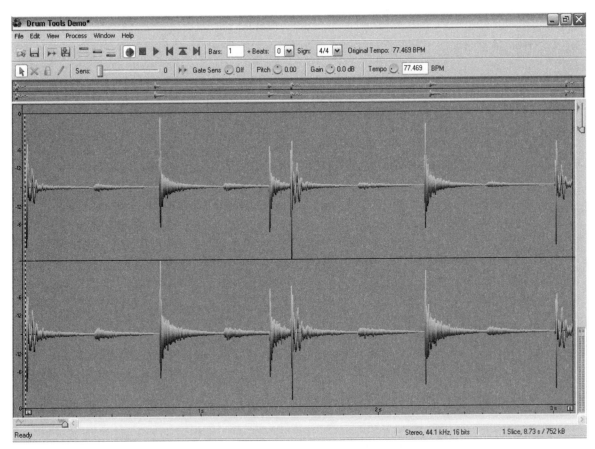

Figure A.5 The ReCycle! graphical interface before slicing.

Figure A.6 The sensitivity slider assigns slices to the audio loop.

With your mouse, click and drag the slider to the right until it reaches 80. Look at your audio loop, and you will see 10 separate audio slices (see Figure A.7). If you want to hear each slice individually, just click on them (see Figure A.8).

7. If you play the loop again, you will still hear the extra beat, which throws off the entire loop. To correct this, you must click and drag the right locator to the 10th slice, as shown in Figure A.9. Press Play again, and this time the loop should sound just fine.

Now that the slices have been created, you are ready to push on and work with the ReCycle! effects. Follow these steps to do so:

1. You must first assign a numeric amount of bars to this loop. Because this tutorial uses the Drum Tools Demo file, this is a one-bar loop.

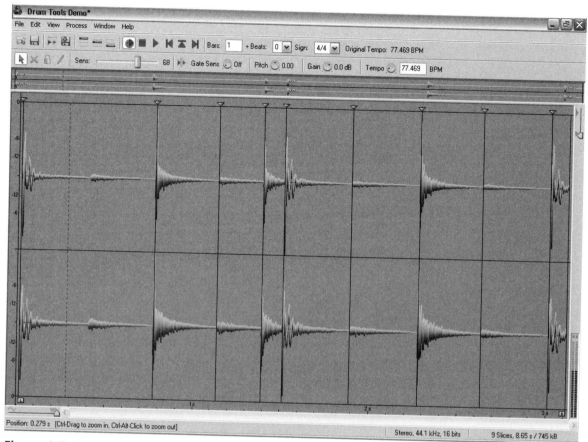

Figure A.7 ReCycle! has now sliced the audio loop.

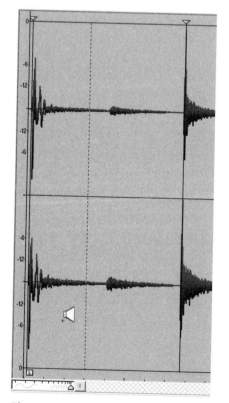

Figure A.8 Click on any slice to preview it.

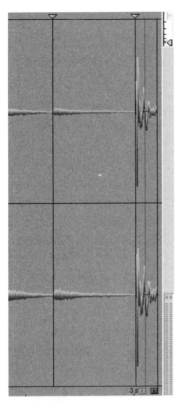

Figure A.9 Click and drag the right locator one slice to the left to correct the timing problem.

Navigate to the upper portion of the ReCycle! interface, where you will find the Bars/Beats/Time Sign toolbar (see Figure A.10). Select the Bars box and enter 1. This will tell ReCycle! that this audio loop is one bar long. Also notice that ReCycle! has automatically assigned a tempo of 80.085BPM to this loop.

Figure A.10 The Bars/Beats/Time Sign toolbar is where you can assign the number of bars to an audio loop.

2.   To the left of the transport controls you will find the Preview Toggle button (see Figure A.11). Click on it once to activate it.

Figure A.11 Click on the Preview Toggle button to allow access to the internal real-time effects or preview your loop at different tempos.

3. After activating the Preview Toggle button, you now have access to the ReCycle! effects as well as other various parameters to edit your loop. If you want to play back the audio loop at a different tempo, click and drag the Tempo knob (see Figure A.12) up or down.

Figure A.12 Use the Tempo knob to preview the ReCycle! loop at a different tempo.

4. To the left of the ReCycle! transport controls is the toolbar containing the real-time effects (see Figure A.13). Click on all three buttons to load the effects into the ReCycle! interface (see Figure A.14).

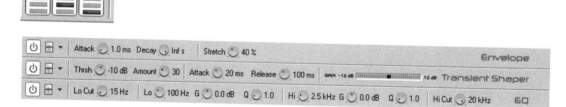

Figure A.13 Activate the ReCycle! real-time effects to load them into the graphical interface.

Figure A.14 Turn on the real-time effects by clicking on their buttons. Now select a preset from the pull-down menu.

5. Activate the Envelope effect by clicking on its button, located to the far left of the interface, and then select one of its presets, located just to the right of the button. A good one to try is the Fake Backwards preset, which creates a reverse effect on the slices by using a combination of Attack and Decay.

6. If you like, you can edit these parameters more to your liking or just activate the other effects, such as the Transient Shaper (or compression) or the EQ (equalizer).

At this point, you can export your audio loop as a REX2 file and import it into Dr. Octo Rex in a couple of clicks.

Before You Export   Before you export your audio loop, make sure that you return the tempo to its original setting. In the case of the Drum Tools Demo file, the tempo is 80.085BPM. Otherwise, ReCycle! will export the audio loop as a REX2 file with a default tempo of whatever the Tempo box reads.

1.   Select Save As from the File pull-down menu.

2.   Select a place to save your REX2 file and give it a descriptive name (see Figure A.15).

Figure A.15   After you have sliced up your audio loop, save it as a REX2 file.

3.   Click the Save button. The audio loop will be saved as a REX2 file.

4.   Start Reason and load a Dr. Octo Rex loop player.

5.   Click on the Folder icon of Dr. Octo Rex to locate a REX2 file to import.

6.   Locate your new REX2 file and import it into Dr. Octo Rex.

Although this appendix is quite brief, I'm sure that you "loop addicts" can see the potential that a program such as ReCycle! can offer. Contact your local music software shop, or just visit www.propellerheads.se, for more information about purchasing ReCycle! or seeing a demo.

Appendix B: ReFills

There is a well-known saying that "too much is never enough." Although this saying can be applied to many life situations, it fits the modern electronic musician like a glove. In a digital world of samples, loops, and patches, creative electronic musicians are always on the prowl for more goodies to add to their stash. Although many wonderful and creative samples and patches come with Reason, an experienced user will always clamor for more and more content. To meet this demand, Propellerhead gives you ReFills!

ReFills are compilations of samples, loops, and patches created specifically for use in Reason. Although files of many formats can be used to create a ReFill, such as WAV, AIFF, REX, and patch files, a ReFill is accessed as one single file of a particular type. This is similar to the idea behind an archived file, such as a ZIP or SIT file. Throughout this book, ReFills have been mentioned many times. This appendix sheds more light on what they are, how they work, and, most importantly, how to make your own ReFills.

Freebies   In the ReFill section of the Propellerhead website, you'll find a complete list of available ReFills you can use with Reason. Some titles are dedicated to the NN-XT and NN-19 samplers. Others are dedicated to the Subtractor and Malström synths. And better yet, there are plenty that contain several Combinator patches. Sometimes, you can get lucky and find a fully loaded ReFill that has patches and presets for all of the different Reason devices, including Redrum patches and REX files.

The best part of all is that a lot of these ReFills are free downloads from the Propellerhead website. It's great to see enthusiastic users creating products like this free of charge to keep fueling the flames of creativity.

Of course, there are also many commercially available ReFill titles, and these are great too. Over the last couple of years, Propellerhead has released a few key titles, such as Abbey Road Keyboards, and Reason Drum Kits. Not to worry, though, because these ReFill titles are competitively priced and won't put a huge dent in your wallet.

ReFill Ingredients

This section analyzes a typical ReFill and explains the different samples and presets included:

- REX files

- Redrum and Kong patches and files

- NN-XT and NN-19 patches and files

- Malström, Subtractor, and Thor patches

- Real-time effects patches

- Combinator patches

REX Files

As you read in Appendix A, "ReCycle! 2.1," a REX file is a digital audio file format created by another Propellerhead Software title called ReCycle! This program imports an AIFF or WAV file, slices it up, and saves the slices in an individual file. Once imported into a program that supports the REX format, that REX file can then be used at different tempos.

On the surface, it might appear that Dr. Octo Rex is the only device that supports the REX format, but this is not true. Redrum, NN-19, and NN-XT all support the REX format in their own ways. Although they are mentioned throughout this book, let's take a moment to recap and review.

As you might remember from previous chapters and appendixes, there are several versions of the REX file (such as REX, REX2, and RCY), but to keep things simple, I will just use REX for the remainder of this appendix.

Redrum Your REX

The REX file support in Redrum is especially unique and interesting because it differs greatly from Dr. Octo Rex, NN-19, and NN-XT. Instead of importing an entire REX file as these other devices do, Redrum can import individual REX slices (see Figure B.1). This opens the door to interesting combinations of sounds and styles. On channel 1, you could load up a kick drum REX slice from a techno-styled REX file, and then you could import a snare REX slice from an acoustic-styled REX file. The combinations are endless.

NN-19 and NN-XT

Both of these virtual samplers can import entire REX files and map them across their virtual keyboards, as shown in Figure B.2. Although the parameters of the NN-19

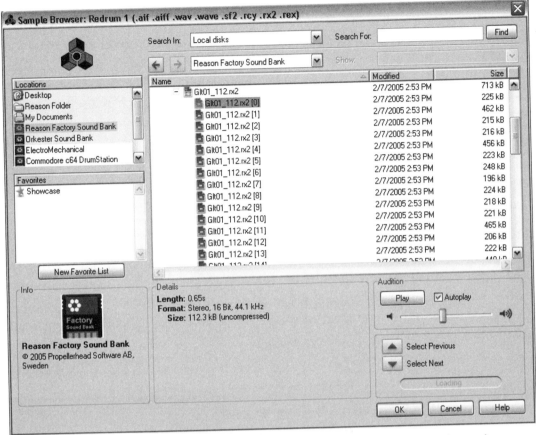

Figure B.1 Redrum can import individual REX slices into each of its 10 channels.

Figure B.2 The NN-19 (left) and NN-XT (right) can both import REX files.

might appear to be quite similar to those found on Dr. Octo Rex, there are a few tricks and treats that clearly set the two devices apart. For starters, the Spread knob found in the upper-left corner of the NN-19 can create a cool auto pan effect, where the REX slices will randomly pan from left to right in the stereo field. The NN-19 envelope, which sounds great, also contains an additional Invert knob, which is used to invert the effect of the envelope. These are just a couple of differences, but you get the picture.

The NN-XT is the sampler's sampler when it comes to handling REX files. Aside from the individual parameters, the NN-XT can assign REX slices to any of its 16 individual outputs (see Figure B.3). Imagine the routing possibilities.

Redrum and Kong Patches

Quantitatively speaking, when it comes to drum samples, they are pretty much a dime a dozen. Just type the phrase **Drum Samples** in your favorite search engine, and you'll see thousands of web pages that contain freeware and shareware samples to download—not to mention the amount of commercially available drum samples you'll find at your local music shop.

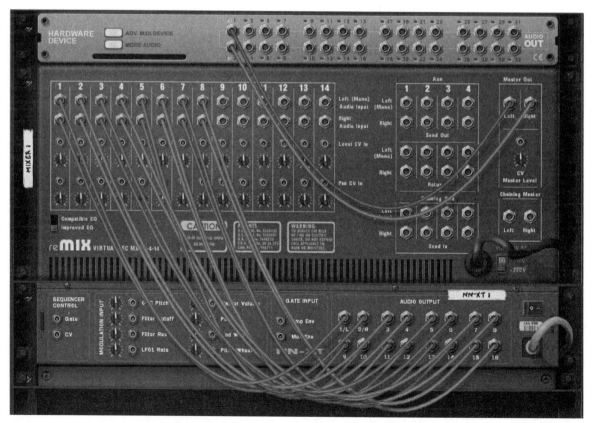

Figure B.3 The NN-XT has 16 individual outputs. By using the NN-XT interface, you can assign each REX slice to its own output.

So, once you have all of these drum samples, how are you going to use them? In Reason, Redrum is your best friend for tackling this challenge. Redrum can import many sample file formats, including:

- AIFF

- WAV

- Sound Fonts or SF2

- REX files

Once you select and import your various samples, you can then save your patch by clicking the Save button on the Redrum interface and creating a DRP file.

NN-19 and NN-XT Patches

Although Reason comes complete with a huge sample library, you may own other sample libraries that you prefer to use on occasion. Both the NN-19 and NN-XT samplers can import various file formats and then save them as individual patches.

Malström, Thor, and Subtractor Patches

If you are a true synth-o-holic, you have probably started to accumulate your collection of patches for Malström, Thor, and Subtractor. These patches are essential to any good ReFill collection. In the ReFill area of the Propellerhead website (www.propellerheads. se), you'll find ReFill collections that are built primarily for these synths.

Real-Time Effect Patches

A ReFill can also include patches for the advanced real-time effects of Reason. These patches are used with the RV7000 Advanced Reverb and the Scream 4 Distortion, which are the only effects devices in Reason that support loading or saving patches. Please note, however, that the settings of any real-time effects used in a Combinator patch will be saved along with that patch.

Combinator Patches

Combinator patches are simply *the bomb*! The Combinator was a new device introduced in an earlier version of Reason, and it is only a matter of time before scads of dope Combinator ReFills begin popping up. In the mean time, why not make your own? You will learn how to make your own ReFills in this appendix, so please read on!

Using ReFills with Reason

Thankfully, using a ReFill collection within Reason is very easy. This section goes through the steps to install a ReFill and shows you how to use it in Reason. Visit the Propellerhead website (www.propellerheads.se/download/refills) and download a free ReFill so that you can follow along with this tutorial.

Downloading and Installing a ReFill

For the sake of simplicity, download a small ReFill from the Propellerhead website. All of the ReFill titles you find on the Propellerhead web page are compressed using the ZIP format. Once you have downloaded the ZIP file, decompress it and place it in the Reason program folder. If you're not sure where that is, let's review:

■ On Windows, you will find it in the Program Files > Propellerhead > Reason folder.

■ On the Macintosh, you will find it in the Applications folder.

Once you have placed the downloaded ReFill in the Reason folder, you should see a total of three ReFills in this folder (see Figure B.4).

■ Reason Factory Sound Bank.

■ Orkester Sound Bank.

■ The new ReFill title you just downloaded, decompressed, and installed. In this example, it is the Commodore-c64-DrumStation ReFill, which I downloaded from the Propellerhead website.

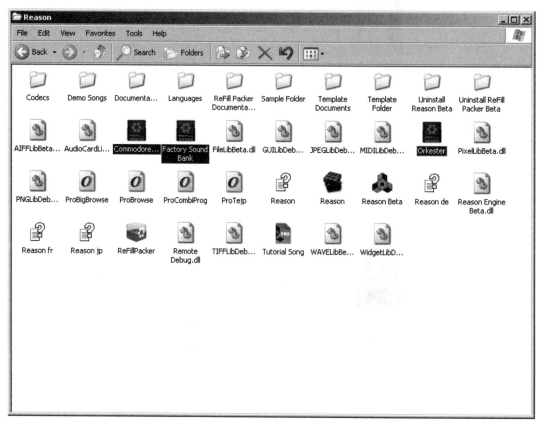

Figure B.4 There are now three ReFills in the Reason Program folder.

Using the ReFill

Now that you have downloaded and installed your ReFill, it's time to learn how to access it and unleash the patches and loops.

Figure B.5 shows that I have created a new song and loaded Dr. Octo Rex, which is set to its default patch. At this point, click on the folder icon. The Patch Browser window will appear (see Figure B.6). Click on Reason folder, which is found in the upper-left corner of the Patch Browser, under Locations. You will see the contents of the Reason Program folder displayed in the main browser window. You should now be able to access the new ReFill by double-clicking on it and opening a patch for Dr. Octo Rex (see Figure B.7).

Figure B.5 Create a new Reason song, and create a reMix device and a Dr. Octo Rex as well.

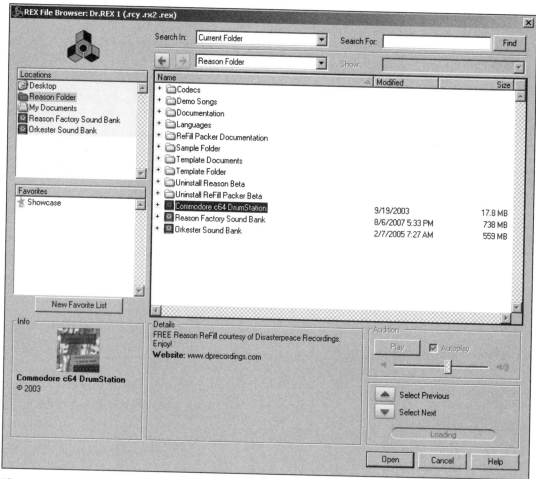

Figure B.6 The Reason Patch Browser is used to locate and load patches and audio files to any Reason device.

Locations

At some point, you will probably want to move your soon-to-be-growing sample collection to a bigger hard drive to save space. If this is the case, Reason has a perfect solution called Locations (see Figure B.8). These are savable presets that contain references to files that can be used within Reason. Say for instance that you have a collection of REX or AIFF/WAV files you like to use. You can specify where these files are and save their location in the Reason Patch Browser. Then when you use the Patch Browser in the future, you can navigate to these locations by just selecting them from the Locations menu. It's an excellent time saver, which is so important when you are trying to channel creativity!

Let's step through an example of working with Locations by using the Commodore-c64-DrumStation ReFill.

1. When you open the Patch Browser, you'll notice that you don't see the Commodore-c64-DrumStation ReFill listed in Locations but you want it listed there

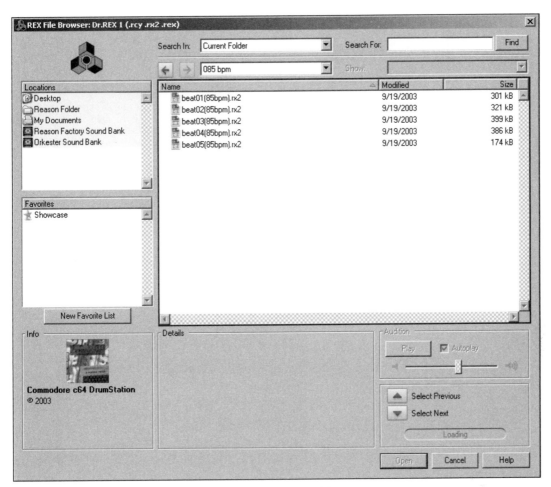

Figure B.7 The new ReFill is now listed and available to use.

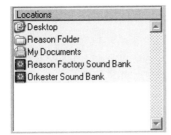

Figure B.8 The Locations menu gives you easy access to your files.

alongside the Orkester and Reason Factory Sound Bank. Start by clicking on the Reason folder. This will display all of the files and folders including the Commodore-c64-DrumStation ReFill (see Figure B.9).

2. Click and drag the Commodore-c64-DrumStation ReFill into the Locations menu (see Figure B.10).

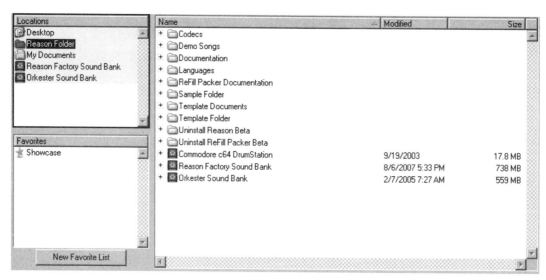

Figure B.9 I want to take the Commodore-c64-DrumStation ReFill and place it in the Locations menu of the Patch Browser so I'll have easy one click access to it.

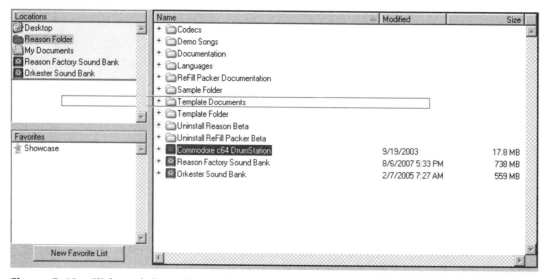

Figure B.10 Click and drag the ReFill into the Locations menu.

3. Drop the Commodore-c64-DrumStation ReFill in the Locations menu, and now you're good to go. The ReFill will now appear in the Locations menu whenever you launch the Patch Browser.

Creating Your Own ReFill

So now that you have had a crash course in ReFills, you might feel the need to throw caution to the wind and try your luck at creating a custom ReFill. This is much easier than it initially looks because Propellerhead has created a free utility program, available at the website, called ReFill Packer.

Remember to Register   In order to obtain access to the ReFills and Propellerhead utility programs mentioned throughout this book, you must register your copy of Reason as soon as possible. This is also a very important step to take if you want to receive technical support and updates to Reason.

The ReFill Packer compiles, compresses, and creates ReFills made of your custom patches, samples, and loops made for Reason. After downloading and decompressing the file, you should run the installer and make sure that it installs into the Reason program folder, so it can be easily found. On Macintosh, there is no installer—you simply drag the decompressed folder into your Reason Application folder. After you have done this, look inside the Reason Program folder, and you should find these additional files and folders:

- The ReFill Packer program

- A ReFill Packer Documentation folder containing a ReFill Packer manual in Adobe Acrobat Reader format (PDF)

- Template and Sample folders, which contain essential templates and examples

The Sample folder is the folder you are going to use for this tutorial. Inside it you will find a JPEG graphics file, a text file, and three folders.

- The JPEG graphics file is the splash-screen graphic that appears when you want to load the ReFill from the Patch Browser window in Reason. It is a very small file, and it can be replaced by any 64×64 pixel JPEG of your own, as long as you name it "splash.jpg."

- The text file, called Info, is used to input the credits for your ReFill, including your website address (or URL) and any additional information.

- The Patch and Sample folders are for specific Reason devices. There is a folder of REX files for Dr. Octo Rex, a folder of patches for the Subtractor, and a folder of samples and patches for the NN-19 sampler. You can create additional folders and subfolders for additional Reason devices, such as Thor or the Malström.

Writing the Info Text   Writing the info text for your ReFill is easy, but you need to make sure that you state everything correctly in order for it to work.

This is how your ReFill info text should by laid out when you create your own. You can change the content to your liking, of course.

```
NAME="My First ReFill"
COPYRIGHT="© 2010 Mi Musique"
URL="www.courseptr.com"
COMMENTS="This is a ReFill that I made"
```

Compiling Your ReFill Files

At this point, it's important to consider how to organize your patches and samples so that you will not experience complications when creating your first ReFill. Although it is not that difficult a task to accomplish, it still needs to be spelled out in detail.

In order to make this as clear as possible, the steps are broken down for each Reason device.

■ **Thor, Subtractor, and Malström**—These devices are fairly simple because the patches are stored in their respective folders. For example, all of your Subtractor patches should be stored in a folder entitled Subtractor Patches. The same goes for the Malström and for Thor. After you have your patches in their correct places, you can then begin to categorize them by creating a subfolder inside the original folder. For example, you could create a Bass or Pad folder inside the Thor Patches folder, and then place the relevant patches into their correct subfolders.

■ **Dr. Octo Rex**—This Reason device's patches can be organized in the same way as the Subtractor and Malström. First compile your REX files and place them in a Dr:rex Drum Loops folder. At this point, you can create subfolders within this main folder and place the relevant REX files into their correct locations.

■ **Real-time FX**—These patches are very easy to understand because there are only two Reason devices that can use them—Scream 4 and the RV7000. When creating your ReFill, you can simply create a folder for each device.

■ **NN-XT, NN-19, Kong, and Redrum**—These are a little more complicated. The basic rule of thumb is that you will need two items to make a ReFill for these devices: first, the NN-19, NN-XT, or Redrum patch file, and then a folder containing the samples that are used for that patch. Figure B.11 shows the contents of the NN-19 Sampler Patches folder found within the ReFill Sample folder. Notice both the patch names and the folder that contain the samples.

Figure B.11 The contents of the NN-19 Sampler Patches folder include the patch names and the additional folder that contains the samples.

■ **Combinator**—These are the most complicated of all (but still not very complicated). In the folder containing the actual Combinator patches (which should be named "Combinator Patches"), you will also need to include folders for patches used by any devices within your Combinator patches, as well as any samples used in those device patches.

Creating the Patches   If you need to review how to create patches for each of the Reason devices, refer to each device's individual chapter.

You Can Pack Your Reason Songs and MIDI Files   In addition to Reason patch files and samples, you can also include Reason songs and MIDI files in your ReFills. Why is this useful? If you create a ReFill and you want to demonstrate its potential to another Reason user, creating a few demonstrations with MIDI and Reason song files will do the trick.

Using Copyrighted Samples   As you begin to compile the samples, loops, and patches for your first ReFill, it might be tempting to add a few samples and loops from your sample CD collection. There is a right way and a wrong way to go about this.

If you plan to use the ReFill just for your personal use, using copyrighted samples is not a problem. You can create a ReFill containing copyrighted samples and loops and use it within Reason to write and produce songs, just as you can with an audio/MIDI program such as Cubase or Pro Tools.

However, you cannot distribute this ReFill to other Reason users, regardless of whether you charge money for it. Doing so results in a violation of copyright law. Musicians, producers, and programmers work tirelessly to create, produce, and distribute these samples. Redistributing these samples in a ReFill is a slap in the face to all of those who worked so hard to create them. It's stealing.

You're almost ready to push forward, run the ReFill packer, and create your first ReFill. But first, you should double-check your organization. Figure B.12 reviews the basic structure of a ReFill. Although you are going to use the pre-made Samples folder for this tutorial, you can always refer to this figure when you create a new ReFill from scratch.

Figure B.12 This is the most commonly found organizational structure in a ReFill.

Using ReFill Packer

In this tutorial, you will launch the ReFill Packer and create your first ReFill by using the Samples folder.

1. Start by launching the ReFill Packer utility, which should be located in your Reason program folder. Once it's launched, you should see the ReFill Packer Program window, which looks just like Figure B.13.

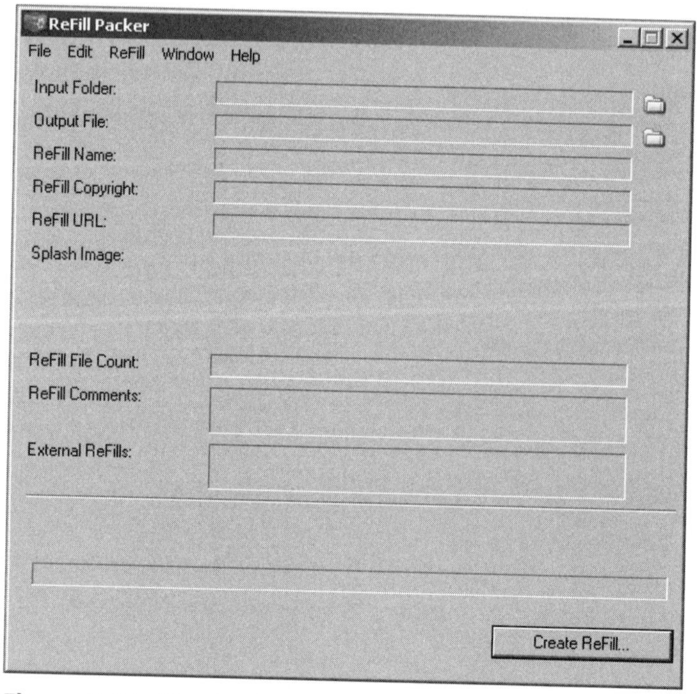

Figure B.13 The ReFill Packer interface.

2. Click on the Input Folder button at the top-right corner of the ReFill Packer interface and select the Sample Folder, which is found within the Reason Program folder (see Figure B.14). Click OK. All of the relevant information should be listed in the ReFill Packer interface (see Figure B.15).

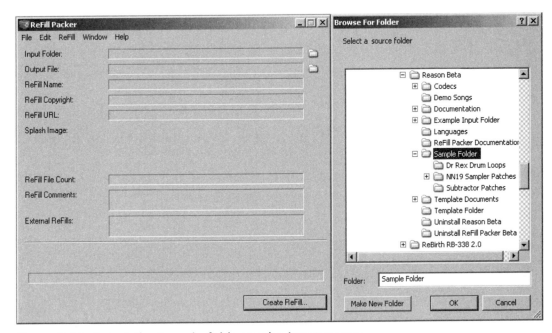

Figure B.14 Select the Sample folder as the input source.

Figure B.15 Now the Sample folder is listed as the input source.

3. Click on the Output File button, which is located just below the Input Folder button. This is where you can select the destination for your ReFill. Because this is your first time, I suggest saving it to the desktop. Once you have selected the destination, the Output File text box will display the name of the ReFill, as shown in Figure B.16.

Figure B.16 Once you select the destination for output, ReFill Packer will display the name.

4. Click on the Create ReFill button at the lower-right corner of the ReFill Packer interface. The ReFill packer should now display a ReFill file count as it compiles. Once it is completed, ReFill Packer will display a message that the ReFill has now been packed successfully (see Figure B.17).

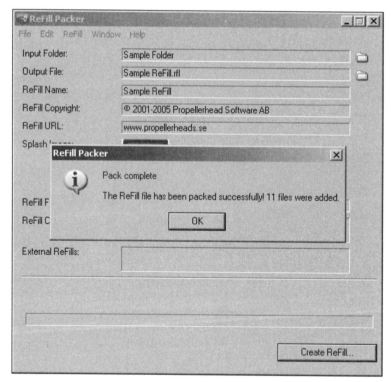

Figure B.17 The ReFill has been successfully created.

5. Locate the ReFill called Sample ReFill on your computer's desktop.

Please note that you cannot make a self-contained ReFill using elements from a previously existing ReFill. If you try to do this, you will get a warning telling you that your new ReFill references an external ReFill, although you will be allowed to go ahead and save your new ReFill if you want. If the external ReFill is in your computer, then it will be referenced when you use the newly created ReFill. However, if you try to use your new ReFill on a computer that does not contain the referenced external ReFill, you will get a message asking you to please insert the CD containing the referenced ReFill. If you have no such disk, you will be unable to use your new ReFill. Bummer! This certainly does discourage ripping off other people's ReFills while designing your own, though!

For More Information   This appendix covers a lot of information within its pages. There are a few additional tips and tricks you can learn by taking a peek at the ReFill Packer PDF file, which is located in the ReFill Packer Documentation folder inside the Reason Program folder.

Index